PRODUCT POLICY

CASES AND CONCEPTS

RICHARD N. CARDOZO

University of Minnesota
Graduate School of Business Administration
Minneapolis, Minnesota

Addison-Wesley Publishing Company
Reading, Massachusetts · Menlo Park, California
London · Amsterdam · Don Mills, Ontario · Sydney

This book is in the Addison-Wesley Marketing Series

Consulting Editor
Yoram J. Wind

Cases in this book are designed as a basis for class discussion, rather than to illustrate appropriate or inappropriate handling of administrative situations.

Library of Congress Cataloging in Publication Data

Cardozo, Richard N
    Product policy, cases and concepts.

    1. Product management--Case studies. I. Title.
HF5415.15.C28   658.5   78-67939
ISBN 0-201-00888-2

ISBN-0-201-00888-2
ABCDEFGHIJ-AL-79

PREFACE

The purpose of the cases in this book is to provide a basis for students to develop skills in analyzing complex problems in product policy and in developing appropriate plans for action. Every case presents a real business problem, along with pertinent background information on the organization and industry involved, and the data to which the decision-makers in the real situation had access. Some cases are disguised, in order to avoid revealing proprietary information. The effectiveness of each case as a vehicle for discussion and instruction has been demonstrated in classroom settings involving graduate students and, for most cases, business executives as well.

The text portions of the book are intended to provide a conceptual framework to aid students in developing generalizations from the study of cases and to provide a basis for further exposition of a conceptual framework and body of knowledge for product policy. The text is intended to be illustrative, rather than exhaustive or definitive.

The book begins with an overview of product policy, then addresses problems involved in modifying existing product lines, and deals last with modification and design of product-market portfolios. The section on modifying existing product lines covers the detailed decisions essential to planning or modifying any product line and enables students to begin the study of product policy by analyzing situations in which not all elements of the marketing mix will vary. After an introduction to product-market portfolios, students have an opportunity to analyze individual ventures, including entire marketing programs, one at a time, to determine whether particular product lines should be added to or deleted from the portfolio. In the subsequent sections on reallocation of resources within the portfolio and portfolio design, students must analyze simultaneously multiple product lines. This sequence parallels the levels of responsibility found in most organizations for product policy decisions, from product management to general management.

For this book I am indebted to Malcolm McNair, Milton Brown, and Walter Salmon of the Harvard Business School who taught me the case method; to the many individuals who worked with me to develop the materials in this book: Lael Berman, Don Blyly, James Clouser, Joyce Grahn, James Haefner, Roger Kerin, Thomas Kindler, Howard Liszt, Peter Lohaus, Bruce Mattson, Cathie Michlitsch, Barbara Nemecek, Gary Purkat, Craig Rockwell, Robert Roden, Richard Sauter, William Solvason, Roger Upson, Orville Walker; to colleagues at other universities whose suggestions on the text and cases have proved most helpful; to the reviewers of the manuscript, Jeffrey Barach of Tulane University and Merle Crawford of the University of Michigan; and to the dozens of businessmen without whose cooperation these cases could not have been developed. I am also very grateful for the skillful and patient support and assistance of Catherine Spreigl, Charlene Duncan, and Connie Hemmingsen in preparing the manuscript itself.

Minneapolis, Minnesota   R. N. C.
January 1979

CONTENTS

ALPHABETICAL LIST OF CASES

OVERVIEW OF PRODUCT POLICY

DEFINITIONS

What Is a Product?

Products or services may be defined by their tangible, physical attributes, such as shape or size or color for a product; or by the specific operations performed in a particular service, e.g., a styled haircut. From a marketing viewpoint, products or services may be more usefully defined in terms of the functions they perform or the benefits they provide, especially as those benefits are perceived by the consumers for whom the products or service is intended. Charles Revson's epigram sharply points up the distinction between physical properties and perceived benefits: "In the factory we make cosmetics. In the store we sell hope." This distinction depends in part on what the manufacturer and retailer have added to the basic physical product: a designer package, advertising to foster a particular image, and the environment at the point of purchase. Manufacturers also augment physical products with services such as software for computers and consulting services for farm supplies and equipment. In these instances, the product-with-services combination is often defined as a "system."

Product Lines In most cases, an organization will offer a line of products or services, rather than just a single product or service. The leading salt company offers not only its standard salt but also a salt with less sodium content, and regular salt in a variety of packages. An increasing number of barbershops, most of which used to offer only a single haircut service, now offer "standard haircuts" and "style cuts," the latter frequently in several variations. The product line is a more useful unit of analysis than the single product, because almost all individual products are managed as members of a product line.

Product/Market Portfolios A set or collection of product lines, together with the markets they serve, constitutes an organization's product/market portfolio, the largest unit of analysis in product policy. An organization's portfolio includes investments in product lines and markets, the latter including building of customer loyalties, relationships with resellers, and expertise in dealing with problems peculiar to particular markets. The number and diversity of product lines and markets included in a portfolio differ among organizations. A manufacturer like General Motors offers several dozen different product lines; General Electric, more than 1,000 different lines. Such portfolios of products or services may be quite closely related, as in the case of a supermarket or General Electric, or may be highly diverse; for example, many large food companies include in their portfolios holdings in the home building, home furnishings, toys, and educational areas.

A portfolio may be described in terms of the return it has historically yielded, or is forecast to yield, and in terms of the variability in that historic or forecast return. Management groups differ with respect to the return levels they seek and the amount and type of variability they are willing to accept in pursuit of their return objectives. In general, however, managers seek to minimize variation for any set level of return from a portfolio, and/or to maximize return for any specified level of variability or risk.

What Is Product Policy?

The objective of product policy is to establish an optimum portfolio for an organization. Product policy consists of the decisions to design or modify the organization's product/ market portfolio to achieve top management's objectives for return on the organization's resources, within the limits of uncertainty or risk top management is willing to accept. Product policy includes decisions on modifying existing product lines. Product policy decisions determine the nature, number, and timing of new products to be offered, and to what markets; the removal of products and markets from the portfolio; and the amount of each of several types of organizational resources to be allocated toward each product line and market.

Product Policy and Corporate Strategy   Because decisions to modify the portfolio or design a new portfolio are central to corporate strategic planning, product policy provides an interface between marketing strategy and overall corporate strategy. Corporate strategy, however, goes beyond product policy in consideration of questions related to manufacturing, financial, and personnel policies and, of course, return objectives and risk preferences for the corporate portfolio.

Product policy is one of the vehicles through which the organization copes with a changing external environment. Almost every organization generates a continuous turnover of products to keep pace with changes in demand, competition, and technology. For some organizations that turnover involves relatively modest annual changes in product specifications; the Volkswagen "bug," for example, remained virtually the same for thirty years. In contrast, many companies observe that more than half of their revenues, and in many instances more than three-quarters, come from entirely new products introduced within the preceding four or five years. Many of these new products replace older ones which the organization has dropped; other new products represent ventures into new businesses.

Product Policy and Marketing Strategy   The decision to enter a new business requires decisions not only about the product itself, but also about the entire marketing strategy to be employed for the venture. Similarly, questions involving reallocating resources or removing investments from the portfolio ordinarily include all elements of the marketing mix—not just the product line itself.

A product line is itself a variable in the marketing mix, like price, promotion, or distribution, but it is the most important. An inappropriate product seldom succeeds, no matter how brilliant the pricing, promotion, and distribution policies that support it may be. The composition of a particular product line may be varied, just as price, promotion, or distribution policies might be. To obtain the full impact of the product line as a variable in marketing strategy, an organization must have a clear definition of its business—a definition not bound up with existing products. The president of a firm which manufactures a wide and continuously changing variety of devices which enable telephone operators and service personnel to obtain access to individual telephone lines illustrated this point for his firm as follows: "If we're in the business of providing access to telephone lines, then we must examine all the ways 'accessing' is performed, not just the ways our current products work. We must evaluate the desirability of making a range of freestanding devices to sell to users and a variety of different components to sell to equipment manufacturers. The characteristics and importance of individual products in the line will change in response to technical refinements, users' needs, and the importance of the markets we presently serve or could serve."

Just as one would expect changes in price, promotion, and distribution policies to move the organization's overall marketing strategy toward its objectives, so one should analyze any product proposal in terms of its contribution to enhancing the effectiveness of the organization's marketing strategy. Without using marketing strategy as a guideline, product proposals are frequently evaluated each on its own merits, with short or medium-term profitability as the paramount criterion. In many instances, a proposal which passes a financial screening test and fits moderately well with the organization's present capabilities will be approved, with only limited attention paid to how well—if at all—the proposal fits with the organization's overall marketing strategy. The questions which should be asked, and too frequently are not, include, "How will this product help maintain or increase our share of a particular market?" or, "Should we seek new products which will help increase our penetration into markets in which we are underrepresented, instead of products which will help us increase our dominance in markets where we're among the leaders?"

Product policy acts as a cornerstone of marketing strategy by providing direction for the other elements in the marketing mix, and is in turn influenced by those elements. For example, marketing communications budgets are often allocated most heavily to new products, because those are the ones about which prospective customers are likely to be most interested in receiving information. The decision to introduce a new product or line, then, carries with it an implication for allocation of the organization's marketing communications resources. Marketing communications may also influence product policy. The ability of a particular market to absorb new information and the resources available to disseminate information often limit the number and scope of new offerings which an organization may introduce at a particular time.

Price lines to be offered may be affected by product policy. The addition of a "luxury" or "economy" model to a product line may enable a firm to compete in markets previously unavailable. Development of a product which uses new technology to provide significantly lower prices may expand demand for that product within existing or new markets. Some companies use their customary price lines and competitive price levels to guide the new product opportunities which they explore. It is not uncommon for a design group to be instructed to develop a product which must sell at a predetermined market price to meet resellers' and customers' requirements and to maintain the organization's competitive price position.

Distribution policies are affected by product policy, particularly in situations in which a new product requires a distribution network different form the company's existing channels. Resellers' requests may encourage—or even force—manufacturers to develop particular products or to expand or reduce their lines to meet resellers' interests.

Product policy and marketing strategy are closely interrelated at all levels of product policy decisions. Decisions to modify a product line will affect marketing programs for that line. Evaluation of new ventures which constitute major additions to the portfolio require that a marketing plan be outlined in order to evaluate the feasibility of the new venture and that a detailed marketing program be prepared before the new venture is marketed. Analysis and design of the entire product-market portfolio requires thorough analyses of the marketing programs for each of the investments in the portfolio, and reallocation of resources among product lines typically necessitates alterations in the marketing plans for the affected lines.

SELECTED REFERENCES

HISE, RICHARD T. *Product/Service Strategy.* New York: Petrocelli/Charter, 1977.
KOTLER, PHILIP. *Marketing Management* (3d ed.). Englewood Cliffs, N.J.: Prentice-Hall, 1976.
LEVITT, THEODORE. *The Marketing Mode.* New York: McGraw-Hill, 1969.
SHOSTACK, G. LYNN. "Breaking Free from Product Marketing." In *Journal of Marketing,* April 1977.
SPITZ, A. EDWARD (ed.). *Product Planning* (2d ed.). New York: Petrocelli/Charter, 1977.

PRODUCT LIFE CYCLES

Decisions to add products to the portfolio, remove them from it, or shift resources among product lines typically involve assumptions about the stage of the product line in its life cycle. Even if these assumptions are clearly stated, the product life cycle (PLC) concept should be employed with some caution. A PLC simply plots the sales of a product or line over a specified time period. Product life cycles are customarily divided into four or more distinct stages: introduction, growth, maturity, and decline, as depicted in Fig. 1.

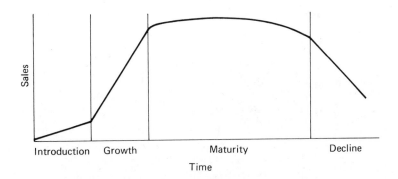

Fig. 1. General PLC model

Sales, indicated on the vertical axis, may be measured in dollars or units. To remove the effects of inflation and population changes, sales are often measured in constant dollars or units per consuming entity (individual, household, or buying organization). Sales figures are often also adjusted for seasonal or cyclical variations. Time, charted on the horizontal axis, is typically measured in years. An alternative form of presentation of PLC data is the use of inflection points, or changes in the rate at which sales are increasing or decreasing among specified time periods.

The widespread use of this general model may obscure the fact that the PLC curve is not just one curve (or relationship), but a whole family of curves. The family includes PLCs for individual items (the 1½ oz. size of Crest, regular-flavor toothpaste), brand (Crest toothpaste, all sizes and flavors combined), product forms (all fluoridated toothpastes), and product classes (all toothpastes). Each member curve of the PLC family may have a somewhat different shape. For example, the product class "cigarettes" is mature and shows relatively minor variation over the past twenty years. In contrast, "filter cigarettes," a product form, has shown dramatic growth, while "nonfilter" forms have declined. But not all brands of filter cigarettes have shared in the growth of the product form: after initial rapid growth, Winston appears to have entered a plateau or maturity stage; Marlboro is still growing; and Kent and L & M appear to be declining from an initial rapid peak in sales. These relationships are illustrated in Figs. 2 and 3.

The sales shown in a PLC curve for a product class represent the sum of the sales of product forms within that product class. Similarly, the sum of the sales of brands within each form constitutes sales of that form; and the sum of items within a brand constitutes total sales of the brand.

Of primary concern to most analysts of PLCs are the causes of the shape of the PLC for a particular item or brand. The marketing strategy supporting a particular item or brand and consumers' reactions to the offering appear to be the principal determinants of the shape of the PLC for a particular brand or item. Substantial marketing support upon introduction can stimulate resellers to stock and display a brand and stimulate consumers

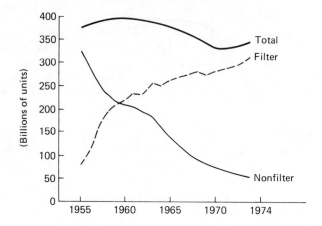

Fig. 2. Sales of all cigarettes and major product forms

Source: Nariman K. Dhalla and Sonia Yuspeh, "Forget the Product Life Cycle Concept!" *Harvard Business Review,* January–February 1976, Copyright © 1975 by the President and Fellows of Harvard College; all rights reserved. ("Total" line added.)

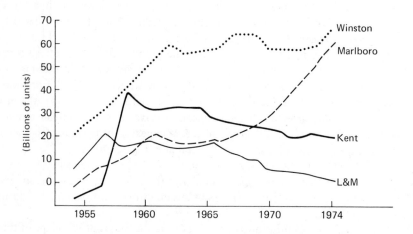

Fig. 3. Sales of individual brands of filter cigarettes

Source: Nariman K. Dhalla and Sonia Yuspeh, "Forget the Product Life Cycle Concept!" *Harvard Business Review,* January–February 1976, Copyright © 1975 by the President and Fellows of Harvard College; all rights reserved.

to try it. If consumers find the new offering superior to what they've been buying, and if resellers consider continued stocking of the product to be profitable, the new offering will likely exhibit growth, at the expense of those other products to which consumers consider the new offering superior. If, however, consumers find that the new product is the same as what they've been using, and resellers foresee limited profit opportunity, then the new product will at best find limited exposure, and very likely will have to be withdrawn.

The life cycles of some items and brands show an initial peak, followed by a decline to a fairly stable sales level. The peak may reflect consumer trial, stimulated by aggressive marketing support. The decline may reflect the failure of some customers to repeat their purchases because they did not find the new offering superior to their present one. The stable portion may reflect continued repeat purchases by that segment of the market to which the new product had lasting appeal.

For some new offerings, the process of trial and repeat (or rejection) will take several years, as in the adoption of new technology or processes in many industries. In such cases, the PLC may approximate in shape the form of a cumulative adoption curve which describes diffusion of innovations. The amount and nature of marketing expenditures will ordinarily reflect this adoption pattern.

A fairly stable level of sales for a consumer durable or an industrial capital goods item, in which repeat sales do not occur, and in which sales of replacements or additional optional features may not occur for several years, may reflect sales to a series of markets, each of which exhibits growth followed by saturation (i.e., few, if any, additional purchases). Figure 4, in which absolute figures and company names have been disguised but relationships unaltered, illustrates this "market life cycle" phenomenon for a new product form, a specialized communications system.

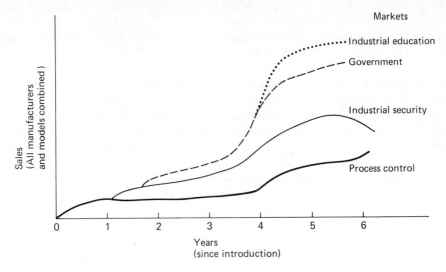

Fig. 4. The market life cycle

The communications system first was accepted in process control applications, then used for security applications in some of the same firms which originally purchased it for process control. One manufacturer saw opportunities for sales to small governmental units for both process control and security applications, and was promptly followed by others; nevertheless, it took almost two years for the government market to begin rapid growth. Most recently, manufacturers have begun to seek sales for industrial education applications.

Uses and Limitations of the Product Life Cycle

The principal applications of PLC analysis occur in planning for new products and in changing marketing strategy for established product lines. When planning for a new venture, many firms attempt to estimate the length of the PLC for the venture, the height of the peak demand, and the general shape of the PLC curve. Historical data on previous new ventures considered similar to the one for which plans are being made are often used as bases for such estimates.

Some marketers use PLC analysis as a basis for planning changes in marketing strategy, such as cutting prices and offering incentives to resellers. Many guidelines for changing marketing strategy as a product moves through its life cycle have been developed; one recent set appears in Table 1.

When a manager believes a product or product line to be past the midpoint of its "growth" stage, he or she may seek ways to extend the life of the product line by adding new products (product line extensions become product life extensions), offering private brands, redesigning, or repositioning the product line.

A forecast that a product is entering its declining stage often leads management to withdraw resources and to divert personnel, facilities, and dollars to products in their "growth" phases. The consequent shortage of resources, coupled with management's clear signal that a particular product line lacks growth potential, may lead operating managers to adopt a passive attitude, thus accelerating loss of sales and market share. If management's intention is to avoid overinvesting resources in mature products, a more appropriate approach is to estimate sales and returns on investment likely to occur for each of several levels of spending and investment. Aggressive management, coupled with modest spending, may be essential to maintaining market share, sales volume, and cash flows in a highly competitive, mature product class. Aggressive operating managers who have access to development funds, and who recognize limitations of growth in present products and markets, frequently generate plans for extending the product life cycle with product modification (e.g., Fab detergent was followed by New & Improved Fab, Fab with Borax, etc.) or penetration of new markets. Markets once considered saturated may be rejuvenated: When Americans regarded watches as "status" items, an individual owned one or two, but in recent years watches have become fashion items, sold to match clothing, resulting in multiple watch ownership and increased industry sales.

The principal criticisms of PLC analysis center on the validity of the PLC model and the predictive accuracy of PLC data. Critics of PLC analysis argue that the PLC concept

Table 1. HOW PLC ADVOCATES VIEW THE IMPLICATIONS OF THE CYCLE FOR MARKETING ACTION

Effects and responses	Stages of the PLC			
	Introduction	Growth	Maturity	Decline
Competition	None of importance	Some emulators	Many rivals competing for a small piece of the pie	Few in number with a rapid shakeout of weak members
Overall strategy	Market establishment; persuade early adopters to try the product	Market penetration; persuade mass market to prefer the brand	Defense of brand position; check the inroads of competition	Preparations for removal; milk the brand dry of all possible benefits
Profits	Negligible because of high production and marketing costs	Reach peak levels as a result of high prices and growing demand	Increasing competition cuts into profit margins and ultimately into total profits	Declining volume pushes costs up to levels that eliminate profits entirely
Retail prices	High, to recover some of the excessive costs of launching	High, to take advantage of heavy consumer demand	What the traffic will bear; need to avoid price wars	Low enough to permit quick liquidation of inventory
Distribution	Selective, as distribution is slowly built up	Intensive; employ small trade discounts since dealers are eager to store	Intensive; heavy trade allowances to retain shelf space	Selective; unprofitable outlets slowly phased out
Advertising strategy	Aim at the needs of early adopters	Make the mass market aware of brand benefits	Use advertising as a vehicle for differentiation among otherwise similar brands	Emphasize low price to reduce stock
Advertising emphasis	High, to generate awareness and interest among early adopters and persuade dealers to stock the brand	Moderate, to let sales rise on the sheer momentum of word-of-mouth recommendations	Moderate, since most buyers are aware of brand characteristics	Minimum expenditures required to phase out the product
Consumer sales and promotion expenditures	Heavy, to entice target groups with samples, coupons, and other inducements to try the brand	Moderate, to create brand preference (advertising is better suited to do this job)	Heavy, to encourage brand switching, hoping to convert some buyers into loyal users	Minimal, to let the brand coast by itself

Source: Nariman K. Dhalla and Sonia Yuspeh, "Forget the Product Life Cycle Concept," *Harvard Business Review,* January–February 1976, Copyright © 1975 by the President and Fellows of Harvard College, all rights reserved.

is an inappropriate biological analogy. Sales of a product over time are not predetermined the way life spans and phases of organisms are. Indeed, sales depend to at least some extent upon actions initiated by marketers. Further, some product classes like distilled spirits, malt beverages, and many basic foods have existed for centuries, and show no signs of permanent decline.

Problems with predictive accuracy arise from two sources: (1) the difficulty in identifying inflection points in a PLC curve, i.e., the moments when a product passes from one stage into another; and (2) the failure of all product forms or brands within a product category to exhibit reliably similar behavior. One of the difficulties in identifying inflection points is that they are ordinarily apparent only after the next stage has been entered. Prediction of, say, the duration and rate of growth for a novel brand or product form is seldom done with sufficient accuracy far enough in advance to provide precise guidance for the marketing manager who seeks to know precisely when the shift from a "growth phase" strategy into a "maturity" marketing strategy for a product or line. This difficulty in prediction occurs in part because, historically, not all items within a brand, brands within a form, or forms within a class behave similarly. The data on cigarettes (above) illustrates this problem.

Despite these limitations, PLC analysis may be useful to the marketer as a planning tool. Effective employment of PLC analysis requires differentiation of items from brands, brands from forms, and forms from the product class and recognition of the fact that consumer response and competitive conditions will likely vary during the time the product line is available.

SELECTED REFERENCES

BROCKHOFF, KLAUS. "A Test for the Product Life Cycle." *Econometrics,* July–October 1967, vol. 35, no. 3–4.

BURQUEST, BRADLEY L. "The Industrial Goods Product Life Cycle: An Exploratory Study." Unpublished MBA paper, Graduate School of Business Administration, University of Minnesota.

BUZZELL, ROBERT J. "Competitive Behavior and Product Life Cycles." *Journal of Business,* 1969, vol. 41, no. 4.

CASS, H.M. "Designing Decay." *Harvard Business Review,* January–February 1966.

CLAYCAMP, HENRY J. "Prediction of New Product Performance, An Analysis." *Journal of Marketing Research,* November 1969, vol. VI.

CLIFFORD, DONALD K.V., JR. "Managing The Product Life Cycle." American Management Association, Inc., New York, 1965.

COX, WILLIAM E., JR. "Product Life Cycles as Marketing Models." *Journal of Business,* October 1967, vol. 40, no. 4.

DHALLA, NARIMAN K., and SONIA YUSPEH. "Forget the Product Life Cycle Concept." *Harvard Business Review,* January–February 1976.

KOTLER, PHILIP. *Marketing Management* (3d ed.). Englewood Cliffs, N.J.: Prentice-Hall, 1976.

LEVITT, THEODORE. "Exploit the Product Life Cycle." *Harvard Business Review,* November–December 1965.

LUCK, DAVID J. *Product Policy and Strategy.* Englewood Cliffs, N.J.: Prentice-Hall, 1972.

MACKENZIE, GEORGE F.K. "MacKenzie of Marketing's 'Missing Link'—the Product Life Concept." *Industrial Marketing,* April 1971.

POLLI, ROLANDO. "Validity of the Product Life Cycle. *"The Journal of Business,* October 1969, vol. 42, no. 4.

PESSEMIER, EDGAR A. "Models for New Product Decisions." May 1969, Krannert Graduate School of Industrial Administration, Purdue University.

SELECTED COMPANY ACCOUNTS. *Marketing Planning: Approaches of Selected Companies.* New York: American Management Association, Inc., 1967.

WASSON, CHESTER R. "How Predictable Are Fashionable and Other Product Life Cycles?" *Journal of Marketing,* July 1966, vol. 82.

————. *Product Management; Product Life Cycles and Competitive Marketing Strategy.* St. Charles, Ill.: Challenge Books, 1971.

WELLS, LOUIS T., JR. "A Product Life Cycle for International Trade?" *Journal of Marketing,* July 1969, vol. 32.

WIND, YORAM. *Product Policy,* Reading, Mass.: Addison-Wesley, in press.

CHARINGTON DISTILLERS, INC.

Presidents' Choice Bourbon

In 1971 Charington Distillers, Inc., was considering marketing a new 86 proof ("straight") Presidents' Choice bourbon as an addition to its well-established 100 proof ("bonded") Presidents' Choice. Charington officials were motivated to consider "splitting" the Presidents' Choice brand by declining sales for all 100 proof spirits and increases in sales of 86 proof spirits, including straight bourbons, vodka, and gin (see Exhibit 1).

Presidents' Choice 100 retailed between $9.50 and $10 a fifth.[1] It was the highest priced bourbon on the market and was very near the top price for any domestically produced spirits. In 1971 the company sold approximately 150,000 cases (12 fifths per case), an increase of more than 75 percent in a three-year period. The most recent budget for Presidents' Choice 100 included $1.1 million for advertising in trade publications and in such consumer publications as *Playboy, Sports Illustrated, The New Yorker, Saturday Review,* and *The Wall Street Journal.* Outdoor ads were also used frequently. (Promotional expenditures for selected distillers appear in Exhibit 2.) Survey data suggested that the typical purchaser bought Presidents' Choice 100 because of its high proof rating, its age (eight years), and the superiority which was associated with a premium-priced bourbon. Characteristics of bourbon drinkers appear in Exhibit 3.

The bourbon market was divided into three categories: premium brands, priced at $5.75 per fifth and higher; medium-priced brands, ranging from $4.75 to $5.75; and low-priced bourbons, retailing for less than $4.75 a fifth. Premium bourbons constituted almost 25 percent of the 29-million-case bourbon market. More than 90 percent of premium bourbon was 86 proof ("straight") whiskey.

Of the three premium brands which accounted for the highest sales volumes in 1971, none was priced above $6.95 per fifth. Both Old Granddad (sales of 1.3 million cases of 86 proof; 65 thousand of 100 proof) and Old Charter (sales of 900 thousand cases of 86 proof; no 100 proof) were priced at $6.95. Old Forester (sales of 900 thousand cases of 86 proof; 100 thousand of 100 proof) was priced at $6.50 per fifth.

Certain data in this case have been disguised.

1. All retail prices include federal and state taxes. A "fifth" was a bottle containing 1/5 of a gallon of alcoholic beverage. "Proof" was a measure of alcoholic content; each proof point represented one-half of one percent of alcohol content. Therefore, 86 proof spirits contained 43 percent alcohol; 100 proof, 50 percent alcohol.

There were certain trends that Charington management wanted to consider before deciding whether or not to market Presidents' Choice 86. At the beginning of 1971 the bourbon market was showing little growth. In contrast, sales of gin and vodka were improving markedly. In 1971, the Liquor Handbook stated, "It would seem apparent that a great many consumers no longer wished to use 100 proof distilled spirits regularly." A projection for 1972 forecast that the market would be deluged by milder, lighter tasting whiskies. Moreover, it was estimated that consumers would continue to substitute non-whiskey distilled spirits for whiskey at an increasing rate.

Despite these apparently unfavorable trends, the distiller of one of the top-selling bourbons, Old Forester, was considering an extensive sales promotion of more than $2 million, aimed primarily at the 25-year-old drinker who would just be starting to form brand habits. The central theme of the promotional campaign was "Old Forester—Formula One"; the campaign featured racing driver Mark Donahue. The company hoped that the youthful, energetic auto-racing image would appeal to the younger drinker and carry over to the more mature drinker.

Although Charington officials had not decided on a price or a budget for the new 86 proof, if it were to be introduced, a company accountant had prepared the following table for internal discussion:

		1/5 gallon ("a fifth")
Price to consumer (assumed)		$9.00
Federal taxes		
(based on alcoholic content)	$1.80	
Taxes in typical state	.65	
Total taxes		2.45
Revenue to retailer		6.55
Retailer/wholesaler margin (combined)		
(approximately 1/3 of retailers' revenue)		2.18
Revenue to Charington		4.37
Production costs (approximately 5% less		
than Presidents' Choice 100)		1.25
Available for marketing, overhead, profit		3.12

Charington personnel knew that the budget for Presidents' Choice 100 included almost $2.50 per fifth for advertising, selling, promotion, and overhead. Costs of selling and promotion to wholesalers and retailers were high because of intense competition for retail shelf space and attention from retail sales personnel. Presidents' Choice 100 generated pretax earnings in excess of 20 percent of sales.

Exhibit 1

CHARINGTON DISTILLERS, INC.
ESTIMATED UNITED STATES CONSUMPTION
OF DISTILLED SPIRITS
1961 AND 1971, BY TYPE

Type	1971	1961
Straight bourbons (86 proof)	20.4%	25.6%
Blends	18.6	29.9
Scotch	13.6	8.3
Canadian	9.5	5.2
Bonds (100 proof)	1.4	3.7
Other	0.3	0.4
Total whiskey	63.8%	73.1%
Vodka	13.2%	8.3%
Gin	9.8	9.6
Cordials	5.1	3.8
Brandy	3.6	2.7
Rum	3.2	1.8
Other	1.3	0.7
Total nonwhiskey	36.2%	26.9%
Total consumption (millions of gallons)	383.1	242.6

Source: Business Week, March 10, 1973, p. 113.

Exhibit 2

CHARINGTON DISTILLERS, INC.
PROMOTIONAL BUDGETS OF SELECTED DISTILLERS, 1969
($000)

	Total	News-papers	Magazines	Bus/trade journals	Outdoor	Point of sale	Miscel-laneous
Seagram's	$20,530	$6,000	$9,000	$400	$5,000	—	$130
Mr. Boston	1,175	500	150	25	—	—	500
Hiram Walker	1,900	150	—	50	650	—	450
Holland House	1,200	120	840	60	—	$60	120

Source: National Register Publishing Company, "Standard Directory of Advertisers," 1969, pp. 337–56.

Exhibit 3
CHARINGTON DISTILLERS, INC.
BOURBON CONSUMER PROFILE

Household income	Percentage of households using or serving bourbon	Every day	Several times weekly	Once a month	Less than once a month	Number of households per segment (000)
$ 3,000 & below	18.9%	0.4%	1.0%	1.4%	16.1%	8,488
3,000 to 4,999	33.4	0.3	1.5	3.6	28.0	8,366
5,000 to 6,999	45.3	0.7	1.9	4.5	38.2	9,699
7,000 to 7,999	50.5	0.7	2.3	6.1	41.4	6,876
8,000 to 9,999	57.0	0.7	2.6	7.3	46.4	9,821
10,000 to 14,999	67.5	2.0	3.5	10.7	51.3	11,492
15,000 to 24,999	75.2	3.0	7.1	17.3	47.8	4,607
25,999 & above	77.3	3.8	9.0	18.4	46.1	1,334
						60,683
Age—head of household						
18-24	58.8%	—	3.2%	9.5%	46.1%	4,308
25-34	60.6	0.5%	3.0	7.9	49.2	10,620
35-49	58.1	1.1	2.9	8.6	45.5	18,569
50-64	46.8	1.7	3.1	6.9	35.1	15,778
65 & above	26.0	1.2	1.3	2.8	20.7	11,408
						60,683
Education—head of household						
Grade school or less	31.7%	0.6%	1.3%	2.6%	27.2%	16,202
Some high school	47.3	0.5	1.8	5.6	39.4	11,530
High school	54.9	1.0	2.5	7.5	43.9	18,022
Some college	61.3	1.6	3.7	11.5	44.5	7,525
College	68.7	2.4	7.9	13.6	44.8	4,066
Postgraduate	68.1	3.5	5.6	13.0	46.0	3,338
						60,683

Source: Starch Reports, "Profile of U.S. Consumer Market Segments," 1969, p. 96.

THE DOW CHEMICAL COMPANY

Liquid Tire Chain

In the summer of 1969, marketing executives of the Dow Chemical Company were deciding whether or not to introduce nationally Dow Liquid Tire Chain traction improver. Liquid Tire Chain is a patented blend of resins dissolved in methanol. The product is sprayed onto the exposed tread of a stuck automobile and the wheels are rotated slowly to bring the sprayed portion of tread in contact with the water on top of the ice. When activated by this water, the resins will come out of solution and cause a gummy layer to set up on the tread. Company officials stated that this gummy extra tread would provide sufficient added traction to get the vehicle unstuck. Liquid Tire Chain was packaged in an aerosol spray can which contained enough Liquid Tire Chain for two complete applications. Liquid Tire Chain had been tested in use by Dow employees at the end of the past winter. Research personnel reported that results of these tests showed Liquid Tire Chain to be successful in helping drivers to get cars unstuck.

Company executives were considering a proposal to market Liquid Tire Chain at a suggested retail price of $1.29 for a four-ounce spray can.[1] The product would be distributed through conventional automotive service outlets such as gasoline and service stations, vehicle and parts dealers, department and hardware stores. Based on the manufacturer's suggested retail price, trade margins for Liquid Tire Chain were at least as great as those for similarly priced automotive products.

On the average, Dow would receive 56 cents for each can sold. Company officials estimated that direct manufacturing and packaging costs amounted to 25 cents per can, leaving 31 cents per can available for sales, advertising, and profit contribution. Sales costs were estimated at $45,000 per year based on the amount of time executives expected the sales force would devote to Liquid Tire Chain. Although no advertising budget had been set, Dow officials knew that a single 60-second television commercial would cost $20,000, and a single full-page, four-color ad in a general circulation magazine such as *Time* would cost about the same amount. Preliminary reviews of vehicle registration statistics indicated that there were between 40 and 50 million passenger cars in snow-belt states.

Dow executives had authorized a budget of $25,000 for further marketing research on Liquid Tire Chain. They had also specified that any research conducted would have to be completed in nine months or less. The company's marketing research department had previously designed three studies which they recommended be carried out. These studies are described briefly in Exhibit 1. Exhibits 2, 3, and 4 show the primary tables which these studies would yield.

Copyright © 1970 by Richard N. Cardozo.
1. Retail price per case of 24 cans—$30.96.

Exhibit 1

DOW LIQUID TIRE CHAIN
PROPOSED MARKETING RESEARCH STUDIES

Table no.	Description of table	Source of data	Collection costs		Purchase*
			Dollars	Months	
1	Telephone survey to determine market size	Telephone survey of 1,000 households in area running from Canadian border to the Mason-Dixon line	2,500	2	_____
2	Field test of product	Interviews with 100 motorists who used product	4,500	9	_____
3	Test market	Five-month test market during winter conducted in city of 2,000,000 people: widespread retail distribution of product; moderate advertising support	20,000	9	_____

*You may wish to keep track of your purchases by using this column.

Exhibit 2

DOW LIQUID TIRE CHAIN—TABLE 1
TELEPHONE SURVEY TO DETERMINE MARKET SIZE
(Sample of 1,000 households)

Time needed: 2 months

Area: New England to the Dakotas, Canadian Border to Mason-Dixon Line.

Cost: $2,500

Number of cars _____

Number of motorists stuck at least once/winter _____

Total number of times stuck/winter _____

Exhibit 3

DOW LIQUID TIRE CHAIN—TABLE 2
FIELD TEST OF PRODUCT AMONG 100 MOTORISTS

Time needed: 9 months	Source: Interviews with 100 motorists who would be given free samples of the product (recipients) *Note:* not all recipients would use the product.

Cost: $4,500

Percent of *Recipients* who used LTC at least once:	_____ %
Percent of *Users* successful in getting unstuck:	_____ %
Main reasons for liking LTC:	(1) _____
	(2) _____
Main negative comments:	(1) _____
	(2) _____

Intent to purchase:
(% of triers)

Very interested	_____ %
Somewhat interested	_____ %
Not very interested	_____ %
Not at all interested	_____ %
Total	100%

Exhibit 4

DOW LIQUID TIRE CHAIN—TABLE 3
TEST MARKET

Time needed: 9 months	Source: Five-month test market in snow-belt city of 2 million population; widespread distribution; advertising equivalent to $250,000 for entire snow belt

Cost: $20,000

Percent of households aware at beginning of test:	_____ %
Percent of households aware at end of test:	_____ %
Percent change in awareness:	_____ %
Percent trial:	_____ %
Percent of triers who repeated:	_____ %

SIMON'S, INC.

Early in 1973, the management of Simon's, Inc., a major department store in Greenfield, Ohio, was reviewing a plan to increase the profitability of its furniture building, one of two separate buildings the store occupied in downtown Greenfield. In essence, the plan suggested that space devoted to home furnishings be reduced, and that the space thereby made available in the furniture building be occupied by the store's men's department, which would be increased in size by about 50 percent and moved from the main building to the furniture building.

Store executives rejected the alternatives of either vacating or substantially remodeling the furniture building. Although executives believed they could get out of their long-term lease on the furniture building, they believed that the owners would have no difficulty renting the space to their major competitor, who already blocked Simon's expansion on two sides. The age and design of the furniture building made major remodeling unfeasible, even if Simon's had owned the property. Executives had ruled out for the foreseeable future the possibility of connecting the two buildings with new construction, because funds would be needed for a branch store in a new suburban shopping center.

THE COMPANY

Simon's, founded more than 50 years ago, enjoyed a reputation for high-quality merchandise and served the middle- to upper-income segment of the Greenfield market. The store carried a full line of women's and girls' apparel and accessories; a limited line of men's and boys' wear, which regularly included accessories and trousers, and occasionally sport coats, but not suits, coats, or shoes; fabrics, sewing supplies, and linens; housewares, china, and gifts; and, in the furniture building, furniture, television, luggage, and books. Operating results for the major merchandise classifications, for the year ending January 31, 1973, appear in Exhibit 1. Exhibit 2 contains a list of the departments within each classification. For the store as a whole, sales had increased more than 2 percent, and gross margin almost 3 percent, over the preceding year.

Simon's occupied two buildings, connected by a parking lot, in downtown Greenfield. The main building faced a newly completed mall, which downtown merchants credited with increasing retail sales volume in the downtown area. The furniture building faced a new one-way Ring Road which circled the heart of downtown Greenfield. Simon's had occupied the furniture building for more than five years. Exhibit 3 shows the location of the two Simon's buildings; Exhibit 4, the floor plan of the furniture building.

THE MARKET

Greenfield is located in a prosperous farming area about 70 miles from Cincinnati. The trading area includes 140,000 permanent residents. Greenfield itself has a permanent population of approximately 40,000, plus more than 12,000 students in two colleges.

Total department store sales in the trade area amounted to $55 million. The seven major competitiors in the area, including Simon's and Patrick's (considered by Simon's officials to be the store's principal rival) made approximately half of this total. Among these major stores, 30 percent of the sales came from the downtown area, 50 percent from a shopping center located several miles from downtown, and 20 percent from other locations. Simon's major competitors dealt mainly in medium-priced goods. The largest department store in the area, a unit of a major national chain, had sales 2½ times those of Simon's.

The market for women's and girls' clothing was estimated at $16 million, much of which was sold by department stores.

The total market for men's and boys' wear in the trade area was approximately $8 million. Apart from the department stores, three men's specialty stores located downtown together did an estimated $500,000 to $600,000 worth of business. There were also several men's specialty stores located in the shopping center.

Retail furniture and furniture accessory sales in the trade area were thought to be about $3.2 million; store officials estimated that 6 percent of this business was lost to Cincinnati merchants. There were 15 furniture stores in and around Greenfield; none but Simon's was located downtown.

PROBLEMS AND OPPORTUNITIES

The furniture building as a whole had been unprofitable for several years. Several combinations of merchandise had been tried over the years, the most recent of which is shown on the diagram of the furniture building, Exhibit 4. The furniture department had varied between being profitable and unprofitable, but the profit trend had been upward during the past five years.

The television department had been reduced in size, but remained unprofitable in spite of high sales per square foot. Losses had decreased as the breadth and depth of stock, as well as floor space, had been decreased. Currently the merchandise display and stock levels were at the minimum allowed by Magnovox, the only line carried. Further reductions in display stock or space would cause Magnavox to withdraw the franchise, and require Simon's to switch to lower-margin known brands or higher-margin brands from little-known manufacturers. The luggage and books department had been marginally profitable. Operating data for departments in the furniture building appear in Exhibit 5.

Store officials had believed for some time that expansion of their profitable men's and boys' operation to include a full line of men's wear (adding suits, coats; expanding current sport coat, slacks, and accessories lines), might provide opportunities for increased profits. Operating data for the men's and boys' department appears in Exhibit 6.

THE PROPOSAL

The proposal, prepared by the Cincinnati consulting firm of KLB, Ltd., contained four principal recommendations, as follows:

1. Eliminate the television department altogether.
2. Move the luggage and books department to the main building. The department would remain approximately its present size.

3. Reduce the space allocated to the sleep shop from 1,500 square feet to 200 square feet, and display springs and mattresses along with bedroom furniture.

4. Move the men's department from its present location on the main floor of the main building, and expand it into a full-line department occupying 3,000 square feet in the furniture building.

Moving and remodeling required by this plan were estimated at a minimum of $20,000–$25,000, and could run as high as $40,000, depending on the merchandise moved and the fixtures added or altered. Additional inventory requirements for the expanded men's department were estimated at $38,000.

The proposed floor plan for the furniture building appears in Exhibit 7. The consultants' estimates of the impact of these recommendations upon operating statistics for the men's department appears in Exhibit 8.

KLB, Ltd., estimated that their proposal would increase sales in the furniture building to $860,000. They estimated that those sales would produce a gross margin of $350,000, and yield a pretax profit of $38,000.

In support of their recommendations, KLB offered the following rationale:

1. The T.V. department is unprofitable and it is doubtful that this department contributes to the traffic flow in the furniture department or the store as a whole.

2. It is doubtful that the luggage and book department contributes to the traffic in the furniture department. However, the department is marginally profitable and may do better in the main store where there is heavier traffic flow.

3. The sleep shop does contribute to the overall furniture department and is necessary when selling bedroom sets. However, the amount of display space necessary to accomplish this is minimal. One brand of mattresses and box springs is carried by the store; three mattresses on display showing size and firmness variations should be adequate for showing the line.

4. The furniture department is the largest single department in Simon's. It is possible that the cost allocation system is biased against the furniture department but this will have to be proven by a cost analysis. Many of the expenses assigned to the department are fixed or semifixed. Thus, if sales per square foot can be increased by increasing the amount of consumer traffic in the store, the furniture area may well prove to be a profitable operation. It is felt that the immediate impact of reducing the amount of space in the furniture area (i.e., sleep shop) will not adversely affect sales of the total furniture division.

5. A men's department was chosen to fill the vacated 3,000 square feet for these reasons:

   a) The men's department is in more need of space than any of the women's departments. The trade area shows a ratio of women's and men's sales of 2 to 1. Simon's ratio is currently 4.4 to 1.

   b) The men's department will draw both men and women into the furniture building. Women will be shopping for boys' clothes (the major increase in boys' clothing will be in the 12–14 year age bracket where there is a void among the present merchants) and men's accessories. Men will be shopping for slacks, sport coats, and accessories. Thus, both parties necessary for a furniture purchase will be drawn into the building. The housewife is necessary for selection and the husband confirms the price and construction. The furniture area may also add to the traffic in the men's department. The furniture building will draw couples who are looking for furniture and are in immediate need of some men's clothing.

c)   If a women's department were put into the vacated space it would necessitate dividing the women's departments between the main store and the furniture building. It is felt that it would be best to keep all the women's areas under one roof.

The proposed solution will result in a profitable furniture building and will free valuable main floor square footage in the main building.

Exhibit 1
SIMON'S, INC.—OPERATING RESULTS (YEAR ENDING JANUARY 31, 1973)

Merchandise classification	Location	Sales ($000)	Gross margin ($000)	Profit (loss) before taxes ($000)	Inventory (at retail prices) ($000)	Square footage (000)
Linens and sewing center	3rd floor	308.3	115.8	(8.1)	165.6	7.5
Women's	2nd floor	388.2	164.0	24.8	114.2	10.0
Women's	1st floor and mezzanine	737.8	302.4	46.6	199.6	10.0
Infants' and girls'	1st floor	191.9	117.4	9.6	77.4	1.6
Men's and boys'	1st floor	251.9	104.4	30.1	99.2	1.9
Housewares, china, gifts	Basement[a] A	310.0	118.0	5.4	91.4	1.5
Toys	Basement[a] B	32.2	10.8	(1.6)	10.5	2.5
Furniture	Furniture building	776.4	277.9	(17.5)	372.9	11.5
Total		$2,996.6	$1,210.7	$88.6	$1,130.8	46.5

Income statement	(000)
Sales	$2,996.6
Cost of goods sold	1,785.9
Gross margin	1,210.7
Operating expenses	1,122.1[b]
Profit before taxes	$ 88.6[c]

[a] The two basements were physically separated by a bearing wall.

[b] About 55 percent of these expenses were charged directly to individual departments; the remainder could not be readily assigned to specific departments, and was allocated among departments in approximate proportion of each department's sales to total sales.

[c] This profit represents a pretax return of approximately 10 percent on owner's equity.

Source: Company Records

Exhibit 2

SIMON'S, INC.

LIST OF DEPARTMENTS

Men's and boys'	*Women's—First floor and mezzanine*
Men's furnishings	Cosmetics
Trousers	Jewelry
Boys' furnishings	Accessories boutique
	Handbags
Linens and sewing center [a]	Lingerie
Linens and domestics	Sportswear (1st floor)
Bath shop	Sportswear (mezzanine)
Bedding	Budget dresses
Patterns	Junior dresses
Yard goods	Daytime dresses
Notions	Shoes
Art needle	
	Women's—Second floor
Housewares, china, gifts	Foundations
Housewares	Hosiery
China and glass	Lingerie
Gifts	Junior coats
	Women's coats and suits
Toys	Better dresses
	Maternity
Infants' and girls'	Bridal
Infants'	Robes
Girls'	
	Furniture
	Sleep shop
	Lamps and accessories
	Shades
	Carpet
	Drapery
	Furniture
	Television
	Luggage and books
	Vacuum cleaners

[a] Offices were also located on the third floor

Source: Company Records

Exhibit 3
SIMON'S, INC.
CENTER OF DOWNTOWN GREENFIELD

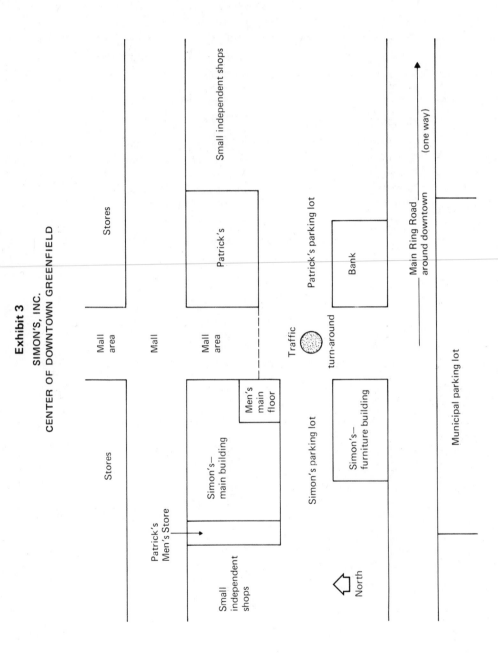

Exhibit 4

SIMON'S, INC.
PRESENT FLOOR PLAN OF FURNITURE BUILDING

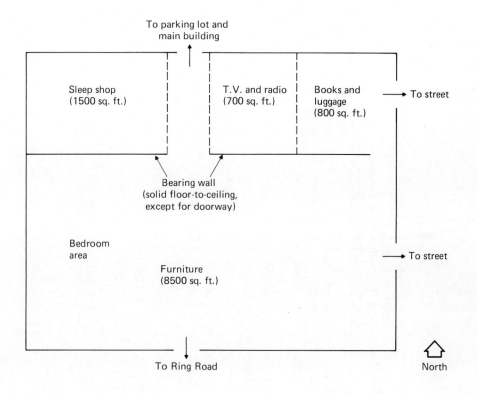

Exhibit 5

SIMON'S, INC.
OPERATING STATISTICS, FURNITURE BUILDING,
Year Ending January 31, 1973

Department	Sales	Cost of goods sold	Gross margin	Expenses	Profit before taxes	Inventory (at retail prices)	Square footage
Sleep shop	$ 26,000	$ 16,200	$ 9,800	$ 14,000	($ 4,200)	$ 13,000	1,500
Lamps and accessories	66,500	38,300	28,200	27,400	800	38,000	
Shades	25,000	13,600	11,400	10,600	800	19,000	
Carpet	108,000	74,200	33,800	41,200	(7,400)	53,000	8,500
Drapery	94,500	56,200	38,300	37,100	1,200	50,000	
Furniture	180,000	101,500	78,500	79,700	(1,200)	67,000	
Vacuum cleaners	21,400	15,700	5,700	6,200	(500)	5,900	
Total furniture	$521,400	$315,700	$205,700	$216,200	($10,500)	$245,900	10,000
Television	185,000	138,750	46,250	53,250	(7,000)	87,000	700
Luggage and books	70,000	44,100	25,900	25,900	—	40,000	800
Total furniture building	$776,400	$498,550	$227,850	$295,350	($17,500)	$372,900	11,500

Source: Company Records

Exhibit 6

SIMON'S, INC.
OPERATING STATISTICS, MEN'S DEPARTMENT,
Year Ending January 31, 1973
(000)

Sales[a]		$251.9
Cost of goods sold		147.5
Gross margin		104.4
Expenses:		
Sales, salaries and fringe benefits	$21.4	
Rent, utilities, and occupancy charges	8.4	
Advertising	1.9	
Other direct expense	1.2	
General overhead[b]	41.5	
		74.4
Profit before taxes		$ 30.0

[a]Sales comprised as follows:

Merchandise classification	Sales (000)	Gross margin (000)	Profit before taxes (000)	Inventory (at retail prices) (000)	Square footage
Men's furnishings	$170.1	$ 70.7	$20.7	$65.5	1,200
Trousers	71.3	30.5	9.8	28.4	500
Boys' clothing	10.5	3.2	(0.5)	5.3	200
Total	$251.9	$104.4	$30.0	$99.2	1,900

[b]Total general overhead of about $510,000 was allocated among departments in approximate proportion of each department's sales to total store sales.

Source: Company Records

Exhibit 7

SIMON'S, INC.
PROPOSED LAYOUT OF FURNITURE BUILDING

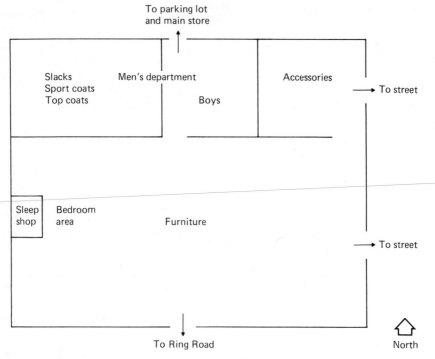

Source: KLB Report

Exhibit 8

SIMON'S, INC.
PROJECTED OPERATING STATISTICS FOR
MEN'S DEPARTMENT IN FURNITURE BUILDING
FOR FIRST FULL YEAR OF OPERATION UNDER PROPOSAL
(000)

Sales[a]		$360.0
Cost of goods sold		210.0
Gross margin		$150.0
Expenses:		
Sales, salaries, and fringe benefits	$29.0	
Rent, utilities, and occupancy charges	12.0	
Advertising	2.5	
Other direct expense	1.0	
General overhead	60.7	
Profit before taxes		106.0
		$ 43.4

[a]Sales comprised as follows:

Merchandise category	Sales	Inventory (at retail prices)	Square footage
Men's furnishings	$154,000	$ 58,500	1,100
Trousers	90,000	34,200	750
Boys' clothing	30,000	11,400	400
Sport coats and suits	56,000	21,300	500
Top coats	30,000	11,400	250
Total	$360,000	$136,800	3,000

Source: KLB Report

MODIFYING EXISTING PRODUCT LINES

OPTIONS FOR MODIFYING EXISTING PRODUCT LINES

A marketing manager may wish to modify an individual product or product line to increase sales or profits, to support the organization's marketing strategy, and to contribute toward the organization's objectives for its entire portfolio. A manager may modify an existing line by altering individually or jointly each of seven distinct attributes of a product line:

1. Position
2. Physical characteristics
3. Package
4. Brand
5. Amount and nature of value added
6. Expansion or reduction of the product line
7. Composition of the product line

The first five attributes—position, physical characteristics, package, brand, and value added—may apply to individual products and/or to product lines. The last two—expansion or reduction and composition—apply only to the sets of products which comprise a product line.

To achieve his or her goals, the marketing manager must see to it that these attributes of the product line are combined into a consistent whole. For example, package and brand must meet the interests of consumers in the market toward which the line is positioned. If a line is to be repositioned and the value added is to be altered, product modification is likely to be needed. Physical characteristics of individual products must be designed so that the composition of the line as a whole includes alternatives which offer consumers and resellers a range of individual products which they consider appropriate. Managers frequently vary these attributes singly or in combination to extend the life of a product line.

Decisions on each of these attributes must be made not only for existing product lines, which this chapter treats, but also as part of the detailed plans necessary for new ventures (discussed in a subsequent chapter). All of these attributes are analyzed in most decisions to reshape the product/market portfolio through disinvestment or reallocation of resources among product lines. The length of this chapter reflects the scope and detail of product line modification decisions, as well as their pervasiveness at all levels of product policy decision making. Nevertheless, it should be recognized that modification of an existing product line is only the first step toward developing an optimum portfolio of product lines and markets for an organization.

REPOSITIONING THE PRODUCT LINE

Every product or line has a definable position, which is typically described in relation to the markets or segments served by the line, and sometimes in relation to competitors' lines within each of the markets or segments served by that product line. For example, Camel and Lucky Strike cigarettes appear to be positioned toward a male market; Virginia Slims, toward a female market. Within the computer market, Control Data positions its product line for scientific and complex industrial applications, whereas Burroughs appears to aim its offerings principally at commercial and less complex industrial applications. BMW has attempted to position its cars against Volvo, Mercedes, and Cadillac Seville in the executive market for compact luxury cars.

The position of a product line may be defined rather differently by the manager responsible for the line, competitors, and consumers. A beer formerly imported into the United States from the United Kingdom was described by the company's export manager as "a European import which offers a lower cost alternative to Carlsberg and Lowenbrau"; the manager expected this brand to appeal to current and prospective drinkers of imported beer who were price conscious. One competitor described the brand as "a national beer without significant export potential." Consumers described it as "English beer," which lacked the appeal of German and Danish beers. Because consumers judged imported malt beverages principally on country of origin rather than on price, the competitor's position statement proved to be the most accurate. What is important to realize here is that position should be described in consumers' terms. And because consumers perceive position differently, it is essential to describe product position for specific market segments—for example, loyal users, sporadic users, and nonusers.

Sometimes a product line can be repositioned simply by altering the position of the line vis-à-vis the positions of competitors within a particular market. Such repositioning may lead to modifications of the marketing program which supports the line, but may not require changes in the product line itself. For example, a manufacturer of a premium-priced deodorant whose line was losing distribution in supermarkets and drugstores, the primary outlets for deodorant products, might decide not to modify the product line in an attempt to sustain distribution in mass-merchandise outlets, but rather to seek distribution of the line through cosmetics outlets, such as department stores, which typically carry lines different from those offered in mass-merchandise outlets. Such a repositioning would involve changes primarily in distribution channels and in the manufacturer's promotional mix. The repositioning might, but would not necessarily, involve catering to different customers; it might simply involve foregoing those customers who would have purchased the deodorant in a supermarket but would not do so at a department store.

A product line may also be repositioned by changing the markets toward which the line is directed, without significant alterations in the product line itself. A manufacturer or reseller can offer the existing line in a new market, with whatever repositioning may be necessary for the new market, while retaining the present position in existing markets or by repositioning the line to shift it from one market to another.

In some cases, the addition of a market involves little more than added advertising, selling, and sales promotion activity, e.g., taking a consumer packaged good from one regional market to another as part of a national "roll-out." Of greater interest, however, are instances in which the addition of a market involves a complete repositioning of the product. A regional Canadian brewer, dominant in his home provinces, attempted to enter the Massachusetts market. In his home market, the brewer's product was comparable to many nationally distributed Canadian beers. In Massachusetts, however, because the brewer had to cover freight and customs costs he was forced to price above the large-selling domestic beers, to compete with established Canadian and European imports, and to carve out a position as a premium-quality imported beer. The costs of developing this position required a share of market larger than that held by all the Canadian beers combined, and required taking a significant share from the European imports. These high costs ultimately led the brewer to withdraw from Massachusetts.

Markets may be added as a product line matures and both marketer and new consumers perceive that the product line has become appropriate for a new market or application. Many home-workshop tools have followed this pattern, starting first with professional craftsmen, then being marketed to and accepted by "do-it-yourselfers" for home-maintenance and improvement projects. Addition of new markets in this manner represents one method of extending the life cycle of a product line. Changes in distribution and promotion programs are ordinarily essential to such market additions; changes in the physical characteristics of the product (another method frequently employed to extend product line life) may or may not be needed.

The decision to shift a product line from one market to another may require an investment much larger than that necessary to add a market. Several years ago Marlboro cigarettes served a market largely composed of women and of men who preferred a milder image. Philip Morris undertook to change the image of Marlboro to a masculine, Western image, and thereby to shift the brand from its original market to one composed of men who favored this image. The repositioning succeeded, but only through an extensive advertising campaign.

Sometimes shifting markets takes the form of specialization in a particular "niche" in the market or concentration on a particular market segment. In the early days of air freight, pioneering air freight firms attempted to serve the needs of companies which used air freight for emergency shipments only, as well as those who were experimenting with the new mode for routine shipment of certain types of products. As users refined their requirements and air freight firms discovered their own particular strengths and weaknesses, the firms repositioned themselves as specialists, some concentrating on emergency shipments and others on routine product distribution.

Repositioning may be deliberate, as described above, or inadvertent, as in the case of an independent supermarket operator who maintained a certain merchandise mix and prices despite the exodus of a middle-income ethnic group from the neighborhood and its replacement by lower-income families, many of whose tastes in food were distinctly different from those of the ethnic group that had left. By failing to change with the market, the retailer inadvertently "traded up," operating a store whose products and prices differed from what the new residents wanted and could afford. (Unresponsive both to neighborhood committees of new residents and to threats from those who accused him of "profiteering," the retailer ultimately saw his store burned.)

Several factors stimulate decisions to add, shift, or withdraw from markets, including changes in size and importance of particular market segments, competitive pressures and opportunities, channels of distribution, and costs. The niche specialization of air freight firms occurred in response to increased size of each of the major market segments, along with responses to competitors' service and price moves. The change of some traditional lumber yards into mass-merchandisers of home-building and improvement products and the demise of other yards forced manufacturers of paint and hardware items to remerchandise their lines consistent with the reduction in personal selling help available to the consumer at the retail level and the greater reliance on self-selection. The cost of servicing hundreds of small users led a manufacturer of transformers and telecommunications equipment to withdraw from the small-user market by adopting a quantity-discount pricing schedule.

In general, entering or shifting a product line to a new market is most likely to be profitable when that market is relatively large and growing, when the firm has a distinct competitive advantage, when the channels which serve the new market are increasing their penetration, and when the incremental costs of serving the market are low. Conversely, shifting a product line away from a market may be indicated when the market is small and shrinking, when the firm lacks any clear competitive advantage, when the channels which reach the market are losing penetration, and when the costs of remaining in that market are relatively high.

Marketing managers contemplating repositioning of their lines frequently encounter difficulty in defining and segmenting prospective additional markets. Some useful dimensions for defining and segmenting markets for this purpose include the following:

- The user: Will adults or children be primary users of a particular breakfast cereal? Will men, women, or the whole family use a particular deodorant?

- The purchaser: Who will purchase the cereal or the deodorant—the user, or someone else (typically the housewife-purchasing agent in the family)?

Users and purchasers may be defined on several different dimensions, including physical characteristics (age, sex, height, weight, etc., for individuals; size, location, ownership [private vs. public], etc., for organizations); educational and occupational characteristics of individuals; Standard Industrial Classification (SIC) designation, Original Equipment Manufacturer (OEM) vs. user, for organizations; attitudes and information preferences; patterns of purchase and use.

- Use of application: Will a particular pet food be used as a treat or a staple food?

- Appeal: Some toothpastes stress cleanliness and dental hygiene, while others emphasize sex appeal.

- Price/feature combinations: In automobiles and wristwatches, there appear to be two distinct markets—the first composed of persons who want acceptable performance at minimum price (Ford, Chevrolet; Timex); and the second, of those who prefer the best and are willing to pay for it (Cadillac; Omega).

- Brand preference: Some individuals are fiercely brand loyal, others continually switch brands.
- Performance characteristics: Some shampoos are intended for dandruff conditions, others for dry scalp, and still others for oily hair.
- Knowledge: Some buyers (both consumers and organizations) recognize their purchase objectives, while others do not; both groups may be divided again into those who understand differences among the available alternatives quite precisely, and others who lack that knowledge. Some men, for example, feel perfectly confident buying their own suits; others cannot do so without the help of a female companion.

These dimensions illustrate, but by no means exhaust, possible bases for defining and segmenting prospective markets. Entry into markets defined on these dimensions will likely require changes in marketing communication programs, and perhaps in price and distribution as well.

Trading Up and Trading Down

One important method of repositioning a product line involves "trading up" or "trading down." Trading up involves adding value to the product through additional features, higher quality materials, and the like, and raising the price. Trading down involves reducing the number of features and/or quality, and reducing the price. Trading up or down may involve either shifts within an existing product line or adding or withdrawing products at the extremes of the price range spanned by the product line. Addition of a deluxe model, with more features, higher quality, and a higher price than present offering, represents a trading up in the position of the entire line; withdrawal of a deluxe model, a trading down. Chrysler's discontinuation of the deluxe Imperial models is an example of such a trading down. Addition of a "promotional" model to extend the price/feature spectrum downward involves trading down; withdrawal of such a model, trading up of the entire line.

Trading up or down may yield short-term gains, but create long-run problems. During the depression of the 1930s, the Packard Motor Car Company, which until that time had offered a product in the "luxury car" class, significantly reduced both the price and the features of its cars, making them competitors in the medium-price/medium-quality automobile market. Although the company survived the depression, it faced a difficult time competing in that intermediate market and was unable to trade back up into the luxury car class. Shortly after World War II, the Packard disappeared from the market.

Trading up is sometimes attempted through image enhancement, i.e., a promotional campaign and a price increase without an accompanying change in product features. Such a strategy is less likely to be effective than one that involves both promotion and product modification.

Trading up or down may be accomplished with no change in prices or product characteristics if the market itself shifts. A midwestern "low overhead" apparel retailer maintained the price and quality levels he offered in the late 1940s through 1970, when the firm became insolvent. During that period, consumers in the market served by the retailer had themselves "traded up" to more costly, higher quality apparel, and no longer had significant interest in the lower price and quality levels they had formerly sought. Other stores moved to meet the consumers' changing interest, and gradually took the market away from the original "low overhead" operator.

In the examples cited above, repositioning occurred because the revised product line had a different position vis-à-vis competing product lines and because the altered line served a different set of markets. Trading up (or down) may also be undertaken in order to avoid inadvertent repositioning. During the 25 years after World War II, the major American automobile manufacturers regularly increased engine size, features, and prices to meet the changing interests of the markets they served and to keep pace with one another. In the energy shortage of the early 1970s, however, these manufacturers reduced engine size and prices on many models, again to keep in step with a changing market. In this instance, trading up and down occurred, but repositioning did not necessarily occur for all manufacturers.

SELECTED REFERENCES

MAGGARD, JOHN P. "Positioning Revisited." *Journal of Marketing,* January 1976.
WIND, YORAM. "The Perception of a Firm's Competitive Position." In Franco M. Nicosia and Yoram Wind (eds.), *Behavioral Models of Market Analysis,* Hinsdale, Ill.: The Dryden Press, 1975.
YANKELOVICH, D. "New Criteria for Market Segmentation." *Harvard Business Review,* March–April 1964.

CHANGING THE PRODUCT CHARACTERISTICS

Of central importance in managing the existing product line is the question, "What changes should be made in the characteristics of current products in the line, and under what circumstances?" A product characteristic is any definable physical feature of a product. Changes in product characteristics may include changes in quality type and level, changes in performance features, or changes in features which alter the appearance of the product. The term "quality" is distinct from "qualities" or "features" of a product.

Quality

Quality of a product may refer to the type of material used to manufacture the product or to the level, grade, or purity of materials used. Changes in the type of materials used include the use of nylon versus polyester for making binding tape and the use of steel, aluminum, fibergalss, or wood for tennis racket frames. An example of a change in the level or grade of materials is the use of 12-guage steel as opposed to the thinner and lighter 16-guage steel in the manufacture of waste cans.

Alterations in the type or level of quality of materials used in manufacturing may result in changes in performance of a product. The type of thread used to make binding tape affects the stress it can withstand in certain situations. The material used to make a tennis racket frame affects the performance (playing) characteristics of the racket. And the thickness and weight of steel used in a waste container affects its durability under particular use conditions.

Quality of a product may also be defined in terms of the degree of technical perfection of design, which may manifest itself in performance, appearance, or ease of service of the product; the manufacturing and quality control procedures and requirements (e.g., number of defective units per thousand made); and the degree of particular attributes possessed (e.g., tensile strength of tape, maximum speed and torque of an electric motor, etc.). Because technical definitions of some quality attributes may differ considerably from consumers' definitions, the latter must be interpreted and translated into technical terms with care. For example, the market research department of a manufacturer of household paper goods asked consumers to evaluate a new formulation for a tissue which it was considering to replace the company's present formulation. Consumers responded favorably to the prospective product with one exception—they thought it wasn't soft enough. Company technical personnel set about "softening" the product in terms they understood—by weakening the fibers and reducing the density of fibers. When the revised product was use-tested, it literally fell apart. Market research and technical personnel subsequently discovered that the way to make this particular tissue feel "soft" to consumers was actually to *increase* the strength and density of the fibers—just the opposite of what technical personnel originally thought consumers had meant.

A marketing manager may alter type or level of quality in response to changes in legal or regulatory codes, changes in accepted industry standards, pressures from consumer groups, or changes initiated by a highly visible competitor whom consumers consider a pacesetter in terms of quality. A marketing manager may also seek to modify type or level of quality in the product line when planning a change in performance or appearance features of a product or when planning to modify the combinations of prices and features offered within the product line.

A level of product quality that is perceived high by customers may enhance a firm's profitability. Results from the PIMS (Profit Impact of Market Share) Program suggest that businesses with high quality products and strong market positions enjoy high average returns on investment, and that a high quality product may compensate for a weak market position.

Performance Features

Changes in performance features may include changes in the type or method of performance of a component or the whole product, or changes in the particular combination and arrangement of components which comprise the product. For example, use of a rotary engine instead of a conventional internal combustion engine represents a change in method of automobile propulsion. An example of a change in combination of components is the substitution of a microwave oven for the second conventional oven in a line of kitchen ranges.

Changes in method of product performance may affect the kind of performance a product delivers. The use of a rotating ball instead of a moving carriage on electric typewriters (a change in the method of performing the typing function) has increased the capability of typewriters to provide a variety of scripts and spacings previously unavailable. Some motorists believe that rotary engines deliver a type of automobile performance different from that of a conventional internal combustion engine.

Changes in performance features may affect the durability, versatility, and utility of particular products in specific applications. Consequently, such changes may lead to the repositioning of products in current markets, or permit their entry into new markets. Thus a change in material of manufacture may lead to a change in type of performance, which may in turn lead to a new market opportunity.

Perhaps the most frequent stimulus to change in performance features is the appearance of new technology, either from within a firm's own laboratory or from a competitor, either outside or inside the industry. Because the appearance of a new technology may threaten the very basis of a company's existing product line, it is worthwhile to ask what happens to existing products when a new, presumably superior technology is introduced. Data from a variety of industries ranging from razors to locomotives indicate the following: If sales of current products (i.e., those based on existing technology) do not decline sharply within a year of the commercial introduction of the new technology, sales may either (1) decline gradually over a period of more than five years, or (2) continue to expand in dollars, if not in market share. Reasons for the slow decline or even continued expansion include, among others, the following: (1) the new technology is unrefined at first, and therefore not always commercially suitable; (2) users may be slow to accept the innovation, primarily because use habits (perhaps including work rules embodied in labor agreements) require considerable time and persuasion to modify, and because commercializing the new technology may require substantial capital outlays: (3) although the new technology may initially appear promising for a wide range of applications and market segments, it may not become technically or economically feasible for many of them.

Nevertheless, because consumers may gradually accept the new technology as it becomes more refined, firms whose product lines are threatened by new technology may pursue what Levitt calls a policy of "innovative imitation"; that is, as soon as they become aware of new technology that is likely to impact present product lines, they begin exploring the possibilities of acquiring the technology either through internal research and development or through acquisition. In some instances, the time required to duplicate a competitor's technical advance may be too short, or the capital requirements too great, for a firm to copy directly the first-generation product based on the new technology. In such instances, a company may wish to employ a strategy of "technological leapfrog"; that is, to begin immediately to develop the second-generation product, either for the entire market or for a segment that appears to be particularly appropriate for the specific product the firm believes it has the best chance to commercialize successfully.

Just as some firms deliberately follow a policy of attempting to maintain technical leadership, so others intentionally pursue a policy of "watchful waiting," hoping to imitate, either directly or through a "leapfrog" strategy, the particular features and technology of the leaders. Although this strategy may be quite profitable and relatively free of risk for the second or third firms to offer a particular feature or technology, for subsequent imitators the strategy is likely to involve high marketing costs with limited possibility of gaining market share.

In addition to changes in technology and market conditions, changes in government regulations and laws may stimulate changes in or the addition of performance features. Examples of such changes include the replacement of two-pronged electrical plugs with three-pronged, grounded plugs and the addition of emission control systems to automobiles. Because changes in regulation or law seldom occur without warning, companies whose product lines may be affected by such changes are frequently advised to work with the appropriate government agency in drawing up the revised requirements and to begin planning for possible revisions or additions to products well in advance of the time at which the new requirement is likely to become effective.

The financial impact on a firm of changing or adding a performance feature depends on several factors. Among the most important appear to be (1) the cost of changing or adding the feature; (2) the probability and speed with which competitors will copy the feature; (3) the size of the market segment to which the specific feature appeals; (4) the importance of performance features in determining consumers' preferences among alternatives; (5) the size of the market segment that may dislike the new feature.

The cost may be analyzed in terms of comparing the increased expenses associated with providing the feature (and servicing it after sale, if appropriate) with the increased revenues and units which must be sold to recover the cost. The lower that break-even point, the more attractive the new feature is likely to appear to the firm.

It is very likely that competitors will copy any feature which they consider to be successful in a particular market segment which they serve or hope to enter, provided that adequate patent protection is unavailable. The speed with which performance features are copied by numerous competitors has varied from months (or less) in the life insurance and furniture industries, to several years in wristwatches and major appliances. In general, the more rapidly competitors copy, the less likely the new feature is to provide a competitive advantage.

The larger the segment to which a new feature appeals, the more profitable it is likely to be, provided that the firm has sufficient resources to capitalize on that appeal. The size of the segment to which a particular feature appeals may change over time. In 1950, a television manufacturer offered a device that enabled the viewer to magnify the image in the center portion of the screen. Because few consumers were interested, the feature was dropped. But in 1975 the feature reappeared and has remained available.

If performance features are important influences on consumers' choices, changed or added features may help increase—or at least avoid erosion in—market share. If performance features are relatively unimportant, as in bedroom furniture, for example, where styling is considered a more powerful determinant of choice, new performance features are not likely, to enhance profits.

If a significant segment of the market is apt to dislike a performance feature, a firm may choose to forego that segment in favor of the segment to which the feature is thought likely to appeal or, more often, to make the feature optional on some or all models. Because the television magnification device or a remote control device for home television receivers appeal to limited segments, and because the increased cost of television receivers so equipped would discourage many consumers, manufacturers have made those features optional.

In sum, a firm will likely find it profitable to add or change a performance feature when the incremental cost of doing so is low, the probability of competitive duplication is low, the speed of competitors' copying is slow, the appeal is to a broad segment to whom performance features are important determinants of choice, and the number of consumers who will be alienated by the new feature is small. Although it is tempting to make changes in or additions to performance features when the cost of doing so is minimal, such a practice may lead to a series of trivial product changes which are unimportant to most consumers (and may even alienate some) and may unnecessarily diffuse the marketing and engineering efforts of the firm.

Appearance Features

Changes that affect the appearance, but not the performance, of a product are often referred to as "cosmetic" changes. Such changes may include changes in color of component parts subsequently incorporated into (perhaps even hidden within) industrial machinery; the size or shape of controls on industrial equipment; and handles, knobs, and a variety of other builders' hardware items. Perhaps the most visible type of appearance change is the seasonal or annual fashion or style change, which may involve changes in design, color, pattern, texture, and other determinants of appearance. Many such changes, especially in wearing apparel, involve no significant change in performance capabilities. Annual fashion changes in automobiles, however, frequently involve some performance changes along with appearance changes.

Marketing managers may alter the appearance features of their product lines in response to changes in consumers' preferences and changes in the appearance of competing products; along with changes in materials or performance features (a change in material or performance may require a change in product appearance); or in order to obtain savings in design, factory labor, and associated manufacturing costs.

The timing of changes in appearance may be crucial to the success of the product line, as in the apparel industry; or relatively unimportant, as in the case of industrial capital equipment. Similarly, the frequency of major changes in the appearance of a product line varies from seasonally for apparel and home furnishings to more than a year (or even several years) for certain types of industrial equipment.

Some companies plan major model changes on a periodic multi-year cycle, in addition to more modest periodic or occasional product modifications. Other companies do not plan such major redesign efforts to occur on a regular basis, but only as alterations in customers' requirements, changes in competitors' products, other modifications in the product line, or cost pressures may require them to respond.

SELECTED REFERENCES

COOPER, ARNOLD C., and DAN SCHENDEL. "Strategic Responses and Technological Threats." *Business Horizons,* February 1976.

KUEHN, ALFRED A., and RALPH L. DAY. "Strategy of Product Quality." *Harvard Business Review,* November–December 1962, vol. 40, no. 6.

LEVITT, THEODORE. "Innovative Imitation." *Harvard Business Review,* September–October 1966, vol. 44, no. 6.

"NEW PRODUCT MIDDLE AGE." *Sales Management,* November 1962.

"SOME PIMS PROGRAM FINDINGS." *Marketing News,* July 1976.

STAUDT, THOMAS A. "Higher Management Risks in Product Strategy." *Journal of Marketing,* January 1973, vol. 37, no. 1.

STEWART, JOHN B. "Functional Features in Product Strategy." *Harvard Business Review,* March–April 1959.

VAN DYCK, KENNETH. "New Products from Old: Short Cut to Profits." *Industrial Marketing,* November 1965.

VILLANI, KATHRYN A., and DONALD G. MORRISON. "A Method for Analyzing New Formulation Decisions." *Journal of Marketing Research,* August 1976.

CHANGING THE PACKAGE

The package has essentially five functions with respect to the product line: to store the product, to protect it, to facilitate use of it, to help position or reposition it, and to help sell it. Marketing managers may alter the functional characteristics or appearance of the package to improve the performance of one or more of these functions or to reduce costs.

Storage functions must be performed at the manufacturer, reseller, and user levels. In recent years, many manufacturers have changed both the size of the packages of their products and the number of individual packages enclosed in bulk shipping cartons to conform to the changes in palletizing, desired lot size, and other materials-handling changes adopted by resellers. In some instances, the manufacturers themselves initiated these changes in an attempt to reduce handling and storage costs throughout the entire channel of distribution. A dramatic example of a package redesign which reduced the total cost of the product was achieved by Millipore, which sells membrane filters and filtering equipment to the pharmaceutical, wine, and beer industries. The company changed its package from individually-wrapped cushioning materials to a shrink-wrapped plastic on a tray. The redesigned shipping cartons increased the speed of order processing by almost 170 percent, and in its first 16 months the package had suffered no damage in transit. In addition, a savings of 20 percent on materials and $10,000 in overtime on shipping line labor was realized. Customers were also satisfied; the containers are easier to unpack with less trash to discard, and the products remained dust free in transit and storage. Uncertainties about availability and costs of packaging materials will likely lead to increased interest in package material changes.

To protect the product against vibration, pressure, changes in temperature, and other hazards during shipment from manufacturer to reseller, some manufacturers perform an extensive series of tests on alternative package formulations. The package may also serve to protect the product on the shelf. In the early 1970s one sugar processor added a resealable aluminum foil envelope inside the traditional paper carton used to hold brown sugar to protect the contents from exposure which would cause the sugar to harden and become difficult to use.

Packages may facilitate use by serving as dispensers for a product. In recent years, an increasing number of household cleaners have become available in spray-dispenser containers. One manufacturer based a series of television commercials on the advantages claimed for the shape of its dispenser compared with the shape of that of a leading competitor. Packages may also facilitate use by providing clear and concise instructions for the preparation and use of the product. Several manufacturers based outside the English-speaking world have switched from presenting on (or in) the package translations of instructions originally prepared in the native language to having instructions written by individuals for whom English (or American) is a native language. The copy on the package constitutes a very important source of information to the consumer in many product lines. In pharmaceutical products sold over the counter (without prescription), for example, the message on the package conveys important information on the use and the risks of particular products. Manufacturers of pharmaceuticals are facing increased regulatory attention to the content of that package information; the influence of regulations on package copy in this and other industries is likely to increase significantly in the next decade.

The marketing manager may use the package to help position or reposition a product. The distinctive shape of the Taster's Choice Freeze-Dried Coffee container is credited with differentiating that product from Maxim, a competing brand, and helping Taster's Choice to carve out its own specific niche in the market. A small publisher, left because of disappointing sales with a large inventory of a book on American folklore, packaged the book in a slip-on box, had it wrapped in cellophane, and sold substantial quantities which were purchased principally as unusual gifts, rather than for the subject of the book.

A package can stimulate sales of a product through gaining shelf space and through employing a distinctive shape or material and/or more powerful graphic design. Several years ago, Bristol-Myers packaged Ban roll-on deodorant in a shadowbox package that effectively more than doubled the shelf space for the product, which by itself was so slender that even several facings could well be passed up by a consumer. Distinctive shapes or novel materials may draw attention to a product and enhance its image. Ritter uses a glass jar to package asparagus; the jar is designed to rest on its cap. The unusual material and configuration of the package dramatize the line on the grocery shelf. Janitor-in-a-Drum household cleaner is packaged in a plastic container resembling a miniature drum of industrial cleaning chemicals to project its image. Improvement of package graphics is credited with stimulating a significant improvement in sales of Nice 'n Easy hair coloring. But changes in illustrations may adversely affect sales. A manufacturer of frosting mix attempted to improve the appearance of the package by changing the illustration of the frosted cakes. The brand's share fell dramatically; consumer interviews revealed that a change in color of the illustration of the frosted cake had signaled a change in chocolate flavor to the consumer.

SELECTED REFERENCES

SCHWARTZ, DAVID A. "Research Can Help Solve Packaging Functional and Design Problems That May Be Costing You Sales." *Marketing News*, January 16, 1976.
NOTE ON PRODUCT POLICY. Boston: Intercollegiate Case Clearing House, ICH10M67.
KLUGE, ELEANOR S. "Modification of Product Lines Through Packaging." Working Paper, Center for Experimental Studies in Business, Graduate School of Business Administration, University of Minnesota.

MODIFYING BRAND POLICIES

A brand is "a name, term, sign, symbol, or design, or combination of them which is intended to identify the goods or services of one seller or group of sellers and to differentiate them from those of competitors."* Brands may be identified by names or by distinctive trademarks or, in the case of some products, simply by the name of the seller. An *individual brand* is one unique to a particular product, which may include multiple flavors or styles, and multiple sizes, e.g., Gainesburgers. A *family brand* is one applied to an entire line of different products, e.g., Del Monte canned peas, beans, beets, carrots, etc. A *manufacturer's brand* is one which is owned by a manufacturer, who possesses the exclusive right to use or control the use of that brand. A manufacturer's brand may be national or regional, depending upon the scope of distribution coverage of the brand. A *reseller's brand* (or "private label" or "house brand") is one which is owned and controlled by a reseller—a retail institution, an integrated wholesaler-retailer, a wholesaler or industrial distributor. Ownership and control of a brand ordinarily coexist with authority to control the marketing strategy for the brand. An exception to this general statement is the *controlled brand,* which the manufacturer owns, but makes available exclusively to one reseller.

Manufacturers face four distinct decisions with respect to brand policy: (1) whether to offer the product under their own label, under resellers' labels, or both; (2) whether to offer their own branded products under individual or family brands; (3) at what levels of quality (and price) to offer branded products; (4) how many different brands to offer at particular quality levels. Resellers have parallel options.

Manufacturer or Reseller Label

The circumstances under which manufacturers would find it desirable to increase emphasis upon or offer a reseller's brand in addition to their own brands are similar to the circumstances that would encourage resellers to request products packed under private label. (Nevertheless, the negotiations between manufacturers and resellers involved in private label programs may be prolonged, because each may analyze present and prospective

---

Marketing Definitions: A Glossary of Marketing Terms. Chicago: American Marketing Association, 1960.

market conditions differently and each will be concerned about self-interest.) These circumstances include the following:

1. The product class is past the midpoint in the "growth" stage of the life cycle; some market segments may already be saturated. In product classes in which private labels have a significant market share, that share (for all private labels combined) typically increases during the latter half of the growth stage of the product class life cycle and stabilizes thereafter.

2. Consumers are beginning to consider alternative offerings within the product class as undifferentiated substitutes for one another; i.e., the product class is approaching "commodity" status. This perception of equivalence is likely to occur only after the product class begins to mature, but will not be shared by all consumers, some of whom will still prefer manufacturers' brands. In such mature product classes as power lawn mowers and canned vegetables, resellers' brands have significant, but by no means total market shares. But resellers' labels do not play major roles in such mature product classes as toothpaste and beer.

3. The reseller becomes more important than the manufacturer as a source of assurance of quality or style or both to the customer, and has greater economic power than the manufacturer. In recent years consumers have increased their reliance on the reseller as a source of advice and assurance in the purchase of paint. At the same time, changes in the channels of distribution have increased the concentration of paint sales in chains of large, self-service home-improvement centers, and decreased paint sales in paint stores or lumber yards. Most paint manufacturers, historically modest in size and regional in market, faced large, highly visible retail organizations which desired private or controlled labels. As a result of these changes, sales of paint under resellers' labels have taken market share from manufacturers' labels.

4. Changes in the competitive environment stimulate manufacturers to provide private labels, lest they lose distribution to competing manufacturers who will do so. Failure to provide a private brand to resellers who offer only one brand in a product class may result in a manufacturer's losing distribution among those resellers. A manufacturer of fireplace fixtures recently lost distribution in a chain of home-improvement centers because he was unwilling to supply products under the reseller's label; the chain found other manufacturers willing to do so. Even when resellers offer both manufacturers' brands and their own brands, manufacturers are often reluctant to provide private label merchandise, fearing that sales of the private label might take sales away from the manufacturer's label, either because the reseller will reduce support (display and sales promotion) for the manufacturer's brand or because consumers will recognize that they may obtain identical products under either the manufacturer's or the reseller's label. Because private label sales are typically less profitable to manufacturers than sales of their own brands, they will ordinarily offer a private label only when they consider it more desirable to have their own private brand "cannibalize" sales of their manufacturer's brand, rather than to have another manufacturer's private brand do so.

5. Economic slowdowns cause consumers to seek lower-priced products. Historically, manufacturers and resellers in numerous product classes have increased emphasis on private labels or introduced new private labels during periods of economic recession, partly to stimulate sales and partly to avoid compromising the quality images of established brand names (i.e., to avoid "trading down"). Nevertheless, the argument that private label products offer lower prices to the customer is not always supported. In many product classes, prices of manufacturers' and resellers' brands overlap one another in the medium and lower price ranges.

6. The resellers' volume becomes adequate to permit economic production of a custom product by the manufacturer and stocking and promoting by the reseller; and the changes in production, distribution, stocking, and promotion will not require extraordinary commitments of physical, technical, financial, or human resources by either manufacturer or reseller. For a reseller, emphasizing private labels implies a backward vertical integration, involving the assumption of certain functions formerly handled by the manufacturer. Resellers large in size or dominance in particular product classifications are likely to find private label programs most attractive.

For a manufacturer, greater emphasis on private brands shifts a portion of the marketing function to the reseller. Such a shift may be most attractive to small companies whose marketing resources are limited and for whom the smoothing of production schedules and improved cash flow ordinarily associated with private labeling can be particularly attractive. Indeed, manufacturers with excess capacity often aggressively seek private label contracts in order to make use of that capacity. Such contracts may be negotiated at prices (to the reseller) very little above marginal costs of producing the private label product.

Individual vs. Family Brands

The shifting of emphasis from individual brands to family brands often represents a fairly subtle change, partly because the distinction between the two categories is not always clear-cut. General Motors, for example, promotes Chevrolet as an individual brand, but, through some promotional activities and in certain distribution areas, links Chevrolet closely with other individual brand names offered by the company. Although General Mills promotes Wheaties principally as an individual brand, the package also displays the "Big G" trademark (the family brand) common to all General Mills breakfast foods. Over the years, the "Big G" trademark has assumed varying degrees of prominence in the company's promotional efforts. Other brands, such as General Foods' Gainesburgers or Jello-O, are almost wholly individual brands. In contrast, brand names like Green Giant, Smucker, and Presto are associated not just with individual products, but with entire product lines.

Emphasis by manufacturers on individual brands, as distinct from family brands, may be more appropriate for product lines composed of unlike products, of products whose individual characteristics are more important to the consumer than characteristics of the manufacturer or family, and of products which might be confused with other offerings different in quality of the same manufacturer. Emphasis on family brands, on the other hand, may be appropriate for product lines in which the individual items are similar in type and quality, in which the reputation of the vendor is more important than that of the particular item, in which individual products might be confused with similar offerings of competing vendors, for which an "umbrella" advertising and promotional strategy offers higher impact and/or greater economy than a series of individual campaigns, and in which manufacturers wish to facilitate frequent additions (each modest in scale) to the product line with minimum risk. Thus General Foods might well consider it inappropriate to put Gainesburgers—food for dogs—under the same common family brand name as Jello-O—food for humans. But the company's Post division emphasizes the "Post" family name to differentiate its breakfast foods from the camparable offerings of Kellogg's and General Mills. Processors of canned and frozen vegetables place even more emphasis on the family brand—e.g., Green Giant, Del Monte—in order to differentiate their items from the virtually identical peas, beans, or carrots of competing manufacturers. Manufacturers of portable appliances may benefit more from advertising the family brand than from individual brands, because a household ordinarily purchases an iron, coffemaker, or toaster infrequently, even though it may purchase a series of portable appliances over a period of years. Consumer familiarity with a family brand may facilitate the introduction of new appliances that manufacturers typically offer each year. Given that purchase pattern, emphasis on the quality and reliability of the manufacturers, rather than on the individual item, appears appropriate.

Resellers ordinarily use family brands for related items rather than individual brands for items under their own private labels, e.g., Craftsman tools (Sears). Only in rare instances would a reseller have a large enough market for one individual product, but not for other similar items, to justify the costs of building brand recognition and stocking an individual brand.

Levels of Quality

Manufacturers and resellers frequently use different brand names to differentiate levels of quality within a particular product class. General Motors offers five distinct brands of automobiles differentiated in terms of sets of features and quality (Chevrolet, Pontiac, Oldsmobile, Buick, and Cadillac). Sears, Wards, and other retailers who make extensive use of their own brands identify "good," "better," and "best" levels of quality in products ranging from men's underwear to metal fence materials. Such distinctions are intended to provide the consumer with pertinent information on which to make his or her choice.

Number of Brands at a Quality Level

Manufacturers may offer multiple brands, which differ little with respect to quality and features, in order to maintain limited distribution of a particular brand. For example, Hickey-Freeman makes men's clothing both under its own name and under the Walter

Morton label. Both brands are sold by exclusive men's stores in the same geographic areas, but the manufacturer attempts to avoid offering the same brand to stores which compete directly with one another in a particular shopping center or metropolitan area. The purpose in limiting distribution of each brand is to protect retailers' margins, by avoidance of price cutting, so that retailers will be able to provide the extensive display and inventory, fitting, delivery, and credit services desired by most men who buy high-priced clothing.

Changes in the structure of the distribution channels may motivate manufacturers to change the number of brands offered at a particular quality level. When discount houses first emerged as threats to conventional retailers of appliances and similar items, manufacturers faced pressure from their established resellers to withhold manufacturers' brands from the new type of retailer. The discounters, many of which were growing rapidly, pressed the manufacturers to sell them established brands so that the discounters could convince customers of the savings they could obtain compared to traditional retailers. In an effort to placate their established outlets, yet participate at least to some extent in the growth of discount houses, many manufacturers adopted a two-brand policy: the established manufacturer's brand for the traditional outlets, and a new brand for the discounters. Occasionally some features of the product in addition to the nameplate were changed, but frequently the same product, identical but for the nameplate, was offered through both channels. As the discount house matured into the mass-merchandise outlet and to a major extent replaced traditional outlets for appliances, many manufacturers gradually abandoned the two-brand policy and offered their own branded items to both types of outlets, which by that time had begun to price comparably to one another at the retail level.

The offering of multiple brands within a quality range may be intended to manage an existing or changing distribution system, as described above, or to reach multiple market segments that do not differ by retail outlet preference. In the latter case, multi-brand entries represent an expansion of the product line.

SELECTED REFERENCES

COOK, VICTOR J., and THOMAS F. SCHUTTE. *Brand Policy Determination*. Boston: Allyn and Bacon, 1967.

KOTLER, PHILIP. *Marketing Management* (3d ed.). Englewood Cliffs, N.J.: Prentice-Hall, 1976.

LEVITT, THEODORE. "Branding on Trial." *Harvard Business Review*, March–April 1966, vol. 44, no. 2.

MOREM, JOSEPH A. "Shift From Brand to Product Line Marketing." *Harvard Business Review*, September–October 1975, vol. 53, no. 5.

CHANGING THE AMOUNT AND NATURE OF VALUE ADDED

In this context, the concept of "value added" refers to the change in the physical characteristics of the product from the time the constituent ingredients of the product enter the organization to the time the product is sold by the organization. Most of the value added that affects the physical characteristics of the product occurs at the manufacturer or processor level. Some distributors, particularly of industrial goods, perform limited processing and customizing functions which alter the physical characteristics of the product, and some retailers—particularly in the automotive and apparel industries—perform final assembly and alteration functions which customize the physical product for each purchaser.

Changes in amount and nature of value added are sometimes described as changes in the level of manufacture engaged in by the firm, i.e., raw materials supply, component manufacture, and finished goods manufacture. Changes in the physical value added to the product line in most, but not all, cases involve repositioning the line because either markets or competitors or both differ from one level of manufacture to the next.

A manufacturer may change the amount and type of value added by offering components instead of semifinished or raw materials, or completed products instead of components. Such changes, sometimes described as "vertical forward integration," involve taking over functions previously performed by customers or shifting markets to customers who had not performed those functions. In either case, those manufacturers who do integrate forward are likely to face different competitors from those they faced before and will have to position their offerings somewhat differently. Indeed, after adding value to their product lines, manufacturers may be competing with their customers. Such competition may produce little conflict or may force manufacturers to choose between serving customers for materials or components and serving customers for finished goods. Many such conflicts among manufacturers and their customers can be resolved provided that the customer's survival is not threatened.

A firm that offers finished products may go beyond selling individual products to selling completely assembled systems which include several individual products and may include elaborate software or support services. One firm that did so is NCR, which in the early 1960s shifted from offering separately to large accounts three product lines—cash registers, accounting machines, and computers—to offering integrated systems, coupling cash registers (input devices) with computers (processors) and accounting machines (processors and output devices). In contrast, many manufacturers of home sound equipment, for example, have continued to offer one type of component—speakers, record players, or receiver/amplifiers—and have left to retailers the function of assembling those components into systems. (Other manufacturers in that industry have elected to offer complete systems, although many such systems include components purchased from other manufacturers and simply assembled into the final product.)

Organizations heavily involved in research and development activities are faced from time to time with the decision of whether to offer their expertise in the form of (1) consulting and design services, (2) development of prototypes or initial applications, (3) manufacture of customized products for specialized applications, or (4) manufacture of standard products.

Although the markets for design services and prototype development may overlap, as may those for initial and custom applications, ordinarily the number of customers increases and their technical sophistication decreases as one moves away from the market for consultation and design and toward that for standard products. The specific competitors and the bases of competition differ substantially from one market to the next. As a result, the decision to move from one level to another involves a major repositioning of the product line. MTS Systems, a manufacturer of testing equipment, has moved from one level of manufacture to another by adding markets as particular technologies matured.

Opportunities for increasing the amount of value added—i.e., offering a product in a more complete stage—may arise as a result of changes in consumers' desires, changes in the distribution structure, or changes in technology. For example, the increased interest of consumers in "convenience foods" during the past 25 years has provided opportunities for flour millers to produce cake mixes and refrigerated and frozen flour-based products for home consumption. In this instance, the value added by flour millers replaced value formerly added by consumers.

The rapid expansion of franchised fast-food outlets with needs for uniform quality and portion control on a national basis stimulated those chains to seek suppliers other than the local meat processors on whom restaurants had previously relied. The chains encouraged some operators of large slaughterhouses, who formerly shipped raw carcasses of fresh meat to local butchers for cutting and resale, to add value to their product by cutting and forming it into individual portions, freezing the portions, and shipping them directly to the restaurants or frozen-food distribution points that served these restaurants. The value added by the large slaughterhouse operators replaced that formerly added by local processors and resellers, or by the users (restaurants) themselves.

Development of new technology may tempt companies which have developed the new knowledge to exploit it themselves in the marketplace. A consulting firm whose employees developed a programmed learning device attempted to manufacture and market the device itself, rather than selling or licensing the technology; the firm eventually withdrew the product. Notable in its resistance to this temptation is du Pont, which has consistently sold such products as nylon and corfam to manufacturers of end products, rather than attempting to add value to the fabricated material by engaging in the manufacture of end products.

A manufacturer may find it desirable to offer finished products instead of components, or components instead of semifinished materials in situations in which: (1) the user has a stronger incentive than an intermediary processor (a wholesaler who performs some processing functions, or a manufacturing firm which processes basic raw materials into semifinished parts or components) to accept a particular product; (2) competition with intermediary processors—the manufacturer's traditional customers—is minimal; (3) intermediary processors or resellers lack the resources to exploit market opportunities; (4) the manufacturer has access to a marketing organization adequate to distribute and sell the finished product; (5) the manufacturer's competitive position in components or semifinished materials will not be jeopardized by diverting from that core business the resources necessary for offering a more finished product; (6) the manufacturer can anticipate a viable competitive position in the new market; (7) the manufacturer can add the value more economically than can a channel intermediary or the final user.

Manufacturers as a group add value to their products more frequently than they decrease the value added. In situations in which manufacturers find their positions in a finished-goods market no longer viable, they typically withdraw entirely, rather than merely dropping back to the position of suppliers of materials or components. Total withdrawal may be appropriate not because the remaining manufacturers do not wish to do business with a former competitor but, more likely, because the remaining manufacturers already have established strong relationships with their own sources of supply.

SELECTED REFERENCES

COREY, E. RAYMOND. "Key Options in Market Selection and Product Planning." *Harvard Business Review,* September–October 1975, vol. 53, no. 5.

EXPANSION AND REDUCTION OF THE PRODUCT LINE

A manufacturer or reseller may increase or decrease the number of items in an individual product line by adding or withdrawing particular models, styles, flavors, size and price ranges, accessories, or closely related items. These changes, often referred to as changes in breadth of line, are typically made at the operating division level. In contrast, adding or dropping an entire product line ordinarily involves top corporate management to a far more significant extent and is more appropriately considered a portfolio issue than a simple breadth of line decision. Nevertheless, the distinction is not always clear-cut, for some breadth of line decisions are major "horizontal integration" decisions which may involve items very similar to the existing product line, but also involve commitments of organization resources so significant that a major corporate decision must be made.

Changes in breadth of line are ordinarily accomplished by one of two approaches: multibrand entries or brand extensions (or withdrawals). "Multibrand entries" refers to the practice of offering several distinct individual brands to a defined market. For example, Procter and Gamble offers several brands of detergent (Tide, Cheer, Gain, and others), each of which possesses some distinctive characteristics. "Brand extension" refers to the practice of adding to a line a product which bears the same brand name but differs in certain product characteristics. Ivory soap, for example, is offered in bar, liquid, flake, and powder form.

In general, multibrand entries are intended to capture multiple segments of a particular market, with the objective of increasing total company penetration of that market. Brand extension through proliferation of sizes, flavors, and the like, also attempts to attain that objective. But brand extension through changes in product form or type may be intended to penetrate multiple markets. Ivory soap in bar form competes in the hand- and bath-soap market. Ivory Liquid is used for washing dishes (and hand washing delicate fabrics) and Ivory Snow for machine washing delicate fabrics. In addition to this difference in objective, multibrand entries may be more effective than brand extensions in situations in which the product(s) to be added differ in quality and price levels from the established brand, or the image of the established brand is perceived as inappropriate by consumers for the new entry. A manufacturer of baby food, for example, recently abandoned plans to extend its brand by adding a low-calorie, highly nutritious drink for overweight preteens and teen-agers when results from marketing research showed that consumers responded favorably to the product when the brand name was not shown, but negatively when the brand name was included. Further analysis revealed that consumers could not believe that a brand that helped babies grow and gain weight could help older children lose weight.

Expanding the Product Line

The benefits likely to accrue from adding a product to an existing product line depend upon several factors, among them consumers, competitors, cost structure, marketing strategy, and demand relationships within the product line.

Consumers   Consumers' desires for a wide variety of styles from which to select and the heterogeneity of consumers' tastes affect opportunities for broadening the product line. The greater the consumers' concern for wide selection and the more varied (heterogeneous) the consumers' tastes, the greater the opportunity to broaden the product line. Consumers' desires to decorate their kitchens in different schemes provided an opportunity for appliance manufacturers to add colors such as copper, gold, and avocado to the traditional white. Consumers' interests in variety provided manufacturers of breakfast cereals, snacks, and other frequently used products with opportunities to add to their lines new flavors, textures, and shapes. Major breakfast cereal manufacturers continue to add items to their lines, in part to provide costomers with a chance to "try something different" for breakfast. Some of these manufacturers offer prepackaged sets of individual servings to meet this desire for variety. Addition of multiple brands may help a manufacturer gain attention, shelf space, and trade support for an entire line, as well as increase total penetration of a particular market.

Another reason manufacturers add multiple brands is to attract consumers who regularly switch brands, either because those consumers seek variety or because they seek a taste, performance, or some other characteristic in a product that existing offerings have not provided. The consumer who switches for variety may respond best to a continuing proliferation of brands ("multibrand entries") or items within a brand ("brand extension"). Consumers searching for particular combinations of product characteristics will respond favorably to those certain additions which meet their needs, but not to others. Thus manufacturers or resellers attempting to serve the needs of segments of the consumer market who are not entirely satisfied with present offerings and who seek different combinations of characteristics must estimate the size and profitability of the additional segments they intend to reach with an addition to the line. Several years ago a Canadian motor manufacturer faced this problem when a major user, whose lead was likely to be followed by other customers, developed specifications for an oil-well-pumping motor which differed from standard specifications. The manufacturer had to decide whether the number of motors which would be purchased for this application would be large enough to support development and marketing of an additional motor, and whether compliance with this request would lead to a host of similar requests from markets too small to support specialized products.

In some instances, one segment of a market will outgrow the technical capabilities of a product before other segments. In such cases, simply replacing the less sophisticated product with the more sophisticated item might result in loss of sales to the users who had not outgrown the product and had neither the technical expertise nor the economic need to purchase a more complex and costly model. Consequently, manufacturers of such products as computers, control and testing equipment, communications equipment, and the like, regularly add more sophisticated products to their lines, but continue to offer for some time the existing equipment. Some analysts argue that this procedure extends the life of the entire product line, but shortens the life cycle of a particular product.

Consumers' desires to purchase from a single reseller and resellers' or users' desires for a single source of supply provide opportunities for broadening the product line. Consumers' desires for comprehensive decorating help have led many home-furnishings retailers to add a variety of accessory items. Consumers' interests in "one-stop shopping" contributed to the evolution of supermarkets' nonfood offerings and to the emergence of the "superstore"—a combined food–mass-merchandise outlet. Consumers who want extended credit on the purchase of durables and prefer to deal with a small number of creditors have encouraged retailers of recreational vehicles to add a variety of costly sports and camping equipment. A similar phenomenon occurs in industrial purchasing when a supplier who enjoys a long-established and satisfactory relationship with the buying organization is encouraged to bid on projects or add to its line items outside its traditional field of expertise. The desire for a single source may reflect the buying organization's desire to deal with a limited number of resources, independent of special competence of the supplier. This latter phenomenon has led many distributors to broaden their offerings to a "full line" capability from an originally limited line of products. A "full line" may be defined as one that covers a wide range of price points; of styles; of accessories or complementary items; or of brands or items, each of which is intended to meet a somewhat different customer requirement.

The status enjoyed by an established industrial supplier has its counterpart in brand loyalty at the consumer level. Control of a strong brand provides the manufacturer (or reseller, in the case of private labels) with the opportunity to add products not always clearly related to the existing product line. For example, Smucker, long known as a manufacturer of jams, jellies, and dessert toppings, added catsup to its line; Sara Lee, an established manufacturer of frozen pastries, added frozen meat entrées; and Welch Foods, prominent originally in the grape juice business, has added cranberry and prune products. These examples of brand extension are apparently intended to increase the number of markets in which the manufacturer operates, rather than to increase penetration of an existing market.

Competition   Competitive forces may also stimulate addition of products to the line. For example, major mass merchandisers have followed one another in establishing automobile-service facilities in new shopping centers. Apart from such "defensive" product additions, manufacturers may add new brands in order to make inroads on competitors' brands in a manner their established brands connot. Major coffee makers pursue this strategy from time to time.

Cost Structure   Of major significance, of course, in determining the likely profitability of adding a product are the costs associated with that addition. Some companies deliberately structure their operations so that the incremental costs of adding new items are low; others strive for minimum cost on a selected number of items. A major manufacturer of electric motors converted its manufacturing system to a "modular" basis so that a wide variety of motors could be added, each at a competitively advantageous cost, even for short production runs. As a result, the manufacturer was able to compete far more effectively than before against high-quality, high-cost custom "job shop" producers, but was underbid on long production runs of standard motors (and those nonstandard items for which quantities were large enough to support special tooling).

Marketing Strategy   Organizations that must choose, because of limited resources, among high-demand, low-cost additions to the product line may make the choice on the basis of the organizations's overall marketing strategy. A manufacturer of components for OEMs in the electronics industry wished to establish itself as a major supplier to four firms which were expected to offer the company its most attractive market over the next five years. Consequently, the company responded to requests from those manufacturers to broaden its line with marginally profitable products, while turning down other opportunities which offered greater immediate return.

Some firms may deliberately choose to increase share in a particular market, frequently through multibrand entries. Others may prefer to expand their activities to multiple markets, often by brand extension.

Demand Relationships   Analysis of the benefits and risks of broadening a product line depends in part upon whether the demand for the added item(s) is independent of, complementary to, or competitive with other products in the line. Demand may be independent if the product to be added is purchased by different customers from those who purchase the remainder of the line or if the same customers purchase the product in question for entirely different purposes, applications, or uses from the rest of the line (i.e., if they do not consider that particular item a substitute for other items in the line). For example, consumers who use mushrooms ordinarily purchase either fresh or canned mushrooms. If the same person buys both, he or she rarely substitutes fresh mushrooms for canned in specific dishes. Therefore, an integrated mushroom grower and canner could expect that, apart from any transfer of favorable brand image from one product to the other, demand at the customer level for fresh and canned mushrooms would be independent. Consequently, the processor could analyze the decision to add fresh mushrooms by itself, without concern about consumer reaction to the broadened line. Because different buyers in grocery chains typically purchase fresh and canned mushrooms, trade support for one product would likely be affected only marginally by addition of the other.

Demand may be complementary if the product considered for addition is purchased or used along with other products in the line and if competing lines are not considered interchangeable by the consumer or trade. In analyzing market potential the manufacturer would likely project an increase in sales of the present item as a result of addition of the new item. At the reseller level, addition of an item might stimulate increased reseller support.

In situations in which consumers purchase and use related items jointly, but in which brand is relatively unimportant, demand at the manufacturers' level may resemble independent demand, although it will likely be complementary at the reseller level. For example, most consumer purchases of paint are accompanied by the purchase of one or more sundry items, such as sandpaper, brushes, or other surface preparation, application, and clean-up equipment. Almost all paint retailers carry at least a limited line of sundries; rarely are sundries offered without paint at the retail level. Nevertheless, most consumers do not have strong brand preferences for sundries, nor do they insist that the brush be manufactured by the maker of the paint. Because there are numerous sources of sundries available to most paint retailers, neither consumers nor retailers would likely react sharply to the decision of a paint manufacturer to add sundries. In that case, the paint manufacturer could likely forecast no increase or decrease in paint sales as a result of the addition of sundries.

Nevertheless, there is one important difference between truly independent demand and demand that is complementary in product type, though not in brand. In the paint example, demand for sundries may be considered derived from demand for refinishing; i.e., sundries will be purchased primarily with paint or some other finishing, coating, or covering material, rather than independently of such material. A consumer who wants to repaint a room may have a brush; if not, he or she will likely pay far more attention to the selection of the paint, and buy the brush as an accessory item. In derived-demand situations, sales of the primary item (paint, in this example) may offer a guide to the upper limit of sales of the secondary item(s) (brushes, sandpaper, etc.).

Demand of a prospective addition to the product line may be considered competitive with other products in the line if the item in question is a substitute for another item in the line. "Substitute" in this context means used interchangeably by a specific consumer in a specific situation. Although chocolate and white cake mixes may appear to be substitutes in an aggregate sense, there are some consumers who regularly buy chocolate for family use, but serve white cakes on occasions when guests outside the family are invited. For this segment, addition or withdrawal of nonchocolate flavors in the line will have no effect on purchasing habits (so long as at least one plain white mix is available). Proliferation of chocolate-flavor alternatives, however, might simply have the effect of dividing the purchases of this segment among multiple varieties of chocolate instead of one, with the result that each flavor has quite limited sales. Such a proliferation may be necessary, however, if the consumers want a variety. Withdrawal of all chocolate flavors would not result in a shift to white cake, but to different alternatives altogether.

Manufacturers frequently worry that addition of another model, style, size, or brand will draw sales from existing products, or "cannibalize" the existing product line. Sometimes such cannibalizing is inevitable, as when a competitor threatens to displace an existing product if the manufacturer does not do so. In many instances, however, cannibalizing can be avoided if the manufacturer analyzes carefully the customers and applications for existing products and positions the addition toward different customers and/

or different applications. Resellers ordinarily attempt to balance the varied interests of their customers and the costs—in space and inventory—of carrying lines that are substitutes for one another, and therefore in competition with each other. In analyzing prospective additions to the line of products which compete with others in the product line, both manufacturers and resellers must estimate how much of the projected sales of a new addition would come from existing products, whether existing products would remain profitable by themselves, and, if they might not, whether the combined profitability (plus other benefits) of the new and existing products exceeds that of either offered by itself.

Summary In sum, a manufacturer will likely find it most advantageous to add those products for which demand is likely to be substantial, either because customers seek variety or because a viable market segment whose needs are unmet exists; for which a competitive advantage may be maintained; for which resellers will provide support; for which incremental costs are low; addition of which will help advance the firm's marketing strategy; and demand for which is complementary, or at least not competitive with other products in the line.

Even though a prospective product appears to meet these criteria, it still may not be added to a particular product line. Organizations do not have limitless resources and often must choose among additions to one or more product lines. Even though the addition of products may stimulate trade support, motivate the sales force (by having something new to talk about), encourage technical personnel (by showing that the company thinks highly enough of their new development to add it to the line), and generally excite the whole organization, proliferation of products may, apart from any competition with one another, diffuse the efforts of company personnel in all departments, with the result that not all the new additions to the line will receive adequate support in the form of product literature, sales force briefings, and the like.

Reducing the Product Line

Most organizations expend far less effort on pruning their product lines than on expanding them and lack a formal, structured approach to product-line reduction. Because the decision to drop a product typically encounters organizational inertia or resistance, many product-management groups at either the manufacturer or reseller level explore the possibility of dropping a product only after such moves as decreasing price, increasing promotion, repositioning, and changing product characteristics have been tried.

Despite organizational resistance to product discontinuation, there are several warning signals that indicate that the possibility of dropping the product exhibiting these symptoms should be explored. These signals include decreases in sales, primary demand, market share, price, product effectiveness, average order size, profit, and return on capital employed; and increases in promotional expenditures following a period of stable expenditures, manufacturing costs, inventories, and executive time devoted to the product.

These and other factors peculiar to individual businesses may be, but all too often are not, incorporated into a systematic product-audit procedure which may be built into an organization's marketing information system. The existence of such a routine procedure permits management to forecast the possibility of product discontinuance, or even to plan for product demise by forecasting market saturation or replacement of the product with a newer mode. One such model uses accounting and marketing data to estimate the value to the firm of each of several products in specified lines. *

Occasionally, managers can anticipate the appearance of these signals by forecasting the impact on particular products of changes in consumers' tastes and preferences, entry of a new competitor or major attacks on a product by an existing competitor, structural changes in channels of distribution, or the emergence of new technology. Indeed, withdrawal of a product may be advisable under conditions just the opposite of those that favor addition of a product to the line.

Because both the signals and the environmental changes may indicate problems which may be addressed by methods other than product discontinuation, even a product that appears to exhibit all the symptoms should not necessarily be dropped. Careful analysis of the likely continued viability of the product is, nevertheless, indicated.

Determination of cost savings that would occur from discontinuing a product in many cases requires analysis different from that ordinarily possible through use of data provided by an organization's accounting or information system. One argument often advanced for retention of a product in the line is that withdrawal of the product would result in savings of only minor variable costs; that semifixed overhead expenses would continue, and would have to be borne by other products. Although that argument may rightly prevail in many instances, the savings in manufacturing, order-handling costs, inventories, and other assets resulting from a substantial cutback in breadth of line may be significant, at both the manufacturer and the retailer levels. In recent years, manufacturers and resellers of such diverse items as home fireplace equipment, paint, and electronics equipment have found this to be the case.

One of the reasons most often cited for retaining a product that is obviously losing money is that the product supports the other products in the line; that sales of other products would decline if the particular product were withdrawn. Nevertheless, the interdependence of demand among products in the line is frequently overemphasized, except in cases where demand can very clearly be shown to be complementary. For example, withdrawing unprofitable skin conditioner from a line of cosmetics proved costly for one manufacturer who subsequently discovered that women were using skin conditioner and particular cosmetic items together as a "system." When one component was discontinued, customers shifted brands altogether, jeopardizing the profitability of the entire line.

An organization that wishes to withdraw a product has several options, including: (1) consolidating the product with others in the line, so that fewer styles, sizes, or finishes are offered; (2) replacing the product with a newer model which will perform the same function in a slightly different manner, in addition to other jobs, or at lower cost;

*See Paul W. Hamelman and Edward M. Mazze, "Improving Product Abandonment Decisions," *Journal of Marketing,* April 1972.

(3) discontinuing manufacture of the product, either retaining existing inventories or liquidating them. The first two options are the most commonly used. Nonetheless, there is no guarantee that demand for the withdrawn product can be shifted to the replacements that the manufacturer offers. When the third option, ceasing manufacture without replacement, is chosen, the organization will very likely retain inventories of replacement parts to help assure continued operation throughout their useful lives of units already sold. Such diverse items as sterling flatware for home use and industrial capital equipment follow such a policy.

In sum, the most likely candidates for withdrawal from the product line are those that are losing money, for which another product in the line may be substituted with little or no redesign or effort on the customers' part, and demand for which is independent of that for other existing and prospective products.

SELECTED REFERENCES

BROWN, MILTON P., et. al. *Problems in Marketing* (4th ed.). New York: McGraw-Hill, 1967.

GAMBLE, THEODORE R. "Brand Extension." In Lee Adler (ed.), *Plotting Marketing Strategy,* New York: Simon and Schuster, 1967.

HISE, RICHARD T. *Product/Service Strategy.* New York: Petrocelli/Charter, 1977 (chapter 10).

HAMELMAN, PAUL W., and EDWARD M. MAZZE. "Improving Product Abandonment Decisions." *Journal of Marketing,* April 1972.

KOTLER, PHILIP. *Marketing Management* (3d ed.). Englewood Cliffs, N.J.: Prentice-Hall, 1976.

KRATCHEM, STANLEY H., RICHARD T. HISE, and THOMAS A. ULRICH. "Managements' Decision to Discontinue a Product." *Journal of Accountancy,* June 1975.

MOREM, JOSEPH A. "Shift from Brand to Product Line Marketing." *Harvard Business Review,* September–October 1975, vol. 53, no. 5.

ROTHE, JAMES T. "The Product Elimination Decision." *MSU Business Topics,* Autumn 1970.

YOUNG, ROBERT W., JR. "Multibrand Entries." In Lee Adler (ed.), *Plotting Marketing Strategy,* New York: Simon and Schuster, 1967.

(See also references on Removing Investments from the Portfolio)

CHANGING THE COMPOSITION OF THE PRODUCT LINE

A marketing manager may change the composition of a product line by altering the set of individual products that constitutes that line. Changes in composition of a product line may result from changes in the number and specific types or styles of products offered; from changes in the size, color (or texture or flavor) of products included within the line; from modifications in options or accessories; and from changes in the number, range, and spacing of particular combinations of features and levels of quality offered in the line. Composition of the product line may also change through time.

Style and Product Characteristics

Manufacturers or resellers may attempt to cover uniformly the entire range of styles or types included within the range spanned by their product line, or they may wish to concentrate their offerings more heavily in certain portions of the range. For example, some furniture manufacturers offer multiple designs in each of several styles ranging from French provincial through contemporary. Other manufacturers offer several suites in one style, and only one in each of several others. Manufacturers and retailers ordinarily shift their concentrations along a style or design dimension in response to expected changes in consumer tastes. Such shifts are more comprehensive and frequent for retailers in such lines as apparel, where style concentrations may shift from season to season, than for manufacturers of capital equipment.

Within any group of styles or product types, manufacturers and resellers may vary the range of such dimensions as sizes and colors offered. Munsingwear, for example, manufactures a wide range of colors and sizes of undergarments, although the company does not ordinarily produce very large sizes in many styles. Venus Foundations, on the other hand, produces medium and large sizes only, and offers a full range of very large sizes. Most mass-merchandise outlets like Target and Zayre carry the most frequently demanded sizes, and not very large or very small sizes of undergarments. Retailers like Lane Bryant or the House of Large Sizes, however, specialize in large sizes. Manufacturers generally alter the range of colors or finishes they offer in response to forecast changes in consumers' tastes. Manufacturers may shift the range of sizes offered in response to shifts in the size composition of the population. Makers of theater seats and restaurant chairs have discontinued smaller sizes and added larger ones as the American population has grown broader-beamed. Retailers make similar adaptations in response to changes in the characteristics of population in their particular trade areas.

Options and Accessories

Of central importance to the composition or merchandising of the product line in such products as automobiles are the issues of what performance features are to be standard versus optional, and what levels of optional features are to be offered. Cadillac makes air conditioning and automatic transmissions standard on its automobiles. Volvo offers automatic transmission as an option at the time of purchase, and air conditioning as an option at purchase or any time thereafter (the Volvo system is comparable to factory-installed air conditioning on domestic cars). Oldsmobile offers three levels of shock absorber options: standard, heavy duty, and adjustable.

Manufacturers' decisions to make certain features optional and to offer different levels of options depend on their estimates of the desires and size of particular market segments. Although Cadillac buyers demand the comfort of air conditioning and ease of automatic transmission in a luxury car, Volvo evidently reaches two distinct market segments: one which values the comfort and convenience of air conditioning and automatic transmission; and another which values economy and, perhaps, the "feel" of a standard transmission. Some Oldsmobile buyers will travel only city streets and well-surfaced highways and will not have occasion to carry heavy loads; others will face rougher driving conditions with heavier loads; and still others will face a mixture of the two and desire the flexibility of adjusting the riding characteristics of their cars to each. In each of these examples, the manufacturer considers each market segment large enough to support the offering of the option.

The availability of a wide range of options and different levels meets the needs of many different market segments, provides customers greater variety, and affords manufacturers and resellers opportunities to increase their sales per customer. In durable goods industries, such increases in revenue per customer may make an important contribution to a firm's profitability, particularly when the firm serves a limited number of customers each month or year. As a general rule, then, manufacturers may make more options available both to attract additional market segments and to enhance the profitability of the resellers that handle their lines. There is, of course, the risk that making optional some features that formerly were standard will result in lower sales revenue per customer. This risk is frequently managed by changing features from "standard" to "optional" only a few at a time and, in some cases, simultaneously increasing the price of the "standard" or basic product. In either case, thorough analysis of the costs of adding or withdrawing an option, or of converting a feature from standard to optional (or vice-versa) should be made in order to ascertain whether the additional segments attracted (or lost) will be likely to affect profitability at the manufacturer or reseller level.

Price Points

A central issue in determining the composition of the product line is the number of price levels spanned by the product line and the distance among those price points. In this context, price levels or points reflect combinations of features (the fewer features included in the combination, the lower the price, for any specified level of quality), levels of quality (the higher the quality, the higher the price), or both.

Manufacturers and retailers in many industries consider it desirable to have numerous price points with modest intervals or steps between each price-feature combination or quality level and the next, so that larger price jumps do not deter customers from considering higher quality or more fully equipped products. Modest intervals provide marketers the opportunity to segment the market more precisely on a price basis, by meeting the needs of consumers whose interests in the product and willingness to pay differs.

Some industries have established or customary price points at the retail or user level. In such instances, a manufacturer's or retailer's decision involves simply which price points to serve. For example, manufacturers of apparel ordinarily offer products at each successive price point within the range they serve, such as $19.95, $29.95, $39.95, for men's trousers. Modifications of these intervals ordinarily occur as a result of cost increases, changes in resellers' requirements, or changes in customers' interests and willingness to pay.

Manufacturers or resellers may vary the composition of their lines to meet customary price points or to establish new ones by developing new combinations of standard and optional features. Another technique occasionally employed to provide a series of price intervals is to charge different prices for different styles or for different finishes.

Changes through Time

The composition of a product line may change through time as individual products are phased out and new ones introduced. This turnover of products within a line may be 100 percent per year for product lines which undergo annual styling or model changes.

Of greater interest than annual restyling, however, is the turnover, or appearance and disappearance, of specific sets of products. Manufacturers of small electric appliances, for example, periodically add and discontinue such items as electric carving knives, electric toothbrushes, electric combs, and curling irons. Other items, such as electric coffee-makers, toasters, and irons, typically remain in a manufacturer's product line on a more or less permanent basis. Thus, analysis of a product line such as small electrics should distinguish between specific products with shorter and longer life cycles. The composition of such a product line will vary through time because of the phasing in and out of shorter life cycle products. Those shorter life cycle products typically appeal to a smaller consumer group and generate low demand for replacements, parts, and accessories. In planning for such products, managers typically attempt to estimate their expected life and to develop business plans accordingly (e.g., heavy promotion and distribution emphasis in the first year; followed by transition to a "milking" strategy).

Manufacturers who turn over products in their lines on a continuing basis, apart from annual model changes, frequently state that between 25 and 75 percent of their sales come from products that have been introduced within the preceding five-year period. This range is wide in part because definitions of "new" vary among firms and studies, and in part because manufacturers' product turnover policies differ. To the extent that manufacturers may control turnover rate, they may be able to influence profitability significantly.

Summary: Modifying the Existing Product Line

The manufacturer or reseller who wishes to modify the organization's existing product line has several techniques available. He or she may reposition the product line; alter the amount and nature of value added to the product line; modify the performance or appearance characteristics of the product or the package; change brand policies; extend or narrow the line; and modify the composition of the line. A marketing manager may combine several of these techniques. For example, to reposition the product line by trading up, a manager may modify some product characteristics and change the composition of the line. A manager may also trade up by adding a deluxe model to the line (extending the product line), at the same time changing the package and brand. In general, decisions to extend or reduce the product line will affect other dimensions of composition of the product line. Almost all decisions to modify a product line will involve repositioning to some extent.

The principal factors that affect executive action on those decisions include changes in consumers' preferences and in the size and growth of particular markets or segments; changes in technology; changes in the channels of distribution and/or the structure of the industry at the manufacturing level; changes in the bases and intensity of competition; and changes in costs and profitability of existing product lines.

CASES ON MODIFYING EXISTING PRODUCT LINES

JAMESTOWN FOODS CORPORATION

InstantRice

After reviewing InstantRice[1] sales data for 1973, Mr. Earl Swarthol, product manager for InstantRice, was concerned when he discovered that sales were continuing to decline (see Exhibit 1). (InstantRice and other "quick" rices contain rice that has been processed and precooked, so that the user need boil the rice for less than 5 minutes before serving. Regular long-grain rice had to be boiled for 20 to 25 minutes before serving.)

Sales of InstantRice in 1973 were just under $12.5 million. Sales of the company's regular rice products, which were the responsibility of a senior product manager and his staff, were more than six times that amount. Sales of specialty rices, responsibility for which was divided between two different product managers, were slightly less than $20 million. Responsibility for all Jamestown rice sales lay with a product group manager, to whom Mr. Swarthol and his three colleagues reported.

In 1973 Jamestown total sales exceeded a quarter of a billion dollars, 70 percent of which came from within the United States. Sales had recently been growing at an annual rate of 10 to 15 percent. Earnings after taxes had increased slowly to more than 4 percent of sales. In addition to rice, Jamestown marketed a wide variety of specialty foods.

InstantRice was sold through grocery stores which accounted for more than 90 percent of sales of rice in the United States. Retailers typically priced the popular 16-ounce package at 88 cents, and earned a margin of 18 percent on InstantRice. Direct manufacturing costs amounted to approximately 72 percent of the revenues received by Jamestown for InstantRice. Sales and sales support costs amounted to 6 percent of sales. Trade and consumer advertising and promotion accounted for about 7 percent. InstantRice contributed 15 percent of its sales to allocated general expenses and profit. Company officials believed that the expense and profit structure of InstantRice was fairly typical of that for many long-established packaged foods.

Approximately half of the total advertising and promotion budget for InstantRice was devoted to consumer advertising. Trade promotion accounted for about 30 percent of the budget. The balance was divided about equally between consumer promotion and direct administrative costs.

1. InstantRice was Jamestown's brand of precooked (or "quick") rice.

Consumer advertising for InstantRice was intended to increase consumption among present users by stressing the multiple uses for InstantRice. Although more than one of every three households stocked some brand of precooked rice at one time or another, the typical user employed the product for only one or two different foods. In addition to picturing different uses on the package itself, the company advertised InstantRice in women's magazines.

Consumer advertising expenditures for InstantRice during 1973 amounted to less than 10 percent of total rice advertising (See Exhibit 2). InstantRice advertising was divided between print and television. Advertising for competing precooked rices was concentrated in local newspapers. Regular rice and specialty rice products were advertised primarily on television and, to a limited extent, in magazines and newspapers.

COMPETITION

Company officials believed that InstantRice competed against several different types of product including (1) other precooked rices; (2) specialty rices, e.g., Spanish rice, onion rice, etc.; and (3) regular long-grain rice. (Shorter-grain rice was important primarily in the South for specific uses.)

Precooked rice accounted for 14 to 18 percent by weight of the 550 to 600 million pounds of rice purchased in grocery stores. Total volume of precooked rice had declined over the past three years. InstantRice accounted for approximately 25 percent of dollar sales of precooked rice, and ranked second to the leading brand which held an estimated 35 to 40 percent share. One other major brand held approximately 15 percent of the market; the remainder was divided among more than five brands. According to company officials, the average retail price of some competing precooked rices generally offered retailers margins which were at least as great in dollars as that of InstantRice.

Specialty rice sales had risen markedly during the past three years, and currently amounted to about twice the volume of precooked rice. Specialty rice mixes typically included regular long-grain rice, together with the dried vegetables and spices necessary for a particular food. To serve a specialty rice dish, the consumer ordinarily added liquid to the mix and heated it. (Wild rice, which was classified as a specialty rice product, could not be duplicated by any precooked rice, and had to be prepared in a manner similar to long-grain rice.) Specialty rices cost 30 to 50 percent more than precooked rice plus the individual ingredients necessary to prepare an equivalent amount of a specialty-rice dish. Jamestown personnel believed that InstantRice, when combined with individual ingredients, produced foods that were superior to those made from some specialty rice mixes, but that other specialty mixes produced dishes that the consumer could seldom match with InstantRice.

Long-grain rice accounted for more tonnage than any other type of rice, and the volume of long-grain rice purchased by consumers had remained relatively stable during the past several years. Many consumers preferred the taste and consistency of long-grain rice to precooked rice and/or to specialty rice mixes. Regular long-grain rice was priced substantially below all brands of precooked rice.

The importance of these three sources (precooked, specialty, and regular rice) varied somewhat among the dishes for which rice was used (see Exhibit 3). Historical changes in the relative importance of these sources for selected foods appear in Exhibits 4 through 8. In addition, Mr. Swarthol noted that the popularity of rice and of particular rice dishes varied considerably among different regions within the United States. Rice purchased through retail stores exceeded four pounds per person in the West, but amounted to just two pounds in the Midwest (see Exhibit 9). Plain rice was most popular in the South; Spanish rice and ethnic rice dishes (e.g., fried rice and certain flavored rices used with Chinese or Indian foods) in the West; and rice pudding, in the Midwest (see Exhibit 10).

The competitive position of InstantRice varied both by food and by region. Nationally, InstantRice accounted for more than 75 percent of sales of precooked rice used in selected plain rice dishes, but for less than 15 percent of precooked rice used in Spanish rice (See Exhibit 3). But in the West, according to consumer panel data, use of Instant-Rice for plain rice dishes was 1.8 times the national average for the brand; for Spanish rice, more than twice the national average for InstantRice. Mr. Swarthol believed that, for all food uses combined, InstantRice enjoyed greater market penetration in the West, and less in the Midwest, than the brand's national market share. He noted that some 35 percent of InstantRice shipments went to the West; 30 percent, to the East; 20 percent, to the Midwest; and 15 percent, to the South.

CONSUMER PROFILE

Data from a variety of sources indicated to Mr. Swarthol that use of InstantRice was related to family size, age, and income. Relationships between family size and InstantRice consumption appear in Table 1.

<table>
<tr><th colspan="3" align="center">Table 1</th></tr>
<tr><th colspan="3" align="center">FAMILY SIZE AND INSTANTRICE USE</th></tr>
<tr><td>Family size</td><td>Percent of InstantRice sales</td><td>Percent of families</td></tr>
<tr><td>1 or 2 individuals</td><td>30</td><td>42</td></tr>
<tr><td>3</td><td>22</td><td>20</td></tr>
<tr><td>4 or 5</td><td>34</td><td>28</td></tr>
<tr><td>6 or more</td><td>14</td><td>10</td></tr>
</table>

Source: Company Records

<table>
<tr><th colspan="2" align="center">Table 2</th></tr>
<tr><th colspan="2" align="center">AGE OF HOUSEWIFE AND INDEX</th></tr>
<tr><td>Age</td><td>Purchase index</td></tr>
<tr><td>under 25</td><td>67</td></tr>
<tr><td>25–34</td><td>96</td></tr>
<tr><td>35–44</td><td>108</td></tr>
<tr><td>45–54</td><td>106</td></tr>
<tr><td>55–64</td><td>106</td></tr>
<tr><td>65 and over</td><td>104</td></tr>
<tr><td>all age groups combined</td><td>100</td></tr>
</table>

Source: Company Records

Older consumers were somewhat more important to InstantRice than were younger consumers. An index of InstantRice usage, by age group, appears in Table 2.

A 1970 study of housewives indicated that income and use of precooked rice (all brands combined) were positively correlated (see Table 3).

Table 3

INCOME AND PURCHASE OF PRECOOKED RICE

Family income level	Purchase index
less than $4,000	79
$4,000-$8,000	90
$8,000-$12,000	105
more than $12,000	134
all income levels combined	100

Source: Company Records

ALTERNATIVES

One alternative to remedy declining sales was to develop a slightly different product formulation for the western United States. Some company officials believed that a large market in the West that was currently using regular long-grain rice to make Spanish rice would offer InstantRice an opportunity for a significant increase in sales volume. It appeared that the Spanish rice now being made from InstantRice did not meet the tastes of Westerners, who preferred rice of a different texture and flavor from that desired in other parts of the country for Spanish rice. Mr. Swarthol knew of one study which indicated that Westerners made Spanish rice from scratch (i.e., by preparing from fresh foods the ingredients to be added to regular long-grain rice) as often as they made it with precooked rice; nationally, almost twice as much precooked rice as regular rice was used to make Spanish rice. Specialty Spanish rice mixes, including that made by Jamestown, enjoyed only limited success in the West.

Jamestown food technicians had formulated a precooked rice that appeared to satisfy Westerners' tastes in Spanish rice. This new formulation could be prepared by baking the rice with liquid and other ingredients in Spanish rice, rather than by first boiling the rice and then combining it with other ingredients and baking it in a Spanish rice casserole. If the new formulation were to be served as plain rice, it could, like the present Instant-Rice, be prepared by boiling.

Taste tests indicated, however, that Westerners preferred the present product to the new formulation for all dishes except Spanish rice, and that consumers in other regions preferred the present product over the new formulation for all uses.

If the new formulation were to perform well in consumer-use tests, Mr. Swarthol could recommend test marketing it in selected areas in the West. If test market results warranted, he could recommend introducing the new product throughout that region.

Up to $150,000 in new equipment would be required to produce the new formulation. The new formula would require the use of ingredients which would increase manufacturing costs by about two cents per pound. Some company marketing personnel believed that Jamestown could charge considerably more for the new formulation, but others doubted that InstantRice could increase consumer prices above the present premium level. Mr. Swarthol estimated that the amount spent on advertising and promotion in the West would have to be twice the $125,000 now being allocated to that area, if the new formulation were to succeed. If the new formula were introduced in the West, the present product formulation would continue to be sold in the rest of the United States. Mr. Swarthol had not determined whether the present InstantRice would be withdrawn from the Western market once the new formulation was introduced.

Other alternatives were to utilize a specialized advertising strategy in each region, but without a product change; or to reduce expenditures for trade and consumer advertising and promotion. If spending were cut, Mr. Swarthol believed that InstantRice sales would likely continue to decline gradually. He believed that a proposal to increase promotional expenditures would meet considerable skepticism from senior Jamestown executives unless persuasive justification were presented.

Mr. Swarthol knew that in some long-established product categories, such as coffee and ketchup, price reductions and private brands were employed in an attempt to secure sales increases. Although he was not certain whether either or both approaches would be appropriate for InstantRice, he recalled that representatives of major grocery chains had individually approached Jamestown about packaging precooked rice under their own store labels.

Within six months, Mr. Swarthol would have to submit a proposed budget for InstantRice for the coming year. If he were to decide against test marketing or introducing the new formula in the West, Mr. Swarthol believed he had to recommend some plan which would reverse the decline in InstantRice sales. "There's a lot of pressure on me to produce," he commented. "I'm due for a promotion in a year, and I may not get it unless I can show some positive results with this brand. In fact, corporate (Jamestown's top management group) has set some almost unbelievably high sales targets for each product management group. My boss (the product group manager) has let it be known that product managers who don't help him meet his quotas may as well start sending out their resumés. It's a 'grow or go' plan."

Exhibit 1

JAMESTOWN FOODS
INSTANTRICE SHIPMENTS, 1964–1973
(Millions of Pounds)

Year	16-oz. package	8½-oz. package	24- and 32-oz. packages (combined)	Total
1964	14.9	2.6	1.7	19.2
1965	15.0	2.4	1.9	19.3
1966	15.0	2.5	1.9	19.4
1967	14.8	2.7	1.8	19.3
1968	14.6	2.7	1.9	19.2
1969	14.4	2.6	2.0	19.0
1970	14.2	2.5	2.2	18.9
1971	14.0	2.1	2.5	18.6
1972	13.7	1.9	2.7	18.3
1973	13.2	1.6	3.1	17.9

Source: Company Records

Exhibit 2

JAMESTOWN FOODS
ANNUAL ADVERTISING EXPENDITURES FOR MAJOR RICE PRODUCT CLASSES
FOR ALL ADVERTISERS
(000)

Year	InstantRice	Total Precooked rice[a]	Regular rice	Specialty rices
1970	$635	$ 682	$1,987	$ 970
1971	600	1,105	2,216	2,002
1972	370	930	1,973	3,200
1973	450	1,045	1,480	3,068

[a]Totals include InstantRice

Source: Company Records

Exhibit 3

JAMESTOWN FOODS
SOURCES OF SELECTED RICE–BASED FOOD, 1973
(Millions of Pounds)

Foods	Sources				
	Instant-Rice	All Precooked rice[a]	Regular long-grain rice	Specialty rice (includes wild rice)	Total sources
Plain rice dishes	8.6	11.1	117.9	67.4 (chiefly wild rice)	196.4
Spanish rice	3.6	27.1	14.3	14.3	55.7
Ethnic rice	1.7	7.1	3.6	15.0	25.7
Other flavored rice	0.4	0.7	5.3	9.3 (includes	15.3
Rice pudding	0.9	1.6	1.0	1.1 flavored plain rice and flavored wild rice)	3.7
Total	15.2	47.6	142.1	107.1	296.8

[a]Includes InstantRice

Note: Figures in Exhibit 3 represent foods accounting for approximately 85 percent of InstantRice sales; and about half of all sales of rice through retail outlets.

Source: Company Records: Estimates based on Consumer Diary Panel Data

Exhibit 4

JAMESTOWN FOODS
SOURCES OF PLAIN RICE DISHES
(Millions of Pounds of Precooked Rice or Equivalent)

Year	InstantRice	All other brands of precooked rice	Regular rice	Specialty rice	Total
1964	8.9	2.1	217.5	14.5	243.0
1965	8.8	2.1	201.6	17.0	229.5
1966	8.8	2.1	187.0	21.6	219.5
1967	8.7	2.2	175.4	28.2	214.5
1968	8.7	2.2	161.1	34.0	211.0
1969	8.5	2.2	158.5	39.8	209.0
1970	8.6	2.3	147.9	46.2	205.0
1971	8.6	2.4	135.3	55.7	202.0
1972	8.7	2.3	128.9	60.6	200.5
1973	8.6	2.5	117.9	67.4	196.4

Source: Company Records

Exhibit 5

JAMESTOWN FOODS
SOURCES OF SPANISH RICE
(Millions of Pounds of Precooked Rice or Equivalent)

Year	InstantRice	All other brands of precooked rice	Regular rice	Specialty rice	Total
1964	2.1	25.4	14.9	—	42.4
1965	2.2	26.3	15.3	—	43.8
1966	2.1	27.4	15.3	—	44.8
1967	2.2	27.7	15.3	—	45.2
1968	2.9	27.0	15.8	1.4	47.1
1969	3.3	26.2	15.8	3.7	49.0
1970	3.5	26.0	15.5	5.1	50.1
1971	3.6	25.0	15.5	7.3	51.4
1972	3.7	23.8	15.3	10.2	53.0
1973	3.6	23.5	14.3	14.3	55.7

Source: Company Records

Exhibit 6

JAMESTOWN FOODS
SOURCES OF RICE PUDDING
(Millions of Pounds of Precooked Rice or Equivalent)

Year	InstantRice	All other brands of precooked rice	Regular rice	Specialty rice	Total
1964	1.2	0.1	2.9	0.3	4.5
1965	1.1	0.2	2.8	0.4	4.5
1966	1.0	0.3	2.6	0.5	4.4
1967	1.1	0.3	2.3	0.6	4.3
1968	1.2	0.3	2.0	0.7	4.2
1969	1.3	0.2	1.8	0.8	4.1
1970	1.2	0.4	1.5	0.9	4.0
1971	1.1	0.5	1.3	1.0	3.9
1972	1.0	0.6	1.2	1.0	3.8
1973	0.9	0.7	1.0	1.1	3.7

Source: Company Records

Exhibit 7

JAMESTOWN FOODS
SOURCES OF "ETHNIC" RICE DISHES
(Millions of Pounds of Precooked Rice or Equivalent)

Year	InstantRice	All other brands of precooked rice	Regular rice	Specialty rice	Total
1964	1.8	5.6	6.1	4.0	17.5
1965	1.8	5.6	6.0	5.1	18.5
1966	1.9	5.5	6.0	6.3	19.7
1967	1.8	5.4	5.6	8.2	21.0
1968	1.8	5.5	5.2	9.7	22.2
1969	1.7	5.4	4.8	11.7	23.6
1970	1.8	5.4	4.5	12.4	24.1
1971	1.7	5.5	4.0	13.4	24.6
1972	1.7	5.4	3.8	14.2	25.1
1973	1.7	5.4	3.6	15.0	25.7

Source: Company Records

Exhibit 8

JAMESTOWN FOODS
SOURCES OF FLAVORED RICE DISHES
(EXCLUDING SPANISH RICE, "ETHNIC" RICE DISHES)
(Millions of Pounds of Precooked Rice or Equivalent)

Year	Instant Rice	All other brands of precooked rice	Regular rice	Specialty rice	Total
1964	0.8	0.7	8.1	3.1	12.7
1965	0.8	0.8	7.6	3.6	12.8
1966	0.8	0.7	7.4	4.1	12.9
1967	0.8	0.6	7.2	4.8	13.4
1968	0.8	0.6	6.6	6.0	14.0
1969	0.7	0.7	5.8	7.3	14.5
1970	0.6	0.6	5.6	8.1	14.9
1971	0.5	0.5	5.3	8.8	15.1
1972	0.4	0.4	5.3	9.1	15.2
1973	0.4	0.3	5.3	9.3	15.3

Source: Company Records

Exhibit 9

JAMESTOWN FOODS

The geographic regions referred to throughout the case and
exhibits are defined as shown on the map below. Approximate
populations, total rice purchased through retail stores and
per capita consumption are given for each region.

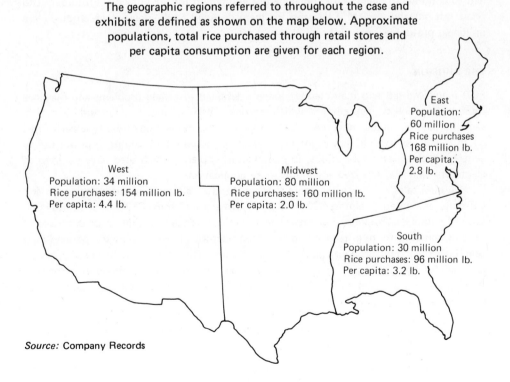

East
Population:
60 million
Rice purchases
168 million lb.
Per capita:
2.8 lb.

West
Population: 34 million
Rice purchases: 154 million lb.
Per capita: 4.4 lb.

Midwest
Population: 80 million
Rice purchases: 160 million lb.
Per capita: 2.0 lb.

South
Population: 30 million
Rice purchases: 96 million lb.
Per capita: 3.2 lb.

Source: Company Records

Exhibit 10

JAMESTOWN FOODS

REGIONAL INDEX OF SERVINGS OF SELECTED RICE FOODS

Food	East	Midwest	South	West	Total United States
Plain rice	25[a]	30	300	50	100
Spanish rice	80	105	80	125	100
Ethnic rice	85	85	85	145	100
Rice pudding	150	200	75	60	100

[a] Average per capita consumption of plain rice in the East was one-fourth the national average. These regional index numbers reflect differences among regions, and are not meaningful for comparing different foods within a particular region. These numbers do not necessarily reflect total volumes served in each region, because of differences in sizes of regions.

Source: Consumer Diary Panel

PROCESS CONTROL DIVISION

Late in 1975, Robert Clifton, President of Process Control (PCD), an autonomous division of a half-billion-dollar conglomerate, wished to decide whether to proceed with development of a series of test devices which would be installed permanently in a customer's plant. The new series might supplant Process Control's present portable test equipment to some extent, particularly among larger customers. PCD management planned to continue to manufacture portable test equipment for the immediate future, but to phase out portable devices if demand for them declined to the point at which they were no longer profitable.

THE DIVISION

PCD manufactured and marketed equipment designed to isolate problems and diagnose causes of problems on circuits which carried electrical impulses, including cables, switches, and terminal connections. Circuits which required testing of the type performed by PCD and competing equipment were found in certain applications in power utility generating plants and substations, in manufacturing plants which used large volumes of electricity, and in specialized communications applications.

Division sales had increased more than two and a half times in the past decade, and currently amounted to almost $20 million. Of this amount, some $12 million represented sales of complete "packages" or sets of test equipment; the remainder was comprised of sales of components to original equipment manufacturers (OEMs) who incorporated PCD gear into their own products and of sales of parts. The proportions of total sales accounted for by "packages" and components had remained fairly stable during the past three years. Export sales had increased gradually over the past several years, and in 1975 exceeded 20 percent of PCD's total sales.

This case was prepared in cooperation with an organization which prefers to remain anonymous. Consequently, certain data are disguised.

PCD's most recent series of equipment, first introduced in 1973, currently carried a price of about $40,000 for a typical "package," which consisted of a set of electronic testing devices mounted on a cart. When trouble became evident, the cart was wheeled to a point where the difficulty was suspected, and a technician trained in the use of PCD equipment performed a variety of tests on the circuit to isolate and diagnose the difficulty. Either that technician or a repairman subsequently made the necessary repairs. Large utilities or manufacturing plants might have several PCD carts and a like number of their own personnel trained to operate the equipment.

In the United States PCD sold its products through its own field sales force of 30 people plus a headquarters selling staff. In markets outside the United States, the division sold its products through sales representatives, directed by a headquarters executive. The division shipped its products directly to purchasers. PCD maintained a service staff of two persons at headquarters, but because of the straightforward design of PCD equipment and rigorous quality control procedures, service personnel were "underutilized," according to one executive.

An income statement for the year ending June 30, 1975, appears in Exhibit 1. Expense percentages for 1975 were similar to those for recent years. The parent company estimated that PCD employed more than $17 million in assets, divided approximately equally between current and fixed assets.

PRODUCT MODIFICATION AND DEVELOPMENT

Because PCD's sales of components were comprised of hundreds of relatively small orders from dozens of customers, and because specifications differed among customers and among orders for particular customers, PCD technical personnel spent considerable time modifying basic designs for individual orders. Aware of this problem, management was continuously working to standardize designs and develop modules for use in a variety of parts without compromising PCD's position of technical leadership or standards of quality. Nevertheless, division officials foresaw little likelihood that applications engineering costs for components or packages could be reduced further.

PCD research and development activities included development of new components and packages, as well as research into new testing methods and novel equipment designs. The division's R & D budget was thought to be greater than that of any of its competitors except Circuitrex, the largest manufacturer of this type of testing equipment.

PCD had regularly upgraded its products by introducing modified products every 9 to 18 months, and by introducing an entirely new series of models approximately every three years. Price increases accompanying these product improvements had averaged 5 to 8 percent per year. In the opinion of division engineers, each new series represented a technical advance which enabled users to perform more complex tests, and to perform them more quickly. Customers typically bought the new series for testing in new or expanded facilities, but in many cases would simply replace older PCD products with newer models. As plant and equipment expansion slowed in the early 1970s, more PCD sales were "replacement" sales. Consequently, more secondhand—but still perfectly usable—PCD equipment was finding its way into inventories of dealers in used business equipment.

PROPOSED PRODUCTS

Process Control engineers were currently developing two new series of products. Both represented what one division engineer described as ". . . a significant advance over what we've been doing. We've pushed portable equipment about as far as it can go—the move to centralized testing is the next step." The first series, which could be ready for market within a year, included a central bank of testing equipment wired to all the locations within a customer's site where a cart could have been connected. The central bank of equipment would include an expanded, updated version of devices heretofore mounted on a cart. Only one trained technician would be needed to operate the equipment on any shift, and he or she could do so without leaving the central office. Maintenance of the connections from the central location to the peripheral connection points was expected to be simple and routine. Savings from use of the new systems depended upon the incidence of trouble, the difficulty of isolating and diagnosing the difficulty, and prevailing labor costs. Customers with whom PCD personnel had worked closely on the new system estimated that these savings could range between $20,000 and $60,000 per site per year.

Approximately $100,000 had already been spent on developing the first system. An additional $75,000 would have to be spent to prepare the system fully for market. In addition to development costs, division officials believed they would have to add a field service force of two to four persons to oversee installation, provide on-site warranty service (because system failure could occur either if the test equipment malfunctioned or if the connections to peripheral points became unsatisfactory), and supervise routine system maintenance for the first several months. These service personnel might office at headquarters, or with a salesperson in a location where installations were concentrated. In either case, service personnel would have to travel, and would be able to do so, since no one installation would need continuous supervision.

Cost data to date indicated to PCD officials that the manufacturing cost of this new system would range from two to three and a half times that of the current portable package. In addition, customers would incur installation costs estimated at $25,000 to $35,000 per site. This estimate included costs of $2,000 to $12,000 for assistance from PCD's proposed field service force. PCD officials expected to recover these costs, but to earn no profit on field service activities.

The second system, which could be ready in three to five years, depending upon the number of personnel assigned and their success in completing design and engineering, also called for a central bank of testing equipment, connected to peripheral testing sites. The centrally located testing devices would, however, be connected to a small computer, which would be programmed to function automatically. In case of trouble, the computer program would activate the test devices to perform their problem-isolation and diagnosis tests. This feature permitted the system to handle up to twice as many problems as a manually operated central system.

At a second stage, thought to require yet another year's development time, the computer would be programmed to evaluate circuits periodically on a routine basis to detect incipient malfunction. Although difficulties with circuits could be detected before actual malfunction occurred, existing test procedures did not provide information which allowed one to predict how long after the initial indication of improper function actual breakdown would occur. Consequently, PCD technical personnel were working with consultants and university scientists to refine existing testing methods. These methods would likely require more sophisticated test equipment than that currently available. Routine evaluation and detection of trouble before actual malfunction occurred had been a goal of many customers' engineers for some time. The savings from routine maintenance instead of "crisis repairs," combined with the reduction in downtime for repairs, were not known, but some industry personnel speculated that savings could amount to tens to hundreds of thousands of dollars per year per site.

Development costs of the second system would amount to an estimated $350,000 in addition to the $75,000 already invested. Another $350,000 was likely to be needed to develop the additional tests, equipment, and programs for the computer-based routine evaluation procedure. Once installations of the second system began, the field service force might have to be augmented with another two to four persons.

The second system was likely to have a manufacturing cost 25 percent greater than the first proposed new system, plus $150,000 for a computer on which PCD would take a negligible markup. Installation would cost a customer up to $65,000 for the system (including computer installation). Process Control executives had not decided how they might price the computer programs for the routine evaluation.

THE MARKET

A division market research study indicated that there were thousands of individual sites in the United States alone in which equipment of the type made by Process Control or its competitors could be used. (No reliable figures on the size of the market outside the United States were available.) Of these sites, some 5,000 were operated by 350 large multiplant companies; another 300 companies accounted for 2,000 sites. The remaining sites were operated by hundreds of small, typically single-location firms, most of which could not afford even a portable system, but used trial-and-error methods supplemented by components when necessary. The large companies typically made capital expenditure decisions and approved equipment designs at headquarters, but left plant managers discretion in implementing those decisions. Annual plant and equipment expenditures of the 350 largest companies averaged $4 to $5 million per company and were typically stable from year to year, although the particular items purchased would vary gradually over time.

Apart from buying testing devices directly, these companies could purchase from OEMs equipment which might have PCD or a competitor's testing devices already incorporated within it. OEM customers who purchased PCD components for installation in equipment which they sold to users were demanding increasingly sophisticated and specialized components to monitor the increasingly complex equipment which they made. Some division technical personnel predicted that sales of components to OEMs would in time replace sales of systems to users, as users acquired equipment designed to monitor itself. Other technical personnel disagreed, arguing that even the most sophisticated equipment still had to be connected to other, less complex, devices and that advanced testing systems of the type PCD proposed offered more effective, more flexible testing and lower total cost than did built-in monitoring devices. No clear indication of which way the market might go was available.

Competition came primarily from three firms. Each of these, like Process Control, was a division of a larger, well-financed organization and operated internationally. The dominant competitor, Circuitrex, held 50 to 55 percent of the United States market. Schocken A.G., a German firm with worldwide operations, had 15 to 20 percent of the domestic market. PCD and General Testing each held about 10 percent of United States sales; the remainder was divided among several firms. Circuitrex and Schocken employed their own salespeople in most markets. General Testing, like PCD, used its own sales force domestically, and representatives abroad. Smaller firms used various combinations of salaried sales personnel and representatives.

Division officials believed that PCD dominated the market among customers who were technically sophisticated, but that Circuitrex was considered the leader in the remainder of the market. Customers ordinarily purchased a single make of testing equipment, and did not switch makes, in part because customer personnel required about four weeks of training to operate a particular brand of test equipment. Nevertheless, buyers had switched from one manufacturer to another when an alternative to their present equipment appeared markedly superior. Although exact price comparisons were difficult because specifications differed among makes, PCD, Circuitrex, and Schocken were comparably priced; other manufacturers priced about 5 to 10 percent below those firms and stressed low price in their sales presentations.

Process Control management knew that Circuitrex would soon announce a new system which would be permanently installed. PCD engineers learned from prospective customers that the Circuitrex system possessed many features like those in Process Control's first proposed system, but the two were thought to differ in several respects. Process Control engineers believed that their system would be superior in certain installations; Circuitrex's, in others. Although Circuitrex's future development plans were not definitely known, the substantial investment Circuitrex was believed to have made in development of permanent systems convinced PCD officials that Circuitrex would continue to pursue its interest in permanent installations. PCD personnel charted Circuitrex's historical introduction of new models, and discovered that Circuitrex had begun about eight years ago to offer new models every 30 to 33 months. Within two years, the other competitors had adopted a similar schedule.

Although PCD executives agreed that the new Circuitrex system represented a "trading up" in terms of technical sophistication, they were divided in their estimates of its impact on PCD. One executive was worried: "They're going after our core business—and with their name and organization, they can get coverage and impact we can't. And they're ruthless. They'll underbid like crazy to get some of our customers." Another executive acknowledged the competitive power of Circuitrex, but argued that their "trading up" augured well for PCD: "They know their customers' requirements well. If they're trading up, the market's becoming more sophisticated, and we have the best record and reputation for the more sophisticated gear. They'll help us increase our penetration."

Exhibit 1

PROCESS CONTROL DIVISION
INCOME STATEMENT
YEAR ENDING JUNE 30, 1975
(Millions of Dollars)

Sales	$19.7	100%
Cost of sales	11.9	59
Gross margin	8.0	41
Sales, sales support, and service	3.2	16
Applications engineering	0.8	4
Research and development	0.2	1
Administration	2.0	10
Earnings before taxes	1.8	9

MISSOURI MILLS, INC.

Commercial Division

In October 1970, managers of the Commercial Division of Missouri Mills, Inc., St. Louis, submitted to the corporate management of Missouri Mills a proposal to buy Buttersweet Bakeries, Inc., as a vehicle for entering the frozen bakery products business. The proposal to negotiate acquisition of Buttersweet for $800,000–$900,000 was approved, but in July 1971, Buttersweet Bakeries' officials informed Missouri Mills management that a food manufacturer had offered to buy Buttersweet for a price in excess of $2 million. Missouri Mills' executives were convinced that the other offer was genuine and that Buttersweet would accept the offer unless Missouri Mills could match it.

Late in the summer of 1971, executives of the Commercial Division met to discuss the alternative courses of action open to them:

1. Propose to Missouri Mills corporate management that the acquisition price for Buttersweet Bakeries be increased to $2 million. Although the Commercial Division executives were confident that Buttersweet would accept an offer of $2 million, the executives were not certain that Missouri Mills corporate management would authorize the expenditure.

2. Develop their own frozen bakery products business by building one or more bakeries. Division management believed that four to six bakeries in strategic locations could serve the major markets in the United States. Each of these bakeries would cost from $3 million to $5 million, depending upon size and equipment.

3. Develop their own frozen bakery products business by buying and re-equipping conventional bakeries at a cost of $2 million to $4 million per bakery, depending upon size and equipment.

4. Have frozen bakery products manufactured under contract for sale through the Commercial Division marketing and sales organization. Division officials estimated that a contract manufacturer would have to price frozen bakery products at a level which would present a 20 to 25 percent return on investment on contract sales to the Commercial Division. Officials speculated that manufacturers with excess capacity might, however, be willing to provide frozen bakery products at prices only slightly higher than the supplier's cost of manufacturing those products. Division officials noted that a contract manufacturer might limit their discretion in scheduling production and their direct control over uniformity of product quality. Missouri Mills' investment, if any, would probably not exceed a few hundred thousand dollars.

5. Postpone, for the present, any attempt to enter the frozen bakery products business.

THE COMMERCIAL DIVISION

The Commercial Division operated as an autonomous division of Missouri Mills, which manufactured a variety of consumer food products, including baking mixes, snack products, and flours. These products were sold through the company's Consumer Division to the grocery trade. Missouri Mills' sales, income, and return on equity had increased steadily over the past five years. In 1970, net sales exceeded $650 million, and income (before taxes) was more than $40 million. Return on stockholders' equity exceeded 12 percent (after taxes).

The Commercial Division's product line included bulk flour, bulk bakery mixes and baking equipment, flour and bakery mixes packaged for sales to institutions, and a variety of other specialty products. The Commercial Division ranked among the three largest firms in the bakery mix market, and among the top five suppliers of flour to commercial bakeries. The division's sales, margins, and earnings had increased 20 percent since 1966, and in 1970 were as shown in Table 1.

Table 1

Product	Sales	Gross margin	Pretax profit
		(Millions of Dollars)	
Bulk flour*	$150	$ 7.8	$2.8
Bulk bakery mixes and bakery equipment	15	3.0	1.0
Food service packages of flour and mix	15	3.5	1.1
All other	5	0.2	0.1
	$185	$14.5	$5.0

*Approximately half of the division's flour production was transferred at prevailing market prices to the Consumer Division of Missouri Mills.

The Commercial Division sold its products through two separate sales forces, one selling to the food service market (institutions) and the other to commercial bakeries.

The institutional sales force included forty-one salespeople (six of whom were also qualified as technical service representatives), four regional managers, a national account sales manager, a general manager, three sales promotion specialists, and a home economist. The institutional salespeople sold both the Commercial Division's products and frozen chicken to distributors which in turn sold these products to food service operations. Of the 135 distributors nationwide, Commercial Division officials considered 10 to be key accounts (based on sales volume) and another 10 to be potentially key accounts. Apart from sales through distributors, the institutional sales force also handled a small number of sales direct to food service operations. Direct sales amounted, however, to less than 10 percent of all sales made by the institutional sales force.

The commercial bakery sales force consisted of thirty-five salespeople, six headquarters personnel, five resalers who serviced distributors, and fourteen technical-service personnel. The commercial bakery salespeople sold flour, mixes, and baking equipment to a total of 4,000 independent wholesale bakeries and bakeries owned and operated by supermarket chains, and to several hundred distributors (wholesalers of flour mixes and equipment) which serviced 16,000 retail bakeries.

Company officials noted that in recent years most wholesale bakeries had experienced a severe profit squeeze. In several cases, supermarkets which had formerly been customers of the wholesale bakeries opened their own central bakeries. Industry observers attributed the profit squeeze and growth in supermarket central bakeries to the sharply rising costs of distribution of fresh bakery products. Because supermarkets could deliver fresh baked goods by the trailer-load in their own trucks from a central bakery to their stores, supermarkets' distribution costs were substantially lower than the distribution costs of wholesale bakeries. Wholesale bakeries, on the other hand, made more frequent deliveries of smaller amounts of merchandise through routemen, who took orders and stocked the stores' shelves. Almost all wholesale bakeries were committed, through labor agreements, to continue this method of distribution. Industry observers believed that the combined costs of manufacturing and distribution for fresh bakery products were substantially lower for supermarkets' central bakeries than for other wholesale bakeries.

Although the number of retail bakeries had declined only slightly during the late 1960s, the number of small, one-family retail bakeshops had decreased, while the number of larger, multiunit retail bakeshops had increased. Some multiunit retail bakeries were operated as leased departments in supermarkets.

In recent years, Commercial Division officials had sought to increase the division's rate of growth in sales and earnings, either through the addition of new products or through acquisitions. A major reason for this search was the continuing decline in per capita consumption of flour (see Exhibit 1).

As a result of this search for new opportunities, Commercial Division management became interested in Buttersweet Bakeries, Inc., which was heavily involved in the frozen bakery products market. Management viewed this company as an opportunity for entering the growing frozen bakery products market, and in September 1969, began an investigation of both the company and the market for frozen bakery products.

THE FROZEN AND REFRIGERATED BAKERY PRODUCTS INDUSTRY

The frozen and refrigerated bakery products industry consisted of three generic product classes: (1) refrigerated dough, (2) frozen dough, and (3) frozen prebaked products. Refrigerated dough products, which included cookies, sweet rolls, and dinner rolls, had to be baked before serving. Icing or topping, if any, could be applied after baking, while the cookie or roll was still hot. Frozen dough products required proofing (a process in which fermentation of dough by yeast resulted in expansion of dough volume), baking, and application of icing or filling, if any. Frozen dough products consisted primarily of bread and rolls, the recipes for which resembled bread recipes. Prebaked frozen products, which consisted primarily of coffee cakes, frosted layer cakes, and similar sweet or dessert items, needed only to be thawed before final consumption.

Prebaked frozen products commanded a higher price than did frozen dough items. For example, a manufacturer might sell 14 pounds of prebaked frozen donuts for $4.00. An equivalent amount of frozen donut dough would be sold for $3.12. Typically, on either type of item a manufacturer would obtain a gross margin of 25 to 30 percent.

The major markets for frozen and refrigerated bakery products included the consumer market, the food service market, and the bake-off market. (The bake-off market involved sales of frozen prebaked and frozen dough products to supermarkets for their on-premise baking operations.)

THE CONSUMER MARKET

Although considerable uncertainty surrounded estimates of the market for refrigerated and frozen bakery products, industry analysts believed that in 1970 the consumer market for frozen and refrigerated bakery products combined amounted to more than $100 million at manufacturers' prices, most of which represented sales of refrigerated products. The consumer market for refrigerated dough was dominated by the Pillsbury Company, which held the largest share of that market; Campbell-Taggart, a producer of private-label refrigerated products; and the Borden Company. These three firms were believed to hold more than 90 percent of the market for refrigerated dough products. Almost all refrigerated dough products were sold through the grocery trade to consumers; virtually no refrigerated dough was sold to the food service or bake-off markets.

Only limited sales of frozen dough items were made to the consumer market. Buttersweet Bakeries sold frozen bread dough to consumers through the grocery trade. Bridgford Foods, which operated plants in New Jersey, Texas, and California, made both frozen bread dough and frozen roll dough for the consumer market. In addition, some smaller manufacturers sold limited amounts of frozen dough products to local consumer markets.

The consumer market for frozen prebaked products, which was thought to be several times the size of that of the consumer frozen dough market, was dominated by Sara Lee, which offered a full line of frozen prebaked items and was believed to hold 30 percent of that market. Other full-line firms included Awrey's and Burny Brothers (Beatrice Foods), each of which was believed to have no more than 10 percent of the consumer market for frozen prebaked products. Five other companies offered limited lines of frozen prebaked products (typically cakes and pies). None of these firms, however, held more than 10 percent of the consumer market for frozen prebaked products.

Division officials noted that competition for frozen bakery products came not only from within the frozen bakery products industry but also from products made by consumers from scratch or mixes, from products of local retail bakeries, and from products manufactured by wholesale bakeries and sold through retail grocery outlets. These "shelf stock" items, such as Wonder Bread and Hostess Cupcakes, represented, in the opinion of division officers, by far the largest market for consumer baked goods.

THE FOOD SERVICE MARKET

In 1970, total sales of food service operations exceeded $35 billion. The food service industry had been growing at a 6 to 7 percent annual rate, and industry observers expected this rate of growth to continue. Industry sources estimated that sales to all food service operations of frozen bakery products had in recent years amounted to $30 to $50 million (at manufacturers' prices), and might increase to more than $150 million (manufacturers' prices) by 1977. Frozen prebaked products were thought to account for more than two-thirds of current sales.

Food service operations ordinarily purchased frozen bakery products, together with other frozen and nonfrozen products, from distributors. Distributors' margins on sales of frozen bakery products typically amounted to 20 percent of the distributors' selling price.

The food service market consisted of two major segments, the "eating out" segment and the "captive" segment, which together accounted for 85 to 95 percent of sales made by food service operations. The "eating out" segment of the food service market accounted for 55 to 60 percent of total food service sales. This segment included free-standing restaurants, restaurants in hotels or motels, snack bars associated with such amusement facilities as bowling alleys or movie theaters, and delicatessens. The "captive" segment, which accounted for 30 to 35 percent of all food service sales, included food service in factories, educational institutions, hospitals, prisons, and federal government facilities; and on airlines, railroads, and ships.

Both segments of the food service market faced a shortage of reliable labor to handle the present volume of industry sales. The labor force needed to service the planned expansion of the industry was expected to grow more slowly than the industry itself. Furthermore, because the educational and experience levels in this labor market were expected to increase, the average cost per labor-hour was expected to continue to rise over the next five years. Substantial technological breakthroughs which could reduce these higher labor costs were not expected. Food service operators were, therefore, interested in forms of food which required fewer labor-hours to prepare and serve. Restaurants in many chain hotels, for example, were beginning to serve entrées that were produced in central commissaries, frozen, and then thawed and garnished before serving.

These trends made on-premise baking, even from prepared mixes, increasingly costly. Furthermore, operation of a full bakery required a food service operator to devote considerable space and capital to baked products, which typically contributed little to the operator's profits. One possible solution for the food service operator was to buy ready-to-serve products from a local bakery. Even when users provided specifications, however, they could get a broad range of cost and quality from different local bakers in their marketing area. Nor were there bakers in or near every local market who could supply the quantities required. Buying from several bakeries could often result in the loss of cost economies obtained through centralized buying operations.

Another way for the food service operator to save on labor costs was to use frozen dough and prebaked frozen products. According to industry sources, there were several reasons why food service firms were unable to buy the type of product and service they desired. First, the most likely manufacturer to provide frozen dough and frozen prebaked items, the commercial baker, was typically reluctant to alter his or her product line. This reluctance stemmed from the investment in equipment, drivers, and trucks for the delivery of fresh baked goods. Second, for many such manufacturers, there were problems of distribution. Frozen dough or prebaked frozen items were bulky; for retention of freshness, they had to be kept at zero degrees from point of manufacture to actual use. The greater the distance between those points, the greater the cost of transport and the dangers of mishandling. Third, the lack of freezer space, both in the distributor's warehouse and in the user's back room, limited the use of frozen dough or prebaked frozen items.

Despite these limitations, industry sources expected sales of frozen dough and frozen prebaked products to food service operations to continue to grow. Principal suppliers of frozen dough to the food service market included Bridgford Foods, Palmer, and (to a much more limited extent) Buttersweet Bakeries. Sara Lee was the dominant supplier of frozen prebaked products to the food service market; Sara Lee was believed to account for one-third of all the sales of frozen prebaked products to food service operations. Sara Lee was known to be investing $16 million in new plant and equipment, primarily to supply the food service market. Although Buttersweet Bakeries and Awrey's sold frozen prebaked products to the food service market, neither firm was believed to account for more than a small percentage of the sales of frozen prebaked products to that market.

BAKE-OFF MARKET

Bake-off operations constituted a third market for frozen dough and frozen prebaked products. In attempting to offer one-stop shopping to the consumer, many supermarkets established some kind of bakery operation on their premises. Some installed an in-store bakery, making most of their items as the local retail bakery shop did, while others utilized a bake-off operation. Experience in supermarkets throughout the country suggested that installation of an in-store bakery—either traditional or bake-off—could result in increases of 10 percent in sales and traffic, and increases in net profit of 5 to 7 percent.

Because the products used in a bake-off operation were already in a more convenient form, less labor and plant investment were needed to conduct a successful bake-off operation than for a traditional bakery. According to a research report prepared for the Commercial Division, a bake-off operation, which used primarily unbaked frozen dough, required no skilled labor, fewer people, less floor space, less supervision and control, and an initial investment only a quarter to half as large as that needed for a complete on-premise bakery. The report also indicated that profits from bake-off operations might exceed those from the traditional in-store bakery operation, and return on investment would be substantially greater. Several industry sources believed that, because of these advantages, many supermarkets might in the future install bake-off operations.

Industry analysts also stated that supermarkets might produce their own frozen dough products if they went into the bake-off operation. Super Valu Stores, a large grocery wholesaler which serviced several hundred franchised supermarkets and grocery stores, had recently begun to offer to its stores a complete line of frozen dough products for bake-off operations. Industry sources estimated that Super Valu might account for 10 to 15 percent of the bake-off market for frozen dough products.

Estimates of current sales of frozen bakery products to bake-off operations ranged from $50 million to $80 million, an estimated 75 percent of which represented sales of frozen dough products. Bridgford Foods, Country Home Foods, Palmer, and Buttersweet Bakeries each supplied a complete line of frozen dough products for bake-off operations. Industry sources indicated that products from all four had received a favorable response from the trade. The suppliers had, however, experienced difficulty in providing products of uniform high quality.

The market for frozen prebaked products to bake-offs was dominated by five firms. Burny Brothers, Country Home Foods, and Buttersweet Bakeries together held 40 to 50 percent of that market, although sales of each of these firms were concentrated in the regions surrounding its manufacturing facilities. Sara Lee and Awrey's together accounted for another 10 percent of this market.

BUTTERSWEET BAKERIES

Buttersweet Bakeries was a family-owned bakery located in Peoria, Illinois. In 1970, the firm employed more than 400 persons and had sales in excess of $8.6 million.

Buttersweet's product line included (1) fresh baked products (breads, sweet rolls, danish items, and most other items typically produced by a wholesale bakery), (2) frozen dough products (including bread, donuts, cookies, and danish), and (3) some prebaked frozen items (donuts, cakes, and cupcakes). In 1970, Buttersweet was one of the few firms in the United States that offered a full line of bake-off items. The company was also one of the nation's largest producers of frozen bread dough. In addition to its manufacturing activities, Buttersweet operated five retail bakeries.

The company's largest-selling item was fresh baked bread, which was distributed to the grocery trade in the Peoria area. Buttersweet also sold frozen bread dough to the grocery trade for resale to consumers. The company sold frozen dough and frozen pre-baked products to the food service and bake-off markets. Buttersweet's sales were handled through a network of brokers. The company distributed its products through a fleet of 25 refrigerated trucks and trailers. Buttersweet's market for frozen products extended to

Pittsburgh in the East, Atlanta in the South, Minneapolis in the North, and Denver in the West. Most of the company's sales of all products came from the five states of Illinois, Indiana, Missouri, Iowa, and Wisconsin.

Buttersweet's total sales had increased steadily for the past five years. The increases in frozen sales to all three main market segments were primarily responsible for the overall growth (see Exhibits 2 and 3).

Buttersweet Bakeries' sales and net income before taxes increased steadily over the past three years. A comparative income statement appears in Exhibit 4; a balance sheet for the year ending December 31, 1970, appears in Exhibit 5.

ACQUISITION ARRANGEMENTS

The Commercial Division had originally proposed to negotiate an option for cash or an exchange of stock in the range of $800,000 to $900,000 for the business and assets of Buttersweet Bakeries, Inc. In addition to the acquisition price, $750,000 was to be spent in modernization and expansion of the plant and its equipment. If it acquired Buttersweet Bakeries, the Commercial Division intended to sell all of Buttersweet's fresh bakery operations, which Commercial Division officials considered unprofitable.

Using Buttersweet's projections for growth and adding their own projections for nationwide sales to the food service market of prebaked and frozen dough products, Commercial Division officials projected the income statement which appears in Exhibit 6. This income statement was based on projections of prebaked and frozen dough forms of frosted sheet cake (one layer, rectangular cake) frosted round cake (two or more layer circular cake), sweet rolls, donuts, and dinner rolls.

Product specification sheets were developed for the products involved, which the Commercial Division intended to test market in three major cities in the United States. Buttersweet's network of brokers for its baked and frozen products was to be discontinued.

With the Commercial Division's sales force handling frozen and baked products, executives realized that conflict could result with some existing customers such as commercial bakeries. Management estimated that profits of approximately $200,000 would be lost by the bakery mixes and flour sales force because of their handling of competing products. It was also estimated that $50,000 in profit would be lost in food service dry mixes when the institutional sales force began handling frozen products. This would result from a deemphasis of dry mixes by that sales force.

SHELF-STABLE TECHNOLOGY

While still seeking to enter the frozen bakery goods market, the Commercial Division was also attempting to develop a new technology which would permit the development of a shelf-stable product (one which would retain the taste and texture of a fresh-baked product for six months or more). Research and development personnel at the company estimated that within five years bakery products high in dough content and low in moisture content, such as bread, could be made shelf stable. Technical specialists doubted that such products as cream pies and fruit-filled products could satisfactorily be made shelf stable within the foreseeable future. Industry observers believed that shelf-stable products would cost about the same per unit as fresh baked goods, but would require less costly distribution, storage, and preparation than either fresh or frozen dough products.

Executives in the Commercial Division had diverse opinions concerning the impact of shelf-stable products on frozen bakery products. Some executives believed that shelf-stable products would remove the need for any frozen products, while other executives thought that there would always be a sizable market for frozen bakery products. This latter group pointed out that extensive educational efforts might be needed to convince consumers that bakery goods that had been on a grocer's shelf for several weeks could still be perfectly fresh.

Exhibit 1

BUTTERSWEET BAKERIES, INC.

POPULATION AND FLOUR CONSUMPTION, 1950-1974

Year	Population (Millions)	Total flour consumption (Millions of Pounds)	Per capita consumption (Pounds)
Actual			
1950	151.7	20,631.2	136
1951	154.3	20,676.2	134
1952	157.0	20,881.0	133
1953	159.6	20,588.4	129
1954	162.4	20,624.8	127
1955	165.3	20,497.2	124
1956	168.2	20,520.4	122
1957	171.3	20,556.0	120
1958	174.1	21,240.2	122
1959	177.1	21,429.1	121
1960	180.7	21,322.6	118
1961	183.8	21,688.4	118
1962	186.7	21,470.5	115
1963	189.4	21,591.6	114
1964	192.1	21,899.4	114
1965	194.6	21,989.8	113
1966	196.9	22,052.8	112
1967	199.1	22,498.3	113
1968	201.2	22,735.6	113
1969	202.9	22,927.7	113
1970	204.9	22,948.8	112
Estimated			
1971	206.9	23,172.8	112
1972	208.9	23,187.9	111
1973	211.0	23,421.0	111
1974	213.1	23,441.0	110

Source: Company Records

Exhibit 2

BUTTERSWEET BAKERIES, INC.
FRESH AND FROZEN GROSS SALES HISTORY
(000 Omitted)

	Frozen sales	Fresh sales	Total sales
1970	$3,923	$4,680	$8,603
1969	2,808	4,853	7,661
1968	1,733	4,765	6,498
1967	1,337	4,796	6,133
1966	1,022	4,087	5,109

Source: Company Records

Exhibit 3

BUTTERSWEET BAKERIES, INC.
FROZEN GROSS SALES HISTORY
(000 Omitted)

	1968	1969	1970
Frozen consumer products	$1,180	$1,737	$2,158
Bake-off operations	412	731	1,215
Food service	141	340	550
Total frozen	$1,733	$2,808	$3,923

Source: Company Records

Exhibit 4

BUTTERSWEET BAKERIES, INC.
COMPARATIVE INCOME STATEMENT, 1967–1969
(000 Omitted)

	1968	1969	1970
Gross sales	$6,498.0	$7,661.0	$8,603.0
Returns, allowances, and distribution	570.0	711.5	870.0
Net sales	$5,928.0	$6,949.5	$7,733.0
Cost of sales	4,548.6	5,233.4	5,592.0
Gross margin	1,379.4	1,716.1	2,141.0
General selling and administrative expense	1,299.6	1,625.3	2,046.4
Net income before taxes	79.8	90.8	94.6

Note: Expenses were allocated to each product line on the basis of sales. The same percentage alloca-tion (expenses as a percent of sales) was used for all products. Therefore it was not possible from accounting records alone to determine the profitability of individual products or product lines.

Source: Company Records

Exhibit 5

BUTTERSWEET BAKERIES, INC.
BALANCE SHEET, DECEMBER 31, 1970
(000 Omitted)

Cash	$ 165
Accounts receivable	450
Inventories	250
Fixed assets	935
Total assets	$1,800
Current liabilities	900
Long-term liabilities (mortgage)	150
Owner's equity	750
Total liabilities and equity	$1,800

Source: Company Records

Exhibit 6

PROJECTION OF BUTTERSWEET BAKERIES, INC.
SALES AFTER ACQUISITION
(000 Omitted)

	1971	1972	1973	1974	1975
Gross sales	$11,125	$15,445	$19,235	$24,110	$29,660
Depreciation	200	175	155	140	125
Profit before tax	$ 675	$ 1,515	$ 2,085	$ 2,765	$ 3,590

Source: Company Records

THE DAYTON-HUDSON CORPORATION

Dayton's Downstairs Store in the Ridgedale Shopping Center

In the spring of 1970, the management of Dayton's department stores faced a decision concerning the retail strategy to adopt for the "downstairs" or basement portion of a planned new department store. The proposed department store was to be situated in a newly planned shopping center called "Ridgedale" located in a suburb of Minneapolis. Dayton's executives realized that evaluation of alternatives for the Ridgedale store might lead to an analysis of the role of downstairs operations in the merchandising strategy of all Dayton's stores, and of the Dayton-Hudson Corporation as a whole.

Certain quantitative information in the case has been judged useful for purposes of class discussion, but does not necessarily reflect the Corporation's experience.
Copyright © 1971 by Richard N. Cardozo.

Several alternative proposals concerning the Ridgedale downstairs store were being considered. One proposal was to include in the new store a downstairs operation similar to those now operated in all other Dayton's stores. A second proposal under review was to expand the downstairs store to include a larger number of "budget" items presently carried in upstairs departments. A third suggestion was to eliminate many of the product lines sold in present downstairs stores and carry only a few expanded product lines in the Ridgedale basement store. A final alternative was to include no budget downstairs store at all in the Ridgedale department store, but rather to move a number of upstairs departments to the lowest floor. This plan would allow a number of upstairs departments to increase substantially the presentation and display of the products they carried.

THE DAYTON-HUDSON CORPORATION

The Dayton-Hudson Corporation was formed in 1969 following the merger of the Dayton Corporation and the J.L. Hudson Company, Detroit. The corporation operated department stores, low-margin stores, shopping centers, and specialty stores which sold books, jewelry, and electronic products. At the end of fiscal year 1970, it had 183 stores in 26 states, including 58 franchised electronics-equipment stores. A statement of income and balance sheet for the corporation for fiscal year 1969 appear in Exhibits 1 and 2.

In 1970, in the Twin Cities metropolitan area (Minneapolis, St. Paul, and suburbs), Dayton-Hudson operated three regional shopping centers; five Dayton's department stores (three within the shopping centers and one each in downtown Minneapolis and St. Paul); six low-margin Target stores; five J.B. Hudson jewelry stores; and two B. Dalton book stores.

Additional department stores were planned both in Ridgedale and in south suburban St. Paul. Plans were also being developed to open several new Target stores in suburban areas. Exhibit 3 indicates the location of existing department stores and discount stores, as well as additional stores planned by Dayton-Hudson in the Twin Cities area.

Dayton's Department Stores

Dayton's was the dominant department store in the area which includes Minnesota, western Wisconsin, Iowa, and the Dakotas. In Minneapolis, Dayton's has been a leading department store since 1902. Dayton's expanded to Rochester, Minnesota, in 1954, and in 1956 opened a store in the Southdale Shopping Center—the first of the company's regional shopping centers and one of the first fully enclosed centers built in the country. In 1963, Dayton's opened a new department store in downtown St. Paul. The company opened a new branch store in the Brookdale Shopping Center in 1966. The most recent Dayton's store was opened in the new Rosedale Shopping Center in 1969. The sixth Dayton's store in the Twin Cities was expected to open in the Ridgedale Center in 1974. Exhibit 4 presents an income statement for each of the five Twin Cities Dayton's Stores.

According to company executives, quality and fashion were the hallmarks of the Dayton's stores. Numerous fashion and specialty shops were included in each store.

Within such areas as women's clothing and men's clothing, the stores operated several such shops, each of which emphasized particular styles within limited price ranges. In addition, each department store offered customers a wide range of services, including restaurants, repair services, a travel agency, a driving school, and a car-rental service. According to a recent image study conducted by Dayton's Research Group, the department stores were viewed by customers as being primarily stores for women that sold fashion merchandise of high quality at relatively high prices.

The merchandising philosophy of the Dayton-Hudson Corporation was summarized in the following statement:

> Dominance, quality, and fashion are the key concepts of Dayton-Hudson's Merchandising Philosophy.
>
> Dominance is sought through large stores, broad assortments of merchandise, and the continued striving to create an exciting atmosphere.
>
> Quality applies to merchandise, service, and facilities. We seek quality in all operating groups, in low-priced lines as well as high-priced lines.
>
> Through dominance, quality, and fashion we seek customers of every taste and budget. Customers at Dayton's . . . department stores, for example, can shop from a broad assortment of merchandise in widely diversified departments, ranging from high-fashion specialty boutique shops to economy-priced bargain departments. Target attempts to satisfy growing customer demands for convenience, price, and everyday merchandise.

Dayton's executives believed that the store faced significant competition from specialty stores (in practically every merchandise line) and department stores in particular markets.

Like a great many large department stores, Dayton's was organized into four major merchandise areas, each of which included numerous departments grouped into divisions, and several functional areas. Responsibilities of each major merchandise area and functional area had become well established over time. Rarely was responsibility for a particular department transferred from one of the four major merchandise areas to another.

Each of the four major merchandise areas—fashion, home furnishings, general merchandise, and the downstairs store—was headed by a vice-president–general merchandise manager, who was responsible for the profitability of his or her area in the branch stores as well as in the downtown store. The general merchandise managers reported directly to the president of the store who, together with them, determined the merchandising, promotional, and general strategy for Dayton's downtown department store and its branches. Within this group the position of the general merchandise manager for the downstairs store was generally the least powerful, in part because that area produced less sales and profit than the other divisions and because sales were increasing much less rapidly than sales in the upstairs departments.

The general merchandise manager for the downstairs store supervised four divisional merchandise managers, who in turn managed the activities of several buyers. The four divisional merchandise managers included one for fashion apparel and children's wear; one for men's and boys' wear and home furnishings; one for accessories, women's shoes, and intimate apparel; and one for leisure merchandise (see Exhibit 5). Each divisional merchandise manager and buyer was responsible for his or her particular area in the downstairs stores of both the downtown and the branch stores.

Activities in the functional areas, including the controller, personnel and customer service, and branch store operations, were the responsibility of the executive vice-president. Branch store operations came under a senior vice-president for branch stores, to whom the general managers of each of the branch stores reported. These general managers were assisted by managers of personnel and operations, and by group sales managers (see Exhibit 5). A primary responsibility of the branch management function was to maximize sales in each store. In carrying out this responsibility, store managers had to balance the interests of the several general and divisional merchandise managers, each of whom was concerned with securing facilities and attention for his or her departments.

Dayton's Downstairs Store

In 1970, all Dayton's department stores in the Twin Cities area included downstairs budget operations. The combined sales volume of the downstairs stores in the two downtown and three suburban locations exceeded $20 million in 1969. Of that total, approximately 22 percent represented sales of women's clothing; 26 percent, women's shoes and accessories; 20 percent, children's clothing; and 27 percent, men's clothing and furnishings. The remaining 5 percent was divided among five unrelated departments.

Apart from the Minneapolis store, each of Dayton's downstairs operations encompassed an area of approximately 25,000–30,000 square feet. The downtown Minneapolis downstairs store was much larger. Except for the downstairs operation located in the Brookdale store, none of the downstairs stores had entrances leading directly to the parking areas. Only in the Brookdale store could a customer enter the downstairs area without first passing through a portion of the upstairs store.

Although there was some variation in the types and sizes of departments included in the various Dayton's downstairs stores, most of the stores were similar in their product offerings. Exhibits 6 and 7 list the departments typically included in the downstairs stores, and give the size, sales, gross margin, total expense, and profit figures for each downstairs department in the Brookdale and Southdale shopping centers, respectively.

Dayton's attempted in its downstairs stores to convey an image of a full-line merchandising operation with low prices. The downstairs stores typically carried many of the same merchandise categories as comparable upstairs departments. Seldom, however, were identical products carried in both locations. There were many instances in which price lines overlapped and the highest quality product downstairs was priced higher than the lowest priced line in the corresponding upstairs department. Exhibit 8 presents several illustrations of the range of prices included in downstairs departments and their upstairs counterparts.

To maintain a wide range of departments and merchandise, some downstairs departments were operated at little or no profit. Other departments, though profitable, had sales and profits far below their upstairs counterparts. Downstairs departments typically had higher turnover rates and lower profit margins than the store as a whole. Total profit and profit/square foot were usually substantially greater in the upstairs departments. The vice-president and general merchandise manager in charge of downstairs operations believed that a detailed analysis of this type of data for existing stores might suggest that several downstairs departments should be expanded, and a number eliminated or decreased in size in a Ridgedale downstairs store. Exhibit 9 includes sales and profit data for several downstairs and comparable upstairs departments for Dayton's Southdale store. (Net profit figures for each department and the total downstairs operation were calculated using a full costing system. Gross margin was computed by subtracting from net sales the cost [net, after any discounts] of merchandise purchased for resale. Direct and indirect expenses were subtracted from gross margin to arrive at a net profit figure. Exhibit 10 indicates the expenses included in the direct and indirect expense categories and shows how these expenses are allocated.)

In most instances, expense items were not determined for individual downstairs departments but rather for a group of departments. Exhibits 11 and 12 indicate the expenses incurred as a percentage of sales for selected downstairs department groups in the Brookdale and Southdale stores, respectively. Although data for identical groupings of departments in the upstairs stores were not available, Exhibit 13 provides expense data for similar upstairs department groupings. The data in these exhibits and the table illustrate that both gross margins and expense items varied widely across different types of merchandise lines as well as between similar merchandise groupings in the upstairs and downstairs locations.

Turnover rates also varied substantially among different departments, as indicated in Exhibit 14. These rates varied from a low of 2.4 for Children's Shoes to a high of 7.6 for Junior Dresses. Because turnover data were not available for individual stores, the data in Exhibit 14 indicate the rate of merchandise turnover by downstairs department for department stores with volumes similar to Dayton's.

The advertising campaigns for Dayton's downstairs stores were distinct from those of the upstairs stores. In each advertisement run by a downstairs department, the logo "Dayton's Downstairs" was prominently displayed. The National Retail Merchants Association (NRMA) reported that, for stores whose total volume exceeded $50 million per year, expenditures on advertising typically amounted to 3.8 percent of sales for all downstairs departments combined, compared to an average of 3.6 percent for the store as a whole.

Although precise figures were not available, the vice-president in charge of downstairs operations estimated that more than 90 percent of the customers who patronized Dayton's downstairs also shopped in Dayton's upstairs departments. Of all the customers who shopped upstairs, however, the percentage who also shopped downstairs was considerably less than 90 percent, according to his estimate.

An analysis of sales to charge account customers revealed both overlap and differences in demographic profiles of shoppers between comparable downstairs and upstairs departments. This analysis indicated that demographic profiles of customers varied among downstairs departments, and that the differences between downstairs departments and their upstairs counterparts varied among pairs of departments (see Exhibit 15).

Another study Dayton's carried out indicated that a substantial number of upstairs shoppers were not aware that a downstairs budget operation did exist. The vice-president in charge of downstairs operations hypothesized that many shoppers who were aware of the downstairs store did not perceive it to be lower priced than the upstairs store. He believed that Dayton's downstairs store did not have an image distinct from that of the upstairs store. He thought that the problem of indistinct image was further complicated by the fact that in surburban stores, downstairs store departments shared the lowest building level with departments which were located upstairs in both downtown stores.

COMPETITION

Dayton's executives classified direct competitors of Dayton's downstairs stores into five major categories:

1. *Dayton's upstairs departments.* The vice-president in charge of downstairs operations believed that the major competition faced by many of Dayton's downstairs departments was the departments offering similar merchandise in the upstairs store. His major reasons for this belief were (a) that all merchandise categories carried in downstairs departments were also carried upstairs and (b) that the total downstairs store lacked an image distinct from the upstairs store.

2. *Other local department stores.* In 1970, there were two major competitive department stores operating in the Twin Cities area in addition to Dayton's. Donaldson's Department Stores operated stores in downtown Minneapolis and St. Paul and branch stores in Brookdale, Southdale, and Rosedale. Powers Department Stores had a major facility located in downtown Minneapolis; a branch in Knollwood Plaza in the Ridgedale trading area; and a branch in Highland, a shopping center in a residential area of St. Paul.

Only the Donaldson's stores located in downtown Minneapolis and St. Paul and the Powers store located in downtown Minneapolis, however, had downstairs budget stores. Because these downstairs stores had only limited product lines and little was spent on promotion for these operations, Dayton's executives believed that these downstairs stores offered little competition to Dayton's budget operations.

3. *National chains.* The major national chains competing with Dayton's were believed to be Sears, Penney's, and Wards. Sears operated major stores in south Minneapolis and the Brookdale shopping center. Penney's operated major outlets in downtown Minneapolis and Brookdale, and planned a new store in the Southdale Shopping Center. Wards operated complete department stores in St. Paul, and in the south, west, and north Minneapolis suburbs. (See Exhibit 3 for the locations of all Sears, Penney's, and Wards full-line department stores.) These national chains also operated numerous catalog and smaller stores in the suburban areas. According to the vice-president in charge of basement operations, the merchandising approach used by the Dayton's downstairs store was more

promotional than Penney's, Sears, and Wards, in that much more emphasis was placed on price specials in downstairs advertisements.

Of the three major national chains, company executives believed for several reasons that Penney's was the strongest competition for the downstairs store. Penney's merchandise mix and philosophy was believed to be closer to Dayton's downstairs store than either Sears or Wards, both of which were believed to be following a policy of "trading up" in many of their merchandise lines. In addition, Sears and Wards were also believed to be strongest in merchandise lines that Dayton's downstairs store did not carry. These included such items as appliances and tools. Finally, Dayton's studies had shown that customers perceived Penney's to have excellent values in many of the same soft-good lines that Dayton's downstairs store also carried.

A survey conducted by Dayton's showed that the demographic characteristics of Dayton's shoppers and those of Penney's, Sears, and Wards did not differ significantly. In fact, as Exhibit 16 shows, there was very little difference between the demographic characteristics of the Dayton's shopper and those of any major competitors.

4. *Discount stores.* There were several major discount operations in the Twin Cities area, including Target stores, owned by the Dayton-Hudson Corporation; Holiday Stores; Shoppers' City; Gem; and Spartan-Atlantic.

The six Target stores located in the Twin Cities area were one-floor, freestanding units which offered both "hard" and "soft" line merchandise at discount prices on a self-service, cash-and-carry basis. Target's major merchandising emphasis was on faster moving items such as everyday needs, health and beauty aids, and recreational items. Grocery items were also offered through leased departments. Target stores did not carry furniture and major appliances. Management of Target stores was known to be considering expansion of its lines of men's, women's and children's clothing.

The Target stores were typically located in high-traffic sites in or near established shopping centers or areas. However, no Target stores were located in the major shopping centers which housed Dayton's department stores. The most recently constructed stores encompassed 160,000 square feet of floor space, which included 30,000 square feet of leased supermarket area. Most Target stores were open seven days a week.

Executives believed that Holiday and Shoppers' City were Target's principal competitors, but did not perceive the discount stores to be major competitors of Dayton's downstairs operations. One basis for this opinion was that discount stores and Dayton's department stores were never located in the same shopping centers.

5. *Specialty shops.* Numerous clothing, furniture, appliance, and other stores were located in all suburban and downtown locations. Dayton's executives did not perceive these stores to be primary competitors, however, because of their limited product offerings and higher prices.

Dayton's major competition varied substantially according to both the particular products or product lines considered and the specific store location. Overall, Dayton's management believed the major competitors of the downstairs stores, in order of intensity of competition, were Dayton's upstairs departments, Penney's, Sears, Target, and

Wards. In areas such as children's apparel and linens and bedding, Penney's was thought to be the major competitor, while Sears was believed to be the major competitor in ready-made draperies.

As one estimate of Dayton's competitive position within the Twin Cities metropolitan area, management cited a study in which each of 600 adults was asked to name the store at which he or she made his or her most recent purchase in each of several merchandise categories. The results showed that Dayton's was the single store most frequently mentioned and in most categories was mentioned far more often than any other store (see Exhibit 17). For any particular trading area, however, the figures varied from five to ten percentage points from those shown in Exhibit 17. Exhibit 18 contains the figures for the Ridgedale trading area.

THE RIDGEDALE TRADING AREA

The Ridgedale trading area appeared attractive to Dayton's management both because of its relatively affluent population and because of its lack of retail facilities.

Customer Characteristics

The Ridgedale area was differentiated significantly from the other Dayton's trading areas by the income characteristics of its residents. Exhibit 19 indicates that the Ridgedale area had a large number of families in the upper-income brackets. This factor led some Dayton's personnel to suggest that a budget operation may be less necessary and less profitable in the Ridgedale store than in the other branch facilities. A survey of frequent customers of the one Target store now located in the Ridgedale area, however, indicated that a high percentage of upper-income families in this area did shop at discount stores (see Exhibit 20). In the opinion of some Dayton's executives, this factor supported the contention that a downstairs budget operation would appeal to upper-income families as well as the lower-income segments of the trading area.

Exhibit 21 shows the percentage of residents in each of Dayton's existing and proposed trading areas who *usually* shopped at Dayton's for selected types of merchandise. This table shows that, for many types of goods, a large percentage of Ridgedale residents shopped at Dayton's, even though no Dayton's store was located in their trading area. Company officials expected that these percentages would increase significantly once the Ridgedale store opened.

Competition

In the Ridgedale trading area, there were no large regional shopping centers, and Dayton's executives knew of none planned except their own. The managers of Dayton's planning division did expect that one or more additional discount and specialty stores might be built in the Ridgedale area. For example, Target stores had plans to locate a new discount store in the Ridgedale vicinity and Boutells, a large furniture outlet in the Twin Cities, also planned to construct a store near the proposed Ridgedale shopping center.

The major competitive shopping area in the Ridgedale area was a "strip center" known as Knollwood Plaza. This center had a branch of Powers department stores, a Target store, a Penny's store, and a Sears Catalogue store. A number of other small shopping centers were located in the Ridgedale vicinity, but these centers contained only small specialty shops.

The director of Dayton's marketing research department stated that the major competition for a new Dayton's store at Ridgedale would be the other major outlets in that shopping center and the department stores in Brookdale, Southdale, and Downtown. If a downstairs bargain operation were included in the new Ridgedale store, the vice-president in charge of downstairs operations believed that the major competition for downstairs merchandise would come primarily from Dayton's upstairs departments and from any Sears, Penney's, or Wards stores located in the center, rather than from discount stores.

Tentative Plans and Major Alternatives for Ridgedale

Tentative plans for the new Ridgedale Shopping Center called for a three-story facility comprised of approximately one million square feet, about the same size as Brookdale. In addition to Dayton's, Donaldson's, Sears, and Penney's were expected to operate full-line department stores in the center. Other expected occupants included 80 to 100 women's and men's stores, and several types of specialty shops.

Preliminary plans for Dayton's Ridgedale store called for a total of approximately 220,000 square feet, built on three levels. Both the first and second levels would be accessible from a parking lot. In no case would the downstairs store, if included in Ridgedale, occupy floor space which would be entirely below ground. If a complete downstairs store were included, it would encompass about 25,000 square feet. This size would make the Ridgedale downstairs store very similar in size to the other Dayton's downstairs stores (apart from downtown Minneapolis) located in the Twin Cities area.

In attempting to structure a merchandising strategy for the new Ridgedale store, a number of Dayton's personnel questioned the policy of including in this store a downstairs operation similar to those operated in the other outlets. These individuals believed that some other "downstairs" strategy might lead to a more optimal utilization of space and, thus, a more profitable total department store operation. Therefore, in addition to operating a downstairs store similar to those now in existence in the other Dayton's stores, three other proposals were being considered.

One proposal under consideration was to blend the lower priced lines now sold in the upstairs departments with those traditionally available in the existing downstairs stores. This would make the Ridgedale store a more complete budget operation and further segment its offerings from the upstairs departments. If there were to be no overlap in either products or prices in the downstairs departments and their upstairs counterparts, a major issue would be to decide where the price breaks should be on merchandise carried in each of the two departments.

Another suggestion was to modify the product mix in the Ridgedale downstairs store and offer a much smaller number of product lines than were now available in existing downstairs stores. For example, some Dayton's executives were in favor of carrying only men's items in the Ridgedale downstairs operation. One issue raised concerning this alternative was the question of what sales impact the elimination of certain downstairs lines would have on sales of comparable upstairs departments.

A final alternative being examined was to include no "budget" operation at all in the Ridgedale store. Rather, lower priced lines would be added to existing upstairs departments, whose floor space and merchandise presentation would be expanded. Executives noted that not all of the department store branches opened throughout the country in recent years included budget operations. According to some analysts, the absence of these budget floors in suburban department stores created a void that was eventually filled by modern day discount stores:

> However, these large department stores in their move to the suburbs did not always take one fundamental fact into account, namely, that many of their new customers in outlying areas were the same people that they had been serving for years in their downtown units. Moreover, these suburban branches did not have a bargain basement, which has become an important feature of the downtown department store. Much to their chagrin, large retailers found that the trend toward "trading up" among suburbanites did not blot out the need for staple items at attractive prices. Hence, the growing suburban areas created a ready-made haven for discounters which they were eager and willing to occupy.[1]

Several executives agreed with this argument, and stated that elimination of a budget store would mean the loss of a certain customer segment to competition such as Sears and Penney's. Also, if no downstairs store were included in the Ridgedale operation, or if a store were included that carried only a limited number of product lines, some executives were concerned about customer reactions if certain downstairs store advertised specials were available in all stores except Ridgedale.

Dayton's management was evaluating these alternative proposals to determine which, if any, was appropriate for the new Ridgedale store. If they recommended one of these alternatives or developed a different plan, Dayton's executives knew that they would have to prepare a detailed recommendation for review by senior executives and staff of the Dayton-Hudson Corporation.

---

1. Walter R. Keay, "The Revolution in Department Store Merchandising," *The Magazine of Wall Street* **115** (Oct. 3, 1964), p. 60.

Exhibit 1

THE DAYTON–HUDSON CORPORATION
DAYTON–HUDSON CORPORATION AND SUBSIDIARIES
STATEMENT OF INCOME

	Fiscal Year	
	1969 Year ended January 31, 1970	1968 Year ended February 1, 1969
Revenues	(000)	
Net retail sales, including sales of leased departments	$868,335	$795,243
Rental income	15,251	13,338
Realized gain from real estate sales	4,772	3,400
	$888,358	$811,981
Costs and expenses		
Cost of sales and expenses, exclusive of items listed below	$773,829	$704,632
Maintenance and repairs	4,128	3,832
Depreciation and amortization of property and equipment	16,176	14,022
Rentals of real property	7,458	7,005
Interest	12,150	6,381
Taxes other than income taxes	22,278	20,056
Contribution to retirement plan	4,265	5,073
	$840,285	$761,001
Income before income taxes	$ 48,073	$ 50,980
Income Taxes	24,400	26,422
Net income	$ 23,673	$ 24,558

Source: Annual Report

Exhibit 2

THE DAYTON–HUDSON CORPORATION
DAYTON–HUDSON CORPORATION AND SUBSIDIARIES
STATEMENT OF FINANCIAL POSITION

	End of fiscal year	
	1969 January 31, 1970	1968 February 1, 1969
Assets		
Current Assets		
Cash	$ 22,986	$ 19,104
Short-term government obligations—at cost		17,416
Accounts receivable	132,744	116,483
Merchandise inventories	137,194	124,696
Supplies and prepaid expenses	2,332	3,009
Total current assets	$295,256	$280,709
Investments and other assets	13,018	8,737
Property and equipment		
Land and improvements	$ 72,073	$ 51,182
Buildings and improvements	250,285	210,586
Fixtures and equipment	70,712	60,187
Construction in progress	35,987	23,241
Less allowance for depreciation and amortization	(116,550)	(106,479)
	$312,510	$238,716
	$620,784	$528,162

Exhibit 2 (Cont.)

	End of fiscal year	
	1969 January 31, 1970	1968 February 1, 1969
Liabilities		
Current liabilities		
Notes payable to banks—unsecured:		
Finance subsidiary	$ 16,450	$ 15,800
Other		9,300
Accounts payable	54,183	57,229
Taxes other than income taxes	21,906	19,070
Accrued liabilities	16,961	13,639
Income taxes, currently payable	11,470	10,314
Deferred taxes on income reported on the installment basis	14,682	13,230
Long-term debt due within one year	10,791	7,105
Total current liabilities	$146,442	$145,687
Long-term debt	193,745	118,832
Deferred credits	10,893	7,835
Shareholders' investment		
Preferred stock	352	352
Common stock	15,805	15,827
Additional paid-in capital	34,731	35,353
Retained earnings	218,815	204,277
	$269,703	$255,808
	$620,784	$528,162

Source: Annual Report

Exhibit 3

THE DAYTON–HUDSON CORPORATION
LOCATION OF DAYTON'S TRADING AREAS, DAYTON'S DEPARTMENT STORES, AND MAJOR COMPETITORS' OUTLETS IN THE TWIN CITIES METROPOLITAN AREA

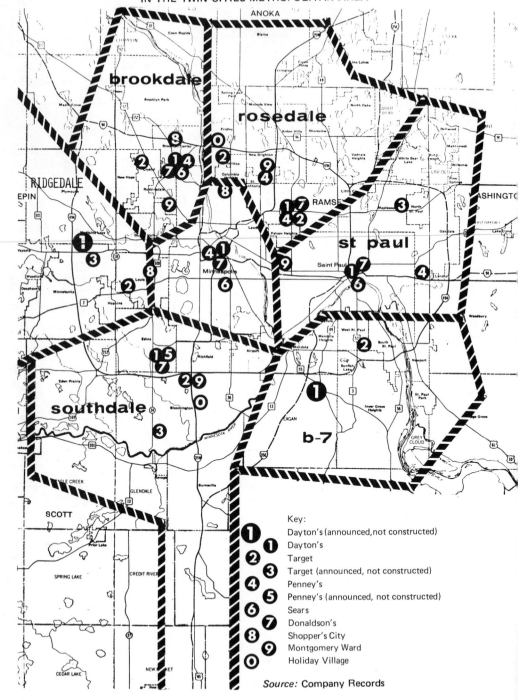

Key:

1 Dayton's (announced, not constructed)
1 Dayton's
2 Target
3 Target (announced, not constructed)
4 Penney's
5 Penney's (announced, not constructed)
6 Sears
7 Donaldson's
8 Shopper's City
9 Montgomery Ward
0 Holiday Village

Source: Company Records

Exhibit 4

THE DAYTON–HUDSON CORPORATION
INCOME STATEMENT FOR EACH OF DAYTON'S FIVE TWIN CITIES
DEPARTMENT STORES
TWELVE MONTHS ENDING JANUARY 31, 1970

Income and expenses	Store location				
	Minneapolis	St. Paul	Southdale	Brookdale	Rosedale[a]
Index of sales (Minneapolis = 100)	100	39	54	25	20
Gross margin (% of sales)	37.2%	32.1%	39.9%	40.0%	40.6%
Operating expenses (% of sales)	33.7	27.8	28.0	30.3	36.2
Operating profit (% of sales)	3.5	4.3	11.9	9.7	4.4
Square feet	1,354,180	338,003	349,341	195,285	189,118

[a] Opened August 1, 1969

Source: Company Records (figures disguised)

Exhibit 5

DAYTON–HUDSON CORPORATION
ABRIDGED ORGANIZATION CHART

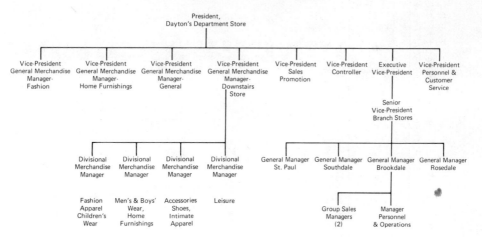

Exhibit 6

THE DAYTON-HUDSON CORPORATION
SALES, TOTAL EXPENSES, GROSS MARGIN, PROFIT, AND SIZE DATA
FOR SELECTED DEPARTMENTS IN DAYTON'S BROOKDALE DOWNSTAIRS STORE

Department no.	Name	Net sales	Gross margin and discount (% of sales)	Total expense (% of sales)	Profit ($)	Profit (% of sales)	Square feet	Profit/ sq. ft.
1	Women's Coats, Suits	$ 83,554	38.7	37.1	1337	1.6	1,035	$ 1.29
2	Misses Dresses	60,465	37.9	37.7	120	0.2	959	0.13
3	Women's Dresses	10,148	36.4	35.6	91	0.9	560	0.16
4	Maternity Shop	18,079	40.4	39.4	180	1.0	240	0.75
5	Junior Coats	44,047	39.8	31.5	3655	8.3	100	36.56
6	Junior Dresses	43,792	36.5	29.6	3021	6.9	190	15.90
7	Infants	90,395	36.5	32.7	3435	3.8	960	3.58
8	Toddlers	47,082	38.3	35.4	1318	2.8	200	6.59
9	Children's Shop	94,110	39.4	31.8	7152	7.6	700	10.22
10	Girls' Wear	105,409	39.1	30.9	8643	8.2	860	10.05
11	Junior High Shop	31,232	36.1	32.0	1280	4.1	800	1.60
12	Child. Underwr. and Access.	69,935	36.8	32.2	3217	4.6	450	7.15
13	Blouses, Sweaters	258,250	39.1	29.0	26083	10.1	2,015	12.95
14	Junior Sportswear	63,014	39.2	25.4	8695	13.8	190	45.77
15	Housewares, Aprons	74,373	41.8	39.4	1785	2.4	700	2.55
16	Notions	13,408	37.0	36.7	40	0.3	100	0.40
17	Men's Suits and Coats	64,146	33.4	32.4	641	1.0	522	1.23
18	University Shop	209,764	41.9	28.0	28947	13.8	1,850	15.64
19	University Shop	70,856	39.5	29.8	6873	9.7	732	9.39
20	Men's Work Clothes	68,831	36.9	30.2	4611	6.7	684	6.74
21	Men's Furnishings	213,269	40.5	26.3	29004	13.6	1,664	17.43
22	Boys' Clothes	192,746	37.9	33.0	9444	4.9	1,824	5.18
23	Floor Coverings	36,766	37.7	34.1	1323	3.6	200	66.12
24	Draperies and Curtains	66,921	38.3	38.0	200	0.3	1,340	0.15

Operating data

Exhibit 6 (Cont.)

Department		Net sales	Gross margin and discount (% of sales)	Operating data Total expense (% of sales)	Profit ($)	Profit (% of sales)	Square feet	Profit/ sq. ft.
no.	Name							
25	Linens and Towels	70,958	40.9	38.0	2057	2.9	765	2.69
26	Domestics	75,218	36.7	36.0	526	0.7	465	1.13
27	Bedding	47,842	41.4	41.0	190	0.4	665	0.29
28	Dress Accessories	37,227	52.2	29.1	8599	23.1	416	20.67
29	Leather Goods	51,509	45.1	35.3	5047	9.8	444	11.37
30	Millinery	31,828	49.0	34.3	4678	14.7	244	19.17
31	Women's Hosiery	145,325	41.4	33.7	11190	7.7	1,012	11.06
32	Gloves	19,867	52.2	30.3	4350	21.9	216	20.14
33	Lingerie	119,505	42.8	39.9	10635	8.9	1,222	8.70
34	Corsetry	73,085	44.1	38.4	4165	5.7	784	5.31
35	Men's and Boys' Shoes	56,960	42.4	36.6	3303	5.8	702	4.70
36	Women's Comfort Shoes	127,330	41.1	38.1	3819	3.0	1,078	3.54
37	Children's Shoes	70,958	41.6	38.7	2057	2.9	996	2.06
Totals		$2,950,004	40.0	32.8	211,730	7.2	27,884	$ 7.59

Sales Volume by Category

	(000)	%
Women's Clothing (Depts. 1–6, 13–14)	$ 581.3	19.7
Women's Shoes and Access. (Depts. 28–34, 36)	605.7	20.5
Children's (Depts. 7–12, 37)	501.1	17.0
Men's and Boys' (Depts. 17–22, 35)	876.6	29.7
Household Goods and Misc. (Depts. 23–27, 15–16)	385.3	13.1
Total	$2,950.0	100.00

Source: Company Records (figures disguised)

Exhibit 7

THE DAYTON-HUDSON CORPORATION

SALES, TOTAL EXPENSES, GROSS MARGIN, PROFIT, AND SIZE DATA

FOR SELECTED DEPARTMENTS IN DAYTON'S SOUTHDALE DOWNSTAIRS STORE

Department no. Name	Net sales	Gross margin and discount (% of sales)	Operating data Total expense (% of sales)	Profit ($)	Profit (% of sales)	Square feet	Profit/ sq. ft.
1 Women's Coats, Suits	$ 125,545	38.7	31.5	9039	7.2	780	$ 11.59
2 Misses Dresses	87,696	37.9	34.0	3332	3.8	852	3.91
3 Women's Dresses	15,568	36.4	35.9	77	0.5	479	0.16
4 Maternity Shop	17,808	40.4	34.5	1015	5.7	235	4.32
5 Junior Coats	41,664	39.8	29.2	4374	10.5	385	11.36
6 Junior Dresses	63,168	36.5	26.9	6064	9.6	587	10.33
7 Infants	88,655	36.5	32.2	3812	4.3	1,081	3.52
8 Toddlers	26,208	38.3	34.1	1126	4.3	380	2.97
9 Children's Shop	99,960	39.4	32.1	7197	7.2	1,271	5.66
10 Girl's Wear	138,550	39.1	30.4	12053	8.7	1,599	7.54
11 Junior High Shop	52,416	36.1	27.4	4162	8.8	479	8.69
12 Child. Underwr. and Access.	98,900	36.8	32.5	4153	4.2	573	7.25
13 Blouses, Sweaters	284,920	39.1	27.7	32480	11.4	2,475	13.12
14 Junior Sportswear	85,596	39.2	24.3	12573	14.9	789	16.16
15 Housewares, Aprons	80,750	41.8	35.3	5168	6.4	731	7.07
16 Notions	17,920	37.3	36.0	215	1.2	94	2.29
17 Men's Suits and Coats	96,730	33.4	29.1	4159	4.3	594	7.00
18 University Shop	289,095	41.9	26.2	45538	15.7	1,792	25.41
19 University Shop	127,160	39.5	25.4	17802	14.0	1,076	16.54
20 Men's Work Clothes	85,456	36.9	26.6	8887	10.4	471	18.87
21 Men's Furnishings	369,410	40.2	23.7	60952	16.5	1,951	31.24
22 Boy's Clothes	271,745	37.9	28.8	24728	9.1	1,897	13.03
23 Floor Coverings	4,704	37.7	37.6	4	0.1	–	–
24 Draperies and Curtains	16,464	38.3	38.0	49	0.3	94	0.53

Exhibit 7 (Cont.)

Department no. Name	Net sales	Gross margin and discount (% of sales)	Total expense (% of sales)	Profit ($)	Profit (% of sales)	Square feet	Profit/ sq. ft.
			Operating data				
25 Linens and Towels	87,734	40.9	35.7	4562	5.2	200	22.81
26 Domestics	92,406	34.7	34.5	184	0.2	150	1.23
27 Bedding	42,076	39.3	38.7	252	0.6	150	1.68
28 Dress Accessories	86,576	52.2	21.8	26319	30.4	535	49.15
29 Leather Goods	81,760	45.1	28.1	13899	17.0	604	23.01
30 Millinery	27,664	49.0	25.9	7165	23.1	115	6.23
31 Women's Hosiery	366,605	41.4	27.4	51324	14.0	1,150	44.63
32 Gloves	32,256	52.2	25.8	8515	26.4	44	193.53
33 Lingerie	173,655	28.7	19.8	13973	13.3	1,443	9.68
34 Corsetry	105,060	44.1	33.1	11451	10.9	798	14.35
35 Men's and Boys' Shoes	93,744	42.4	39.6	2624	2.8	622	4.21
36 Women's Comfort Shoes	130,135	41.1	40.2	1172	0.9	1,239	0.95
37 Children's Shoes	93,184	41.6	40.8	745	0.8	1,106	0.67
Totals	$3,999,023	39.6	29.3	411,105	10.3	28,821	$ 14.26

Sales Volume by Category

	(000)	%
Women's Clothing (Depts. 1–6, 13–14)	$ 722.0	18.0
Women's Shoes and Accessories (Depts. 28–34, 36)	1,003.7	25.1
Children's (Depts. 7–12, 37)	597.9	15.0
Men's and Boys' (Depts. 17–22, 35)	1,333.3	33.3
Household Goods and Misc. (Depts. 23–27, 15–16)	342.1	8.6
	$3,999.0	100.0

Source: Company Records (figures disguised)

Exhibit 8

THE DAYTON–HUDSON CORPORATION

PRICE RANGES FOR SELECTED DOWNSTAIRS AND UPSTAIRS PRODUCTS

	Low price		High price	
Product line	Downstairs	Upstairs	Downstairs	Upstairs
Men's Suits	$39.00	$55.00	$79.00	$300.00
Women's Junior Size Dresses	$ 7.00	$13.00	$25.00	$100.00
Sheets (double-bed size)	$ 2.00	$ 4.00	$ 6.00	$ 10.00
Bath Towels	$ .99	$ 3.00	$ 4.50	$ 15.00

Source: Company Records

Exhibit 9

THE DAYTON-HUDSON CORPORATION
COMPARISON OF OPERATING DATA* FOR SELECTED† DOWNSTAIRS AND UPSTAIRS DEPARTMENTS
IN DAYTON'S SOUTHDALE STORE

No.	Department	Sales	Location	Profit (% of sales)	Square ft.	Turnover‡	Gross margin net of cash discount (% of sales)
21	Men's Furnishings	$369,410	Downstairs	16.5	1,951	3.7	40.2
		580,343	Upstairs	25.4	1,944	3.5	46.4
35	Men's and Boys' Shoes	93,744	Downstairs	2.8	622	2.6	42.4
		485,125	Upstairs	17.5	1,397	2.2	46.0
13	Sweaters and Blouses	284,930	Downstairs	11.4	2,475	N.A.	39.1
		457,027	Upstairs	20.4	2,885	N.A.	44.3
14	Junior Sportswear	85,596	Downstairs	14.9	789	7.5	39.2
		346,976	Upstairs	18.7	2,591	4.3	43.0
25	Linens and Towels	87,734	Downstairs	5.2	200	4.5	40.9
		247,058	Upstairs	19.9	1,858	2.6	48.4
27	Bedding	42,076	Downstairs	0.6	150	N.A.	36.3
		308,921	Upstairs	15.5	2,509	3.0	43.3
24	Drapery	16,464	Downstairs	0.3	94	2.8	38.3
		261,147	Upstairs	10.8	2,007	2.6	48.5
3	Women's Dresses	15,568	Downstairs	0.5	479	5.7	36.4
		143,194	Upstairs	21.4	523	5.7	41.7

* Data presented are for 1969.
† Departments were selected on the basis of comparability between product lines carried in upstairs and downstairs departments.
‡ NRMA estimates based on stores of similar volume.
Source: Company Records (figures disguised)

Exhibit 10

THE DAYTON-HUDSON CORPORATION
FACTORS USED IN THE COMPUTATION OF DIRECT AND INDIRECT EXPENSES
AND METHODS USED TO ALLOCATE THESE EXPENSES

Expenses	Basis of allocation
Direct	
Total selling wages	*
Total direct advertising	*
Rent	Square footage
Maintenance	Square footage
Buying	Sales
Receiving and marking	Time
Interest on inventory	*
Taxes on inventory	*
Stock boy wages	Time
Wrapping and packaging	Time
Delivery	Size and number of units
Indirect	
Institutional advertising	Sales
Corporate staff salaries	Sales

*Charged direct, not allocated

Exhibit 11

THE DAYTON–HUDSON CORPORATION

DIRECT AND INDIRECT EXPENSES AS A PERCENTAGE OF SALES FOR
SELECTED DOWNSTAIRS DEPARTMENT GROUPINGS

(Brookdale Store)

Sales and expense categories	Department groupings*						
	Women's wear (1, 2, 3, 4, 5, 15)	Women's sportswear (6, 13, 14)	Women's access. (28, 29, 30, 31, 32)	Lingerie and corsetry (33, 34)	Children's, girls' wear (7, 8, 9, 10, 11, 12)	Men's wear (17, 18, 20, 21)	Boys' wear (19, 22, 35)
Sales ($)	$290,666	$365,056	$285,756	$192,590	$438,163	$556,010	$320,562
Gross margin and discount	39.4%	38.8%	44.6%	43.3%	38.0%	39.7%	38.9%
Total selling wages	6.8	5.1	8.3	6.9	5.6	5.1	6.6
Total direct adv. (net)	0.1	—	—	—	—	—	—
Rent	6.8	5.1	5.0	6.5	5.8	4.8	5.8
Maintenance	1.8	1.3	1.3	1.7	1.5	1.3	1.4
Buying	3.4	2.5	2.3	2.6	2.2	1.9	2.3
Receiving and marking	0.2	0.2	0.2	0.2	0.2	0.2	0.2
Interest and tax on inv.	0.4	0.2	0.8	0.9	0.7	0.7	0.8
Stock people's wages	0.4	0.3	0.4	0.5	0.3	0.2	0.3
Wrap and packaging	0.9	0.4	0.6	0.8	0.8	0.7	0.6
Delivery	—	—	—	—	—	—	—
Other direct	2.8	2.9	2.6	2.5	2.2	2.0	2.3
Indirect (store)	1.6	1.3	1.4	1.5	1.5	1.4	1.5
Multi-store allocation:							
Buying	2.6	2.0	2.5	2.8	2.2	1.9	2.5
Advertising	3.5	2.0	2.0	2.3	2.7	2.4	2.4
Delivery	—	—	0.1	—	—	0.1	0.1
Other	6.8	5.2	5.8	6.4	6.3	5.5	6.0
Total expenses	38.1	28.5	33.3	35.6	32.0	28.2	32.8
Profit (net)	1.3	10.3	11.3	7.7	6.0	11.5	6.1

*Departments are grouped according to their physical proximity in a store. Because of this, certain groupings may not include all departments that would logically fall under each heading or may include departments that would better fit in a different grouping. Group headings such as "Women's Wear" are only meant to reflect the general nature of the departments which comprise each group or the departments that dominate the sales of a group.

Source: Company Records

Exhibit 12

THE DAYTON-HUDSON CORPORATION

DIRECT AND INDIRECT EXPENSES AS A PERCENTAGE OF SALES FOR

SELECTED DOWNSTAIRS DEPARTMENT GROUPINGS

(Southdale Store)

Sales and expense categories	Women's wear (1, 2, 3, 4, 13, 15)	Junior wear (5, 6, 11, 14)	Department groupings*			Boys' wear (22)	Men's wear (17, 18, 19, 20, 21)
			Women's access. (28, 29, 30, 31, 32)	Lingerie and corsetry (33, 34)	Children's girls' wear (7, 8, 9, 10, 12)		
Sales ($)	$612,287	$242,844	$594,861	$278,715	$452,273	$271,745	$967,851
Gross margin and discount	39.2%	38.1%	43.9%	43.3%	38.1%	37.9%	39.7%
Total selling wages	6.8	6.0	7.8	7.1	6.6	7.0	5.3
Total direct adv. (net)	—	—	—	—	—	—	—
Rent	4.4	3.9	2.0	3.5	4.8	3.6	2.5
Maintenance	1.6	1.3	0.8	1.4	1.9	1.0	1.0
Buying	1.4	1.4	1.4	1.6	2.2	1.4	1.4
Receiving and marking	0.1	0.1	0.1	0.1	0.1	0.1	0.1
Interest and tax on inv.	0.6	0.6	0.8	0.9	0.7	0.7	0.7
Stock people's wages	0.5	0.3	0.2	0.5	0.3	0.4	0.2
Wrap and packaging	0.5	0.7	0.5	0.6	0.7	0.7	0.6
Delivery	—	—	—	—	—	—	—
Other direct	1.8	1.9	1.9	2.0	2.0	1.6	1.6
Indirect (store)	1.3	1.0	1.1	1.3	1.3	1.3	1.3
Multi-store allocation:							
Buying	2.6	1.5	2.2	2.8	2.2	2.3	2.3
Advertising	2.8	2.2	2.0	2.4	2.9	2.3	2.3
Delivery	—	—	0.1	0.1	0.1	—	—
Other	6.3	5.4	5.7	6.6	6.0	6.4	6.2
Total expenses	30.7	26.3	26.6	30.9	31.8	28.8	25.5
Profit (net)	8.5	11.8	17.3	12.4	6.3	9.1	14.2

*Departments are grouped according to their physical proximity in a store. Because of this, certain groupings may not include all departments that would logically fall under each heading or may include departments that would better fit in a different grouping. Group headings such as "Women's Wear" are only meant to reflect the general nature of the departments which comprise each group or the departments that dominate the sales of a group.

Source: Company Records

Exhibit 13

THE DAYTON-HUDSON CORPORATION

DIRECT AND INDIRECT EXPENSES AS A PERCENTAGE OF SALES FOR
SELECTED UPSTAIRS DEPARTMENT GROUPINGS

(Brookdale and Southdale Stores)

Sales and expense categories	Department groupings*					
	Brookdale women's wear	Southdale women's wear	Brookdale junior wear	Southdale junior wear	Brookdale men's wear	Southdale men's wear
Sales ($)	$615,397	$1,141,974	$692,921	$545,934	$1,406,075	$3,594,124
Gross margin and discount	43.2%	41.5%	43.4%	43.5%	43.1%	42.2%
Total selling wages	5.4	4.9	4.0	6.3	4.0	5.8
Total direct adv. (net)	–	–	–	–	–	–
Rent	5.6	5.3	4.7	5.5	2.7	2.6
Maintenance	1.3	1.3	1.2	1.8	0.7	0.7
Buying	1.4	1.0	1.5	1.8	0.7	0.7
Receiving and marking	0.2	0.1	0.2	0.1	0.1	0.1
Interest and tax on inv.	0.6	0.5	0.2	0.2	1.0	1.3
Stock people's wages	0.3	0.1	0.2	0.3	0.1	0.1
Wrap and packaging	0.5	0.5	0.3	0.4	0.4	0.4
Delivery	–	–	–	–	–	–
Other direct	2.7	1.5	2.4	2.7	6.5	2.1
Indirect (store)	1.4	1.1	1.5	1.5	1.2	1.2
Multi-store allocation:						
Buying	1.6	1.6	1.5	1.9	1.1	1.1
Advertising	1.0	1.2	0.7	1.1	0.7	0.8
Delivery	0.1	0.1	–	–	–	0.1
Other	5.8	5.5	6.1	7.0	6.5	6.3
Total expenses	27.9	24.7	24.5	30.7	19.7	23.2
Profit (net)	15.3	16.8	18.9	12.8	23.4	19.0

*Departments are grouped according to their physical proximity in a store. Because of this, certain groupings may not include all departments that would logically fall under each heading or may include departments that would better fit in a different grouping. Group headings such as "Women's Wear" are only meant to reflect the general nature of the departments which comprise each group or the departments that dominate the sales of a group.

Source: Company Records (figures disguised)

Exhibit 14

THE DAYTON–HUDSON CORPORATION
MEDIAN TURNOVER RATE BY DEPARTMENT FOR
LARGE–VOLUME DOWNSTAIRS STORES
(Main Stores and Branches Combined)

NRMA classification	Turnover rate[a]
Women's, Misses', and Junior Coats, Suits	6.0
Daytime Dresses	5.7
Women's, Misses', and Junior Dresses	7.6
Infants	4.3
Toddlers	3.4
Girls' Wear	4.2
Women's, Misses', and Junior Sportswear	7.5
Housewares, Aprons	7.0
Notions	4.7
Men's Dress and Business Outerwear	3.2
Men's Work Clothes	3.7
Men's Furnishings	3.7
Boys' Clothes	4.3
Floor Coverings	3.4
Coverings—Window, Furniture, Bed, and Table	2.8
Linens and Towels	4.5
Domestics	4.2
Adult Female Accessories	4.2
Female Handbags and Leather Goods	5.4
Millinery	5.3
Women's Hosiery	4.3
Women's Gloves	4.3
Lingerie	5.1
Corsets and Bras	3.9
Men's and Boys' Shoes	2.6
Female Footwear	3.6
Children's Shoes	2.4

[a] Turnover is defined as: $\dfrac{\text{Sales}}{\text{Average Inventory (at retail prices)}} = \text{Turnover}$

Source: National Retail Merchants Association/Merchandising and Operating Results of 1968

Exhibit 15

THE DAYTON–HUDSON CORPORATION
PERCENTAGE DISTRIBUTION OF CHARGE ACCOUNT SALES BY DEMOGRAPHIC CHARACTERISTICS
WITHIN SELECTED COMPARABLE DOWNSTAIRS AND UPSTAIRS DEPARTMENTS (All Stores Combined)

Demographic characteristics	Women's dresses Downstairs	Upstairs	Women's sportswear Downstairs	Upstairs	Sheets and bedding Downstairs	Upstairs	Men's clothing Downstairs	Upstairs
Age								
Under 35	22%	3%	39%	23%	24%	26%	32%	38%
35–54	26	33	50	47	49	49	52	45
Over 54	52	64	11	30	27	25	16	17
	100%	100%	100%	100%	100%	100%	100%	100%
Annual Income								
Under $7,000	58%	40%	40%	35%	33%	22%	32%	24%
$7,000–15,000	39	43	49	44	33	46	57	52
Over $15,000	3	17	11	21	14	32	11	24
	100%	100%	100%	100%	100%	100%	100%	100%
Occupation								
Professional, managerial, sales	36%	59%	66%	66%	66%	78%	67%	79%
Craftsman, operative, and miscellaneous	64	41	34	34	34	22	33	21
	100%	100%	100%	100%	100%	100%	100%	100%
Trading area in which home located								
Minneapolis	28%	24%	16%	21%	19%	15%	18%	18%
St. Paul	16	7	15	10	11	14	10	13
Southside area	29	39	26	38	31	34	32	33
Brookdale area	12	6	23	14	19	9	20	12
Rosedale area	11	14	9	7	9	9	7	9
Ridgedale area	4	8	8	9	8	15	9	11
B-7 area	—	2	3	1	3	4	4	4
	100%	100%	100%	100%	100%	100%	100%	100%

Source: Company Records (figures disguised)

Exhibit 16

THE DAYTON-HUDSON CORPORATION

DEMOGRAPHIC PROFILES OF SHOPPERS OF DAYTON'S AND MAJOR COMPETITORS

(Upstairs and Downstairs Stores Combined)

Demographic characteristics	Dayton's	Donaldson's	Powers	Penney's	Sears	Wards	Target	Holiday
Age
Over 55	26%	29%	35%	24%	23%	23%	19%	15%
35–54	35	37	38	35	35	37	37	37
25–34	24	21	15	26	28	26	28	31
Under 24	15	15	12	15	14	14	16	17
Occupation
Professional	17	16	17	15	17	16	16	16
Managerial	10	11	11	9	37	8	10	7
Clerical/sales	22	21	23	20	21	18	23	19
Craftsmen	31	30	25	30	9	42	37	45
Retired/other	20	22	23	17	16	16	14	13
Income
Over $15,000	19	19	25	16	16	14	18	17
$10,000–15,000	33	32	30	33	34	33	34	33
$7,000–10,000	23	24	20	26	26	29	27	31
$4,000–7,000	12	11	12	14	13	12	12	13
Under $4,000	13	14	13	11	11	12	9	6
Education
Completed college	27	28	30	22	23	22	26	20
Some college	23	22	23	23	22	22	23	26
Completed some high school	39	39	38	44	44	46	43	46
Completed some grade school	11	11	9	11	11	10	8	8

Source: Company Records (figures disguised)

Exhibit 17

THE DAYTON-HUDSON CORPORATION

PERCENT OF METRO ADULTS MENTIONING DAYTON'S AND COMPETITION AS THE
STORE AT WHICH MOST RECENT PURCHASE MADE IN SELECTED MERCHANDISE CATEGORIES
ALL TRADING AREAS COMBINED

Merchandise category		Retail stores					
	Dayton's[a]	Penney's	Wards	Sears	Donaldson's	Target	All other
Women's suits and dresses	40%	8%	5%	4%	6%	3%	34%
Women's sportswear	34	12	6	5	4	4	35
Linens and bedding	31	22	10	7	7	6	17
Children's apparel	25	24	5	8	6	7	25
Draperies	22	9	9	13	7	—	40
Men's suits	16	5	4	4	2	—	69

[a]Mentions of Dayton's did not differentiate the downstairs store from Dayton's as a whole.

Source: Company Records (figures disguised)

Exhibit 18

THE DAYTON-HUDSON CORPORATION

PERCENT OF METRO ADULTS MENTIONING DAYTON'S AND COMPETITION AS THE
STORE AT WHICH MOST RECENT PURCHASE MADE IN SELECTED MERCHANDISE CATEGORIES
RIDGEDALE TRADING AREA

Merchandise category		Retail stores					
	Dayton's[a]	Penney's	Wards	Sears	Donaldson's	Target	All other
Women's suits and dresses	40%	7%	5%	10%	2%	2%	34%
Women's sportswear	26	12	5	10	2	7	28
Linens and bedding	36	17	5	5	2	21	14
Children's apparel	24	26	—	12	7	2	29
Draperies	19	14	2	19	7	—	39
Men's suits	19	2	2	2	—	—	75

[a]Mentions of Dayton's did not differentiate the downstairs store from the store as a whole.

Source: Company Records (figures disguised)

Exhibit 19

THE DAYTON-HUDSON CORPORATION
DEMOGRAPHIC PROFILES OF
SOUTHDALE, ST. PAUL, ROSEDALE, BROOKDALE, AND RIDGEDALE RESIDENTS

	Southdale	St. Paul	Rosedale	Brookdale	Ridgedale
Age					
18-24	15%	11%	6%	11%	13%
25-34	26	20	30	32	24
35-44	22	14	25	25	34
45-54	17	19	16	10	16
55 and over	20	36	23	22	13
	100%	100%	100%	100%	100%
Education					
Some/completed grade school	11%	14%	11%	8%	5%
Some/completed high school	28	46	50	57	45
Some college	26	20	17	18	17
Completed college	35	20	22	17	33
	100%	100%	100%	100%	100%

Exhibit 19 (Cont.)

	Southdale	St. Paul	Rosedale	Brookdale	Ridgedale
Income					
Under $4,000	6%	27%	13%	7%	4%
$4,000–$6,999	12	13	13	18	5
$7,000–$9,999	22	28	30	26	22
$10,000–$14,999	38	25	34	33	34
$15,000 and over	22	7	10	16	35
	100%	100%	100%	100%	100%
Occupation					
Professional/technical	22%	15%	17%	12%	15%
Managerial/official	12	8	8	5	22
Clerical/sales	22	14	15	24	22
Craftsmen	16	12	21	22	14
Operatives	6	19	18	19	14
Service workers	6	4	7	4	5
Other	16	28	14	14	8
	100%	100%	100%	100%	100%

(Statistics compiled for the year 1969)
Source: Company Records (figures disguised)

Exhibit 20

THE DAYTON–HUDSON CORPORATION
A DEMOGRAPHIC COMPARISON OF FREQUENT [*]
TARGET SHOPPERS WITH PRIMARY TRADE AREA RESIDENTS

	Knollwood [†]	
	Frequent Target shoppers	Primary trade area residents
Age		
Under 25	20%	5%
25–34	28	20
35–44	28	40
45–54	17	25
Over 54	7	10
	100%	100%
Income (adjusted)		
Under $4,000	3%	1%
$4,000–$7,000	10	1
$7,000–$10,000	25	15
$10,000–$12,000	25	34
$12,000–$15,000	13	26
$15,000–$20,000	13	17
Over $20,000	11	6
	100%	100%
Occupation		
Professional/technical	19%	19%
Managerial	19	24
Clerical/sales	19	22
Craftsmen/operatives	22	15
Laborers	4	8
Service	10	3
Other	7	9
	100%	100%
Family Size (if married)		
No children	23%	20%
One	11	14
Two	33	30
Three	11	16
Four or more	22	20
	100%	100%

[*] Twice a month or more

[†] Knollwood is a shopping center and trading area located within the Twelve Oaks Trading Area.

Source: Company Records (figures disguised)

Exhibit 21

THE DAYTON–HUDSON CORPORATION
PERCENTAGE OF METRO ADULTS FROM EACH TRADING AREA* MENTIONING DAYTON'S
AS STORE USUALLY SHOPPED FOR VARIOUS MERCHANDISE CATEGORIES

Merchandise category	Trading area							
	St. Paul	Southdale	Rosedale	Brookdale	Ridgedale	B-7	Minneapolis
Women's Suits and Dresses	30%	50%	28%	50%	40%	18%	43%
Women's Sportswear	27	41	18	41	26	25	46
Linens and Bedding	30	41	16	30	36	22	36
Children's Apparel	19	37	10	21	24	22	32
Draperies	17	23	24	26	19	10	26
Men's Suits	13	17	10	20	19	15	16
Carpeting	15	17	9	14	17	12	21
Major Appliances	15	25	26	30	38	18	42
Furniture	13	10	6	21	10	10	20
Housewares	21	31	17	29	21	35	30

* See Exhibit 3

Source: Company Records (figures disguised)

UNIVERSITY OF MINNESOTA PRESS

In early 1975, Mr. John Ervin, Jr., director of the University of Minnesota Press, was exploring ways to modify the list of publications offered by the press, in order to eliminate the need for university subsidies for operations and to pay the university a fair rate of interest on the funds which it provided to the press. University officials had asked Mr. Ervin to meet these objectives by 1980 and to submit a plan for doing so within the next few months. Despite increasing pressures on the university budget, university officials had indicated that additional resources could be made available to finance additions to or changes in the publications offered by the press, provided that such additions or changes promised to be profitable. For the year ending June 30, 1975, Mr. Ervin expected the press to receive nearly $110,000 in general subsidies from the university, an amount equal to approximately 25 percent of the press's operating expenses.

UNIVERSITY PRESSES

The 70 or more university presses within the United States, together with the Oxford and Cambridge University Presses, operate as part of their respective universities. Most American university presses are supported in part by the universities with which they are affiliated. Traditionally, the function of university presses has been to provide outlets for scholarly works which are considered likely to change ways of thinking about particular subjects or contribute to human knowledge, but which are likely to have markets too small and specialized to be of interest to commercial publishers.

In addition to scholarly works such as professional commentaries, critiques, reference books, and reports of research studies longer than those ordinarily published in scholarly journals, many university presses publish books of regional interest intended primarily for general readers in the state or region served by the university with which the press is affiliated. Three presses whose lists of regional general-interest publications were considered adequate to gain attention from wholesale and retail book buyers are those at the Universities of Minnesota, Texas, and Washington.

Certain university presses, notably Chicago, Harvard, and California, have attempted to be more active than other university presses in trade publishing, i.e., in publishing books intended for sale to general readers through retail bookstores. These presses have large budgets for trade promotion and make considerable use of media advertising. The success of this strategy is not known, although one large university press active in trade publishing did report a deficit of more than $500,000 for 1972, and acknowledged at that time that it was reviewing its entire operation. Industry sources confirmed that a university press or a commercial publisher needs a large list of trade books to receive attention from buyers for retail bookstores.

Some university presses (e.g., Chicago, Cambridge, Wisconsin) are heavily involved in the publication of scholarly journals, which contribute 10 to 25 percent of those presses' total revenues.

University presses receive most of their manuscripts from scholars, and few from professional writers or their agents. Professional writers generally prefer to place manuscripts with commercial publishers, which typically have broader distribution coverage and larger sales promotion budgets, and therefore yield higher sales and revenues to the author. In addition, commercial publishers are often willing to advance to authors substantial sums against prospective royalty income; those advances need not be repaid if royalty income fails to achieve forecast levels. University presses ordinarily make small or no advance payments. Commercial publishers are typically, but not always, able to offer a more attractive royalty schedule to authors than are university presses.

In 1974, total sales for university presses exceeded $46 million, more than double their level in 1963 (see Exhibit 1). Consistent with the pattern of earlier years, in 1974 most university presses required subsidies to cover losses in their operations.[1] Exhibit 2 presents income statements for 34 university presses of all sizes, together with income statements for smaller numbers of presses similar in size to the University of Minnesota Press. (An income statement for the University of Minnesota Press is included for comparison.)

Average unit sales for university presses in 1974 were $7.10 for hardbound books, and $1.73 for paperbound books. The latter accounted for approximately 23 percent of the sales of university presses. Sales within the United States accounted for 87 percent of total sales. Revenue from subsidiary rights, e.g., permission sold to others to publish and distribute works originally published by a university press, accounted for less than 3 percent of sales.

During 1974, inventories for university presses of all sizes increased from 62 percent to 74 percent of 1974 sales. For presses with sales from $250,000 to $1 million, inventories rose from 89 percent to 99 percent of 1974 sales.

Of the 34 university presses which together accounted for about 90 percent of sales of all university presses, most of the sales were concentrated among the 14 largest presses (see Exhibit 3).

---

1. Most commercial publishers with sales under $1 million experienced financial problems similar to those of university presses. Small commercial publishers typically operated with very limited capital; some rented office and warehouse space, and subcontracted entirely their manufacturing operations. Small publishers of general trade books (popular fiction and nonfiction, of the type usually found at retail bookstores) frequently incurred losses ranging from 2 to 20 percent of sales, and seldom earned large profits. Small publishers of professional books (books intended for practicing physicians, engineers, attorneys, and the like) seldom earned more than 3 percent (before taxes) on their sales. Publishers of college texts with sales up to $3 million frequently posted losses in excess of 10 percent of sales. Inventory turnover for small commercial publishers ranged from about one turn per year for trade publishers to little more than 1.5 turns per year for college publishers. Receivables of small commercial publishers turned between three and four times per year.

DISTRIBUTION

University presses sell their books directly, through reciprocal marketing arrangements with other presses, and through independent commission salespeople to general book wholesalers, retailers, libraries, and consumers. Although other publishers use the same outlets, the percentage distribution among those outlets of books from university presses during the years 1972–1974 differed from that for the publishing industry as a whole (see Exhibit 4). Approximately 350 major academic libraries had standing orders with wholesalers for automatic purchase of every title published by every university press, provided the list price was less than $50. For costlier books, wholesalers requested specific approval before shipping.

Information on both manufacturing and distribution practices in the publishing industry are described in an appendix to this case.

THE UNIVERSITY OF MINNESOTA PRESS

The University of Minnesota Press operates as an administrative and budgetary unit of the University of Minnesota, whose mission is defined as teaching, research, and service. In 1974–1975, the university enrolled more than 51,000 students and operated on an annual budget in excess of $350 million. According to Mr. Ervin, the role of the press was to make knowledge available and to encourage research by providing an outlet for scholarly research. An additional role of the press was to reflect and represent the intellectual quality of Minnesota and its university, through the quality of the press imprint.

The director of the press, who reported directly to the University's second-ranking officer, the vice-president for academic administration, supervised a staff of 19 employees (see Exhibit 5). In addition to the director, the press management group included the assistant to the director and four department heads. Mr. Ervin, the director, came to his present position in 1957 at age 30, following five years on the editorial staff of the Princeton University Press. The assistant to the director, Paula Ruddy, had experience in religious publishing and in the Journals Division of the University of Chicago Press. She joined the University of Minnesota Press in 1973. Robert Taylor, head of the design and production department, worked for many years in magazine design with Curtis Publishing, and also had experience in book publishing before coming to the press in 1971. Jeanne Sinnen, the press' senior editor, has worked for the press since receiving her Master's degree in the late 1940s. Janet Salisbury, head of sales and promotion, had many years of experience in newspaper, radio, publicity, and magazine work before joining the press in 1950. Minnie Matsuura, the press business manager, has been associated with her department for 30 years.

In the year ending June 30, 1974, the press had net sales of more than $483,000, and incurred an operating loss of $98,100. University subsidies of $132,800 and donations/subsidies from outside sources of $21,000 resulted in net income of $55,700 in 1974. Sales and operating losses had varied substantially since 1970 (see Exhibit 6). In general, the press' expense percentages were very similar to those of other university presses of comparable size. Exhibit 7 contains press balance sheets from 1969 through 1974.

Paperbound books accounted for less than 11 percent of press sales in 1974, compared to more than 16 percent in 1973. Press personnel attributed the decrease to the discontinuation of a paperbound series on American Writers. Average receipts for paperbound books in 1974 were $1.22; for hardbound books, $6.32. Domestic sales accounted for 89 percent of all University of Minnesota Press sales in 1974.

The press ordinarily published 20 to 34 titles per year, and typically printed 2,000 to 4,000 hardbound copies of each title. Exhibit 8 contains printing and profitability data by title for press publications for the year ending June 30, 1973, exclusive of the American Writers Paperback Series, which was discontinued in 1974. Aggregate printing and profitability data for earlier years are included for comparison.

About a third of the press's total output for a particular year was sold within that year; the remainder was carried forward in inventory. Approximately half of the 1,180 books, pamphlets, and tests published by the press since its beginning in 1927 were still "in print," i.e., available from press inventories.

Of the titles in print in 1975, fewer than 50 hardbound books, and a somewhat greater number of paperbound books and pamphlets, had sold more than 2,500 copies since their dates of publication. Eleven had sold more than 10,000 copies in the last ten years. Six of these eleven sold primarily through trade channels; three, principally to libraries; and two, primarily as texts. These eleven had all been published before 1973.

Analysis of sales histories of individual high-volume press books (i.e., those with sales in excess of 2,500 copies since date of publication) indicated no clear relationship of sales and time since publication, either within particular subject categories or for all subject areas combined. Some titles enjoyed high sales within a year of publication and then declined rather sharply. Sales of other titles increased gradually after publication and then remained relatively stable; some others displayed wide fluctuations instead of stability of sales.

The percentage of total press sales attributable to high-volume books appeared to have increased from 1971 to 1973. Titles which had sold 2,500 or more copies since publication ("high-volume" titles) accounted for 17 percent of press sales in 1973, compared to less than 10 percent in 1971 and 1969. Among the high-volume titles, those with sales since publication of 2,500 to 5,000 copies accounted for 40 percent of sales of high volume titles in 1973, compared with more than 60 percent in 1971 and 1969; those with sales of 5,000 to 10,000 copies, for 40 percent of sales of high-volume titles in 1973, versus about 30 percent in 1971 and 1969; and those with sales in excess of 10,000, for 20 percent of high-volume sales in 1973, compared with less than 10 percent in 1971 and 1969.

PRESS PUBLICATIONS

Press officials grouped press publications, most of which were considered "scholarly works," into three general categories: social sciences, humanities, and natural sciences. Social sciences included history and political science, psychology, anthropology, and other social sciences such as sociology, law, business and economics, and area studies. The humanities category included literary history and criticism, creative literature, philosophy and religion, and other humanities topics, such as music and biography. Natural science included biological science, medicine, and other natural science areas, such as geography. Exhibit 9 summarizes press output by topic area from 1967 through 1974.

Titles in humanities and in social science together accounted for approximately 75 percent of press sales; the humanities category had traditionally been somewhat larger than social sciences in sales volume. Natural science books accounted for the remaining 25 percent of sales.

Like other university presses and most commercial publishers, the press enjoyed a reputation as an important source of books and other publications in particular topic areas. According to press officials, the press's strongest list of publications (i.e., most salable, most significant impact on the discipline) was in psychology, especially psychometrics (tests, measurement devices, and associated literature), and, to a somewhat lesser degree, developmental psychology. Half of the press' $30,000 income from subsidiary rights came from royalties on the Minnesota Multiphasic Personality Inventory (MMPI), first published by the press. Press personnel believed that commercial publishers, rather than other university presses, were their chief competitors in psychology. Press managers also thought that a substantial market potential existed in psychology, because of the large number of practitioners in the field, and therefore allocated most of their exhibit budget to the annual professional meeting of psychologists.

Press officials considered their press a leader among university presses in philosophy, especially the philosophy of science. Although the number of philosophers was limited, according to Mr. Ervin, they purchased books to own, rather than depending upon libraries.

The press had historically had strong positions in American literature, in history, and in music reference books. The large number of professionals in music made this last market attractive to press managers.

The press had developed books in Scandinavian Studies. An institution which operated like a book club assisted the press in obtaining extensive coverage of this limited market.

Mr. Ervin considered the University of Minnesota Press less strong than other university presses in certain topic areas. In science, for example, Harvard and MIT presses held leadership positions. In linguistics, such presses as Michigan and MIT had specific strengths. In art history, Princeton, Pennsylvania State University, and the University of California presses all had strong lists of publications. In general economics, Columbia University, MIT, and the University of Chicago presses all had much stronger lists than Minnesota, according to Mr. Ervin, but Minnesota had a strong list in agricultural economics.

DEVELOPING THE LIST

To develop its list of publications, the press encouraged submission of manuscripts, screened them carefully for editorial content, and then evaluated their likely profitability.

Each year the press received some 1,500 completed and partial manuscripts, outlines, and inquiries. The press attracted these materials through promotional materials which stressed the reputations of current press books, authors, and the press itself, and through personal contact.

Most materials submitted were scholarly in nature and came directly from professors or professionals in particular fields. Although these authors were specialists in particular fields of knowledge, they were not professional writers; their literary output ordinarily arose as a by-product of their principal vocation. Like most university presses, the Minnesota Press attracted about half of its titles from scholars at its own university.

Roughly one of every four titles published by the press came from manuscripts which Mr. Ervin solicited through correspondence or personal contact. Mr. Ervin contacted authors who had published successfully with the press or whose scholarly works appeared to have been successful elsewhere, recipients of foundations' research grants, and professionals who he believed might have promising materials but had not made plans for publication. Mr. Ervin hoped to encourage successful authors and grant recipients to publish through the press results of projects in which they were engaged. By encouraging authors with promising materials to put them into publishable form and by suggesting a schedule on which they might do so, Mr. Ervin might commit an author to the press even though the materials might have a market broad enough to interest a commercial publisher. Mr. Ervin considered personal contact particularly important when seeking manuscripts in fields other than those in which the press had established a reputation. In the latter fields, authors would frequently contact the press, but in topic areas in which the press was not known to be interested, Mr. Ervin had to seek out prospective authors.

Agreements between authors and the press were embodied in a formal contract, which typically specified the rights and obligations of each party, including the royalty the author was to receive. Royalty payments, which were negotiated by the author and the press, typically started at 3 to 10 percent of the press's net selling price, and increased with the number of copies sold. For a number of books, royalties were deferred in the contract because of uncertainties with respect to costs and income for those specific titles.

All promising completed manuscripts passed through three stages of editorial screening: preliminary, in-house, and outside reader. Partial manuscripts, outlines, and inquiries which contained ideas for book-length manuscripts received preliminary screening; authors of promising partial materials were encouraged to develop their materials into completed manuscripts for subsequent evaluation.

In preliminary screening, the press editorial staff rejected manuscripts and materials in categories the press did not publish, e.g., fiction, children's books, personal memoirs; and in nonscholarly areas, such as astrology, extrasensory perception, and mortuary science. Materials from authors who lacked scholarly credentials were far less likely to be accepted than were those from authors who held doctorates.

Some 20 percent of all materials passed preliminary screening and received further in-house consideration. The press staff wrote reviews for Mr. Ervin of partial and completed manuscripts which showed promise in content and style. Mr. Ervin encouraged authors of incomplete manuscripts to finish them, and frequently offered editorial assistance. Of the promising completed manuscripts, those which Mr. Ervin and Ms. Salisbury expected to have sufficient sales during the life of the book went to outside readers for review. Approximately 50 manuscripts went to outside readers each year. A preliminary financial analysis, similar to that described below for manuscripts evaluated favorably by outside readers, was performed on many manuscripts which passed in-house screening, to determine whether they should be sent to outside readers.

Readers who were specialists in the topic area of the manuscript reviewed and evaluated each manuscript with respect to its scholarly contribution and soundness; its appropriateness for publication as a book instead of one or more articles in scholarly journals; and its likely sales to professionals, to general readers, and to students in undergraduate courses and in graduate courses. Reader fees per manuscript ranged from $50 to $150. Each manuscript received one or more independent readings. Ordinarily 30 to 40 manuscripts received favorable reader evaluation.

For all manuscripts that outside readers evaluated favorably, press personnel estimated profit potential according to the following formula:

Number of salable copies times *net receipts per copy;* minus *royalties, estimated manufacturing costs,* and *allocated operating expenses;* equals *profit.* Throughout the financial evaluation, press personnel made multiple estimates of price and volume combinations.

Number of salable copies equalled the number of copies to be printed (print size), less copies distributed free of charge. Ms. Salisbury's estimates of sales of a prospective title during the life of a first printing (ordinarily five years) determined print size. Her estimates considered the magnitude and trend of sales associated with the particular category (e.g., psychology, creative literature) to which the title belongs, the current interest in the specific topic of the manuscript, the visibility and popularity of the author, and the potential for sales as a textbook. In recent years 3 to 4 percent of all books printed have been sent free to reviewers, authors, and other persons.

Net receipts amounted to the list price less applicable discounts (described in the following section on pricing). The list price itself was estimated by Ms. Salisbury on the basis of her experience and appraisal of the particular market for which the book was intended, and in consideration of costs.

Royalties varied among titles. For trade books, the press attempted to meet or approach commercial publishers' royalty schedules, which typically began at 10 percent of the list price for hardbound books and increased to 15 percent for 10,000 or more copies, with lower rates being typical throughout the industry for paperbound editions. The press's own royalties were usually based on net proceeds (list price less dealer discount), but in meeting or approaching commercial rates, royalty percentages were used which would yield approximately similar amounts in dollars to authors. The press attempted to be competitive on textbook royalties, and generally paid the equivalent of 5 to 10 percent of list price (more at very high volumes) as a royalty. On most scholarly works, press royalties, like those of other university presses, ranged from no royalties till a break-even point was reached, up to 10 percent of the press's net proceeds. Royalties might, however, be somewhat higher for particular titles.

Manufacturing costs were estimated largely from historical average costs for a typical six-by-nine-inch text. Books which contained complex composition, oversize material, or elaborate illustrations were ordinarily more costly to produce. Average cost data for a six-by-nine-inch text appear in Table 1.

Table 1

AVERAGE MANUFACTURING COST,
UNIVERSITY OF MINNESOTA PRESS

Print size (number of copies)	Manufacturing cost per page
1,500	$18.70
2,000	20.40
2,500	22.10
3,000	23.00
4,000	24.70
5,000	26.70
7,500	30.55
10,000	34.80

For example, costs of printing 4,000 copies of a 300-page book would be $7,410 (300 pages $\times$ $24.70/page = $7,410).

Allocated operating expenses: Editorial (copy editing and evaluation) and production costs other than manufacturing (proofing, art work, and scheduling) were charged at $900 per title plus a per-book-page variable rate. Editorial costs accounted for roughly 65 percent of that amount. Other operating expenses—marketing, fulfillment, general and administrative—were charged according to projected operating expenditures for each new title.

If a manuscript appeared unprofitable, a new list price was established and the financial evaluation reiterated.

Before January 1974, some books that were expected to lose money were accepted for publication because of their scholarly merit alone. Since that time the press has accepted only those books that have reasonable prospects of being profitable during their lives, or of breaking even with the press bearing less than the full cost of publication. Some titles may be profitable or break even despite quite limited sales, provided that an organization other than the press bears some of the production and marketing costs, or provides a grant to defray some costs. For example, the press might incur the costs of producing a title for which another publisher guaranteed to purchase a certain number of books and bear the marketing expenses for these books in its geographic area. The press might publish a title for which a fixed dollar subsidy were received, provided that subsidy appeared sufficient to enable the press to break even on publication of the title. Approximately twenty titles accepted for publication in the three years before January 1974 were expected to be unprofitable. Six or seven of these titles were scheduled for publication during the present year and each of the coming two years.

Once a manuscript was accepted, production usually took between nine and twelve months, the average time for university presses. Because the screening process took two to six months (for a completed manuscript which required little revision) to more than two years when resubmission after revision was necessary, publication could occur from one to more than three years after an author's initial contact with the press.

Mr. Ervin presented manuscripts that he and press staff considered appropriate for publication to the press committee, which was chaired by the university vice-president responsible for the press. The 15-member committee, which included deans and faculty members from various collegiate units within the university, served as an editorial policy-making body. In that role, the press committee approved all titles before publication. In addition, the committee served as a sounding-board for other matters Mr. Ervin brought before it. The committee did not, however, have any responsibility for the press's budget, which was controlled by the vice-president's office.

PRICING AND RETURN PRIVILEGES

According to press officials, list prices of press books had been about in the middle of the range of prices for university press books, but were likely to rise to the higher end of that range with new titles introduced during the coming two years.

Wholesalers and retailers received a 20 percent or "short" discount off of list price for most press titles. On a small number of those titles the press offered an additional discount, for a total of 40 percent off list, to resellers who ordered quantities of twenty or more copies of a single title, and promoted that title in printed material.

Resellers received a 40 percent or "trade" discount on titles press managers believed were likely to be stocked in quantity by wholesalers and retailers for sales to the general public. Quantity discounts could increase the total discount received by resellers from 40 percent (for five or more copies, assorted titles) to 50 percent for 1,000 copies, assorted titles. The press offered trade discounts on only two or three titles in a typical year.

Libraries and individuals who purchased directly from the press did so at list price. This practice was similar to that of some other university presses, and the press's discount schedule was similar to that of most others.

Like most other university presses, the press allowed all titles that carried short (20 percent) discounts to be returned for full refund within 90 days of purchase. Titles that carried trade (40 percent) discount could be returned for full credit any time within one year of purchase.

PROMOTION

Each year from 1970 through 1974 the press spent between $35,000 and $40,000 to promote newly published and backlist (i.e., published before the current year) titles. Approximately one-third of that amount was devoted to media advertising; slightly less, to catalogs. More than half of the balance was spent on direct mail; the remainder, on exhibits at trade shows and professional meetings. The promotional budget was not formally allocated among individual titles or groups of titles, although estimated promotion expenses were included in the financial evaluation of prospective titles.

In addition to catalog listings and announcements of additions to its list, the press employed four basic promotional programs, two for trade books; another, for trade-and-text books; and one for scholarly books. For a recent trade book advertisements were run in newspapers and magazines ranging from the *New York Times Book Review* to *Publishers Weekly* (a trade publication) to small but influential journals in the subject area of the book. Although the author was not available for national television or other personal appearances, the director of the press and others associated with the book were scheduled for local television programs. The press placed a selection from the book in a prestigious monthly magazine. The press sent more than a hundred copies of this book to book-review media, both general-reader magazines and newspapers and special-interest journals. Direct-mail advertising was also used to reach the specialists in the field of the book. Posters were prepared for use in exhibits and retail bookstores. The press typically published one or two general trade books in a year.

The promotion program for regional trade books relied on cooperative advertising, in which the press paid 75 percent of the cost of a retail bookstore's advertisements of the title. In addition, the press did limited advertising entirely at its own expense in local media, provided brochures for retailers, and distributed a modest number of review copies. The press historically offered one or two new regional trade titles each year.

A recent title that press officials believed to have potential both as a trade book and as a textbook received some media advertising and a substantial amount of direct-mail promotion. In addition, a higher-than-average number of free copies of the book was distributed both to book-review media and to teachers in universities and colleges around the country who were asked to consider the book for course use. One of the authors appeared in a series on an educational television station and was also interviewed on local talk shows. This author was active as a lecturer around the country and brought his book to the attention of adult study groups, business and industrial groups, and civic groups, as well as organizations of which he was a member. Comments on the book were solicited from well-known people for use in advertising and news releases. Arrangements were made with an industrial firm to adopt the book in its communications program.

Approximately four titles each year that press managers believed to have potential for use as textbooks (as well as general or regional trade books) were published in paperback editions as well as hardbound.

Scholarly books, which most press publications were considered to be, were ordinarily promoted to specialists in the pertinent field and to libraries through a modest amount of advertising in specialized journals and through direct mail. The latter method received greater emphasis whenever lists of specialists in the particular field were available.

SALES ORGANIZATION

Ms. Salisbury and her assistant, together with three independent domestic sales representatives and three foreign sales agencies, handled sales of press publications. Ms. Salisbury's office provided the sales representatives and agencies with descriptions of current and forthcoming titles, as well as the promotional activities planned for particular titles. A succinct description of new titles was essential for the sales representatives who typically had to present to resellers in one or two hours new titles in all the lines they represented.

Each domestic representative carried several noncompeting lines within a particular region. The Midwest representative handled five or six other university presses in addition to the University of Minnesota Press. The Eastern representative carried one other university press and lines of five or six commercial publishers. In the West, the press was represented by a small publisher, which sold its own (noncompeting) line and one or two others. Sales representatives received commissions of 10 percent on net sales to retail accounts and 7½ percent on net sales to wholesalers.

Sales representatives covered their territories twice each year. In January the representatives presented the books to be released in spring; in July they presented those to be published the following fall. Representatives ordinarily called on large-volume accounts more than once during each seasonal trip and called on smaller accounts at least once each season.

DISTRIBUTION

Like most other university presses, the Minnesota Press sold its books to general and library wholesalers, college and general retail bookstores, libraries, and (by mail) direct to consumers. Exhibit 10 shows estimated sales of press publications to these several purchasers for 1973, 1971, 1969, and 1967. Estimates in Exhibit 10 came from two separate sample surveys of press invoices. Data from these surveys, which yielded very similar results, indicated no consistent differences in sales to different purchasers among social science, humanities, and natural science titles.

One of these sample surveys showed that library wholesalers ordered an average of five items each time they placed orders with the press. All other purchasers ordered only one or two items on each purchase. The average order placed with the press by library wholesalers was approximately $90, and consistently ran many times larger than the average from any other type of purchase.

FUTURE PLANS

Mr. Ervin forecast that the press would, during the coming two years, gradually increase its sales to more than $600,000 primarily by increasing the number of titles published and the average price per copy. During that period he expected the general operating subsidy from the university to decrease slightly in dollars, and decline as a percentage of sales and of operating expenses. Mr. Ervin believed that the press would lower (or at least prevent increases in) printing costs by using a typesetting process which could be operated by a typist, instead of the traditional hot lead and photo-typesetting processes which required substantial investment and skilled specialized operators.

To move toward financial self-sufficiency, the press management group had formulated a plan which involved increasing the size and changing the composition of the press's publication list. The plan called for publication of thirty to thirty-five titles each year, all but two to five of which would be handled entirely by the press. Those two to five would be published jointly with other presses (likely foreign), then marketed by the press in the United States. Adding "imports" to the press's list would enable the press to increase volume without concomitant increases in editorial and production costs. Proceeds from each "import" were shared with the other publisher involved.

Mr. Ervin considered the "ideal" list for the press one which included three types of books: (1) high quality, highly salable text or regional trade books; (2) books that promised to have substantial academic impact, by altering traditional ways of thinking or by adding to knowledge; and (3) books that possessed potential both for high sales volume and for scholarly attention. Press managers expected the number of scholarly books published to be about 50 percent of the total publication list over the next several years. They planned to increase the number of reference books and textbooks, to limit regional trade books to one or two per year, and to forego attempts to penetrate the national trade book market. A list with such composition represented, in Mr. Ervin's judgment, a movement toward a "higher-risk, higher-return" philosophy for the press. He considered the markets for scholarly monographs, which traditionally had comprised most of the press's list, secure but only marginally profitable. The decline in libraries' purchases from the early 1970s had led the press to reduce average printings of scholarly books to about 1,500 per title, a number which press managers were confident they could sell, because of the lack of directly competing titles. In contrast, books with larger markets and sales potential outside of libraries and small groups of specialists held the promise of higher profits, provided that these books were unique or could compete successfully against other publishers' entries in particular fields. Competitive pressures could be particularly keen in textbooks, where several publishers could each be promoting a text for a specific course. Competition came not from identical content or presentation (inasmuch as the press would not knowingly publish books that did not provide a new approach or new material); rather, competition was intense because of the limited number of textbook dollars available for specific courses.

The press staff considered reference books promising, even though the libraries which constituted the primary market for such books had recently experienced significant reductions in appropriations. Press managers believed that, with limited budgets, librarians would attach high priority to books that promised to serve many users over a long period of time. Although the number of volumes sold by university presses as a whole to libraries had decreased in recent years, a respected industry source forecast no further decline.

To expand the press' textbook offerings, Mr. Ervin planned to seek manuscripts that could be used in upper-level undergraduate or graduate courses in specialized fields, such as physical therapy, applied statistics, and nutrition.

Mr. Ervin planned to reduce slightly the number of regional trade books published each year (from two or three to one or two), because he believed that the higher number exceeded the regional markets' "ability to absorb" regional trade books. National trade books appeared unattractive financially because of the high break-even points associated with such publications.

Although he wished that the press could publish more books in biological science and linguistics, Mr. Ervin recognized that development of a strong list and commensurate reputation would have to be a gradual process. He was cautious about some works in art history because of the high publication costs associated with books that contained numerous finely detailed four-color illustrations. Although the press was continuing to develop its list in agricultural economics, Mr. Ervin had heard from economists that fewer books, and more journal articles, would be published in general economics in the coming years, thus diminishing the opportunities for the press to grow in general, as distinct from agricultural, economics.

As possible means of implementing this general plan, Mr. Ervin was currently reviewing three proposals for specific publications: a textbook; a regional trade book; and a major new venture, a comparative economic history of fourteen Western nations.

Textbook: This book would be used as a text in introductory courses in food science and technology, nutrition, and related subjects; as a reference work in agricultural and food processing industries; and in libraries. The book covers product standards, food ingredients, additives, labeling, nutritional and antinutritional factors, and other aspects of food processing.

Continuing developments in the field of food science and technology, together with changing standards and governmental regulations, will mean that the book will need revision in about three years.

Food science and technology professors at two leading universities indicated that the book would be appropriate for introductory course use, and that such courses were becoming increasingly popular. Nevertheless, substantial competition from other works could be expected. One advisor said that, if the book met his expectations, it would probably be used in courses at his university with annual enrollments of 500–800 students.

The book could be published in both hardbound and paperbound editions. The paperback would be intended primarily for student use; the hardbound edition, for sale to libraries, institutions, and others who would purchase it primarily as a reference work. Sales of 3,000 hardbound copies at a list price of $15 less short discount, plus 4,000 paperbound at $7.95 less short discount would yield from $12,000 to $15,000, after deduction of all costs except an allocation for general and administrative expenses.

Regional trade book: A book on Minnesota place names would be used by natives and tourists as a popular handbook providing brief information about the derivation of place names in the state—names of cities, towns, counties, rivers, lakes, and other geographical entities. Similar books have been published for their home states by other university presses. One such book, published in a state like Minnesota, sold almost 10,000 copies (at a list price under $7.00) in its first year. That book received considerable promotion as "entertainment." Another book, published in a sparsely populated state, sold more than 4,000 paperbound copies, partly through promotion to tourists, over a six-year period.

If 10,000 copies were sold at the rate of 4,000 the first year and 1,500 per year for the succeeding four years, at a list price of $8.95 with a trade discount, then the book would show a loss in its first year of $14,000, and a profit of about $21,000 for its second through fifth years combined. Comparable estimates for total sales of 7,000 copies were a loss of almost $13,000 in the first year and a profit greater than $15,000 for the subsequent four years combined. Increasing the list price to $9.50 would reduce the first-year loss to less than $12,000, and increase profits for the next four years to more than $16,000. (All estimates include all direct costs plus an allocation for general and administrative expenses.)

Comparative economic history: This book would include hundreds of detailed charts, tables, time series, and maps, as well as text, describing the economic (and to some extent social) activity of fourteen nations from about 1750 to the present. The market could include a wide range of professional and academic specialists and students, including those concerned with economic forecasting, business planning, international trade, government fiscal and monetary policy, sociology, and political science, as well as historians of all types. Professional specialists might purchase the volume either for themselves or through their business firm or government agency; academicians, either for personal use or through university libraries; students, primarily for their own use. Because of the long time span covered, the book would likely not need revision for five to ten years.

The large size of the volume and the numerous colored graphs, charts, and maps indicated a manufacturing cost of almost $72,000 for 2,500 copies. All other expenses, including a substantial promotion budget, could amount to almost $60,000, for a total cost between $130,000 and $135,000. The International Federation of Historians (IFH) had assembled, from various governmental sources in the countries to be included, a sum sufficient to defray half of the production costs. In return for this contribution, IFH would receive a third of the profits after all expenses, including overhead, were covered.

Although no strictly comparable volume existed, press personnel learned that an economic atlas prepared for a region within one Western country had sold more than 4,000 copies within less than five years, at a price equivalent to $80. Another volume on economic history, which contained a considerably smaller amount of detailed data than the proposed publication, had sold fewer than 2,500 copies in eight years. That volume had been priced initially at more than $100, but was thought to be available at a substantial reduction in price.

To estimate market response to this proposed publication, press personnel interviewed several persons knowledgeable in the subject area, including prospective purchasers. An official of a government planning agency responded that the volume would be useful, that price would not be a consideration in purchasing the volume, and that government agency libraries at all levels would very likely buy the book. A legislator responded that the volume would be useful and that the "premium" price such a volume would require would pose no problem for government agencies.

An executive of a respected private economic forecasting firm responded very favorably to the concept of the volume, but indicated that, for widespread use (i.e., by students, manufacturers, bankers, etc.) the volume should be priced at $25 or less. Other consulting economists and their counterparts in business firms doubted the utility of the book, citing their needs for information that was current and even more detailed than that proposed for this volume, and available from various governmental agencies.

If the volume carried a list price in the $100 range, the press would sell it to wholesalers and retailers at a 10 percent discount, half of the "short" discount carried by most press books. The IFH would also receive this discount. To stimulate advance orders, that 10 percent discount would also be offered in advance of publication to libraries and individuals, who ordinarily purchased at list price. After publication, only wholesalers, retailers, and the IFH would receive the 10 percent discount. On the other hand, if the volume were to carry a list price below $50, wholesalers and retailers would receive the typical "short" discount of 20 percent; the IFH would receive a 10 percent discount.

Exhibit 1

UNIVERSITY OF MINNESOTA PRESS
NET SALES OF ALL UNIVERSITY PRESSES 1963, 1967, 1969–1974
(DATA FROM OTHER YEARS NOT AVAILABLE)

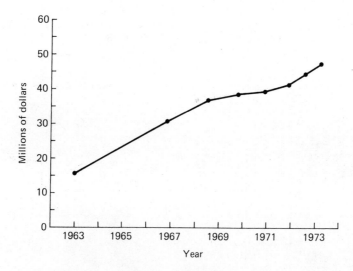

Source: Association of American Publishers (AAP)

Exhibit 2
UNIVERSITY OF MINNESOTA PRESS
OPERATING DATA OF UNIVERSITY PRESSES, 1974

	34 Presses — Average percent of net sales	Operating data of 6 presses with net sales from $500,000 to $1 Million — Average percent of net sales	Operating data of 7 presses with net sales from $250,000 to $500,000 — Average percent of net sales	University of Minnesota Press $	University of Minnesota Press %
Gross sales[a]	113.0	110.5	108.7	509,687	105.3
Returns and allowances	13.0	10.5	8.7	25,867	5.3
Net sales[a]	100.0	100.0	100.0	483,820	100.0
Cost of sales (net of title subsidies of approximately 5¼%)	48.4	48.9	52.3	236,169	48.8
Press-owned books	45.0	46.4	50.4	226,081	46.7
Commission books	3.4	2.4	1.8	10,088	2.1
Gross margin on sales	51.6	51.1	47.7	247,651	51.2
Other publishing income (primarily subsidiary rights)	2.0	1.0	3.4	35,147	7.3
Operating expense					
Editorial (includes proofreading)	8.1	8.4	14.1	76,685	15.8
Production	3.0	4.1	5.4	29,812	6.2
Marketing	17.1	20.0	21.1	95,729	19.8
Fulfillment	12.6	16.4	14.1	63,103	13.0

Exhibit 2 (Cont.)

	34 Presses	Operating data of 6 presses with net sales from $500,000 to $1 Million	Operating data of 7 presses with net sales from $250,000 to $500,000	University of Minnesota Press	
	Average percent of net sales	Average percent of net sales	Average percent of net sales	$	%
General and administrative expense[b]	20.1	22.0	28.0	115,613	23.9
Total operating expense[c]	60.8	70.8	82.7	380,942	78.7
Other (nonpublishing) income (or exp.)	1.2	1.2	0.8	—	—
Net income (or loss) from operations[d]	(6.0)	(17.5)	(30.8)	(98,144)	(20.2)

[a] Sales figures include books published by the presses as well as books for which the presses acted as commission sales agents.

[b] Actual or imputed rent and occupancy expenses are included in this category. The University of Minnesota Press, like most other university presses, was supplied with space, utilities, and maintenance services at no cash charge by the university. The basis for imputing such occupancy costs varied among universities and, hence, among university presses.

[c] In general, expense percentages in all categories varied inversely with sales volume; percentages were lowest for the largest presses and highest for the smallest presses.

[d] Losses of university presses were ordinarily covered by subsidies from other university funds. These general or operating subsidies were in addition to occupancy subsidies and title subsidies.

Exhibit 3

UNIVERSITY OF MINNESOTA PRESS
COMPARATIVE SALES VOLUMES OF UNIVERSITY PRESSES
REPORTING TO AMERICAN ASSOCIATION OF PUBLISHERS

Estimated annual sales volume	Number of 34[*] university presses reporting	Total sales of presses in volume class (000)	Examples
More than $1 million	14	$33,247	California, Cambridge, Chicago, Columbia Harvard, MIT, Yale
$500,000 to $1 million	6	4,482	Michigan, Wisconsin, Texas, Washington
$250,000 to $500,000	7	2,662	Minnesota, Kentucky, Notre Dame, New York University
Less than $250,000	7	930	Duke, Ohio State, Southern Methodist University

[*] These 34 presses represent an estimated 90 percent of the sales of all university presses.
Source: Estimates by University of Minnesota Press personnel

Exhibit 4

UNIVERSITY OF MINNESOTA PRESS
PERCENTAGE DISTRIBUTION OF BOOKS FROM UNIVERSITY PRESSES
1972-74, AND FOR ALL PUBLISHERS, 1972-73

| | University presses | | | All publishers |
	1974	1973	1972	1972–1973
Wholesalers	32%	35%	32%	18%
College bookstores	22	20	17	25
General bookstores	16	16	18	
Public libraries	1	6	3	
College and university libraries	8	7	10	9
Other libraries	3	4	5	
Direct to consumers	15	10	9	29[a]
Special sales and miscellaneous	3	2	6	19
Total	100%	100%	100%	100%[b]

[a] These sales were divided approximately equally among book clubs, door-to-door sales, and mail-order sales.
[b] Total sales amounted to almost $3 billion.
Source: Association of American Publishers and estimates based on AAP statistics

Exhibit 5
UNIVERSITY OF MINNESOTA PRESS
ABRIDGED ORGANIZATION CHART, 1973-1974

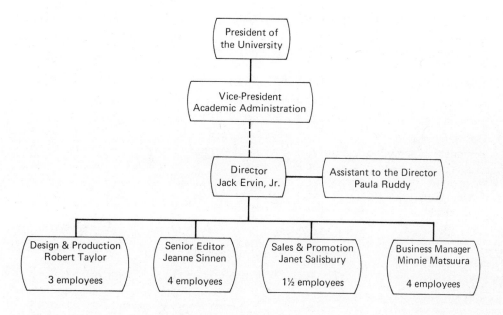

Source: University of Minnesota Press

Exhibit 6

UNIVERSITY OF MINNESOTA PRESS
INCOME STATEMENTS, 1970-1974, FOR YEARS ENDING JUNE 30
(000)

	1974	1973	1972	1971	1970
Gross sales	$509.7	$474.2	$424.8	$427.4	$437.4
Returns and allowances[a]	25.9	27.7	13.2	27.5	25.6
Net sales	483.8	446.5	411.6	399.9	411.8
Cost of goods sold[b]	236.1	189.4	262.7	208.2	215.9
Gross margin	247.7	257.1	148.9	191.7	195.9
Other income[c]	35.1	30.7	31.2	28.3	29.0
Operating expenses					
Editorial[d]	76.7				
Production[e]	29.8				
Marketing[f]	95.7	n.a.	n.a.	n.a.	n.a.
Fulfillment[g]	63.1				
General and administrative[h]	115.6				
	380.9	349.8	351.3	356.0	327.5
Income (loss from operations	(98.1)	(62.0)	(171.2)	(136.0)	(102.6)
University subsidies and donations[i, j]	153.8	134.2	132.9	139.9	132.3
Net income (loss)	55.7	72.2	(38.3)	3.9	29.7

Exhibit 6 (Cont.)

[a] Returns and allowances of paperbound books ran about 3.5 percent of net sales of paperbound books; for hardbound books, about 6.5 percent of net hardbound sales.

[b] Cost of goods sold includes direct manufacturing costs, including labor, materials, and allocated overhead expenses; royalties; less subsidies provided for particular titles. Title subsidies from 1969 to 1974 were as follows:

	(000)		(000)
1969	$55.0	1972	23.6
1970	8.3	1973	33.8
1971	22.0	1974	24.1

[c] Primarily from subsidiary rights, i.e., payments for permission to reprint and distribute materials originally published by the press.

[d] Editorial expenses consisted almost entirely of salaries, and fees paid outside specialist-readers and proofreaders. Editorial expenses for each title varied directly with the number of pages.

[e] Production expenses included that portion of the salaries of senior staff in the design and production department which was not charged to general and administrative expense, plus a small amount of specialized proofreading expense. All other costs associated with production were included in cost of goods sold.

[f] Marketing expenses included salaries of press sales and promotion staff; commissions paid sales representatives; free copies of books (charged at cost) distributed for promotional purposes; and advertising and sales promotion expenditures, which had amounted to $35 to $40 thousand per year in recent years.

[g] Fulfillment expense was comprised about equally of costs of warehousing and physical distribution, which was handled by an outside firm at a charge of 7 percent of sales; and of salaries of the press business office staff (exclusive of the department head and her assistant), equipment and supplies.

[h] General and administrative expense included administrative salaries ($54,000 in 1974) and fringe benefits for the entire press staff (approximately $26,000 in 1974); other general expense (about $20,000 in 1974); and noncash charge of $15,800 for occupancy (rent and utilities) provided by the university.

[i] University subsidies included occupancy subsidies ($15,800 in 1974), a subsidy for manufacturing costs, and partial support for an administrative and an editorial salary. These latter subsidies, which varied from year to year, together amounted to approximately $117,000 in 1974.

[j] Donations were difficult to forecast, and highly variable, amounting to only $400 in 1969, and $21,000 in 1974.

Source: University of Minnesota Press

Exhibit 7

UNIVERSITY OF MINNESOTA PRESS
BALANCE SHEETS FOR YEARS ENDING JUNE 30
(000)

	1974	1973	1972	1971	1970	1969
Assets						
Cash[a]	$ 56.9	$ 88.4	$111.7	$140.4	$191.3	$162.5
Restricted funds[b]	330.8	251.3	210.2	239.6	214.8	152.4
Accounts receivable[c]	119.2	121.2	107.4	100.9	95.3	103.6
Inventory[d]	349.9	363.3	308.0	307.5	292.9	328.5
Furniture, equipment and advances on royalties	43.7	47.0	38.4	30.3	25.2	24.1
	$900.5	$871.2	$775.7	$818.7	$819.5	$771.1
Liabilities and retained earnings						
Accounts payable	$ 62.4	$ 2.9	$ 1.3	$ 0.6	$ 0.1	$ 0.4
Other current liabilities[e]	149.6	163.1	140.9	154.5	149.0	129.7
Retained earnings[f]	688.5	705.2	633.5	663.6	670.4	641.0
Total liabilities and retained earnings	$900.5	$871.2	$775.7	$818.7	$819.5	$771.1

[a]The cash account included minor cash assets such as petty cash and postage, and funds supplied by the university for the press' operations.

Because university policy required the press to set aside in advance funds which were needed to produce books in a particular year, and because revenues from those books would not flow in until about a year after production began, the university provided the press with operating funds. Balances in this operating fund at the beginning and end of fiscal years 1970–1975 were as follows:

(000)
Year ending June 30

	1970	1971	1972	1973	1974	1975
Beginning of year	n.a.	$350.0	$300.0	$350.0	$450.0	$500.0
End of year	$190.9	140.3	111.4	88.0	55.9	18.4

The difference between the ending balance one year and the beginning balance the next represented the amount advanced to the press by the university for books to be published during that coming year. In the past, press officials had intentionally maintained high initial balances, in order to provide for publications of up to 40 titles per year. In years when fewer books were published, an ending balance accumulated in the operating account.

[b]Under university policy, the press must encumber funds designed for specific services to be performed or products to be purchased.

[c]Average collection period is 90 days, slightly less than the average for university presses as a whole.

[d]Inventory was valued at cost when printed, subject to adjustment for age. Inventories remaining two years after printing were valued at 60 percent of cost; those remaining after three years, at 40 percent; those after four years, at 20 percent; after five years, 10 percent; and were completely written off at the end of the sixth year. Reprinted titles were written down on a straight-line basis within four years.

[e]Obligations to organizations (or departments) which have provided funds. This account is the obverse of the "restricted funds" asset. The obligations for which restricted funds have been established may, but do not necessarily, fall due within one year.

[f]Changes from year to year in retained earnings may differ slightly from net income (loss) shown on the income statement, because of minor adjustments to the income statement, to conform to industry-wide reporting procedures.

Source: University of Minnesota Press

Exhibit 8

UNIVERSITY OF MINNESOTA PRESS
PRINTING AND PROFITABILITY DATA BY TITLE,
JULY 1972–JUNE 1973
EXCLUSIVE OF AMERICAN WRITERS SERIES[a]

Title classification	Title	List prices	Number of copies printed	Sales from date of publication to June 30, 1973[b]		Average revenue per unit	Average mfg. cost per unit printed	Gross margin per unit[c]	
				Units	Dollars			Dollars	Percent
Social science									
History, Political science	Cuba: The Measure of a Revolution	$10.00	2994	1901	$11,461	$ 6.03	$2.35	$3.68	61%
	Federal Judges: The Appointing Process	10.00	4000	3092	14,199	4.59	2.45	2.14	47
	Fighting Ships and Prisons: The Mediterranean Galleys of France in the Age of Louis XIV	16.50	2078	491	5,156	10.50	4.45	6.05	58
	The French Campaign in Portugal, 1810–1811: An Account by Jean Jacques Pelet	18.50	2219	369	4,470	12.11	5.95	6.16	51
	Capital Cities of Arab Islam	7.95	2996	661	2,963	4.48	2.05	2.43	54
Psychology	Minnesota Symposia on Child Psychology, Vol. 6	7.50	2980	1039	6,023	5.80	1.94	3.86	67
	Transfer, Memory, and Creativity: After-Learning as Perceptual Process	7.50	2501	677	3,453	5.10	1.65	3.45	68

Exhibit 8 (Cont.)

Title classification	Title	List prices	Number of copies printed	Sales from date of publication to June 30, 1973[b]		Average revenue per unit	Average mfg. cost per unit printed	Gross margin per unit[c]	
				Units	Dollars			Dollars	Percent
Psychology	Social Adjustment and Personality Development in Children	$ 8.50	2538	863	$ 5,178	$ 6.00	$2.03	$3.97	66%
	An MMPI Source Book: Basic Item, Scale, and Pattern Data on 50,000 Medical Patients	9.50	3462	424	2,400	5.66	1.53	4.13	73
	Contemporary Approaches to Interest Measurement	10.00	2003	231	1,384	5.99	3.22	2.77	46
Anthroplogy	The Settlement of Polynesia: A Computer Simulation	10.75	2528	841	4,105	4.88	4.10	.78	16
Other social science	The Minnesota Messenia Expedition: Reconstructing A Bronze Age Regional Environment	22.50	2043	478	7,102	14.86	9.59	5.27	35
	Soybeans and Their Products: Markets, Models, and Policy	10.00	1939	828	5,945	7.18	4.18	3.00	42
	Lifeway Leap: The Dynamics of Change in America	{ 6.95 { 3.95	3040 cloth 3108 paper	922 669	8,397 2,035	9.11 3.04	1.89 1.40	7.62 1.55	84 51

Exhibit 8 (Cont.)

Title classification	Title	List prices	Number of copies printed	Sales from date of publication to June 30, 1973[b]		Average revenue per unit	Average mfg. cost per unit printed	Gross margin per unit[c]	
				Units	Dollars			Dollars	Percent
Other social science	*Returns in Over-the-Counter Stock Markets*	$ 7.95	2534	93	$ 482	5.18	$1.61	$3.57	69%
Humanities									
Literary history and criticism	*Milton's Earthly Paradise: A Historical Study of Eden*	12.50	2141	1161	10,427	8.98	3.39	5.59	62
	Aldous Huxley, Satirist and Novelist	7.95	1909	1275	7,000	5.49	2.10	3.39	62
	Charles Dickens: Radical Moralist	9.50	2027	1018	5,747	5.65	3.28	2.37	42
	Seven American Literary Stylists from Poe to Mailer: An Introduction	10.50	5968	663	3,904	5.89	1.75	4.14	70
Creative literature	*The Government Inspector*	5.75	1502 cloth	424	682	1.61	.98	.63	39
		1.95	5006 paper	1285	1,346	1.05	.68	.37	35
	Oedipus the King	5.95	1345 cloth	542	2,210	4.08	1.17	2.91	71
		1.95	4948 paper	2228	2,468	1.11	.73	.38	34
	The Dramatization of 365 Days	5.95	2049 cloth	551	1,894	3.44	1.73	1.71	50
		1.95	3356 paper	582	689	1.18	1.24	(.06)	negative
	Playwrights For Tomorrow: A collection of Plays Volumes 8 and 9	8.95	2111 cloth	732	4,116	5.62	2.18	3.44	61
		2.95	3144 paper	393	671	1.71	1.74	(.03)	negative
	Candle in the Wind	6.95	4968	804	2,949	3.67	1.39	2.28	62

Exhibit 8 (Cont.)

Title classification	Title	List prices	Number of copies printed	Sales from date of publication to June 30, 1973[b]		Average revenue per unit	Average mfg. cost per unit printed	Gross margin per unit[c]	
				Units	Dollars			Dollars	Percent
Philosophy, Religion	A Companion to the Study of St. Anselm	$10.50	2166	680	$ 4,938	7.26	$3.55	$ 3.71	51%
Other humanities	The Linguistic Atlas of the Upper Midwest, Volume 1	17.50	1997	234	3,087	13.19	2.85	10.34	78
Natural science									
Biological science	—	—	—	—	—	—	—	—	—
Medicine	The Comparative Anatomy and Histology of the Cerebellum: The Human Cerebellum, Cerebellar Connections, and Cerebellar Cortex	17.50	2011	579	7,645	13.20	7.40	5.80	44
	Frontiers in Comparative Medicine	4.75	2213	596	1,949	3.27	1.46	1.81	55
Other science	—	—	—	—	—	—	—	—	—
Totals	29		91,824	27,326	$146,475	$ 5.36	$2.37	$ 2.99	56%

Totals for prior years[d]

	Number of booklets (all booklets together counted as one title)	Total number of copies printed	Sales from date of publication to June 30, 1973		Average revenue per unit	Average mfg. cost per unit printed	Gross margin per unit	
			Units	Dollars			Dollars	Percent
1971–1972	19	57,391	22,115	$129,631	$ 5.86	$2.54	$3.32	57%
1970–1971	22	62,372	22,138	118,322	5.34	2.31	3.03	57
1969–1970	19	50,048	15,405	69,298	4.50	1.93	2.57	57
1968–1969	31	86,510	23,684	79,094	3.34	1.71	1.63	49

[a] Data for the American Writers Series, discontinued in 1973–1974, appear below:

Title classification	Number of booklets (all booklets together counted as one title)	Total number of copies printed	Sales from date of publication to June 30, 1973		Average revenue per unit	Average mfg. cost per unit printed	Gross margin per unit	
			Units	Dollars			Dollars	Percent
1972–1973	3	32,555	10,560	$ 6,628	$.63	$.14	$.49	77%
1971–1972	3	28,370	9,515	6,299	.66	.15	.51	77
1970–1971	5	48,425	14,793	9,602	.65	.14	.51	78
1969–1970	12	128,510	37,226	23,341	.63	.11	.52	83
1968–1969	14	156,629	40,211	25,816	.64	.10	.54	84

[b] Date of publication could be as early as July 1, 1972 and as late as June 30, 1973. The sales figures presented here include approximately 12 months' sales for books published in July 1972, and less than one month's sales for books published in June 1973.

[c] Unit gross margin equals unit revenue (i.e., net sales @ average price received) less unit manufacturing cost.

[d] These totals also exclude the American Writers Series.

Source: University of Minnesota Press Records

Exhibit 9

UNIVERSITY OF MINNESOTA PRESS

SUMMARY OF TITLE OUTPUT, 1967–1974

Year ending June 30	Number of different titles[a]	History, political science	Psychol-ogy	Anthro-pology	Other social science	Literary history and criticism	Creative literature	Philosophy, religion	Other human-ities	Biolog-ical science	Medi-cine	Other sciences
1967	25	6	—	—	8	6	3	1	—	—	1	—
1968	34	6	2	—	3	13	5	1	3	1	—	—
1969	32	4	2	—	4	10	2	3	2	4	—	1
1970	20	5	2	1	6	3	4	—	—	—	—	—
1971	23	7	2	—	3	6	1	1	1	—	1	—
1972	20	5	4	—	2	8	—	—	—	1	—	—
1973	30	4	5	1	5	5	6	1	1	—	2	—
1974	20	5	3	—	1	3	2	—	4	1	1	—

[a] All titles falling under American Writers Series (listed under Literary history and criticism) are counted as one title, even though more than one title might be published during a particular year. The American Writers Series was discontinued in 1974.

Source: University of Minnesota Press Records

Exhibit 10

UNIVERSITY OF MINNESOTA PRESS
ESTIMATED SALES BY PURCHASER

Sales to:	1973	1971	1969	1967
Wholesalers				
● General	11%	2%	2%	3%
● Library	49	55	55	52
Retail book outlets				
● College	10	9	8	9
● General (including book departments)	10	8	10	11
Libraries				
● Public	2	1	2	2
● University and institutional	5	6	6	7
● School	1	4	2	4
● Other	7	8	10	6
Direct to consumer	5	7	5	6
Total	100%	100%	100%	100%

Source: Sample surveys of press invoices

APPENDIX

Note on the Book Publishing Industry

This appendix describes the publication and distribution of books in the United States. The contents of the appendix are listed below:

Book Publishing

In 1973, book-publishing industry sales amounted to some $3.5 billion, double the level of a decade earlier, and 1.4 times the level of 1967–1969. Some analysts, however, attributed almost all the increase from 1967–1969 to 1973 to price inflation, rather than to real growth. Fifty of the 1,200 American publishers accounted for more than 75 percent of industry sales.

Encyclopedias and textbooks together accounted for almost half of industry sales (see Exhibit A.1). In recent years the output of new titles had been largest in sociology and economics, followed by science, juveniles (i.e., books for children), and fiction (see Exhibit A.2).

Industry sources ordinarily divide book publishing into four broad areas: (1) trade, (2) educational, (3) professional, and (4) subscription reference. Although distinctions among these categories are by no means always clear-cut, trade publishing typically includes both hardbound and paperbound fiction, nonfiction, and religious books sold through retail book outlets, book clubs, and mail-order houses. Educational publishing includes materials intended for use in elementary and high schools (elhi) and in colleges. Professional publishing comprises books intended for use by practitioners in a particular professional field. Subscription reference publishing involves primarily the publishing of encyclopedias. Books ordinarily referred to as "reference books," such as dictionaries or wildlife guides, are considered "trade" publications

Large firms, such as McGraw-Hill and Prentice-Hall, may publish books in all four areas. Smaller firms usually confine themselves to one area of publishing.

Practices vary among the four types of publishing. This variation produces income statements which differ from one type of publishing to another (see Exhibit A.3).

In trade publishing profit comes not from the sales of trade books (operating expenses are greater than gross margin) but rather from "other publishing income." This "other" income includes subsidiary rights such as reprint rights, book club rights, movie rights, etc. In general, profits of trade publishers vary with sales volume. Smaller trade houses earn low profits, and frequently sustain losses.

Mass-market paperbacks (low-price paperbound books sold on racks and through newsstand outlets) have a high return percentage, high royalties, and lower editorial and production costs than hardbound and quality paperbound books. Return percentages are high because the mass-market publisher typically prints 30,000 or more copies of each title. If the book does not sell, the returns are great (in fact, books are not returned, as freight costs are too high, but book covers are torn off and sent back to the publisher for refunds). Royalties are high because of the high cost of reprint rights for good hardcover books. These rights must often be obtained in fierce bidding competition. Editorial costs are low, because the original book is already edited. Production costs are low because inexpensive rubber plates are used, and the print size is huge. In this instance mass-market publishers benefit from economies of long production runs.

The salient features of the book club cost structure are the lack of editorial and production costs, and the high marketing costs. Editorial and production costs are minimal, as book clubs either buy books from the original publishers or use their plates to reprint the book. Marketing costs are high; new member offers absorb up to 75 percent of marketing funds.

Elhi publishers have relatively low return and royalty percentages and relatively high marketing costs. Returns are low because sales are made direct to a user, school, or school system which takes some time in deliberating the purchase. Royalties are low because most of the text is developed by the publisher's staff. Marketing expenses are high because elhi publishers use their own direct sales forces and substantial supporting promotional material to sell their texts.

College texts have higher return percentages, higher royalties, and somewhat lower marketing costs than do elhi texts. Returns are higher than elhi because college texts are not purchased by the user or by a central authority, but rather by several competing bookstores serving the students. These bookstores have class size information but not competitors' order quantities. Royalties are higher because a college professor is usually commissioned to write a text. Marketing costs are lower because the sales force necessary for college texts is smaller and accompanying promotion (such as free books) less than for elhi books.

Production and editorial costs are greater for professional publishing because of the extra care needed to assure correctness and accuracy in a text used by professionals such as doctors and engineers.

TRADE PUBLISHING

Although trade books comprise only 30 percent of the industry dollar volume, they are the part that generally comes to mind when book publishing is mentioned. Trade books, as defined by the Association of American Publishers (AAP), are books created for the general consumer and marketed primarily through trade channels, i.e., bookstores and libraries, either directly or through wholesalers and jobbers. The majority of books one sees at a general bookstore are trade books.

Trade books include adult hardbound fiction and nonfiction books, quality paper-backs, juvenile books, religious books, mass-market paperbacks, and book club selections (sales of each category appear in case Exhibit A.4).

Except for juvenile and religious books, sales of almost all trade books rarely continue for more than twelve months. The level of sales of an adult trade book is generally determined during the first six weeks the book is on the retailers' shelves. Sales of juvenile trade books, on the other hand, do not ordinarily accelerate until after the first year of exposure.

Adult Hardbound Books

The process by which publishers develop their lists of publications is similar, but not identical, to that used by university presses. Trade publishers receive manuscripts from authors principally through literary agents. Publishers then evaluate those manuscripts and publish that set which promises to be most profitable.

Authors generate manuscripts or outlines for books either from their own ideas or, in the case of some experienced writers, in response to suggestions from publishers. Very few authors rely on book royalties (which range from 10 to 15 percent of the retail price of trade books) as their primary source of income.

Although the number of would-be authors is unknown, large publishers may receive 15,000 unsolicited manuscripts a year. Three of these 15,000 would, perhaps, be given consideration beyond the initial three-minute review given to all incoming manuscripts. According to industry estimates, more than 90 percent of the trade books published represent manuscripts submitted through literary agents.

Literary agents, who are authors' business representatives, have traditionally served as the connecting link between author and publisher in trade book publishing. Agents screen manuscripts from authors, attempt to place promising manuscripts with publishers, negotiate contracts between authors and publishers, and facilitate fulfillment of those contracts.

Literary agents typically submit manuscripts to one publisher after another until a contract acceptable to both author and publisher can be negotiated. Agents may auction manuscripts sought by several publishers because of the visibility of the author or the topic. The price bid in an auction is the advance paid to the author. Although negotiated, as distinct from auctioned, contracts also include advances, those paid at auctions are typically much larger.

There are more than 100 agents in New York, which is considered the trade publishing capital of America. Agents may operate as a one-person shop or part of a large agency. Most agents do more business with one publisher than with any one client.

Agents generally receive a 10 percent commission on the author's gross royalties from sales of the books, and 20 percent for foreign rights. (Royalties typically amount to 10 percent of the retail price of a book for the first 5,000 or 10,000 copies, and increase gradually to 15 percent beginning with the sale of the 20,001st copy. Authors whose works have previously been published may receive a higher percentage beginning with the first copy of a subsequent book.) Agents generally handle movie, T.V., and radio rights and rights to excerpt or serialize a book. On sales of such rights agents receive a negotiated commission. Agents may handle paperback and book club rights, although those are usually sold by the original hardbound publisher.

Publishers consider expected sales of hardbound copies and of rights in deciding whether to publish a particular title. Factors that industry sources believe to be important determinants of sales of books and rights include (1) the novelty of the manuscript's contribution (either in content or approach) to a particular subject area, (2) the literary quality and content, (3) the popularity and visibility of the author.

Estimation of sales depends upon personal preferences, experience, and intuition of publishers' personnel. The decision is far from being refined to a precise formula; yet most publishers agree that, title for title, nonfiction sells better than fiction, and that the first novel from an unknown author is rarely a moneymaking event.

Publishers ordinarily print fewer than 5,000 copies of the first book by an unknown author, but will print at least 10,000 hardbound copies for a book by an established author. In either case, publishers expect the first printing to provide inventory for one year's sales. According to industry sources, most adult trade books sell 3,000 to 5,000 hardbound copies during their lives. Only a small number of each publisher's titles may sell tens or hundreds of thousands of copies.

Larger publishers have their own sales forces who are paid salary plus commission, and sell only their publishers' titles. In contrast, the independent book salespeople sell books from several small publishers, and receive commission on each sale. Both salaried and independent salespeople work within specified geographic territories. Salespeople typically present their publishers' new titles to wholesalers, retailers, and selected libraries twice each year. One industry source observed that salespeople had to present three books per minute to buyers to acquaint buyers with the entire line.

In addition to catalog listings and announcements of new titles on publication dates, publishers may allocate promotional funds in substantial amounts to particular books which they expect to be "best sellers." Although exact promotion budgets for specific titles were rarely made public, industry sources acknowledged that expenditures of tens of thousands of dollars for prospective "best sellers" were not uncommon. Ordinarily 5 to 10 percent of a publishers' titles would receive almost all of these promotional funds.

Substantial promotion budgets may also be allocated to books that initially received minimal promotion but whose higher-than-forecast sales levels during the first six weeks of retail exposure warrant commitment of promotional monies to increase sales. Only very rarely do adult trade books that lack high and increasing levels of sales within their first six weeks attain significant sales volume later in their lives.

Publishers vary in size, organization, and type of books published. Most commercial publishers are considered stronger in certain topic areas or types of books than in others. Large publishers may offer 750 new titles each year; smaller publishers, fewer than 100.

In addition to the original publishers of adult trade hardbound books, there are, apart from book clubs, two other sources of such books: reprinters and remaindering firms. Reprint firms reprint and reissue books of which the original publisher has no current or prospective inventory. Reprint rights, which may or may not include the original printing plates, are generally purchased from the original publisher of the book. In many cases the reprint is difficult to distinguish from the original, although the price difference is noticeable: a $25.00 book will often retail for $12.95 in reprint form. The largest hardbound reprint house in the United States reprints an average of two books a day in addition to publishing 140 new titles each year.

Remaindering firms buy the overstocks of books that the original hardbound publisher could not sell. These books are then sold to book retailers at tremendously reduced prices. In some instances, retailers are able to offer for one or two dollars books which originally retailed for five to fifteen dollars. Retailers frequently seek "remainders," because, ". . . bargain books attract customers in droves," according to one retailer.

Quality Paperbound Books

"Quality" paperbacks may be published concurrently with the hardbound edition, solely as a paperback, or as a reprint much as the mass-market paperbacks. Quality paperbacks are usually published at the same time as the hardbound book if the markets are separate, i.e., general bookstore vs. college text use. More than 25 percent of all quality paperbacks are original manuscripts. For quality paperbacks that are neither copublished with hardbound books nor published as original manuscripts, paperback publishers purchase the right to print the paperback edition of an already-published hardbound manuscript from the original publisher. Paperback sales in most cases exceed the number of copies of the hardbound edition sold.

"Quality" paperbacks retail from three to ten dollars, and are marketed through retail bookstores only. "Quality" paperbacks are sold by publishers' sales forces.

Juvenile

Principal customers for original publication of hardbound children's books are libraries. Publishers typically do not reprint such books in paperbound form until five years following initial publication. Both hardbound and paperbound originals and reprints are sold through normal book channels and through mass-merchandise outlets. Some 80 percent of children's books retail for more than one dollar.

For books for younger children, illustrations are considered very important. Consequently, many publishers of children's books employ their own illustrators. Free-lance illustrators are paid on the same basis as authors. If a free-lance illustrator and author collaborate, they usually divide the total royalties equally.

Religious Books

Religious books are comprised about evenly of Bibles, hymnals, prayer books, and other books of religious content. Most religious books go through several printings before new editions are prepared. Almost all religious books are published by small publishing houses, which typically are affiliated formally or informally with a particular denomination. Profits from publishing activities form an important source of revenue for some religious organizations.

Mass-Market Paperbacks

Mass-market paperback books ordinarily sell at retail prices below two dollars. These books are marketed through bookstores and, like magazines, through newstands, drugstores, and supermarkets. To reach these outlets mass-market paperback publishers use their own sales forces which sell to retailers, book wholesalers, and jobbers and magazine wholesalers which sell these books to their magazine outlets. Some mass-market paperbacks are sold to college stores for educational use.

Mass-market paperbacks have an average print size many time that of the original hardbound editions. Reprint rights, whose cost varies widely, are a major component of total cost. More than 75 percent of mass-market paperbacks are reprints; the remainder are original manuscripts. Shelf life of a mass-market paperback is three to four weeks. If sales during this time do not meet expectations, books are pulled off the shelves, their covers returned to publishers for full refunds, and the books themselves discarded.

Book Clubs

In 1972, book clubs sold 119 million copies for $304 million. This figure represented 40 percent of the total dollar volume of books sold directly by publishers to consumers, and a 160 percent increase in book clubs' sales since 1967. Although there are more than 130 book clubs in the United States, half of them account for 90 percent of book club sales, and the three largest (Book of the Month Club [BOMC], Doubleday-owned Literary Guild and its some 20 satellite clubs, and Reader's Digest Condensed Books) account for more than half of all book club sales. In 1971, BOMC reported net sales in excess of $43 million, a $4 million increase from the previous year. The advertising budget rose from $5.8 million in 1970 to $8.6 million in 1971. Total sales for the Literary Guild and associated clubs are estimated at $70–80 million and are believed to account for nearly half of the total sales of the parent Doubleday Company. Reader's Digest Condensed Books sell more than 10 million volumes per year, almost wholly to subscribers to *Reader's Digest* magazine. Annual sales are estimated between $40 and $45 million. Company sources believe demand will increase as subscribers turn over; one source estimated the turnover in the *Reader's Digest* subscription list at 40 percent per year.

According to industry sources, the major reasons for book club success are (1) the availability, through purchase or rental, of magazine subscription and other mailing lists through which consumers may be contacted; (2) an increase in Americans wanting to read books but not knowing where to get them; (3) poor book distribution ("Books are as hard to buy in the U.S. as they were in 1926," *Publisher's Weekly,* March 13, 1972); and (4) lower prices.

Large areas of the United States do not have bookstores; in addition, book club membership follows population distribution, not rural-urban division. According to one book club executive, "Specialty book stores exist in 2,000 of the nation's zip code areas, with the biggest number of stores concentrated in the East and Far West. A large club like ours serves more than 25,000 zip codes."

Another book club executive argued that "Many people have a fear about bookstores because they just don't know about books. Much of the fear is psychological, irrational perhaps, but it is there. Clubs offer members a convenient and personal bookstore that tells them 'Here's what we've selected. We've read these books, think they're good and recommend them.' Bookstore buying isn't for everyone. There's a real aversion to them (even) in areas where bookstores are plentiful."

Book clubs sell books to members at prices from 40 to 50 percent off the list price. This practice has caused friction with retail booksellers.

Memberships: The book club industry is heavily dependent on obtaining new members. Break even on a membership occurs after one year of membership; average turnover time per membership is two years.

Most book clubs require members to purchase a specified number of books each year. Members ordinarily receive notice of a selected title and a list of alternatives 12 to 15 times each year. If members do not return a coupon specifying an alternate or "no book," the club automatically sends them the selection for the current period. A typical major club requires members to buy four books per year, at prices which it claims represent savings of 40 to 70 percent off of original list prices. In addition, the club offers new members the opportunity to buy, for a total of one or two dollars, two to four books.

Large book clubs offer a broad range of selections; smaller clubs specialize. According to an article in *Publisher's Weekly* (March 1972), "Specialty clubs cater to virtually all tastes except that of the professional pornographer . . . cooks and conservatives, golfers and ecologists, Episcopalians and electronic engineers, mystics and managers, horsemen and humorists, secretaries and salesmen, lovers of wine and of Wisconsin, even writers themselves can get the literature of their choice via the book club route."

Operations: Book clubs are inundated with book submissions from publishers. Generally, a committee within a publishing house decides which books to submit to book clubs, but one large publisher sends more than 75 percent of its books, while another (medium-size) house sends fewer than 15 percent of its new titles.

Most book clubs have a judge selection panel to read, review, and recommend titles to be listed. BOMC buys 250 titles a year for all divisions. A cross-section of fiction and nonfiction is selected, although nonfiction outsells fiction three to two, according to BOMC's editorial director. "Most fiction readers buy paperbacks," he says, "and people who like fiction get a lot of it on TV." Book clubs may pay up to tens of thousands of dollars for rights to republish, as an advance against royalties. Publishers and authors ordinarily divide these royalties equally.

EDUCATIONAL PUBLISHING

Educational publishing may be divided into two areas—elementary/high school (elhi) and college publishing.

Elhi Publishing

Publishing for elementary school (grades K–8) and high school (grades 9–12) involves the development of a complete educational system of texts and collateral materials to provide a smooth transition of material and learning from one grade to the next. Such a system is necessary for each of many topic areas, including math, language, social studies, and science. The textbook ordinarily forms the core of the course. Collateral materials, such as films and workbooks, are added at points specified in the teachers' guides (which form an integral part of the educational system).

To develop an educational system, publishers identify needs of schools on the basis of information from salespeople, consultants, authors of school texts, and the publisher's editorial staff. A publisher then selects a writing team of teachers, university people, and practicing supervisory personnel to draft materials for manuscripts, audio tapes, story books for films, etc. These materials are pilot-tested in schools, and subsequently refined by the writing team, augmented by independent psychologists, designers, artists, content specialists, classroom management specialists, and professional editors. When revisions are completed, sales promotion materials are prepared and presented along with the texts to the sales force.

Educational publishers typically have a sales force to sell their program(s) to private, parochial, and public schools. For private schools salespeople usually call on school administrators; for parochial schools they call upon the archdiocese or comparable authority for area-wide adoption. In the public sector sales and promotion activities depend upon the adoption system used. Three adoption systems exist: (1) state-wide adoption, employed in 23 states; (2) city-wide adoption; and (3) individual school adoption.

Statewide adoptions consists of lists of three types: (1) large adoption lists (meaning mere approval of the program—almost every publisher on list), (2) limited lists (5–12 publishers allowed on list), and (3) restricted lists (3–5 programs allowed on list). The programs that are on lists are selected and approved by a state selection committee. Once on the lists, text publishers are allowed to sell their books to buying groups in the state. Depending on the state, the buying groups may be the individual school, the school district, city, or state agency.

City-wide adoptions are used in large metropolitan areas. City adoption systems may coexist with state adoption systems or may exist independently, i.e., a state may have no adoption system but a large city within the state might. The adoption lists for cities follow a similar pattern to those described in the state system, i.e., large, limited, restricted. The possible buying groups are individual schools, school districts, or a city agency.

Development of an elhi educational system in a particular topic area typically requires two to three years, and costs from two to five million dollars. The life of an elhi program is ordinarily three to four years. Almost all revenues from elhi sales to a particular school system coincide with adoption, and slow to a trickle thereafter. Most sales are made during June, July, and August before the start of the new school year.

In addition to complete programs, schools occasionally adopt texts in particular areas, typically for high school electives. Examples of such special texts include local history and certain college-preparatory courses.

In 1973, sales of elhi materials were approximately $500 million. Sales for both elementary and high school texts had risen slowly but steadily since 1967 (see Exhibit A.4). Enrollment in elementary schools was less than 35 million students in 1973, and had been declining since 1970; high school enrollment had remained about 15.5 million students since 1971 (see Exhibit A.5).

Educational publishing is considered highly competitive. Approximately 200 firms, of which 75 are of major size, vie for the market's attention.

College Publishing

College textbooks are usually developed for an individual course or type of course, rather than for a several-year sequence of courses. Publishers of college texts use three methods to develop textbooks: (1) ask a college professor to write a text on a topic in his or her specialty; (2) define a need in the market, then commission a professor to write a text to meet that need; (3) define a need, then prepare the manuscript with internal staff, seeking input from professors only as needed. The first two methods are used for advanced topics at the undergraduate and graduate levels; methods (2) and (3) are used for undergraduate introductory texts. Needs are defined through information from salespeople, internal research, and published studies. If these sources indicate the existence of a sufficiently large market, an author may be sought to write the manuscript. This definition process takes approximately a year. Once the initial draft of the manuscript is finished, two to twenty topic specialists review the manuscript to ensure technical accuracy, determine pedagogical value, and provide guides for refinement of the original manuscript. In general, the process of review and revision is more extensive for introductory texts than for advanced texts.

College texts are traditionally marketed through publishers' own sales forces, supported by direct mail and advertising in specialized media to professors who select texts for particular courses. In general, visits from salespeople are more important in the adoption of introductory-level texts. For specialized courses or seminars, professors would often rely on direct mail and sample copies to choose a text. Once an individual instructor (or teaching group) chooses a text, he or she will inform local bookstores that the particular book is required for a specific course. Bookstores will then order the text from the publisher, in a quantity determined by the bookstore's estimate of course enrollment and likely sales of competing stores. Bookstores ordinarily receive discounts of 20 percent off publishers' list prices on college texts.

In presenting to a professor a text for adoption, a salesperson typically stresses (1) features the publisher's promotional staff has identified as important, and (2) the other schools that have adopted the book. Sales of college texts are highest in the fall; returns, highest in the spring.

A college text typically has a three- to five-year life before revisions are incurred. For a large college publisher, break-even volume for a hardbound college texts amounts to sales of 7,500 copies over the life of an edition. The price of a text is influenced by several factors, including publishers' sales forecasts, return-on-investment requirements, estimates of demand elasticity, and competitors' prices.

Sales of college texts amounted to more than $375 million in 1973, almost double their level in 1967 (see Exhibit A.6). Approximately 9.5 million students were enrolled in postsecondary institutions in 1973, compared with about 7 million in 1967 (see Exhibit A.7).

Most companies actively involved in elhi publishing also serve the college market. Thirty-two publishers of college texts account for approximately 75 percent of college text sales.

PROFESSIONAL PUBLISHING

Professional books are books intended for use by practitioners in particular professions. The distinctiveness of professional books from other books depends upon the profession. Law and medical books are very distinct as they are not ordinarily usable by the nonprofessional. Books such as those intended for engineers are less clearly distinctive. Business books are even less distinct. Accordingly, the market for law and medical books is well defined; for engineering books, less; and for business books, even less.

The areas of professional publishing are broadly defined as law, medicine, science, technical and vocational, and business. Professional books, as distinct from textbooks in a particular field, emphasize current thinking and recent developments in that profession. Many professional books emphasize "how to . . ." more than do textbooks.

The need for most professional books is identified initially by a publisher, who determines where a book is needed by scanning trade and professional journals and by talking to members of professional societies, subject specialists, and researchers in a particular field.

When a publisher identifies a topic area that appears to have an audience large enough to warrant publishing a new book, the publisher seeks out an author, ordinarily an expert in that area. Although the publisher may specify the length of the book, its contents are determined by the author. Professional books are edited to a higher standard of precision and flawlessness than are most other books, because a mistake in a professional book could cause catastrophic results.

Professional books are marketed largely by direct mail from publisher to professional, since the audience is defined and identifiable. A 10 to 15 percent return on a mailing to a specific target group is considered successful. Professional books are also sold through specialty book stores (business, engineering, medical, etc.), which ordinarily receive a discount of 20 percent off the retail price of the book. Law and medical bookstores order directly from the publishers. Other specialty bookstores usually order through wholesalers.

Small firms are more important in professional publishing than in trade or educational publishing. Many small firms have established reputations in a particular profession (or subspecialty within that profession), and enjoy a large share of one or more limited markets.

SUBSCRIPTION REFERENCE PUBLISHING

The reference book business consists primarily of sales of encyclopedias to three markets: home and office, school and library, and mail order. The contribution of each of these segments to total volume is approximately as follows: home and office, 79 percent; school and libraries, 4 percent; mail order, 17 percent. The growth of encyclopedia sales has been rapid, largely because of increases in population and disposable income.

There are several sizes, levels, and variations in encyclopedias, each meeting specific needs. There are large comprehensive sets with as many as 60,000 entries. A group of moderate-sized encyclopedias about two-thirds this size has been published primarily for student use. There are concise compendia, which are really desk reference books. With changes in school programs and the introduction of a wider range of material in the lower grades, the children's encyclopedia has developed to a high standard. Special-purpose encyclopedias for the general lay reader are appearing in various subject fields including science, the arts, history, etc.

To compile an encyclopedia, articles on the selected topic area need to be written objectively and accurately. Most of the articles are written by the publisher's in-house research-editorial staff, while certain more specialized articles are written by outside topic experts.

Reference publishing today requires a large capital investment, starting with the original cost of new publication and extending through to a yearly update and maintenance as well as financing credit on a subscription basis. Costs can exceed $600 per page. A good quality twenty-volume encyclopedia of 10,000 pages requires an investment of $6 million to compile—before any sets are printed and ready for distribution. Continuous and substantial revision is necessary. A contemporary encyclopedia needs some degree of updating on 20 percent of its pages each year. Also, inasmuch as 95 percent of subscription sets are sold on an installment basis, long-term sales financing is required. A publisher doing $5 million worth of business would need to arrange for $3.5 million to provide funds for paper, printing, binding, commission to salespeople, advertising, etc.

Encyclopedias are primarily sold directly to users through full- or part-time salespersons who receive a commission on each sale. Salesperson turnover is high in the reference publishing industry. One industry source reports a turnover of 75 percent per year. This turnover level requires a publisher to maintain a substantial recruiting and training program. Another industry source believes that competition in this area of publishing is affected substantially by competitors' abilities to recruit, train, and hold sizable sales forces.

Today, four companies in the United States account for approximately 95 percent of the total reference book business through subscription sales, namely: Britannica, Colliers, Field Enterprises, and Grolier. These companies act both as manufacturers and resellers.

Book Distribution

Since World War II book distribution in the United States has been accomplished through a network of wholesalers and retailers, as well as by direct sales from publishers to individuals and libraries. Exhibit A.8 shows the basic distribution structure for the book industry and estimated dollar flows of books for 1973.

WHOLESALERS

In 1973, 877 wholesalers distributed $533 million worth of books in the United States. Of these wholesalers, 588 were magazine wholesalers who distributed mass-market paperback books and magazines through drugstores, chain stores, newsstands, supermarkets, and other similar outlets. The number of magazine wholesalers, each of which served primarily a regional market, had changed little since 1970. Although the mix between magazines and mass-market paperback books varied among magazine wholesalers, the majority derived more than half of their revenues from sales of mass-market paperback books. Magazine wholesalers generally earned markups of 23 to 29 percent on mass-market paperback books.

General book wholesalers distributed hardbound and some quality paperbound books to retail outlets or to libraries and institutions. A few general wholesalers served both. In 1974, there were 276 general book wholesalers, down from 414 in 1970. Some 20 of these general wholesalers together accounted for 75 to 90 percent of the sales of general book wholesalers. Sales of general book wholesalers as a group had declined slightly from 1971 through 1973. More than 72 percent of general book wholesalers' sales of text, professional, and scholarly books were made to colleges and universities, primarily for library use. In contrast, less than 20 percent of those wholesalers' sales of trade books went to colleges and universities.

In addition to the few general wholesalers that served both retail and library markets, some thirteen trade wholesalers served primarily retail markets in 1974. Each of these trade wholesalers operated in a particular region within the United States. Retailers used trade wholesalers primarily to reorder stocks of books after the initial orders from the publishers had been sold out, when volume from subsequent sales of a particular title was expected to be small, or when the title was needed immediately. Occasionally, smaller shops would purchase initial stocks from wholesalers instead of from publishers.

A typical trade wholesaler stocked 6,000 to 8,000 titles at one time. Selection of titles and the quantity stocked depended, according to industry sources, on the publishers' backing as determined by print size and promotion budget, on information from large retail bookstores in the trade area, and on the wholesalers' own estimates of likely sales.

Most trade wholesalers considered their primary competitors to be publishers rather than other wholesalers. One trade wholesaler commented that his principal competitive advantages over a publisher were breadth of line and immediacy of service.

General book wholesalers that primarily served libraries ordinarily concentrated on a single type of library, e.g., college and university libraries, public libraries, school libraries, or specialty libraries. A small number of large wholesalers served all types of libraries.

Wholesalers frequently enjoyed standing orders from libraries to which they sent new volumes and supplements on an automatic basis in any topic area specified by a particular library. In addition, such wholesalers would bind paperbound books in hard cover to help lengthen book life for libraries. Some large wholesalers offered libraries computerized acquisition systems which helped librarians to keep control of their inventories. In addition, large wholesalers' staffs of professional librarians, together with consultants, prepared lists of books that might be of interest to particular types of libraries. The purpose of such lists was to enable librarians to select which books to order from the thousands new on the market each year.

Buyers for large wholesalers determined which titles to stock and the quantity in which they should be stocked on the basis of advance promotion funds budgeted by the publisher, author popularity, publicity and reviews, initial print size and stocking at the retail level, reports of sales of subsidiary rights for book clubs and movies, and the name of the publisher (certain publishers were considered likely to enjoy substantial sales volume in particular fields). Wholesalers generally attempted to stock initially a quantity equivalent to three months' supply of any new title purchased. One very large general wholesaler, more than 75 percent of whose sales were to libraries of all types, operated five warehouses throughout the United States. In total, these warehouses held 250,000 of the 340,000 titles currently in print from all publishers.

The discount structure in the book distribution network differed for trade books and text, scholarly, and professional books. On trade books, publishers typically offered wholesalers discounts ranging from 25 percent off list price for quantities under 10, to 40 percent for quantities from 10 to 25, up to nearly 50 percent for 500 or more copies. Wholesalers offered retailers and libraries discounts of 10 percent on quantities fewer than 10; the discounts gradually increased to 40 percent for 50 or more copies. Publishers offered to retailers discounts which ran about five percentage points less than those offered wholesalers for comparable quantities. Retailers with substantial buying power could often qualify for wholesale discounts.

For text, scholarly, and professional books, publishers' discounts to wholesalers ranged from 28 to 35 percent off of list price. Wholesalers presold to retailers and libraries at discounts of 14 to 23 percent off list price. Publishers typically offered retailers discounts of 20 to 23 percent off list. Some publishers offered standing order plans through which retailers could obtain discounts of 30 percent under limited conditions. Most publishers of text, scholarly, and professional works sold to libraries at 10 percent off list price.

LIBRARIES

In 1973, more than 17,000 libraries in the United States purchased nearly $600 million worth of books. Purchases by libraries had increased very little in dollars since 1971 and, because of inflation, had decreased in real terms. A major reason for this decrease was the slackening in government expenditures for education and, in particular, for library materials.

There were four different types of libraries: public, university, school (elhi), and specialty. Table A.1 shows approximate numbers of libraries and purchases in 1973. Small public libraries and branch libraries served many recreational readers. Large public libraries were often used like academic libraries, which students and faculty relied upon

Table A.1

NUMBER AND ESTIMATED PURCHASES OF LIBRARIES, 1973

	Number (thousands)	Purchases—publishers' prices (millions)
Public library systems	7.1	$229
College and university library systems	2.7	188
School system libraries	n.a.	143
Specialized and miscellaneous libraries	7.3	36

for research purposes. Academic libraries, as well as some large public libraries, ordinarily had extensive breadth of selection in several subject areas. Special libraries were found in a variety of institutions, businesses, and even in private settings. These libraries ordinarily were stocked extensively in a particular subject area (e.g., business, engineering) because their purpose was to serve a particular group of readers with a highly specialized interest.

Almost half of total purchases by libraries came through wholesalers. Much of that business was handled on a formal bid basis. Public and elhi libraries were required to accept the lowest bid. Those "lowest bid" contracts accounted for 20 to 25 percent of the dollar volume sold to libraries. Other libraries chose suppliers on the bases of price, time of delivery, and breadth of line (i.e., ability to fulfill all the needs of a library). Academic libraries were ordinarily more demanding on nonprice considerations than other types of libraries.

For books in certain specified topic areas, or for books of particular types (e.g., specialized dictionaries), some libraries placed standing orders with wholesalers. In some instances, these standing orders, which called for automatic shipment to the library from the wholesaler of the particular type of book in question, were negotiated or bid at a specified discount off of list price.

GENERAL BOOKSTORES

In 1973-1974, there were some 9,200 retail book outlets, excluding college stores, in the United States. Of these, approximately 3,000 were considered general bookstores. The remainder included a variety of outlets whose principal business was in some commodity other than books (e.g., department stores), and some specialized bookstores (e.g., religious, antiquarian).

Retailers ordinarily earned markups of approximately 40 percent of the books they sold. Markups on some higher priced books and on mass-market paperback books could be lower, amounting to 33 percent in many cases and 20 percent in some others.

In determining what titles to stock and sell bookstore buyers relied heavily on recommendations of publishers' salespeople, coupled with information about the print size and promotion budget provided by the publisher for a title. Although most bookstores and book departments did a limited amount of local promotion, usually in newspapers, most booksellers believed that the most effective sales device was word-of-mouth. Most booksellers agreed that publicity, such as authors' appearances on widely watched television show, was far more effective in selling a book than favorable reviews in newspapers and magazines.

The traditional image of most United States bookstores as small, single proprietorships with few employees was rapidly changing. From 1958 to 1967 the number of individual and chain bookstores with annual sales of $500,000 or more increased from 41 to 142. (A chain with central ownership and purchasing was counted as one "store," even though most chains operated more than twenty individual stores.) These 142 bookstores accounted for 40 percent of bookstore sales. Industry sources traced this growth in importance primarily to the emergence of chain bookstore operations such as Waldens, B.

Dalton, and Brentanos. One of the largest and fastest-growing chains, B. Dalton Book-sellers, in 1975 operated almost 150 stores, most of which stocked 20,000–35,000 titles. Although a few specialized bookshops stocked several thousand titles in their particular areas of specialty, it was unusual for a small bookstore or the book department of a de-partment store to carry more than 5,000 titles in stock.

Because there were 350,000 hardbound titles and 100,000 paperbound titles in print, plus almost 30,000 new titles (as distinct from 10,000–12,000 new editions of existing titles) each year, retailers generally ordered only selected new titles each year, and typi-cally offered these new titles for no more than three to six months before returning un-sold copies to the publisher. An executive of one large retail chain noted that fewer than 2 percent of the titles stocked at a particular time would automatically be reordered on a continuing basis. Other titles would be stocked initially, perhaps reordered once, and then special-ordered for customers who requested them. Retailers placed initial orders with publishers, and sometimes with wholesalers. The latter were also used to fill in stock or special orders, although most special orders for customers were placed directly with publishers.

COLLEGE BOOKSTORES

In 1973 there were approximately 2,600 college bookstores located on and off campuses in the United States. College bookstores carried not only textbooks and school supplies but a variety of mass-market and quality paperback books, and frequently many other kinds of merchandise. Because markups on textbooks (and scholarly books) ranged from 20 to 23 percent, and the cost of operations of a college store averaged 23 percent of sales, college store managers sought quality paperbound books and, occasionally, mass-market paperbacks to obtain higher margins. College bookstores generally purchased text and scholarly books directly from publishers.

Although they ordered books not required for class use much in the same manner as any other retail bookstore, college bookstores followed a different pattern when ordering texts and materials to be used in classes. College stores typically had available the lists prepared by professors of required books and materials for particular courses. In addition, they knew either from the college or from past experience the likely enrollment in par-ticular courses, and could estimate the proportion of students who would purchase their texts from the college store instead of from private bookstores near the campus. As a consequence, college store managers were frequently able to order very close to the exact number of texts expected to be needed for the number of the students in the course. If course enrollments exceeded these forecasts, college bookstore managers attempted to place special orders once the class had begun.

MASS-MARKET OUTLETS

Mass-market paperback books were sold principally through magazine outlets and racks in such locations as supermarkets, drugstores, mass-merchandise outlets, and transportation terminals. Retailers received margins ranging from 28 percent to 35 percent of the retail price of mass-market paperbacks. Books with retail prices less than one dollar generally yielded margins near the upper end of the range; those with higher retail prices earned lower percentage margins. Retailers could increase margins on their entire lines by negotiating with the magazine wholesalers who typically handled mass-market paperbacks for the maximum purchase discounts and promotional and special allowances. Most retailers left to the wholesaler the selection of titles to be displayed in the racks or fixtures on their premises, once the retailer and wholesaler had agreed upon general guidelines as to the type of books desired.

OTHER SOURCES

Apart from purchasing books through retail outlets, individuals could buy directly from publishers, book clubs, or mail-order houses. Almost all individual consumers' purchases of encyclopedias and subscription reference works were made direct from the publishers' representatives, typically commission salespersons. Less than $50 million of books from other types of publishers were also sold directly by publishers' representatives. Many publishers conducted direct-mail campaigns for their own books. Professional publishers, university presses, and others who could pinpoint particular audiences for specified titles were likely to use direct mail. In contrast, book clubs and mail-order houses offered titles from a variety of publishers. Book clubs typically produced their own copies, and sold only to their members. Mail-order houses, on the other hand, typically purchased copies from publishers and sold to anyone who received their mailings, without any membership commitment. Some mail-order houses had special editions printed solely for sale through their organizations.

Industry sources estimated that 80 to 85 percent of the $45 million spent on book advertising in 1972 went for books sold primarily through mail-order channels. One major book club reported an advertising-to-sales (A/S) ratio of 6.3 percent. Typical large trade publishers' A/S ratios varied from 2 to almost 6 percent.

Exhibit A.1

UNIVERSITY OF MINNESOTA PRESS
PUBLISHERS' SALES BY CATEGORY OF BOOK, 1971–1973
(Millions of Dollars)

	1973	1972	1971
Trade publishing			
Adult hardbound	264.8	251.5	242.0
Quality paperbound[a]	86.7	79.6	69.6
Juvenile	108.6	110.9	111.1
Bibles, hymnals and religious books	124.7	117.5	108.5
Mass-market paperbacks[a]	285.9	252.8	228.8
Book clubs	262.4	240.5	229.5
Mail-order publications	221.2	198.9	194.6
Educational publishing			
Elhi	547.9	497.6	498.6
College	392.2	375.3	379.1
Standardized tests	28.8	26.5	25.3
Professional publishing			
Technical and scientific	138.4	131.8	122.3
Law, business, and other professions[b]	206.2	192.2	178.3
Medical	60.8	57.0	52.4
Subscription reference publishing	262.2	278.9	301.0
University presses	42.6	41.4	39.3
All other[c]	164.2	154.8	141.0
Total	3197.6	3007.2	2921.4

[a]The distinction between adult trade paperbacks and mass-market paperbacks depended largely on the distribution channels used. Adult trade paperbacks were distributed through the same channels, and marketed in the same manner, as hardbound adult trade books. Most adult trade paperbacks were published by houses which published hardbound trade books, or specialized in quality paperbacks. Mass-market paperbacks were distributed by wholesalers and rack jobbers to drugstores, newsstands, and the like. Many mass-market paperbacks were published in paper only, by houses that specialized in mass-market paperbacks.

[b]Approximately 75 percent were law books; slightly less than 25 percent, business; the remainder, other professions.

[c]Includes sales of unbound copies, remainders, audiovisual, and non-print products.

Source: Association of American Publishers, 1973 Industry Statistics

Exhibit A.2

UNIVERSITY OF MINNESOTA PRESS
AMERICAN BOOK TITLE OUTPUT, BY DEWEY DECIMAL SYSTEM CLASSIFICATION,
1973 AND 1972
(All Publishers Combined)

	1973	1972
Agriculture	292	286
Art	1105	1097
Biography	1369	1086
Business	615	529
Education	999	1041
Fiction	2591	2109
General works	833	802
History	869	906
Home economics	536	479
Juveniles	1834	2126
Language	325	354
Law	494	418
Literature	1249	1398
Medicine	1602	1404
Music	175	215
Philosophy and psychology	858	829
Poetry and drama	1117	883
Religion	1374	1233
Science	2268	2143
Sociology and economics	4644	4688
Sports and recreation	814	686
Technology	1112	1184
Travel	1065	972
Total[a]	28,140	26,868

[a]Total output of American publishers had ranged between 26,000 and 30,000 titles per year since the mid-1960s.

Source: Bowker Publishing Industry Trends and Statistics

Exhibit A.3

UNIVERSITY OF MINNESOTA PRESS
INCOME STATEMENTS FOR DIFFERENT TYPES OF PUBLISHERS
PERCENTAGES OF NET SALES, 1972

	Trade			Educational		Professional
	Hardbound & quality paperbound	Mass market paperbound	Book clubs	Elhi	College	
Gross Sales	116.1	165.0	113.6	103.6	119.8	118.8
Returns and Allowances	16.1	65.0	13.6	3.6	19.8	18.8
Net Sales	100.0	100.0	100.0	100.0	100.0	100.0
Cost of Sales						
• Manufacturing	38.9	31.0	24.4	34.1	30.0	24.4
• Royalties	13.9	23.0	7.0	6.9	15.8	9.4
• Unspecified	—	—	—	—	2.2	7.0
Gross Margin on Sales	43.8	46.0	68.7	65.5	61.0	59.1
Other Publishing Income	7.7	—	—	1.1	0.7	1.0
Operating Expenses						
• Editorial	5.4	1.8	—	5.6	6.1	6.2
• Production	1.7	1.3	—	1.3	1.6	2.0
• Marketing	16.6	13.7	37.3	21.9	14.0	17.8
• Fulfillment	9.7	8.7	8.2	7.3	6.8	6.5
• General and Administrative	11.8	8.6	13.1	11.2	10.7	14.1
Total Operating Expense	45.1	34.1	58.6	53.9	48.2	46.5
Net Income from Operations	6.4	11.9	10.1	12.7	13.5	13.6
Other Income (or Expense)	0.1	(1.3)	1.2	(0.2)	(0.1)	0.6
Net Income Before Taxes	6.6	10.6	11.2	12.5	13.4	14.2
Federal, State, and Local Income Taxes	3.1	n.a.	5.8	6.2	6.6	6.9
Net Income After Taxes	3.5	n.a.	5.5	6.3	6.8	7.3

Note: Operating data were not available on reference/subscription publishing

Source: AAP Statistics (mid-range figures)

Exhibit A.4

UNIVERSITY OF MINNESOTA PRESS
TOTAL SALES OF ELEMENTARY AND HIGH SCHOOL TEXTS, 1967–1973

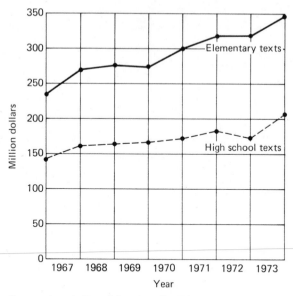

Source: Association of American Publishers

Exhibit A.5

UNIVERSITY OF MINNESOTA PRESS
ENROLLMENT IN ELEMENTARY AND HIGH SCHOOLS, 1967–1973

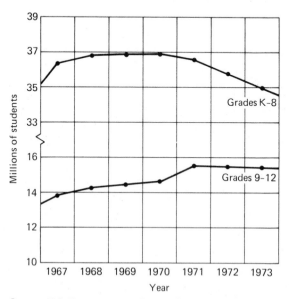

Source: U.S. Department of Health, Education, and Welfare

Exhibit A.6

UNIVERSITY OF MINNESOTA PRESS
ENROLLMENT IN POST–SECONDARY INSTITUTIONS, 1967–1973

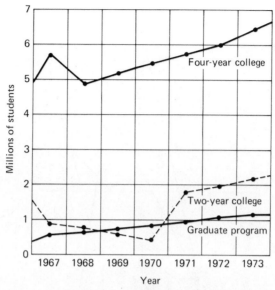

Source: U.S. Department of Health, Education and Welfare

Exhibit A.7

UNIVERSITY OF MINNESOTA PRESS
TOTAL SALES OF COLLEGE TEXTS, 1967–1973

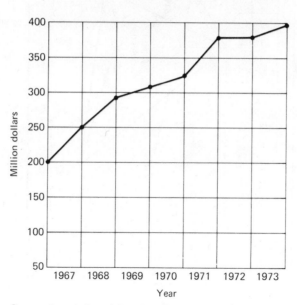

Source: Association of American Publishers

Exhibit A.8

UNIVERSITY OF MINNESOTA PRESS
GENERALIZED BOOK DISTRIBUTION STRUCTURE, 1973
(All figures in publishers' prices. Dollars in millions.)

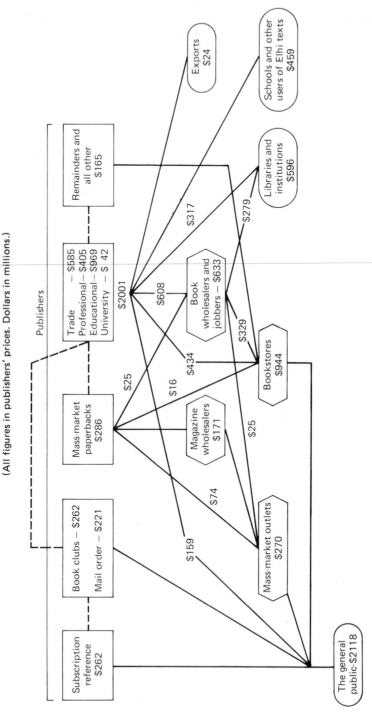

Source: Estimates made from AAP Statistics
Note: Transactions among institutions labeled "Publishers" have been eliminated to simplify and to avoid double-counting. Effects of transfers among publishers have been estimated and included in flows from publishers.

SHAPING THE PRODUCT-MARKET PORTFOLIO

THE PRODUCT-MARKET PORTFOLIO

The preceding cases described situations in which managers were making decisions about modifying individual products or product lines. This section concerns itself with modifications and management of an organization's entire set of products and markets. This set is frequently referred to as a "portfolio" because it represents a collection of investments in product expertise and market position.

The approach used here borrows heavily from analysis of financial portfolios which consist of negotiable securities such as stocks and bonds. Financial portfolio management typically takes as its objective the maximizing of return (yield) for any specified level of risk (variability of return, or uncertainty of return), or the minimizing of risk for any specified level of return. Financial portfolio analysis recognizes two types of risk: (1) market risk, the variability of returns from all investments considered together; and (2) portfolio risk, the return of a subset of investments in comparison with the return from all investments. To manage portfolio risk, financial analysts often include in portfolios investments whose returns have historically varied inversely with one another, in order to smooth the stream of cash flows from the portfolio. (For a discussion of financial portfolio analysis, upon which portfolio analysis in product policy is based, the following references may be useful:

1. *The Stock Market: Theories and Evidence,* James H. Lorie and Mary T. Hamilton, Homewood, Ill.: Richard D. Irwin, 1973.

2. *Portfolio Selection,* Harry M. Markowitz, New Haven, Conn.: Yale University Press, 1970.

3. *Portfolio Theory and Capital Markets,* William F. Sharpe, New York: McGraw-Hill Book Company, 1970.)

Product portfolio analysis employs the concepts of return and risk from financial portfolio analysis, but deals only with portfolio risk, because no single organization could conceivably hold but a small number of investments in potential products, services, and markets. Product portfolio analysis recognizes the interdependence in variation of return among sets of investments, but product portfolio analysts are more likely to forecast these joint variations directly than to rely upon historical data.

As an example of how portfolio analysis helps one to choose among investments, consider an organization which has funds available for two investments among a set of six. For simplicity, assume that the set is comprised of three types of investments, two of each of which are available, and that all six have the same cost. The first type of investment, A, has an expected return of $80,000 with a probable range of returns from $70,000 to $100,000; in other words, it has a limited downside risk and significant upside potential. The second type, B, is expected to return $80,000 with a probable range of $75,000 to $85,000; it offers a predictable return, though limited in potential. The third type, C, has an expected return of $90,000 but that return may range from $40,000 to $120,000; type C typifies a high return, high uncertainty (risk) investment. Assume further that return from A and C vary inversely, i.e., circumstances favoring high returns for A produce low returns for C, and vice-versa. With available funds the organization could invest in any of the combinations whose returns and ranges of returns are listed in Table 1. From analysis of individual investment opportunities alone, it is not immediately clear what combination constitutes the best portfolio. The choice problem may be simplified by application of portfolio theory: for equal returns, the combination with lowest variability is preferable. Alternative combinations AB, 2A, and 2B all have expected returns of $160,000, but 2B has the smallest variability—$20,000—so it is preferred to the other two. Similarly, AC and BC each have expected returns of $170,000 but AC has lower variability than BC; AC is therefore preferable [because returns from A and C vary inversely; if their returns varied directly, the range of returns, $110,000 ($70,000 for A and $40,000 for C) to $220,000 ($100,000 for A and $120,000 for C) would have exceeded the range for BC, and thus reversed the preference for AC]. Note that portfolio analysis considers only the total range around the expected return, and does not differentiate between downside loss and upside opportunity.

Table 1

Portfolio alternative	Expected return (000)	Variability of return (000) Low		High	Range (000)
AB	$160	$145	–	$185	$ 40
AC	170	140	–	190	50
BC	170	115	–	205	90
2A	160	140	–	200	60
2B	160	150	–	170	20
2C	180	180	–	240	160

The choice now comes down to the three combinations listed in Table 2. Investors or managers interested in a relatively "safe and sure" return would choose portfolio 2B; those willing to accept the chance of a return significantly lower than expected in the hope of gaining a return much higher than expected would choose 2C. Other investors or managers might compromise on an AC portfolio.

Table 2

Portfolio alternative	Expected return (000)	Variability of return (000) Low		High	Range (000)
2B	$160	$150	–	$170	$ 20
AC	170	140	–	190	50
2C	180	80	–	240	160

Portfolio analysis, then, can help sharpen the focus of investment decisions by narrowing the alternatives and requiring decision makers to think not only about single estimates of returns, but also about variability of those returns. Portfolio analysis helps pose in fairly precise form the trade-offs investors or managers must make between return and uncertainty. As applied to product policy, portfolio analysis offers an approach to the fundamental issue of product policy—"What product lines should the organization offer?"—sometimes stated in more general terms as, "What businesses (activities) should the organization engage in?" The central question in portfolio analysis in product policy is, "What investments in product lines and markets are to be included in (or excluded from) the portfolio, and how are the organization's resources to be allocated among those investments?"

Describing the Portfolio

It is often convenient to visualize an organization's portfolio of product lines and markets in a "product-market matrix" in which product lines are listed from top to bottom along the left-hand margins and markets arrayed along the top. The matrix shown in Table 3 is an abridged version of one used by corporate planners at Missouri Mills' Commercial Division in analyzing their portfolio.

In this illustration, the division's present business is included in the upper left portion of the matrix. The proposed expansion into the frozen bakery products business envisions addition of some new products to present markets (frozen dough and frozen prebaked products to the food service market), but primarily represents a venture into products and markets new to the division. The consumer market is, however, presently served by Missouri Mills' Consumer Division. In developing a product-market matrix, markets may be described on a wide variety of dimensions, including type of customer, purchasing pattern, or use or application of a product.

An organization's portfolio may be described in terms more precise than "product line" or "market." An organization may offer products and services based on different technologies, which themselves constitute the organization's competitive advantage. In such a case, it may be more useful to think of the portfolio in terms of a set of technologies than a set of product lines.

Table 3

MISSOURI MILLS COMMERCIAL DIVISION PRODUCT/MARKET MATRIX

		Markets			
		Present		New	
Product		Wholesale bakeries	Food service	Supermarket bake-offs	Consumer
Present products	Bulk flour	present line	present line		
	Bakery mixes and equipment	present line	present line		
	Food service packages of flour and mix		present line		
	Frozen chicken		present line		
New products	Refrigerated dough products	(Division planners considered the markets for refrigerated products too difficult to penetrate.)			
	Frozen dough products		prospective addition	prospective addition	prospective addition
	Frozen pre-baked products		prospective addition	prospective addition	prospective addition

Firms whose brands are highly visible and which command loyalty among customers may find it more helpful to think of their portfolios as sets of brands than as sets of product lines. Brands may be used as vehicles to enter new businesses. Smucker based its entry into the ketchup market in part on the acceptance of its brand name in jams and jellies. Toro used its acceptance as a brand in lawn care to enter the snow-removal equipment business.

In some instances, it may be appropriate to consider individual customers, rather than markets, as investments. For example, in industrial purchasing an established and satisfactory relationship between the buying organization and the selling firm may itself be considered an asset capable of producing a stream of revenues in the future. In such an instance, managers might ask, "How might we extend our product lines to capitalize on this relationship?" Apart from adding product lines, a marketer might attempt to increase the yield from customers in his or her portfolio by attracting a greater share of their purchases or by helping them to grow so that their purchases would increase. Utilities which do not face loss of customers to competition may take this latter approach.

Markets may also be defined in terms of channels of distribution. A particularly strong network of distributors may enhance the revenue-producing capability of a manufacturing organization through enabling the manufacturer to add product lines for which he or she could not otherwise have obtained adequate distribution. (In this same circumstance, however, the manufacturer might be foreclosed from such expansion because distributors with established sources of supply would be reluctant to switch suppliers.)

Return and Risk in the Portfolio An organization's investments in product lines and markets may be measured in terms of their return and risk characteristics, in a manner similar to that employed for the analysis of financial portfolios.

Return: Return is simply the yield from the investments in the organization's portfolio. Return is typically measured in net cash flow (NCF), adjusted for the timing of outflows and inflows of funds. Return may also be expressed in relation to the amount of resources employed, i.e., return on investment (ROI), return on assets (ROA), return on capital employed (ROCE). In businesses in which fixed relationships exist between the resource base and sales, return on sales (typically expressed terms of gross margin, direct profit contribution, or net profit divided by net sales) may be used as a proxy measure. Other proxy measures may include percentage market share, or number or percentage of buying points held by the firm in a particular field.

Risk: Risk refers to the uncertainty about the level of return. A low-risk product line is one whose return is virtually certain to fall within a narrow specifiable range. A high-risk, or high-uncertainty, product line is one whose return may fall within a wide range around an average or expected value, or around a point estimate. In the context of portfolio analysis, "risk" takes on both its everyday meaning of a return below a specified level and the additional meaning of a return above a specified level.

Variability in return is by no means always evenly or normally distributed around the average or midpoint value of the return from a particular investment. In many cases, the historical or forecast variability will be skewed to the right or the left. In some cases, the distribution around the average is nearly flat; it is almost as likely that the investment will yield (or has yielded) returns much higher or much lower than the average or point estimate as it is that the expected return will be realized. Ordinarily the possibility of high return is associated with substantial (or high) risk. Lower returns, on the other hand, are more frequently associated with less variability, and variability distributed rather closely around the expected return. Because investors differ in their willingness to take these different types of risk, a thorough definition of risk includes not just a measure of amount of variability, but also of the distribution of that variability.

Variability or uncertainty of return may be caused by several factors, acting singly or in combination. A partial list of such factors includes the following:

- fluctuations in the business cycle, or economic conditions
- changes in social, political, or legal constraints/influences on business activity
- changes in technology
- changes in consumers' preferences, fashion trends
- changes in availability of resellers, including shelf space in self-selection outlets, accessibility of outlets through selling personnel

- changes in competitors' activities
- changes in costs, including costs of product and marketing costs.

Some firms have experience in dealing with certain of these causes (often termed types of risk), and encounter relatively little variation in level of return. Organizations without such experience typically experience relatively wide variations in return levels until they learn how to manage the particular type of risk.

Relationships among Investments   Because the level and variability of return of product lines and markets in the portfolio may be interdependent, portfolio analysis examines various combinations of product lines and markets, rather than simply analyzing individual investments. Three of the most frequently observed types of interdependence include interdependent demand, shared facilities, and environmental factors whose impact differs among product lines or markets.

Demand: Demand interactions may exist among product lines within the portfolio just as they may exist among individual products within a line. In cases in which demand among lines is complementary, the profitability of each may be greater than that of either one if it alone were included in the portfolio. For example, a marketing consulting firm added financial analysis and consulting services to its offering, and found that the new line enabled it to increase substantially the number of clients it served with marketing consultation. The financial consulting services, originally added as a convenience to existing clients, became a profitable activity in their own right, despite the presence of established competitors in the market.

When demand among product lines is competitive, i.e., when customers will buy only one of several product lines, then the several product lines must be analyzed together to develop estimates of sales, expenses, and profitability. Existence of a competitive demand interaction is not always obvious. For example, a small snowmobile manufacturer whose executives were looking for a product to sell in summer decided that importing motorcycles offered an attractive opportunity. Upon analyzing the likely consumer group, however, the manufacturer discovered that the set of potential buyers for its motorcycles would very likely overlap substantially the set of buyers for its snowmobiles, and that consumers within the set could afford only one of the two products. The company thereupon ceased exploring the motorcycle market, despite its apparent attractiveness at the time.

Facilities: Opportunities to share facilities may make apparently unattractive ventures appropriate for a portfolio. The acquisitions staff of a conglomerate company planned to acquire a small manufacturer of playground equipment whose inventory was built during the winter and peaked in spring. The playground manufacturer's production facilities were largely idle mid-spring to mid-fall. Nevertheless, the acquisition appeared attractive until conglomerate personnel realized that production workers at the prospective acquisition would be covered under a union contract which committed the conglomerate to a level of annual wages considerably higher than the playground manufacturer had paid. At that higher cost level, the acquisition appeared unlikely to run at a profit. The conglomerate discontinued negotiations with the playground equipment manufacturer until a member of the acquisition staff discovered that a manufacturer of fireplace equipment, also a prospective acquisition, could use the playground equipment production facilities during the summer. A cost analysis based on the two lines' sharing production facilities and work force indicated that the combined operation would be profitable. The conglomerate thereupon proceeded to acquire both companies. As it turned out, production costs behaved as expected and the joint operation smoothed cash flows. (Unforeseen, however, were the need to add marketing personnel, and difficulties in integrating the selling activities for both lines.)

Environment: Environmental factors, one of the most visible of which is the business cycle, may have different effects on individual product lines. A manufacturer of equipment used for quality control decided against dropping a low-priced line of components which it feared was drawing sales away from its principal line of premium instruments and systems. Market analyses revealed that in two important markets, when the business cycle, as reflected by leading economic indicators, was rising, customers purchased the premium line, and didn't even consider the low-priced components. But shortly after leading indicators headed downward, customers restricted their spending and sales of the premium line dropped dramatically. At such times, company salespeople succeeded in selling many customers components to augment their existing equipment or to keep it serviceable until funds for replacement equipment became available.

Modifying the Portfolio

There are three principal methods for modifying an organization's portfolio: adding new product lines and markets, dropping existing product lines and markets, and reallocating organizational resources among product lines and markets. Decisions to add and remove investments and to reallocate resources within an organization's portfolio influence the design of that portfolio. Historically most organizations' portfolios have evolved as a result of these individual decisions. Once managers have some experience with these individual decisions to add, drop, and reallocate, they are better able to evaluate the organization's entire portfolio as a basis for determining the fate of individual proposals. The text and cases in this section, therefore, begin with analysis of individual projects proposed for addition to the portfolio, move to decisions that involve multiple product lines and markets already included within the portfolio, and conclude with portfolio design.

SELECTED REFERENCES

BURGER, PHILIP C. "A Marketing Model for Selecting Among Interdependent New Product Candidates." Paper presented at the Product Development and Management Association Conference in Chicago, November 1977.

BURSK, EDWARD C. "View Your Customers as Investments." *Harvard Business Review,* May–June 1966.

DAY, GEORGE S. "Diagnosing the Product Portfolio." *Journal of Marketing,* April 1977.

LORIE, JAMES H., and MARY T. HAMILTON. *The Stock Market: Theories and Evidence.* Homewood, Ill.: Richard D. Irwin, 1973.

MARKOWITZ, HARRY M. *Portfolio Selection.* New Haven Conn.: Yale University Press, 1970.

SHARPE, WILLIAM F. *Portfolio Theory and Capital Markets.* New York: McGraw-Hill, 1970.

WIND, YORAM. *Product Policy.* Reading, Mass.: Addison-Wesley, in press.

ADDING INVESTMENTS TO THE PORTFOLIO

The Role of New Ventures

New ventures are ordinarily expected to enrich the forecast total yield of a portfolio within acceptable levels of risk and/or to reduce total portfolio risk (or variability of return) for specified levels of return. The enrichment of yield may be measured in terms of sales or dollar profits and/or in terms of increased productivity of resources, e.g., return on investment. New businesses may be added to the portfolio not only because of their own return/risk characteristics, but also because of their contribution toward an optimum portfolio for the organization.

In the context of this discussion, "new ventures" mean businesses, product lines, or programs entirely new to the organizations planning to offer them, rather than extensions of current product lines or activities, which ventures require significant commitments of organizational resources. In this sense, Pillsbury's entry into the wine business through the acquisition of Sourverain Wines represented a new venture; that company's addition of a line of bundt cake mixes, an extension of current activities. Ventures new to a particular organization may be new to the market (hand calculators in the late 1960s) or already known (General Mills' addition of toys in the 1960s).

Higher Return   Most new ventures are undertaken when managers foresee that opportunities in proposed product lines or markets will yield higher earnings than those available from present product lines or markets. In many instances, the search for such opportunities is stimulated by organizational commitments to growth. Many organizations set sales, profit, and return-on-investment goals higher than historic levels and look to three sources to attain those goals: (1) price increases on current unit volume; (2) increases in unit volume of present products, through growth in primary demand and/or market penetration; and (3) new ventures, which are often expected to fill the gap between stated objectives and gains expected from increases in price and volume of present lines. This practice of goal setting may be based on historical achievement or may reflect a target that is difficult to attain. In the latter case, especially, the pressure to introduce new ventures often becomes intense, and may result in an organization's bringing to market product lines that are not fully developed or, in fact, ought not to have been commercialized at all.

Lower Risk   New ventures may reduce risk in a portfolio by reducing variability of returns. Many organizations attempt to reduce variability of returns through diversification, so that adverse circumstances such as a poor harvest would affect only a portion of the portfolio. Conversely, highly favorable returns in a particular line of business would benefit only a portion of the portfolio. Diversification, then, may be intended to keep returns within an acceptable range, through limiting exposure of the portfolio to any set of environmental factors. Some management groups follow this reduced-exposure approach to the point of refusing to commit themselves to any venture that involves more than a certain percentage of a particular organization's resource base.

Organizations often attempt to reduce variability of returns by seeking new ventures that will help to balance cash flows, production levels, and the like. An organization heavily involved with seasonal products or product lines that vary widely with changes in business conditions may seek contra-seasonal or contra-cyclical ventures to reduce variability of returns, even though these new ventures may promise returns no higher than those from the organization's present lines.

Other Strategic Roles   An organization may undertake new ventures as a preemptive competitive strategy by introducing a product line broader than that which the market can initially be expected to support or by introducing multiple brands in order to forestall entry by competitors. This strategy also may have the effect of enabling the organization to keep pace with the growth of an emerging market.

New ventures may play a defensive role in the portfolio. Organizations occasionally add product lines which themselves appear unlikely to enrich yield, but are considered necessary to avert loss of business in other product lines or to meet competitive threats. Occasionally, organizations enter new businesses in order to gain information to enrich the yield of an existing business. As one example, a manufacturer of soft goods acquired a small chain of leased departments in discount houses to keep itself alert to fashion changes and retailers' needs. Finally, new ventures may be added to support an organization's overall marketing strategy, even though the ventures themselves appear unlikely to enhance the yield of the total portfolio in the immediate future.

No matter what the strategic reason for undertaking new ventures, such ventures may help enhance the value of the portfolio by keeping organizational resources fully employed, through utilizing funds generated from operations, or capacity in manufacturing, technical, or marketing functions which would otherwise be underemployed or diverted to marginally productive activities. Perhaps equally important is the role new ventures play in maintaining management productivity, through enhancing morale, providing new challenges for competent managers, and enabling the organization to learn new businesses.

New Ventures and Society   In recent years increased attention has been focused on the role new ventures play in the economy and in society as a whole. Economic benefits of innovation to individual firms have been recognized, and enjoy the protection of law in such forms as patents, copyrights, and trademarks, which afford firms (or individuals) opportunities to reap economic gain from the development of something unique. Some critics argue that invention and commercialization of inventions would continue whether or not legal protection were provided, and that such protection acts to reduce competition. The presumption that society benefits from innovation, through an improved standard of living, wide freedom of choice for consumers, and vigorous competition, has been challenged by some who argue that many industrialized societies have become too materialistic, and that those societies could better utilize their resources in other pursuits.

Whether one accepts these arguments or not, it must be recognized that the innovative process incurs costs of several types. First, the costs of developing new products are by no means trivial, and up to 70 percent of those costs may be expended on products whose development is curtailed before commercialization or that fail to achieve commercial success. Second, the money costs of introducing a flawed product may be substantial; these may be reflected in costs of product liability insurance and recall campaigns. Third, resellers and consumers alike are less likely to accept subsequent products from firms with a history of unsuccessful products.

Two results of the heightened concern about product safety have been much greater caution on the part of firms and much stricter regulation by government agencies. Both phenomena operate to increase costs associated with innovation and may reduce the number and novelty of innovations brought to market.

What New Ventures to Add

Although the question of what new ventures should be added to a portfolio cannot be answered definitively, portfolio analysis offers one useful approach to that question. The expected returns and variations around those expected returns, i.e., risks, appear to be related to the degree to which a proposed venture "fits" with consumers' interests, competitive offerings, legal or social constraints, and the resources of the organization itself.

The Product-Consumer Fit   In hope of obtaining high returns, organizations often seek to meet hitherto unrecognized or vaguely defined desires of consumers or to fulfill well-known interests of consumers in ways which differ substantially from competitors' existing offerings. For example, Pillsbury's (Space) Food Stick was introduced to meet a need which consumers had not precisely defined in advance, and did not copy exactly existing products in such categories as candy and snack foods. Although General Mills first introduced Bugles, Whistles, and Daisys to meet known consumer interests in snack foods, these products met consumers' interests in ways that potato chips, corn chips, pretzels, nuts, etc., did not. Today puffed, shaped snacks constitute a separate product class within the snack-food category.

Returns from *novel ventures* depend upon the extent and speed with which consumers recognize and define the interests that a new venture may meet, upon the ability of the novel offering to provide superior benefits and/or lower costs than presently used methods of meeting a particular interest, and upon the extent to which consumers must change their purchase and use patterns to obtain the advantages of the novel offering. If the need becomes clear quickly and consumers do not have to alter their behavior to obtain superior benefits, returns are likely to be substantially higher than if considerable consumer education efforts are necessary over a prolonged time period to establish the need, convince consumers of the superiority of benefits, and teach them when and how to buy and use the novel product.

The return from *entries into established product categories* depends upon how a new product line compares with competitive offerings and with consumers' interests on, among others, four dimensions: product features/customer benefits, value, purchase pattern, and use pattern. A return higher than that of established product lines may occur if the new product line offers benefits or value that are visibly superior from the consumer's point of view. But if product features, customer benefits, and value are similar to those of existing products or if benefits are unimportant or cannot be made visible to the consumer, the new venture is unlikely to earn a higher return than products already established in the category. Indeed, the new venture will likely yield lower returns than the established entries which dominate the particular market with the largest shares. A case in point is Chase Manhattan's *Familienbank* in Germany, a bank intended to provide consumer credit and services. *Familienbank* was small, entered the market later than the dominant German banks, and did not respond as quickly as competitors to lowered prices (better value) on consumer credit—a basically undifferentiated commodity which consumers could obtain from many sources. As a result, *Familienbank* incurred losses (*Business Week,* Nov. 1, 1976).

Unless consumers' purchase patterns can be simplified, e.g., by the use of more accessible and more highly utilized channels and media, returns from entries into established product categories are unlikely to exceed those prevailing in the industry. If a new venture offers greater ease of use, does not threaten an established individual or group work or use pattern, and is easy to learn to use, then returns may be greater than those for competing products. On the other hand, a new venture which is complicated to use and involves changes in work and intra-group status patterns may well yield a lower return because of the combined pressures of slow and limited consumer acceptance, and the high costs of consumer education. Many innovations in the printing industry have met this fate. New products which require new methods of use and promise noticeable but modest cost savings or quality improvements frequently encounter resistance, and are accepted only slowly. Delayed recovery of investment and high sales and sales support costs depress returns in these cases.

New ventures which essentially copy established offerings in terms of product characteristics and marketing strategy ("me-too" products) will not necessarily earn the same returns that the established offerings have enjoyed. A "me-too" entry by a powerful firm may divide a market so that both original and new participants earn lower returns. The cost of entering and competing in an established market may result in a smaller market share and consequently lower returns for the late entrant, compared with established firms. Some markets may simply be too small to support an additional entrant, who may find earnings inadequate and therefore withdraw. A "me-too" product is most likely to gain significant market share and concomitant high return in a growing market in which it faces a small number of competitors whose resources (in that market) the new entrant can match or exceed. If the "me-too" entrant can hold only a small share of the market— a typical outcome—its returns will very likely be less than those enjoyed by that dominant competitor.

To estimate the returns a novel product or a new entry into an established product category will earn, precise identification of target markets and thorough analysis of behavior of consumers in those target markets is essential. Managers involved in decisions on new ventures must take the time needed for careful and deliberate analysis and should seek appropriate marketing research data when necessary to facilitate their analyses.

The Product-Competition Fit   The discussion has to this point ignored explicit effects of competitive retaliation upon return. Competitive retaliation acts to lower forecast returns. Its effect depends upon (1) the probability that competitors will react to a challenge and (2) the resources of the challenger vis-à-vis established firms. Retaliation may be expected from firms which have a history of reacting sharply to threats to their market positions and from firms which (history aside) expect the new venture to appeal to their consumers and thus hurt their sales, market share, and profits. Established firms which are small and which face a challenge from a very large organization may, however, elect not to meet the challenge directly. Retaliation may be less likely in a rapidly growing market, in which new entrants may take share points while established competitors nonetheless continue to gain in sales.

If established firms react directly to a challenge, the outcome of such retaliation depends in large part on the technical, marketing, and financial resources of the challenger vis-à-vis those of the established firms. If the new offering is protected by a patent, or supported by proprietary technical knowledge and expertise; if the firm making the new offering has an adequate and appropriate base of channels and customers; and if the firm has adequate funds available to meet competitors' responses, then competitive retaliation may depress returns only in the short run. Without such support capability, however, the new offering may be knocked out of the marketplace by established competitors. Competitive retaliation may take the form of new product development, price cutting, incentives to distributors and salespeople, or substantial advertising and sales promotion, singly or in combination. The costs of establishing a new venture against determined and well-financed competitors may exceed what an organization is willing to commit to a venture. To avoid having later to commit more resources than they wish, or to withdraw the venture, prudent managers attempt to forecast the probability and magnitude of competitors' responses to new ventures before committing themselves to commercialization of a new venture.

The Fit with Legal and Social Constraints   For either novel ventures or for familiar products, variability of return is likely to be directly related to the probability that the proposed venture will encounter resistance from regulatory agencies, consumer activists, or other groups or individuals who may be concerned with the proposed venture. Organizations attempting to build amusement parks, shopping centers, marinas, hotels, or apartments must file a variety of environmental-impact statements, frequently expose the proposal to extensive hearings, and often modify plans on the basis of official and organized informal reaction.

The Product-Company Fit   The degree of fit between the proposed new venture and the organization's present resources and capabilities may affect both variability of return and the return itself. For any level of return, the closer the fit of the new venture with the organization's present capabilities, the lower the variability. (If the resource requirements of a proposed new venture were to fit perfectly in type and capacity with the organization's existing resource base the venture would be more appropriately defined as an extension of the present business.) The less close the fit of the new venture with the organization's present resource base, the more complicated—and costly—is likely to be the task of integrating it completely into the organization's current operation, and the more likely the venture is to incur losses. For example, Gillette, long successful as a marketer of personal-care items through health-and-beauty product outlets, has to date experienced two failures in consumer electronics—pocket calculators and digital watches—in large part because the company lacks technical expertise and supply capability in that field. In situations in which companies try to forestall the probability of low return because of a lack of fit, attempts to add capability or to change the capabilities of the organization itself to meet the requirements of a new venture are quite likely to lead to increased variability of returns or losses associated with that venture.

A close fit between a proposed new venture into an industry new to the firm and the firm's existing resources may lead to a higher level of return than that earned by established competitors in the industry entered, provided that the firm can bring to bear resources and expertise not presently available in that industry. It is not uncommon, for example, for relatively large firms to expect that their managerial and financial resources can produce earnings higher than the average for an industry populated by many small manufacturers. Nevertheless, those expectations are by no means always fulfilled. More than one conglomerate has found its ventures into the housing business—dominated by small, local builders—far less successful than expected.

Dimensions of the Product-Company Fit   The fit of a new venture with the organization which offers it may vary with respect to each of several types of resources: marketing, manufacturing, technical, financial, and management.

1. *Marketing:* The relationship of a new venture with the product lines, markets, and marketing programs presently employed by an organization may have a significant impact on the return that new venture is likely to earn. If the new venture is comprised of products whose demand is complementary to that of the present product lines offered by the organization, then one might expect a higher level of return both on the new venture itself and on the total portfolio. In contrast, if the new venture includes products which are competitive with the existing product line, the total return for the portfolio may decrease and the new venture itself may, but will not necessarily, generate lower earnings than if this competition did not occur.

The duration of the life cycle of the typical product line within the firm may also affect the return earned by a new venture. If the organization is involved with many short life cycle product lines, managers are likely to be engaged in product-line planning, as distinct from planning for individual products, on a regular basis; managers will likely be highly sensitive to marketplace conditions and be able to respond promptly, in part because their technical colleagues will likely be working one step ahead of the products currently in the marketplace. In contrast, those firms that handle product lines whose life cycles are relatively long are more likely to be engaged in the planning for individual products than whole product lines, are likely to make more measured responses to marketplace conditions, and are likely to have an R & D staff accustomed to working with fairly long lead times. The addition to either type of firm of a venture with characteristics opposite to those possessed by the firm is likely to lead to a lower return than that earned by firms whose characteristics match the requirements of the new venture.

The addition of a new venture that requires a different level of value added from that with which the organization is experienced is likely to result in a lower return for that new venture than would have been the case had the new venture been added by a firm with appropriate value-added capabilities. Firms that attempt to increase their yield by bringing forth new ventures that have greater value-added content than their typical products may encounter disappointing and variable returns for some time.

The fit between a new venture and the manner in which an organization customarily develops and markets new product lines may affect return and variability of return for that venture. Four distinct approaches to innovation may be identified: (1) "first to market"–strong research, technical leadership, willingness to take risks; (2) "follow the leader"–strong development resources and marketing capabilities (a firm of this nature could capitalize on the strategy Levitt described as "innovative imitation"); (3) "application engineering"–a strong application engineering section and an ability to serve well-defined segments of the market; (4) "me too"–a strong, cost-efficient manufacturing capability and low-cost marketing operations. The addition of a venture that differs from the capabilities of the firm as described by these different approaches is likely to lead to a return lower than that earned by competitors. A "me-too" firm offering a "first-to-market" venture may have an opportunity to enrich its own yield, but that opportunity will likely be associated with significant variability of return–or even loss–because the new venture will likely require different technical, manufacturing, and marketing skills from those possessed by the firm. A manufacturer of standard industrial clamps, which had consistently copied its competitors' product changes, attempted to introduce a new fastener it had developed. Because the firm lacked the technical support needed to modify the new device to market requirements, and because salespeople had been little more than "order-takers" for years, the company could not gain market penetration with the new fastener. A competitor ultimately developed a similar device and marketed it successfully.

If a new venture is positioned against markets not presently served by the organization, the organization may either have to establish a new division to handle the new markets and marketing programs or change its present marketing activities. Furthermore, some marketing organizations are large and follow standard procedures which permit them to dominate effectively the markets in which they are involved. Other organizations are smaller and capitalize on their ability to respond quickly and to be more flexible in the marketplace. The addition of a new venture which requires a type of marketing support different from that provided for the organization's present product lines may result in the venture's generating returns below those on the organization's existing lines, either because the organization's present marketing capability cannot successfully adapt to the requirements of the new venture, or because the lack of fit is so dramatic that an entirely new division with its attendant high costs must be established.

2. *Manufacturing:* New ventures may fit (or not fit) with a company's existing manufacturing resources on at least three dimensions: plant size and configuration, labor pool and supervision, and raw materials acquisition. Some organizations are set up with large manufacturing plants to make standard products, long runs of which may be highly profitable; in such a configuration, short runs of customized products can be very costly. In contrast, other companies are set up with small, flexible plants which can easily handle custom products in shorter runs. These plants are generally less profitable on longer runs than the larger, more standardized configurations. It follows that the addition of a venture with requirements opposite to those for which a manufacturing establishment is geared is quite likely to result in a lower return than that of competitors whose plants are more appropriate for the product line, or than other product lines manufactured by the firm itself.

Of greater importance in many instances than physical facilities themselves is the experience of the manufacturing labor force and supervisory personnel. Many plant managers find it extremely difficult to introduce into an organization a new venture that requires skills or quality levels markedly different from established product lines without jeopardizing the existing lines. Attempting to mix different quality levels or different quality-control and precision requirements is likely to reduce return on a venture either through "overbuilding" a simple new product line in a plant set up for complex, premium-quality products or by cheapening a premium product through adding it to a work and supervisory force accustomed to mass production of products whose configurations are not complex, nor tolerances critical.

In the acquisition of raw materials, knowledge of markets and access to critical materials may be very important. In such cases, the lack of such knowledge and access may lead to a lower return, or to increased variability associated with returns from a new venture.

3. *Technical:* The amount and nature of technical support required by the new venture may also impact its profitability. The addition of a new venture that requires substantial development but very little research input may not utilize fully the facilities and skills of a research-oriented (as distinct from a development-oriented) technical staff, although the new venture will likely have to bear the overhead charges associated with the research-oriented environment. Similarly, the addition to a development-oriented firm of a new venture that requires significant basic research to become successful or to be maintained

in the marketplace will face a problem simply because the required resources will have to be purchased somewhere else or foregone entirely. In either of these situations, if the new venture requires technical support different from the type the firm is capable of providing, the venture is likely to earn a return lower than that of successful competitors, and perhaps lower than the average for the firm itself. The return is likely to increase only when the venture becomes large enough to support its own autonomous technical group.

4. *Financial:* The fit between the requirements of a new venture and the financial resources of an organization may be summarized in the size and cyclicality of the net cash flows typically managed by the firm vis-à-vis those required by the new venture. If the new venture imposes larger requirements in size than are typical for the company, and/or if the new venture has associated with it a highly cyclical pattern of cash flows, then the return from that venture may well be lower than others in the organization's portfolio, or the return may be associated with higher levels of variability.

5. *Management:* If the amount of cooperation needed among technical, manufacturing, and marketing personnel within an organization is substantial for most ventures, the organization may employ project teams for new ventures. If the coordination ordinarily needed is minimal, functional specialists may provide all the managerial and technical skill that is necessary. The addition of a venture with requirements for project teams to an organization set up on functional specialty lines could well result in a loss or a very low return. The addition to an organization set up on project team lines of a venture that did not require close coordination might lead to a lower return simply because of the unnecessarily high costs that would be incurred.

A general management group may find that particular new ventures will require them to handle problems with which they have limited experience, to cope with market and competitive conditions new to them, and to learn to manage new types of interpersonal relationships—both formal and informal—inside and outside of the organization. For example, many executives who have been involved in acquisitions of firms in unfamiliar businesses report that learning to relate to individuals whose behavior patterns or management styles differ substantially from their own is not an easy task, and may require considerable amounts of their time and energy.

In general, the less close the "fit" of a proposed new venture with a company's ongoing activities, the more difficult the task of predicting and controlling the variation around the expected return. In other words, the less closely the venture fits with present activities, the greater the risk.

Summary In sum, the maximum return on new ventures is likely to come from those that meet emerging or known consumer interests better than available products or processes, those that offer benefits demonstrably superior to competition or significantly lower prices for comparable benefit packages, and those whose requirements fit closely with the resources and capabilities of the present organization. For any specified level of return, variability or risk should be lowest for those ventures that meet recognized consumer needs and require no changes in purchase or use behavior, that competitors are unwilling or unable to counterattack successfully, and that have resource requirements that match closely the available resources of the organization.

Managing the Innovative Process

Once an organization plans to add new businesses to its portfolio, it must manage successfully the process of innovation, each stage of which presents its own opportunities and problems. Management of that process requires recognition of the objectives of each stage and coping with the principal blocks to successful innovation.

Stages in the Process   The process of adding a new venture to an organization's portfolio consists of several stages, frequently identified in time sequence as (1) idea generation, (2) screening, (3) development, (4) evaluation and testing, and (5) commercialization. To yield one commercially successful product, the process may have to begin with some sixty new venture ideas. Of these sixty, some five or ten receive development; half of those may survive to the evaluation and testing stage; two-thirds of these may be brought to market, where one in three will fail. Approximately half of the total dollars and three-quarters of the time expended in the innovative process for a single venture will be spent by the time that venture has passed through the evaluation and testing stage; the remainder is spent in bringing the venture to full commercial development. Of the total expenditures involved in innovation, less than half are typically devoted to plant and equipment, the most visible investment. The bulk of the remainder goes toward research and development, followed by marketing and manufacturing start-up costs. In some industries, the marketing costs overshadow other investments.

Useful though they may be for analysis, in practice these stages are by no means always distinct, and they frequently overlap. Over a period of time individuals in an organization learn what types of ideas are most likely to survive the screening process, and therefore often informally apply screening criteria to their own and their colleagues' suggestions for new ventures. Indeed, the difference between the "screening" and "evaluation" stages rests largely upon the level of detail of the analysis, because there is more to evaluate once development is under way. Many proposed new ventures will pass through more than one cycle of development and evaluation, should initial evaluation reveal the need for further development work before a definite decision on commercialization can be made. In many cases, evaluation and testing includes a test market, which may turn out to be a regional introduction or the beginning of a national introduction of the new venture. Because of the overlap among stages, it may be more fruitful to analyze the innovative process in terms of the functions or activities performed within the process: identification of new venture opportunities, development of new ventures, and analysis of prospective ventures.

Identification of new venture opportunities   The objective of this function is to generate as many potentially suitable ideas as possible for new ventures. Although this activity occurs principally as the earliest stage in the innovative process, the identification of new venture possibilities occasionally occurs in development and even in evaluation and testing stages, as technical and marketing research bring to light previously unthought-of possibilities, either for the extension of the particular new venture under consideration or for altogether different additions to the portfolio.

Investment in generation of ideas may yield a higher return than investment in screening and evaluation procedures. Failure to generate new ideas means opportunity losses ("sins of omission") for the organization. Such losses cannot readily be identified, nor can responsibility for them be easily and quickly assigned. Failure of the screening process means out-of-pocket losses ("sins of commission"), which appear as accounting losses on management reports. It is not surprising, therefore, that most organizations have developed a wide variety of screening, evaluation, and testing techniques, ranging from simple, quick, and inexpensive ones to sophisticated and costly ones, to protect themselves against adding to the portfolio a venture that will turn out not to be successful. Indeed, our management culture today, particularly as evidenced by the type of training provided in graduate curricula in business administration, emphasizes analytical skills intended to help avoid mistakes, rather than entrepreneurial skills to avoid missing opportunities. Because simple, quick, and inexpensive screening techniques are available, and because most managers are inclined to review new venture proposals skeptically, the cost of screening numerous ideas is low, and the likelihood that an idea that turns out to be a "loser" will survive the evaluation process is modest. Many firms, therefore, encourage their employees to generate ideas. Such firms typically provide some or all of their personnel with considerable freedom, encourage risk taking, and tolerate failure. In such a firm, an individual's career will not necessarily be jeopardized by his or her involvement with a venture that fails, provided that he or she has acted in a professional manner in bringing the venture into being. Many organizations employ formal techniques whose purpose it is to generate ideas for new ventures. Among these techniques are formal and periodic review of the product/market portfolio for trends that might suggest opportunities; systematic review of literature and attandance at conferences in industries and technologies outside their own; and a variety of structured and unstructured discussions with groups of technical specialists, consumers, and other groups.

Ideas for new ventures may come from many sources, including marketing personnel, manufacturing personnel, technical specialists, and corporate staff; from resellers and customers; and from senior management. One recent study found that 75 percent of the ideas for new ventures that proved to be successful were stimulated by recognition of a market opportunity or manufacturing or operational problem; fewer than one-fourth of the ideas that ultimately achieved commercial success originated from a technical finding with no market or operational focus.

Development of new ventures   The purpose of the development function is to develop for a product concept specifications, prototypes, and plans for manufacturing and to design a marketing program for that concept. Most organizations seek to perform these functions as effectively, quickly, and inexpensively as possible.

These goals of effectiveness, timing, and cost involve trade-offs, particularly in development of the physical product. If the physical product requires significant advances in technology or its application, it will likely incur substantially greater costs in time and dollars than will a project that utilizes familiar technology and applications techniques. Further, the increase in dollar costs from acceleration of the development schedule for such a project is far more rapid than for projects that employ existing knowledge. For any time and dollar budget projects that require significant technological or applications advances have a lower probability of success than do projects that rest on known technology and applications.

Nevertheless, those projects that involve significant advances are likely, if carefully screened, to have a greater probability of commercial success than projects that depend on current knowledge. This observation implies that there exists another trade-off, between a high probability of commercial success and a lower probability of technical success and/or higher development costs, on the one hand, and a lower probability of commercial success but a higher probability of technical success and/or lower development costs, on the other. An organization with some confidence in its ability to estimate probable returns and risks (i. e., variability of returns) could attempt to balance its research and development portfolio between high technical/low market risk and low technical/high market risk projects.

Although sizable overruns in time and dollar costs are particularly likely to occur in projects that involve extending the state of the art in a particular technology, overruns appear to be a widespread phenomenon among development projects. Dollar cost overruns may range from 20 percent to 100 percent or even more; time overruns, from one-third to three times the initial forecast. The magnitude of overrun depends not only on the technical difficulty of the project, but also on the degree of coordination required and obtained among personnel in development, marketing, and manufacturing. As a general rule, the closer the coordination among these (and other) departments, the lower the overruns in time and dollars. A principal cause of cost overruns, or their alternate— meeting the time and dollar budget but with a marginally suitable product—is a lack of coordination between marketing and technical personnel. Frequently, a product concept which appears to have favorable commercial prospects simply cannot be manufactured feasibly within the initial cost constraints imposed by the price or value statement embodied in the concept. In such instances, either the physical characteristics or the price of the proposed new offering must be revised. If technical personnel make a revision that will in fact reposition the offering, marketing personnel are faced with either demanding that technical work be redone or with attempting to develop a new program consistent with the new position. In either case, development time and costs will increase. The process operates in reverse, too: If marketing personnel fail to communicate very precisely to technical personnel subtle changes in positioning or other portions of the marketing program, technical specialists will have to press for marketing changes or redo technical work. Physical products that differ from the promises conveyed through positioning and advertising ordinarily fare poorly.

Complete alternative marketing programs include specification for product and price policies and for marketing communications and distribution. Product policy will specify position of the offering, including amount and type of value added; physical characteristics; package; brand; breadth of product line; and composition of the proposed new line. Price policy will include statements of objectives for pricing, e.g., skimming vs. penetration; estimates of elasticity of demand with respect to price for both primary and selective demand; and cost and margin requirements. Marketing communications plans will specify, for advertising, the objective, budget, message (copy platform), media, and schedule; for sales promotion, objectives, budget, types of direct activities (trade shows, etc.) and of reseller support activities; for personal selling, objectives, budget, amounts of each of several types of sales activity (canvassing, taking inventory, etc.), types of personnel required, training, compensation, and management. Distribution plans will specify the type and number of outlets at retail and wholesale (if appropriate) levels, the functions they are to perform, and the incentives and management attention required. These alternative programs will among them include different levels of spending and types of activities for each probable environment a particular new venture configuration may face.

The timing of these various marketing activities is important at two levels. The first is when to launch the new venture—at what stage of consumer acceptance, competitive activity and refinement of the physical product and marketing plan. The second involves timing internal to the marketing plan itself. For example, carefully executed marketing programs for consumer package goods ordinarily include provision for assuring that the distribution channels are stocked before intensive consumer promotion begins so that costly media advertising does not draw consumers to empty stores.

To develop marketing programs, most marketers find it useful to outline the process by which particular segments of consumers are likely to purchase and use specific new offerings, and then to develop programs to adapt to or influence that process.

Evaluation and testing of prospective new ventures   The principal objective of the evaluation and testing function is to stop the flow of resources into prospective ventures that are unlikely to meet the organization's criteria for inclusion in its portfolio, and to block the flow as early in the innovative process as possible. Another objective of this function is to refine and revise the new offering so that it enriches the portfolio as much as possible. Most organizations emphasize the first objective—meeting minimum acceptable standards—more than the second—maximizing return on selected criteria.

For most new ventures for large organizations, the criteria are primarily financial and involve the concept of return on capital. Although the definitions of "return" and "capital" vary from organization to organization, most careful evaluators will compare the cash outflows required by the venture to the cash inflows expected from it, appropriately adjusted for differences in the time value of money.

Evaluators to an increasing extent seek ranges or probability distributions of estimates of cash flows, together with explicit statements about the causes for variation within those ranges. To identify clearly principal uncertainties and alternative courses of action, organizations may use such devices as payoff matrices and decision trees.

The criteria used to determine the suitability of a prospective addition to the portfolio, together with factors such as demand, competition, and resource requirements thought to influence performance on the ultimate financial criteria, are often embodied in a checklist or weighted rating sheet which evaluators review. In some organizations, these devices are incorporated into computer simulations which managers may use to evaluate prospective additions to the portfolio.

Whether simple or sophisticated, all these evaluation methods depend upon data about the market, the resources required by the prospective venture, and the response of consumers and competitors to the prospective addition.

The Market Typically, market data for a proposed new venture include forecasts of primary demand, competition, technology, and channel structure. Estimation of relevant primary demand requires rather precise definition and measurement of market segments considered appropriate for the venture under analysis. These definitions and measurements generally become more precise as the evaluation process advances, partly because analysts learn to make discriminations of which they were previously unaware, and partly because more precise knowledge of the physical product and marketing program helps to refine definitions and measurements of appropriate target markets or segments. Estimation of primary demand typically relies on secondary sources, such as government or industry association statistics, supplemented with survey data and, in some instances, interview data. Some of these same sources may be used to develop forecasts of competitive strength and weakness.

Forecasts of the competitive environment require prediction of the number of competitors who are likely to remain permanently in the business. In most industries, by no means all of the firms that initially participate remain after the middle of the growth phase. Managers attempting to forecast their own positions after a "shakeout" occurs must estimate the time advantage they have over competitors, because of holding a patent, possessing proprietary (but not necessarily patentable) knowledge and skill, or having a lead in the time necessary to assemble physical and human resources required for the venture. A time advantage may be important in enabling the innovating organization to make and profit from mistakes before others can capitalize upon them and to gain a secure position with resellers and consumers before competitive threats arise. Managers must also estimate their rivals' interests in the particular venture and their abilities to respond by redirecting their own resources. A small manufacturer entering a precisely defined segment of a market dominated by very large organizations may encounter little competition in that particular segment simply because competitors do not consider retaliation worthwhile.

Forecasts of technology may provide a guide to the expected longevity of a new venture. One that is expected to become technically obsolete within six years, for example, will necessarily have to yield its return on investment in less than six years to remain a viable candidate for addition to the product line.

Changes in the structure of channels of distribution may result in the disappearance of particular institutions and their replacement by others. Obviously, a venture linked primarily to a dying institution (e.g., the local lumber yard) must be expected to have a limited life. Very often, however, distributive institutions that find themselves threatened will modify their practices to adapt to the changing environment, as have lumber yards which have developed into home-improvement centers. In such cases, offerings sold through those channels may enjoy a much longer life.

Resources Most organizations estimate relatively early in the screening process the technical, manufacturing, marketing, financial, and managerial resources likely to be required by a proposed venture. A lack of fit in areas considered critical may result in the proposal's being rejected at this stage.

Response of consumers and competitors to the proposed venture may be estimated at several stages throughout the innovative process. Frequently, concept evaluations will be run before development work begins, both as a screening device and as a guide to the technical and marketing program development work. Concept evaluation involves obtaining, from groups who may represent segments of the prospective market, reactions to a product description, mock-up, or sample, accompanied by a statement of the benefits claimed for the product, position vis-à-vis alternatives, and likely price range. If the groups receive the concept favorably, and if the concept—as it stands or with modifications suggested by the groups—can be developed technically within the constraints imposed by the price range specified, development work may be undertaken.

Once prototypes or samples become available, most manufacturers of both consumer and industrial products conduct (or have conducted for them) use tests, in which consumers who might typify certain segments use the product in their homes, factories, or offices. Sometimes use tests are undertaken first with employees, both because they constitute a friendly group and because they are unlikely to broadcast work of the development activity to competitors, and subsequently with typical users.

Successful use-testing may be followed by introduction of the new offering on a regional, national, or international basis, or by further testing, either in the marketplace or the laboratory. Testing at this stage involves test marketing, i.e., placing the offering, backed by one or more alternative marketing programs, against others available to the consumer. Full test markets in field settings may cost hundreds of thousands of dollars and may require a year or more to yield definitive information. During this period competitors may be able to respond with offerings which capture substantial portions of the prospective market. Because of the costs and competitive risks, manufacturers ordinarily use test markets principally when the costs of failure are substantial, either in dollars, in trade and consumer acceptance of subsequent products, or in injury resulting from improper use; when effective competitive retaliation is not expected to occur for some time; and when substantial need exists for market data to decide on commercialization of the product or to refine the marketing program. Even an organization that stands the costs and risks of competition faces a challenge in interpreting test market data, for test markets are ordinarily conducted with extra effort by salespeople, accompanied by intensive introductory promotion, and trade and consumer interest. Competitors may by accident or design engage in special pricing or promotional activities which can complicate interpretation of results.

The high cost and interpretive problems of field-test markets have led many marketers to skip the procedure entirely or to use controlled laboratory test markets, which cost far less and lead to fewer ambiguities in results. A question many managers raise about controlled experimentation, however, is whether laboratory results do, in fact, predict marketplace behavior.

The Management of Innovation   To maintain a continuing stream of additions to the portfolio, managers must cope successfully with, among others, four major sources of problems in the innovative process: goals, planning, personal commitment, and principal causes of new product failure.

Goals   Goals may be unclear or unrealistic. Lack of clarity of objectives within an organization for a program of innovation in many cases stems from senior management's failure to articulate precisely the role of new ventures in the particular firm's portfolio. Unless those involved in the innovative process themselves present for management approval a clear statement of objectives, the energies of the organization may be fragmented and dissipated in numerous directions, none of which will yield a significant addition to the portfolio. Lack of realism in objectives comes in many, but not all, instances from pressure to catch up with competitors. Under such pressure, timetables for new ventures may be set so short that the organization is forced to offer an imperfect product or to meet criteria such as a certain number of new ventures introduced each year, or a set percentage or dollar amount of sales and/or earnings which must come from additions to the portfolio. This latter kind of pressure often appears in the form of a target increase in sales or earnings set for an operating unit whose existing portfolio promises little or no growth. If those targets require increases that exceed present and prospective markets' abilities to absorb present and extended product lines, the effect of such quotas may be to push the operating unit into product/market areas in which it lacks expertise, and which would be more effectively served by other operating units or a special unit of the organization.

Planning   Managers who know the objectives toward which an innovation program is directed (whether they consider those goals realistic or not), as well as managers who wish to stimulate discussion and clarification of objectives, in most cases find it useful to develop a formal plan for the innovative process for each new venture under serious consideration. Such plans typically list the activities that must occur before the new venture can be brought to market, together with a timetable for those activities. Managers employ a variety of techniques for such plans, ranging from simple lists to elaborate charts using PERT (Performance Evaluation and Review Technique), or related forms of network and critical path analysis. One advantage of these more elaborate systems is that they provide a basis for accelerating the entire innovative process by indicating opportunities to run necessary activities at the same time, rather than one after another. For example, the time required to bring a new consumer package good to market may be reduced considerably if development of the marketing program occurs at the same time as does laboratory work on the physical product. To be effective, however, such a parallel development approach requires close coordination between the two simultaneous activities, lest the product be unable to fill the position toward which the marketing program is directed.

Personal commitment   Personal commitment to a particular new venture on the part of a dedicated or powerful individual or group increases substantially the probability that the venture will be developed and exposed to the market, at least for testing. Individuals who become heavily involved in analysis of a new opportunity are apt to discover many ways in which the new venture can become a commercial success, whereas those not involved will find it relatively easy to point out the pitfalls facing the venture. Nevertheless, those "outsiders" typically are reluctant to attempt to kill the project, in part because they win no organizational medals for stopping a project whose outcome is uncertain. Only after evidence clearly indicates that the venture is unlikely to become successful does one gain credit for opposing it, and by that time no unusually great analytical skills may be needed to ascertain that the venture will fail.

In many instances, those involved with the project will view available market research data differently from those who are not involved with the project. To an individual heavily involved with a new venture, costly test markets represent a vehicle to confirm a "go" decision and to refine the marketing strategy for the venture. To the outsider who has never been keen on the venture, the identical test market data may provide "conclusive" evidence that the venture should be dropped at once.

Causes of failure   In addition to handling problems of goals, planning, and personal commitment, managers attempt to avoid or handle successfully the difficulties most frequently associated with new-venture failures. Identification of the principal causes of failure and laying of plans to avoid them should increase the likelihood of success of prospective additions to the portfolio.

Although the list of reasons why new ventures fail may be infinite in length, four general causes appear to be the major culprits in new-venture failure: (1) inadequate demand analysis, (2) product defects and cost overruns, (3) marketing program deficiencies and excessive costs, and (4) inadequate coordination between marketing and technical personnel. Inadequacies in demand analysis include overestimation of primary demand for the new offering, underestimation of the consumer loyalty to and retaliatory power of established competitors, and incomplete analysis of the purported benefits and costs of the new offering from the point of view of potential customers in each target market segment. Product defects and the cost overruns incurred in attempts to correct those defects may arise from unanticipated difficulties with unfamiliar technology and from inadequate provisions to shift from pilot to full production. Cost overruns themselves may occur during periods of cost increases which cannot be passed through to customers. In many instances, marketing programs for new offerings are incompletely planned and based on inadequate analysis of demand and competition. In other instances, the plan may be sound, but execution of the plan is hampered by such problems as distributors' reluctance to stock an additional line, salespeople's difficulties in learning to handle new accounts or applications or technology, and the like. The most common difficulty in coordination between marketing and technical personnel is that of matching the physical product as it's developed to the original concept believed to have a niche in the market-place. These causes for difficulty with new ventures are likely to become more important in situations in which the new venture requires resources quite different from those of the organization's present activities, i.e., when the new venture lacks close "fit" with the organization's capabilities.

SELECTED REFERENCES

BLOOM, PAUL N. and PHILIP KOTLER. "Strategies for High Market Share Companies." *Harvard Business Review,* November–December 1975.

BROWN, MILTON P. et. al. *Problems in Marketing* (4th ed.). New York: McGraw-Hill, 1967.

BUZZELL, ROBERT D., B.T. GALE, and R.G.M. SULTAN. "Market Share—A Key to Profitability." *Harvard Business Review,* January–February 1975.

COOPER, ROBERT G. "Why New Industrial Products Fail." *Industrial Marketing Management,* vol. 4, 1975.

DAVIDSON, J. HUGH. "Why Most New Consumer Brands Fail." *Harvard Business Review,* March–April 1976.

KLINE, CHARLES H. "The Strategy of Product Policy." *Harvard Business Review,* July–August 1955.

LEVITT, THEODORE. "Innovative Imitation." *Harvard Business Review,* September–October 1966.

PESSEMIER, EDGAR A. *Product Management.* New York: Wiley, 1977.

ROTHBERG, ROBERT R., ed. *Corporate Strategy and Product Innovation.* New York: The Free Press, 1976.

SMITH FOODS, INC. (A)

In May 1967, corporate executives of Smith Foods, Inc., met to decide whether to introduce Smiths Snackers, a puffed, shaped snack food, into one or more test markets, or
into national distribution with a region-by-region "roll-out." In either case, Smith executives could choose to move immediately or to postpone further activity in the marketplace until additional product development work had been completed.

THE COMPANY

Since its founding in 1871, Smith Foods, Inc., of Kansas City had become one of the
largest food-processing firms in the United States. In 1967, the company was in several
businesses, including flour, feed, chemicals, and packaged food products. Packaged foods
included several processed potato products, frozen pastries, and cake and pastry mixes.

Sales of Smith Foods had increased from $450 million in 1960 to $600 million in
1965. In 1967, the company had sales in excess of $750 million and pretax earnings in
excess of $40 million. An income statement and balance sheet for 1967 appear in Ex-
hibit 1. Company officials attributed Smith's growth in the late 1960s in part to a diversification program which was vigorously supported by top management.

Smith Foods was a decentralized company in which each of several divisions had
considerable freedom to manage its business. Responsibility for consumer packaged goods
was shared by the New Ventures Division and the Consumer Foods Division, both of
which were under the general supervision of a vice-president for Consumer Package
Goods (see Exhibit 2).

The New Ventures Division, established in 1966 as part of the company's diversification program, was charged with identifying opportunities for new consumer packaged
foods and then developing products to capitalize on those opportunities. Within the New
Ventures Division each of several teams, which included both marketing and product
development specialists, had responsibility for a particular product. This responsibility
included research, development, and physical testing of the product as well as preparation
of tentative marketing plans. When a product was ready for test marketing, responsibility
for it was transferred to the Consumer Foods Division, which managed the company's
existing products.

The Snack Foods Market

Although no single definition of the snack market was accepted as standard within the food industry, industry sources generally agreed that snack foods included products from at least four categories used in the United States Census of Manufacturers: (1) biscuits, cookies, and crackers; (2) potato chips; (3) corn chips; (4) other chips, sticks, and miscellaneous items. Biscuits, cookies, and crackers was the dominant category, and Census officials forecast that it would remain so (see Exhibit 3).

The markets for most products in those categories, except for potato chips, were dominated by large national food manufacturers. Potato chips were produced and marketed by more than 350 regional firms, known as chippers in the trade. These chippers had adapted their products to local tastes, so that the crispiness, saltiness, size, shape, and texture of potato chips varied greatly among regional markets. Chippers seldom marketed their potato chips outside the areas immediately around their manufacturing facilities. Potato chips had a shelf life of less than three weeks, and were so fragile that they could not withstand normal rail or truck shipment and handling. These freshness and distribution problems had prevented any national manufacturer from dominating the potato chip market. Nevertheless, in the early 1960s, a number of national food manufacturers began to acquire regional chippers.

The market for puffed, shaped snacks (of which Snackers was one example) was not developed until General Mills introduced Bugles, Whistles, and Daisys nationally in 1966. Initial growth of that market was rapid, with General Mills remaining the dominant firm in the market for puffed, shaped snacks.

Although Smith Foods personnel had thought before 1960 that General Mills and other food manufacturers might be developing snack foods, Smith officials first learned of General Mills' specific intentions in 1963 when a Smith employee in the company's Minneapolis District Office was selected at random to participate in an in-home use test of prototype snacks developed by General Mills. From that time on, Smith officials were aware of the development activity at General Mills and followed it with interest.

According to industry sources, General Mills had discovered that, by using technology originally developed in its cereal business, the firm could produce snacks that resembled potato chips but had a shelf life of six to nine months and would not crumble in shipment. Indeed, Daisys had originally been a breakfast cereal that consumers were, however, eating between meals. Upon discovering this usage pattern, General Mills altered the taste and texture of the cereal to make it more suitable as a snack. It was believed that another reason for General Mills' interest in snacks was that it had sufficient capacity to package these snacks without investing the $150,000 to $200,000 typically required for a packaging line.

General Mills stated (publicity release, 1967) that it had prepared four guidelines for development of snack products:

1. The snack product should have a shelf life comparable to other products sold by General Mills, thereby making them available for distribution through chain and wholesaler warehouses.

2. The snack product should have a taste appeal superior or equal to the best-accepted store-delivered products.

3. The snack product should have fundamental characteristics that would be identifiably different to the consumer, either through texture, shape, or color.

4. The snack product should afford the grocer adequate margins and at the same time be competitive in consumer pricing with items in the same category.

General Mills subsequently developed three snacks, Bugles, Whistles, and Daisys, which differed in shape, texture, and color. A brightly colored, droll, cheerful package was designed for each snack. Reflecting General Mills' belief that snacks were used in the evenings and at parties, its advertising light-heartedly promoted the concept that eating Bugles, Whistles, and Daisys was fun and enjoyable. A sample commercial for Bugles stated: "Make noise with Bugles. Bugles are love, truth, beauty, corn, and a little salt."

In January 1965, General Mills introduced all three snacks into test markets in six cities. In some test markets snacks were sold from the grocery shelves; in others, snacks were sold from free-standing racks. General Mills used warehouses to stock the shelves, but hired jobbers, who also sold potato chips and corn chips, to stock the racks.

Distribution through racks and wagon jobbers quickly proved unsatisfactory in comparison to distribution through warehouses to the retailers' shelves. From a survey of 1,000 supermarkets in 50 areas, General Mills determined that shelves were preferable because the product was always in the same place in the store. In contrast, grocers tended to move the rack from place to place, making it hard for the consumer to find the product. In addition, General Mills discovered that grocers did not maintain racks as carefully as they maintained their shelves. Stock-outs were experienced 30 percent of the time on the racks and, still worse, these stock-outs occurred on weekends, when General Mills believed that snacks were sold most often. Finally, General Mills learned that consumers thought that products sold on racks were easily damaged and tended to get stale quickly. For this reason, consumers preferred that the snack be packaged in a clear bag so that they could make sure it was undamaged. When the snack was sold from the shelf, consumers did not hold these opinions as strongly.

Sales of General Mills' snacks exceeded the firm's ability to supply all six test-market cities. When General Mills stopped supplying three cities, retailers in those cities complained that they were losing business because their customers were going to other stores in search of snacks. In August 1965, General Mills ran ads in those three cities apologizing that it did not have enough snacks to sell. Following its test-market success, General Mills early in 1966 began national introduction of the three snacks on a market-by-market basis. Industry sources estimated that General Mills had invested more than a million dollars in production equipment alone prior to May 1967.

History of Snackers' Development

Since the early 1950s Smith Foods personnel had considered developing a snack that would significantly penetrate the market held by potato chips. Early research on a potato chip rugged enough to withstand transportation and handling brought no results. However, Smith researchers continued to look for a snack that resembled a potato chip in flavor, texture, and shape.

Summer, 1966 Work on Snackers began in earnest in June 1966. At that time, Smith Foods executives were concerned about their Payette, Idaho, plant, which milled potato flour and manufactured some of Smith Foods' packaged potato products. In recent years, the plant had operated at capacity only six months each year. In order to obtain the cost savings associated with increased levels of operation, Smith Foods had in 1965 signed a two-year contract to make macaroni for Kawasaki, a Japanese firm. The contract provided an added benefit because macaroni could be made from certain potatoes that could not be used in making packaged potato products. In addition, the Kawasaki firm supplied a macaroni press which was unused nine months during the year. In June 1966, Ralph Winwood decided to see whether the remaining excess capacity of the Payette plant and press could be used in making snack foods out of the potato flour milled at Payette.

Winwood learned that Snackers could be made in two ways using potato flour. If a macaroni press were used, then potato and corn flour had to be mixed in order to produce a dough that would puff when fried. If this press were used, then Smith Foods would have to purchase corn flour from another firm and develop a satisfactory blend of flours. Snackers could also be made completely from potato flour with a special snack press and frying equipment which together cost $105,000 (see Exhibit 4). Winwood decided to use the Kawasaki press, rather than to invest in additional equipment at the Payette plant at this stage of Snackers' development.

Consequently, Smith's Snackers were made from a potato and corn flour batter. The batter was mixed, then pressed through a die on the macaroni press. The extruded product was then cut to the desired length. In this form, called half-product, Snackers were dried for several hours in order to obtain the proper aging necessary for crispiness. This dense, hard half-product had a shelf life of more than 12 months. When the half-product was flash-fried in hot oil, it puffed, lost its remaining moisture, and became soft enough to eat. The resulting Snacker was about 40 percent less greasy than potato chips, had a shelf life of nine months, and was not especially vulnerable to damage during shipping and handling.

Preliminary investigations indicated that if Smith Foods made the half-product, several regional potato chippers could be hired to fry the half-product, package it, and place it on the grocers' shelves. This production method made it unnecessary for the company to purchase frying equipment, and also permitted Smith Foods to tailor its product to local consumer tastes, because each regional chipper could fry the product and season it to meet the local customers' taste preferences. Moreover, the half-product was so durable that only the most ingenious shipper could find a way to damage it.

Because Smith Foods had several prospective new products, in June 1966, Winwood established a new products group to evaluate these products and prepare the best ones for the market. Henry Wotton, a marketing specialist, and Dr. David Bruce, a technical specialist, were named cochairmen of the group. Henry Wotton named Thomas Edmondes, John Ogle, and William Monson to the marketing team for snack foods. Dr. Bruce named Dr. Stephan LeSieur and Dr. Richard Spencer to the snack foods technical team (see Exhibit 2). In the latter part of June, Thomas Edmondes suggested that the company market a line of ready-to-eat french fried snacks, which would include french fried potatoes, french fried onion rings, and french fried shrimp. Winwood and Wotton agreed with Edmondes that the product should tentatively be named Smith's Snackers.

Dr. LeSieur undertook to make prototype snack products using the Kawasaki press with dies patented by Smith Foods, gelatinized corn and potato flour, and the two-step manufacturing process. LeSieur made each shape in three textures, one very crisp, one medium, and one very fluffy.

In July 1966, Edmondes, Ogle, and Monson accepted these prototypes and ordered that development work proceed at once. The Potato Snacker was to have the triangular shape (1½ inches long) with the crispy texture; the Shrimp Snacker was to have the tube shape with the medium texture (same length); and the Onion Ring Snacker was to have the wagon wheel shape with the fluffy texture (1½ inches in diameter). The three men then established preliminary flavors for Smith's Snackers.

Fall, 1966–spring, 1967 In November 1966, results from a test of sample Snackers on a panel of Smith Foods employees became available. The onion-flavored wagon wheel had been tested against an onion-flavored ribbon-shaped snack, Fritos, Bugles, and Lay's Potato Chips. The major conclusion drawn from this test was that Snackers were not yet competitive with leading snack foods. Snackers received an average score of 4.77 on a nine-point "liking" scale (nine was the most favorable score)[1], whereas Bugles, potato chips, and Fritos all scored higher than 6.3 on the "liking" scale (see Exhibit 5).

Smith researchers expressed concern over these results, because the "liking" scale had in the past proved an accurate predictor of market success. Indeed, in product classes similar to snack foods, those products which together dominated a particular market typically received "liking" scores which were clustered together near the favorable end of the "liking" scale. In contrast, products whose shares of those markets were very small received "liking" scores significantly lower than those of the market leaders. Smith researchers noted that the actual "liking" scores received by any product could vary from one time to another, but that the relative positions of products typically changed very little from time to time, unless product formulations themselves were altered.

In December 1966, a second test was conducted among Smith employees. Several onion-flavored Snackers were tested, each with a different salt level. Further, the product had been made fluffier in response to complaints that it was too crispy. "Liking" scores of 5.56 to 6.00 were recorded for these Snacker samples. Dr. LeSieur believed that he could develop a Snacker that would receive higher "liking" scores.

---

1. "Liking" ratings were used to determine whether a new product formulation represented a significant improvement over one or more previous product formulations. This comparison could be made in two ways. One was to test the product formulations against each other. The other was to test each formulation against a set of competitive products.

While this product research was going on, Edmondes made a list of potential competitors of Smith Snackers. He identified 23 major national companies and 11 smaller firms that were participating or could participate in the snack foods market. By late 1966, however, only 9 of these firms had snacks on the market, but activity in the snack market was increasing. From June to December, eight major new products had been introduced into test-market and national distribution had begun for five: Frito's Corn Chips, Allied Foods' Popcorny and Corn Chippy Snacks, and General Mills' Bugles, Whistles, and Daisys.

From the Ziegler survey of warehouse withdrawals for 100 stores from August 1965, to January 1967, Edmondes learned that General Mills had distribution in only 2 stores in August 1965. In September 1966, when General Mills announced that it would sell Bugles, Whistles, and Daisys nationally, 59 stores stocked the products. In November 1966, General Mills had its products in 94 of the 100 stores surveyed. From data for October and November, Edmondes estimated that retail sales of General Mills' snacks for an entire year would be nearly $24 million for Bugles, $10 million for Daisys, and $15 million for Whistles, a total of $49 million, even if General Mills' share of the snack market did not increase. A public statement by a General Mills executive indicated that General Mills officials believed that their snacks had expanded the market:

> We felt we could make a contribution to the growth and acceptance of the entire snack category so that the pie would be bigger for all of us. That's the way it has worked out. There is no indication that we took any chunk of business away from regional operators. The market just continued to expand (*Food Topics,* September 1967).

In February 1967, work began on the Snackers' package, which was expected to require about five months to complete. Consumer tests of the Snackers' package, conducted during the spring of 1967, indicated that the Snackers' package scored as high as Allied Foods' Popcorny and Corn Chippy snacks, and only slightly lower than Daisys, which had been expected to score higher because of its shelf and advertising exposure to consumers. The test results convinced Smith officials that the package design was highly satisfactory.

During March and April 1967, Edmondes undertook research to ascertain whether consumers preferred snacks with or without ketchup. Accordingly, a panel of ketchup users, consisting of 110 adults, 110 school children from grades 4 through 12, all split equally between Denver and Los Angeles, was asked to eat each of four snacks, two with and all four without ketchup. Results from this test appear in Exhibit 6. Edmondes then had a telephone survey conducted on a national probability sample of 370 adults and 199 teenagers to ascertain whether or not they would use ketchup with snacks. Results from this survey are included in Exhibit 7.

While these tests were being conducted, Edmondes also sought basic data on the percent of adults and teenagers who ate particular foods. Results from a telephone survey of a national probability sample of 150 consumers showed that at least 50 percent of the sample ate french fried foods and potato chips, and 25 percent ate General Mills snacks (see Exhibit 8). In addition, 90 percent of all the consumers interviewed in this telephone survey reported that they ate potato chips or Bugles, Whistles, or Daisys between meals; only 10 percent reported eating potato chips or General Mills' snacks with meals.

To explore further how consumers would use Snackers, Smith officials had a panel of 200 respondents in Buffalo examine photographs of Snackers in various settings, taste the product, and then report how they would use Snackers. One hundred respondents were shown color photographs of Potato Snackers in a basket, and 100 were shown photographs of Potato Snackers with hamburgers. After all 200 had tasted the product, they were asked when they thought they would use it. There was no difference in response between the two groups. Entertainment and between-meal family snacking were by far the major two snack occasions chosen. Only 10 percent said they would eat Potato Snackers with meals.

Finally, several positioning statements were tested on 100 respondents in Chicago. These statements were tested for appeal, expected frequency of use of Snackers, expected use of Snackers for specific occasions (e.g., meals, snack entertainment), and for the best description of the product. Using these criteria, Smith research personnel concluded that the statement, "a new snack food that looks like a french fry, tastes like a french fry, but you use it like a potato chip," was the best. Moreover, when this statement was tested on a second panel of 100 respondents, 77 percent identified the product as a french fry. Edmondes interpreted the data to indicate that Smith's Snackers French Fried Potatoes could be positioned against both french fries and potato chips. However, respondents also indicated they would use potato Snackers much more often between meals than at meals. Nevertheless, Edmondes reasoned that if Potato Snackers could score as high on a "liking" scale as potato chips and french fries, then Smith Foods could gain a significant share of both the estimated $400 million potato chip market and the much larger french fry market.

While research into alternative positions for Snackers was under way, members of the Snack Foods team were also evaluating the Smith's Snackers name, which had tentatively been decided upon 10 months earlier. The purpose of the research undertaken in April 1967, was to determine how consumers would respond to the name and what effect, if any, the name would have on the image of Smith Foods, Inc. Until this time, all tests had been conducted without mentioning either "Snackers" or "Smith Foods."

One hundred twenty persons, split equally between Denver and St. Louis, evaluated two flavors of the product and Smith Foods without seeing the name "Smith's Snackers." A similar group of 120 saw the name and then evaluated the products, the name, and Smith Foods, in that order. Both groups then had the opportunity to order the product, which was priced at five ounces for 39 cents, the same as General Mills' snacks. Puffed, shaped snacks were generally 1⅓ to 2 times as costly as potato chips for similar size packages. Smith officials interpreted results from this study as favorable toward both the name and the product (see Exhibit 9).

Also during April 1967, another panel of 200 in Chicago was used to test the product name. Half the sample was not told the name. Of the comments about the product made by these persons, 70 percent were favorable and 30 percent were unfavorable. The 100 persons who were told the name before they tasted the snack made comments 80 percent of which were favorable and 20 percent of which were unfavorable about the name.

Through April 1967, Smith Foods had spent approximately $13,000 on the Snackers' project. That amount was allocated as follows:

Product development equipment	$ 5,000
Employee panels	200
Telephone surveys	800
Ketchup usage (Denver & Los Angeles)	2,000
Taste and concept (Buffalo)	1,000
Name tests	2,000
Package tests	2,000
	$13,000

These figures did not include any costs for time of executives and technical specialists spent on Snackers.

On May 9, 1967, the New Ventures Division team responsible for snack foods formally proposed to corporate management of Smith Foods that the corporation authorize the investment of $55,000 in Snackers. Of this amount, approximately $5,000 would be spent on preparing facilities for manufacturing and packaging Snackers, and the remaining $50,000 would be spent on test marketing Snackers.

Henry Wotton made the presentation for the team:

The snack food industry is one of the fastest growing in the entire food market. By 1968 we expect to see more than $2.6 billion in sales (see Exhibit 10). The fastest growing segment is the puffed snack segment which is dominated by General Mills. General Mills' sales, at the consumer level, rose from practically nothing in August 1965, to an annual rate of close to $50 million in November 1966. We also know some of the details of how General Mills achieved this success. I believe that if we can duplicate General Mills' early successes with their snacks, we will reap similar profits.

We chose a french fried snack line because no other snack maker has one on the market. A great deal of research has been done. The product name is well received by the consumer. Further, we are positioned against potato chips and corn chips. Our latest estimates show that corn chip and potato chip sales in 1965 totalled nearly $420 million. Even a nominal share of this market should mean tremendous sales for Smith Foods.

The Onion Snackers are at an acceptable level of preference right now. They received a 6.4 rating (see Exhibit 9) and 20 percent of the responses were in the most favorable categories. Further laboratory work should be expended not on this product, but on the Potato Snackers. Although the Potato Snackers are improved, they still have very few people rating them in the two most favorable categories on the liking scale. I feel that the potato snack should be improved, but not at the cost of destroying present timing. If necessary, work should be continued on this product right through the test market in order to move more people into the position of strong liking for this product.

General Mills has sold its snacks using television advertising which emphasizes that eating snacks is fun. Our agency has developed a light-hearted commercial which I would like to test. To achieve significant impact in the national market, I estimate that we'd need to advertise at a sustained rate of $2 million per year. (Industry advertising expenditures appear in Exhibit 11.)

Now our potato- and onion-flavored Snackers were tested against both Bugles and potato chips. In analyzing the test it is important to bear in mind that success in the snack category does not require that we overwhelm existing entrants in the field. Considerable success can come from being merely added to the list of items the consumer buys from time to time. A study by Avisco (excerpts from which appear in the Appendix) indicates that consumers often buy several different snacks on a single shopping trip. A small share of this high volume category can equal significant dollar volume. Moreover, there is little investment to be made since we have almost all the equipment we need at our Payette plant. At present, we estimate that we can manufacture, package, and distribute a five-ounce package of Snackers for 15 cents, and sell that package to the grocer for 28 cents. This still permits the grocer to mark up the Snackers 28 percent and sell them for 39 cents per five-ounce box.

In short, Snackers seem to represent a low-risk, high-yield situation. However, there are competitive firms coming to the market with new products. We should try to get our Snackers on the national market as soon as possible so that we can be in an established position when these other new snacks arrive. Therefore, I would like to take the Snackers to test market as soon as possible to learn what levels of repeat we can expect, whether shelves or racks are better for in-store placement of snacks, and whether we can really use regional potato chippers to fry and distribute Snackers for us.

(If this last alternative were followed, investment in special frying equipment could be avoided, but the total manufacturing, packaging, and distribution costs to Smith Foods would increase to almost 20 cents for a five-ounce package.)

Among those present, some wondered whether Snackers should be brought to test-market or national distribution before the laboratory had improved their quality to a level equal to or better than that of potato chips, corn chips, and Bugles. Others agreed with Henry Wotton that competitive pressures required moving forward quickly with the product, and that the risk/return relationship was favorable.

At this point, Smith executives wished to decide whether to postpone further marketing activity, including test marketing, until additional product development work was completed, and whether or not to conduct a test market before taking Snackers into national distribution. A complete marketing plan had to be prepared if either test marketing or national distribution were to be undertaken.

Exhibit 1

SMITH FOODS, INC. (A)—INCOME STATEMENT

For the year ending December 31, 1967

(000 omitted)

Net sales		$752,398
Cost of goods sold		566,132
Gross margin		$186,266
Expenses		
Sales and administrative expense	$124,821	
Interest	7,336	
Depreciation	16,467	
Other expenses	628	
Total expenses		$149,252
Earnings from operations		37,014
Other income		3,820
Earnings before taxes		40,834
Taxes		21,020
Net earnings		$ 19,814

BALANCE SHEET

As of December 31, 1967

(000 omitted)

Current assets		
Cash	$ 34,372	
Receivables	85,418	
Inventories	64,342	
Total current assets		$184,132
French fried heavens—franchises		52,476
Property, plant, and equipment		102,165
Other assets		29,416
Total assets		$368,189
Current liabilities		$ 81,132
Long-term debt		93,080
Stockholders' equity		193,977
Total Liabilities and Stockholders' Equity		$368,189

1967 SALES AND EARNINGS BY BUSINESS AREA

	Estimated sales by business area	Estimated pretax earnings (loss) by business area
	(millions of dollars)	
Consumer products	$327.3	$18.0
Flour milling	181.2	7.5
Industrial chemicals	89.1	3.7
French fried heavens	102.3	6.1
International	52.0	1.6
Other	0.5	(0.1)
	752.4	37.0

Source: Company Records

Exhibit 2

SMITH FOODS, INC. (A)
ABRIDGED ORGANIZATION CHART

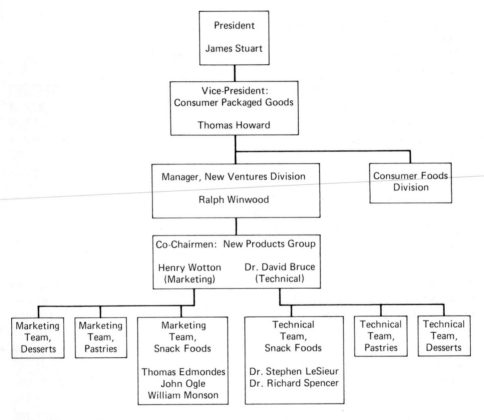

Source: Company Records

Exhibit 3

SMITH FOODS, INC. (A)

MANUFACTURERS' SHIPMENTS OF SNACK FOODS

(millions of dollars)

	Actual			Estimated[*]	
	1954	1958	1963	1968	1973
Biscuits, cookies, and crackers	$805	$ 959	$1133	$1289	$1427
Potato chips	166	263	355	462	601
Corn chips	17	31	63	118	177
Other chips, potato sticks, bacon rinds, and miscellaneous items	n.a.	n.a.	37	56	77
Total	$988	$1253	$1598	$1937	$2295

[*] Estimates based on assumption that each category will maintain current rate of growth.

Source: United States Census of Manufacturers, 1963.

Exhibit 4

SMITH FOODS, INC. (A)

PRICES OF SELECTED PIECES OF MANUFACTURING AND PACKAGING EQUIPMENT

Kawasaki macaroni press[*] (capacity 4 million lbs./year of fried product)	$40,000
Used macaroni press (capacity 2 million lbs./year of fried product; one month delivery)	16,000
Special snack press (capacity 4 million lbs./year; used with frying equipment; six-month delivery)	40,000
Frying equipment (capacity 4 million lbs./year; may be used with either macaroni or snack presses)	65,000
Packaging line[*] depending on speed and exact equipment; present equipment could handle up to 17 million four-ounce packages or equivalents in certain configurations)	200,000–250,000

[*] These items were already installed at Payette. The prices shown are estimated replacement costs.

Source: Company Records

Exhibit 5

SMITH FOODS, INC. (A)

RESULTS OF EMPLOYEE PANEL TASTE TEST, NOVEMBER 1966

A. Average scores nine-point "liking" scale (9 = most favorable) ($n = 60$)

Onion Snackers	Fritos	Bugles	Potato chips
4.77	7.01	6.34	6.66

Note: The difference in average score between Snackers and each of the other three products would have occurred less than 1 time in 100 by random process. There were no statistically significant differences among Fritos, Bugles, and potato chips.

B. Percentage of respondents classifying each of four products on three attributes ($n = 60$)

	Snackers	Fritos	Bugles	Potato chips
Too salty	5%	15%	2%	3%
Not salty enough	58	23	33	38
Just about right	37	62	65	59
Too much oil	24	16	35	19
Not enough oil	12	2	0	5
Just about right	64	82	65	76
Too crispy	39	2	3	0
Not crispy enough	5	10	7	28
Just about right	56	88	90	72

Source: Company Records

Exhibit 6

SMITH FOODS, INC. (A)

SCORES ON "LIKING" SCALE FOR SELECTED SNACKS USED
WITH AND WITHOUT KETCHUP
(Both Cities Combined)

	Adults		Children (grades 4–12)	
	With ketchup	Without ketchup	With ketchup	Without ketchup
Onion Snackers	5.5	6.2	5.3	5.0
Potato Snackers	5.3	5.2	5.5	5.0
John's Potato Chips	*	6.6	*	6.1
GM's Bugles	*	6.8	*	5.7

*Not tested

Source: Company Records

Exhibit 7

SMITH FOODS, INC. (A)
INTENDED USAGE OF KETCHUP WITH SNACKS

Percent of all respondents using ketchup regularly		Percent of regular ketchup users responding to question: "Would you use ketchup with snacks?"		
		Yes	Maybe	No
Adults	45%	25%	42%	33%
Teens	45%	24%	50%	26%

Source: Company Records

Exhibit 8

SMITH FOODS, INC. (A)
PERCENT OF CONSUMERS WHO EAT PARTICULAR FOODS
(Telephone Survey)

Food eaten	Adults	Teens	150 Consumers
French fries	50%	75%	60%
Potato chips	50	75	60
Regularly both	70	70	70
Regularly one but not the other	30	30	30
French fried onion rings	60	60	60
French fried shrimp	No percentages given—equally popular in both groups		
Bugles, Whistles, Daisys	25	25	25

Source: Company Records

Exhibit 9

SMITH FOODS, INC. (A)
RESULTS OF STUDY ON "SMITH'S SNACKERS"
CONDUCTED IN DENVER AND ST. LOUIS
(April 1967)

A. Score on nine-point "liking" scale

	With name	Without name
Potato flavor	6.2	5.9
Onion flavor	6.4	6.2
	(n = 120)	(n = 120)

B. Score on nine-point scale on which adults estimated how well their children would like product

	With name	Without name
Potato flavor	6.8	6.5
Onion flavor	6.0	5.7
	(n = 120)	(n = 120)

C. Percentage of respondents who would/would not serve snack to family

	With name	Without name
Potato		
Would serve to family	86%	83%
Would not serve to family	14	17
Onion		
Would serve to family	77	82
Would not serve to family	23	18
	(n = 120)	(n = 120)

D. Percentage of respondents whose overall reaction to the name "Smith's Snackers" was:

Positive only	57%
Positive and negative	9
Negative only	14
Neutral	20
(n = 120)	

E. Percentage of respondents who saw name and:

Understood main idea	65%
Did not understand	35
(n = 120)	

F. Score on nine-point image scale (9-favorable image): With name: 6.2 (n = 120). Without name: 6.3 (n = 120).

Exhibit 9 (Cont.)

G. Percentage of respondents who considered product a:

	With name	Without name
Good value	25%	29%
Average value	62	61
Poor value	13	10
	(n = 120)	(n = 120)

H. Percentage of respondents classifying products according to specific attributes

	Potato		Onion	
	With name	Without name	With name	Without name
Too much salt	10%	13%	3%	4%
Just right	79	71	80	83
Not enough salt	11	16	17	13
Too much (potato/ onion) flavor	3	4	9	13
Just right	82	76	76	78
Not enough (potato/ onion) flavor	15	20	15	9
	(n = 120)	(n = 120)	(n = 120)	(n = 120)

I. Products for which consumers might substitute Smith's Snackers

	Number of responses			
	Potato		Onion	
	With name	Without name	With name	Without name
French fried onions	—	2	3	4
Fritos	38	33	34	39
Potato chips	83	86	71	74
General Mills' Snacks	23	20	16	28
Crackers	19	17	20	29
French fried potatoes	17	7	3	1
None	9	14	20	9
	(n = 101)	(n = 100)	(n = 90)	(n = 98)

Note: Number of responses may exceed number of respondents because of multiple responses per person.

J. Percentage of respondents who ordered one or more packages of Smith's Snackers: With name: 27% (n = 120). Without name: 23% (n = 120).

K. Percentage of respondents with specific intentions to buy

	Potato		Onion	
Buyer intention	With name	Without name	With name	Without name
Definitely buy	18%	14%	28%	21%
Probably buy	53	57	45	57
Can't say	11	16	10	8
Probably not buy	12	7	11	7
Definitely not buy	6	7	5	8

Source: Company Records

Exhibit 10

SMITH FOODS, INC. (A)

PROJECTED CONSUMER PURCHASES OF SNACK FOODS

(millions of dollars)

	1968	1970	1975	Projected annual growth rate
Potato chips	$ 894.9	$1,002.3	$1,303.0	6%
Cookies	778.0	840.2	1,008.2	4
Nuts	634.6	713.1	954.4	6
Corn chips	226.5	271.8	407.7	10
Pretzels	121.0	123.4	129.6	1
Popcorn	29.5	30.1	31.6	1
	$2,684.5	$2,980.9	$3,834.5	

Note: Puffed snacks are not included in these projections because trend information on puffed snack sales for entire years was not available.

Source: Company Records

Exhibit 11

SMITH FOODS, INC. (A)

ADVERTISING MEDIA EXPENDITURES FOR SNACK FOODS,

BY TYPE OF SNACK FOOD, 1965–1966

($000)

	1965	1966	Percent change
Crackers	$ 4,145	$ 3,996	− 3.6%
Potato chips/corn chips	10,345	7,944	− 23.2
Pretzels	*	23	−
Snacks (including puffed, shaped snacks)	2,280	8,211	+260.1
Total	$16,770	$20,173†	+ 20.3%

*No significant expenditure

†Excludes newspaper expenditures (not available)

PERCENTAGE DISTRIBUTION OF MEDIA EXPENDITURE

	1965	1966
Crackers	24.7%	19.8%
Potato chips/corn chips	61.7	39.4
Pretzels	−	0.1
Snacks (including puffed, shaped snacks)	13.6	40.7
Total	100.0%	100.0%

Source: Advertising Agency Report

APPENDIX

Smith Foods, Inc. (A)

Excerpts from the Avisco Snack Study[*]
Consumer Analysis

In determining trends in snack consumption over a twelve-month period, the survey found that nearly 66 percent of all families were eating about the same amount of snacks. Nineteen percent were eating more, 15 percent were eating less. This pattern holds true for every age group except for children between the ages of six and seventeen. While 64 percent of these children reported eating about the same amount of snacks as in the previous year, 31 percent reported eating more as opposed to 5 percent who reported eating less. Ninety-seven percent of the respondents reported that they ate snacks. Of the 3 percent who did not eat snacks, over half explained that they were dieting.

Potato chips are the favorite snack across all age groups. This percentage drops slightly, however, among persons twenty-five years old and older. The popularity of nuts rises from 12 percent to 23 percent in this age group. In the home, potato chips are the first choice in all situations where snacks are eaten. Cracker sandwiches and corn chips are second. Free from teenage and child influences, snack usage in adult situations reveals that nuts and potato chips are most likely to be served in entertainment situations.

FAVORITE TYPES OF SNACKS BY REGION, 1967

	Total United States	East	Mid-West	South	South-West	West
Potato chips	49.8%	49.0%	51.6%	54.6%	46.3%	46.1%
Index	100	98	104	110	93	93
Nuts	15.2	14.4	15.4	15.0	12.2	17.6
Index	100	95	101	99	80	116
Corn chips	13.5	9.1	13.0	13.9	21.2	16.3
Index	100	67	96	103	157	121
Pretzels	9.3	14.8	9.3	7.7	5.0	5.1
Index	100	159	100	83	54	55
Puffed snacks	3.9	3.0	4.4	3.3	6.2	3.5
Index	100	77	113	85	159	90
All others	8.3	9.7	6.3	5.5	9.1	11.4
	100	117	76	66	110	137
Total	100.0%	100.0%	100.0%	100.0%	100.0%	100.0%

[*] This study, released by Avisco in the first quarter of 1967, involved personal interviews with 4,000 housewives.

When snacks are served with beverages, potato chips are preferred with soft drinks and alcoholic beverages. Cracker sandwiches are used most often with milk. Pretzels are served most frequently with beer. To complement cheese and hors d'oeuvres, snack crackers are preferred. Potato chips are the first choice for party dips. When snacks are served with meals, potato chips are more likely to be served with both hot and cold dishes; corn chips are a strong second choice. Consumers' preferences for different types of snacks vary from region to region across the United States.

More than one-third of the respondents bought two packages of snacks on their last shopping trip. Because they like to provide their families with variety, almost 72 percent of all shoppers bought more than one type of snack. Regardless of their initial snack preference, potato chips will also be among their multiple purchases.

HOW MANY PACKAGES WERE BOUGHT
ON LAST SHOPPING TRIP?

One package	27.0%
Two packages	38.9
Three packages	18.8
Four packages	8.3
No response	7.0

Our expanding economy and population has given rise to the well-stocked, modern, self-service supermarket. And because they now can do all their family food buying in one store, shoppers find it more convenient to buy snacks for the family while shopping for other foods.

WHERE ARE SNACKS PURCHASED MOST FREQUENTLY?

	Total United States	East	Midwest	South	Southwest	West
Supermarket	87.5%	90.9%	87.5%	85.1%	79.2%	89.2%
Neighborhood grocer	16.3	14.0	17.1	18.0	26.0	13.2
Delicatessen	1.4	2.4	0.8	1.2	0.4	1.6

WHY ARE SNACKS BOUGHT AT THIS TYPE OF FOOD STORE?

	Supermarket 87.5%	Neighborhood grocer 16.3%	Delicatessen 1.4%
Convenient	82.6%	59.9%	75.0%
Store location	11.2	58.0	58.3
Variety stocked	20.2	17.7	38.9
Lowest price	16.8	13.3	19.4
Favorite brand	13.8	18.9	22.2
Impulse	10.8	13.8	13.9

Source: Avisco Snack Study, 1967

Over half of all shoppers across the nation report they purchase snacks once a week, or more often—and nearly 25 percent more purchase at least once every two weeks. When questioned how long ago they bought snacks, 63.5 percent said within a week, and 86.7 percent said within two weeks.

HOW FREQUENTLY ARE SNACKS PURCHASED?

Once a week or more often	59.2%
Once every two weeks	24.0
Once every three weeks	4.7
Once a month	7.2
Less often or for special occasions	4.9

WHEN WAS THE LAST TIME SNACKS WERE PURCHASED?

1 to 3 days ago	37.8%	
4 to 6 days ago	25.7	63.5% within a week
7 to 9 days ago	13.1	
10 to 14 days ago	10.1	86.7 within 2 weeks
2 weeks to one month	3.8	
More than one month	9.5	

Source: Avisco Snack Study, 1967

Most shoppers do not decide what brand to buy until they are inside of the store. Since they are motivated to some degree by impulse, snack producers must attract their attention through package design and product display.

IMPULSE BUYING BY BRAND

	Nuts	Potato chips	Corn chips	Puffed snacks	Cracker sand-wiches	Snack crackers	Pret-zels	Other
Planned the brand of snacks	28.3%	48.4%	39.1%	24.8%	22.7%	23.3%	27.9%	15.9%
Decided brand in-side of store	42.9	49.1	35.3	49.8	44.7	52.1	45.2	45.7

When their favorite snack is out of stock, over three-quarters of all shoppers will usually buy the same kind of snack in another brand, another kind in some other brand, or won't buy at all.

WHAT HAPPENS WHEN A FAVORITE SNACK IS OUT OF STOCK?

Buy same kind in another brand	62.2%	
Buy another kind in another brand	10.7	78.6%
Don't buy any	5.7	
Go to another store	11.6	20.3%
Buy another kind in regular brand	8.7	

Source: Avisco Snack Study, 1967

Packaging

The shoppers interviewed said that they prefer snacks to be packaged in printed cellophane bags. A major merchandising consideration for snack producers is a package size that will satisfy the consumer. If the package is too large, it may create storage problems, or the consumer may feel that the snack will become stale over a period of time. On the other hand, being economy-minded, shoppers will tend not to buy packages that are too small because they may think they are not getting a true value for their money. The survey indicates that 92.5 percent of all consumers were happy with the size of today's snack packages. Of the small percentage not satisfied, 3.8 percent wanted larger packages and 3.6 percent wanted smaller ones.

Grocery-Store Displays

Since the snack items offer a good profit potential due to their high average markup (27 to 28 percent average gross margin in chains), most chains will take on most new snack items that show merit. The result is that instead of two or three racks of snacks, the average store now carries literally dozens of different items, and floor space for these displays is at a premium. In smaller stores, where shelf space is even harder to come by, many chains have organized the various rack displays of major snack items into one central location and developed a full-fledged snack department.

SMITH FOODS, INC. (B)

In June 1968, corporate executives of Smith Foods had to decide whether to introduce Snackers (a puffed, shaped snack food) nationally on a region-by-region basis, to postpone any further marketing activity until additional product development and testing were completed, or to cancel the Snackers venture altogether. If they decided to market Snackers, executives had to review the proposed marketing plans and to authorize the necessary capital expenditures.

Since May 1967, when they had previously reviewed the project (See Smith Foods, Inc. (A)), corporate executives had approved expenditures of $50,000 on marketing research, more than $130,000 for production equipment, and an undetermined amount for continuing product development and testing. These figures did not include salaries of Smith Foods personnel involved with Snackers.

MARKET RESEARCH

In May 1967, Henry Wotton was authorized to spend $50,000 to test Smith Snackers in a micro-market and to evaluate commercials, packages, and prices for the product. The funds were to be allocated as shown in Exhibit 1.

The micro-market had three purposes: (1) to determine penetration, repeat rate, depth of repeat, and average repeat consumption likely for Smith Snackers (See Exhibit 2); (2) to determine whether Snackers should be distributed through warehouses or directly to the store; and (3) to discover how well having the local chipper fry, season, and distribute the Snackers would work. The micro-market involved smaller cities and fewer diary panelists than a typical test market, which might cost up to several hundred thousand dollars. In selecting the micro-market, Wotton used several criteria. First, the market had to be near Payette but in a place where competitors would not think to look for a test market. Smith Foods did not want any other firm to discover their plans and then tie up the major local chippers. Second, the micro-market had to have demographic characteristics similar to those of the national market. Third, the micro-market should have its own television station so that Smith Foods could advertise only to that market. Fourth, the executives of Smith Foods did not want any competition from any nationally marketed snacks except General Mills' snacks, Fritos, and potato chips.

The micro-market selected included Klamath Falls, Oregon, and three neighboring communities, referred to collectively as the Medford market. One television station served all four towns. Klamath Falls had a population of 65,000; the three towns in the Medford market together contained 98,000 persons. Klamath Falls' only potato chipper, John's Potato Chips, packaged the Snackers in clear wax-paper bags and used their own salesforce to distribute them to the stores in Klamath Falls. For the Medford market, John's packed the Snackers in bags and then hand-packed the bags in boxes. These boxes were then sold and distributed by Smith Foods salespeople to stores in the Medford market. In both Klamath Falls and the Medford market the suggested retail price for a four-ounce package of Onion Snackers or a five-ounce package of Potato Snackers was 39 cents. The case of twelve packages was sold to the grocer for $3.35 with an "introductory" discount of 45 cents per case. This discount was maintained during the micro-market. With the discount, the price per package to the grocer was 24.2 cents. The grocer could sell the package for 34.5 cents and get a 30 percent markup. Many grocers did, and prices of two for 59 cents and three for a dollar were common. General Mills and Allied Foods snacks, on which grocers typically obtained margins of 27 to 30 percent, sold for 39 cents during the micro-market.

Smith Foods formed a diary panel of 800 persons who said they ate ready-to-eat snacks two or more times per week (400 in Klamath Falls, 400 in the Medford market). Panel members agreed to report their snack purchases every two weeks for ten periods. The diary panel data was to be analyzed to determine brand shares, penetration and repeat rates, and the depth of repeat. Store audits were not planned because Smith officials believed that these expensive audits would only duplicate the diary panel data.

The micro-market test began October 20, 1967. Advertising in the micro-market began in late September, when "teaser" billboards announced the coming of a new snack without naming it. Throughout the micro-market test itself, Smith Foods relied primarily on television advertising (see Exhibit 3).

A two-stage awareness and penetration study was conducted during the micro-market. The study, conducted over the telephone, consisted of asking a random sample of people living in the micro-market area what snacks they were aware of and what snacks they had purchased. The first wave of interviews was completed the week before Snackers were introduced into the micro-market. During that week, the teaser billboards were replaced with billboards announcing the pending arrival of Smith Snackers. The first wave of interviews revealed that 14 percent of the 200 respondents had heard of Smith Snackers, although only 11 percent could remember the billboard. When the second wave of interviews was completed a month later, 80 percent of the respondents had heard of Snackers and 40 percent had tried them.

In the six weeks from October 20, when the micro-market test began, and December 5, Smith Foods sold a supply of half-product which executives had initially expected would last six months. This unanticipated success created a serious problem for Smith Foods. In November, just after the micro-market began, Kawasaki refused to renew its contract with Smith Foods for making macaroni and demanded the return of its macaroni press. Smith Foods found itself in a position where retailers were constantly demanding more and more Snackers and it had no way to make them. During the month of December, more than 35 percent of the stores in the micro-market suffered stock-outs on Snackers. In order to slow demand, Smith Foods purchased only apology ads during the six weeks between November 5 and December 21.

Because a new press could not be delivered in less than six months, Wotton was forced to purchase two second-hand macaroni presses to replace the Kawasaki press. These presses cost $8,000 each, and required another $8,000 each in repairs. With its reconditioned macaroni presses, Smith Foods had capacity sufficient to manufacture half-product for 900,000 cases, slightly less than four million pounds of Snackers a year.

While the micro-market test continued, Smith Foods officials learned that the commercials and package used for Smith Snackers had been judged very successful by an independent testing agency. The agency report stated that one-third of the consumers tested considered the commercial humorous and entertaining, and that the commercial elicited no strong negative reaction. Consumers who were not exposed to the commercial but had the opportunity to exchange coupons for Smith's Snackers as well as other products chose Snackers more frequently than they had ever chosen any Smith Foods product tested by this agency. The redemption rate of those consumers who viewed the commercial exceeded the rate of those who had not been exposed by the greatest margin ever recorded for a Smith Foods product in tests run by this agency.

A separate test evaluated the shelf visibility of the Snackers package. The report on that test indicated that the package was "very effective" in attracting attention and stimulating impulse purchases.

Also, while the micro-market test was still in progress, Smith Foods officials obtained results from a mail-order test of consumer reaction to bag and box at different price levels. This test was conducted by a firm which maintained a panel of 1,100 respondents, equally split between Bridgeport and Sacramento. Panel members ordered products from a catalogue on a weekly basis. For this study the panel was split into four parts. One part was able to order the bag at 39 cents, another at 49 cents. The third part of the panel could order the box at 39 cents, and the fourth could order the box at 49 cents. Smith officials believed that differences in penetration data among panel members would measure price elasticity and that differences in repeat rates would measure satisfaction with the product and package. Results from the mail-order panel showed that the bag was preferred at 39 cents and the box was preferred at 49 cents (see Exhibit 4). Thomas Edmondes regarded these results as inconclusive, but suggested that the box be used to reduce breakage of Snackers. Edmondes also pointed to the higher total revenues earned by the box at 49 cents. He suggested that, when a pricing decision was made, the management group should consider selling Snackers at a higher price than the micro-market price of 33 cents per box. Edmondes suggested that the 39 cent retail price, which he considered very reasonable in light of the mail-order evidence, might be maintained if the introductory discount per case to the grocer were cut from 45 cents to 25 cents per case of twelve boxes.

In January 1968, Wotton reviewed the diary panel data he had received for the first twelve weeks of the micro-market. He noted that Potato Snackers had performed very poorly in Klamath Falls, although they equalled or outperformed Bugles in the Medford market (see Exhibits 5 and 6). Further, he noted that Onion Snackers had shares in both markets equal to or greater than those of Bugles. This performance suggested to Wotton that the Klamath Falls diary panel could be discontinued and that the Medford market diary panel could be relied upon to reflect accurately consumer preferences in the micro-market.

Accordingly, the Klamath Falls diary panel was discontinued in January 1968, and 10 percent of the members were interviewed to determine why they were reluctant to purchase Potato Snackers. From these interviews Wotton learned that John's Potato Chips had not adequately fried the Potato Snackers sold in Klamath Falls, so the product that many of the diary panel members had purchased had been too hard to eat. As a result, few consumers made repeat purchases.

Wotton's personal checks of stores in Klamath Falls showed that Smith's Snackers had poor aisle displays and shelf locations. Wotton attributed this lack of display to the "careless attitude" John's Potato Chip salespeople took toward Snackers. As a result of this micro-market experience, Wotton concluded that Smith Foods would have to handle its own distribution. Dr. LeSieur also indicated that so much time was involved in training John's Potato Chip employees to fry the half-product that he could not conceivably have enough time to train several hundred regional potato chippers. Further, Dr. LeSieur believed that adequate control of product quality required Smith's Snackers to be fried and packaged in Smith Foods' own plants. The arguments of Wotton and LeSieur convinced corporate executives that Smith Foods would have to purchase its own frying equipment and special packaging equipment if the Snackers venture were to be continued. Accordingly, corporate executives authorized approximately $97,000 for purchase of this equipment, which, together with its facilities for making half-product, would enable Smith Foods to manufacture some 900,000 cases of finished Snackers per year.

Robert Cecil had analyzed results from the micro-market and on the basis of those results projected sales for Snackers if they were marketed nationally. Cecil noted that Snackers captured an "astonishing" 60 percent of the snack foods market in Klamath Falls and 77 percent in the Medford market (see Exhibits 5 and 6). Both Potato Snackers and Onion Snackers had a higher penetration rate than any of the General Mills products (see Exhibits 7 and 8).

On the basis of the data from the Medford market, Cecil projected penetration and depth of repeat for Snackers and competing products (see Exhibits 9 and 10). Cecil estimated that Snackers would achieve a penetration of 80 percent by the end of the first year, and that each household purchasing Snackers would buy an average of 2.8 additional packages of Snackers during the year.

Using these estimates, Cecil projected sales of Snackers at approximately 15.2 million cases (182 million packages, packed twelve to a case) for the first year. Of this total, some 4 million cases represented initial purchases by 80 percent of 60 million households (0.8 × 60 million) = 48 million packages ÷ 12 packages/case = 4 million cases). The remaining 11.2 million cases were made up of repeat purchases by these 48 million households who'd tried Snackers (48 million × 2.8 packages = 134 million packages ÷ 12 packages/case = 11.2 million cases).

From the study of these data and available information from General Mills snacks, Cecil stated that sales of Snackers should reach peak volume in the first six months. Sales in the second six months should decline by 40 percent of the sales in the first six months. Sales in the next six months should decline by an equal amount (not percentage). In other words, Cecil stated, Snackers should have a short product life.

Cecil further argued that product life would be extended if product quality were improved. Lower quality, he stated, would cause the product to "wear out" faster.

Cecil stated that the total sales generated during the life of the product depended on the size of the sales peak reached in the first six months of national roll-out.

Based on his estimates of the timing of sales, Cecil projected sales by time period as follows for Snackers, General Mills snacks, and Fritos:

	TIME PERIOD				
	First 6 months (million cases)	Second 6 months (million cases)	Third 6 months (million cases)	Penetration	Depth of repeat
Snackers	9.5	5.7	1.9	80%	2.8[a]
General Mills snacks	8.4	6.4	n.a.	52	4.7
Fritos	11.0	9.2	n.a.	65	5.2

[a] Units per household trying the product

Cecil's report also included a summary of shipments to the micro-market from October 1967, through May 1968 (see Exhibit 11). Smith officials typically considered shipment data for short periods a less sensitive indicator of a new product's performance than diary panel results.

PRODUCT MODIFICATIONS

A consumer survey at the time the Klamath Falls diary panel was discontinued indicated that the sharp decline in sales of Potato Snackers could be traced to the fact that many consumers had initially purchased substandard Potato Snackers and, as a result, did not buy any more.

A more extensive survey of 357 members of the Klamath Falls diary panel showed that both Potato and Onion Snackers scored much lower on the nine-point "liking" scale than Bugles, Fritos, or John's Potato Chips.

Henry Wotton argued that results of the total sample were not valid indicators of Snackers' acceptability. Because the panel was composed of heavy snack users, he argued, its members had preexisting loyalties and preferences for Bugles, Whistles, Fritos, and John's Potato Chips. Therefore, consumers were very likely to prefer their favorite to Snackers and to score it higher than Snackers on the nine-point "liking" scale.

This bias could be compensated for, Wotton argued, if the Snackers scores were broken down into two parts: those scores assigned by the entire sample and those scores assigned by persons who bought Snackers more than once (i.e., the repeat buyers). When the scores assigned by repeat buyers of the six products were compared, Onion Snackers scored as high as Bugles, Fritos, and John's Potato Chips. Wotton interpreted this result to mean that Onion Snackers had sufficient consumer acceptance to be marketed nationally. These same results showed that Potato Snackers still scored significantly worse than any of the other five products. Because Smith Foods did not want to market Onion Snackers by themselves, it was decided that neither Onion Snackers nor Potato Snackers could be nationally marketed until the Potato Snackers "liking" score was as high as the "liking" score for either Bugles or Fritos or Potato Chips.

Wotton immediately prepared to improve Potato Snackers quality. In April 1968, a second Klamath Falls test was conducted with members of the Klamath Falls panel to establish a benchmark against which the progress of product improvement could be measured. Wotton believed that results of the first surveys in February could not provide this benchmark because the Klamath Falls panel members had been exposed to Potato Snackers of varying quality. Further, he did not want to use the February results because many of the respondents in that test had not eaten Potato Snackers for several weeks prior to the interview. On April 12, Wotton completed interviews with 144 members of the panel. The results of this test indicated that the Potato Snackers color was too light.

In May, a new product, darker in color and with less noticeable aftertaste, was developed. Tests on Smith Foods office personnel suggested that it was better than the Potato Snackers used in the April consumer interviews. Wotton immediately assembled 119 Klamath Falls panel members to test this improved product.

Results from this test revealed that the improved Potato Snackers had a slightly stronger flavor and tended to be slightly too crispy. The improved Snackers were rated "just about right" in saltiness and color. Wotton noted that the average score of 5.9 given to Potato Snackers by repeat buyers on the nine-point "liking" scale was not significantly lower than the 6.2 given by the repeat buyers of potato chips to potato chips (see Exhibit 12). Therefore, Potato Snackers had met the decision criterion established in February, and Wotton concluded that both Onion and Potato Snackers could be marketed nationally.

After panel members had given their initial reactions, they were asked to use the improved Snackers at home for two weeks. The purpose of this in-home test was to ascertain whether Snackers would maintain their level of consumer acceptance in actual use.

Results from this in-home test, which were reported at the end of May, showed that flavor was the primary reason for consumers' preferring competitive snacks. Flavor was also the attribute most frequently mentioned as a reason for liking or disliking Snackers (see Exhibit 13).

Smith Foods executives noted that Wotton had based his conclusion that Potato Snackers could be marketed on responses from only 14 persons. Wotton agreed that the sample was small and he stated that he wished it were larger. However, he said, there were only 14 Klamath Falls panel members left who were both repeat buyers of Potato Snackers and willing to participate in the test. Wotton said that while he believed that Potato Snackers had been improved sufficiently to be marketed, nevertheless he thought that work to improve them even more should be done while preparations were being made to enter the national market. Wotton said that he did not think national roll-out could begin before September. Thus research could continue until August and still leave enough time to build up finished product inventories for shipment to the national market.

Early in June, Smith Foods asked Dr. LeSieur, the Snackers chief food scientist, if he thought Potato Snackers could be improved. Dr. LeSieur stated that Snackers improvement had been retarded in the past by three basic problems. First, consumers had not had a well-defined idea of how a good snack product should taste. Second, LeSieur had problems with poor corn flour quality controls. Third, he had had problems with making the triangular-shaped Potato Snackers tender enough to eat. LeSieur said he thought that these problems had been minimized and product improvement was likely.

LeSieur then explained the nature of the three problems. In 1966 and 1967, consumers had not yet been exposed to enough snacks in order to determine what was a good snack and what was a bad one. Because they did not have this personal frame of reference, it was very difficult for them to give any snack a score on the nine-point "liking" scale. However, he added, because so many new products were introduced to the market in 1967 and 1968, consumers had developed firm opinions on what good and bad snacks were. Therefore, LeSieur believed it would now be much easier to develop a pleasing product. Second, equipment requirements, when Snackers research was first begun, caused Snackers batter to be made from corn flour and potato flour. Because Smith Foods did not mill its own corn flour, it had to be purchased from other mills. Making Snackers required corn flour with a quality uniformity greater than these firms were accustomed to providing. Thus, during the micro-market LeSieur said he spent most of his time working with these firms devising quality controls which would supply higher uniform-quality corn flour. Lack of uniformity in the corn flour, he said, was partially responsible for the bad Potato Snackers product sold in the Klamath Falls market.

The third problem was the shape of the Potato Snackers. In order to make the triangle shape tender enough to bite easily, LeSieur had to use at least 50 percent corn flour. The formula of the improved Snackers called for 65 percent corn flour and 35 percent potato flour. This meant that much of the natural potato flavor was lost and the Potato Snackers had a corn flavor which had to be masked. Therefore, LeSieur had to use artificial potato flavoring in order to make the Potato Snackers taste like potatoes. The early problem with Potato Snackers was that the artificial flavor also had an unpleasant aftertaste. The improved Potato Snackers used artificial flavoring which had very little aftertaste and which closely resembled the natural potato flavor. If the shape of the Snackers were changed from a triangle to a cylinder, then LeSieur could use much less corn flour and still have a tender product. Further, because he could use less corn flour and more potato flour, the Snackers with the new shape would have more of the natural potato flavor.

Dr. LeSieur believed that a natural potato flavor was a very desirable product attribute. He argued that certain foods such as Corn Flakes, Wheaties, and potato chips enjoyed continuing consumer acceptance because they had bland, natural flavors. Highly seasoned, artificially flavored snacks and cereals often had short product lives because consumers quickly grew tired of them, he believed.

LeSieur said that a special snack press and additional specialized frying equipment could be purchased for about $100,000. This equipment, which had a capacity of about 1 million cases, would permit Potato Snackers to be made in the cylindrical shape almost entirely from potato flour. The resulting snack would turn out as tender as desired without losing any natural potato flavor. Unfortunately, this equipment could not be delivered for six months. Smith Foods' experience with pilot production facilities similar to those LeSieur described indicated that the production line could become fully operational within a month after delivery. If the shape of the Potato Snackers were changed, then the package and the commercial would have to be changed also because both showed pictures of the triangular-shaped Snackers. These changes would take at least three months to accomplish.

LeSieur acknowledged that his staff had not yet solved one remaining production problem, but was confident they could do so. Because Potato and Onion Snackers puffed up more than planned at random intervals, about 30 percent of the boxes left the packaging machines with lower weights of Snackers than those printed on the boxes. The random puffing phenomenon decreased the weight of affected Potato Snackers from five ounces to four ounces, and reduced the weight of affected packages of Onion Snackers from 3.8 ounces to three ounces. As soon as they discovered this problem, Smith Foods personnel changed the weight byline on packages shipped to the micro-market. Company officials doubted that this change, which occurred at about the time the Medford market diary panel was discontinued, had affected micro-market results.

CHANGES IN THE SNACK MARKET

Between May 1967 and June 1968, Smith Foods executives obtained several pieces of new information about the market for Snack Foods. These data included (1) estimates of the total snack foods market, (2) reports of new entries into the snack market, (3) information on General Mills' strategy, and (4) consumer data.

The September 1967 issue of *Food Topics* estimated total retail snack food sales for 1966 at $2.4 billion. The January 1968 issue of *Snack Foods* published a more conservative series of estimates. *Snack Foods* estimated that the retail sales of potato and corn chips together would top $880 million in 1968 and $1 billion in 1970 (see Exhibits 14 and 15). *Food Topics* reported that the fastest growing segment of the snack food category was puffed-shaped snacks, such as Bugles and Whistles. Many firms were attempting to capture a share of the growing snack foods market. In 1966, 70 new snack foods were marketed in various parts of the United States. In 1967, 150 additional entries appeared, and by June 1968, there were 150 more. General Mills, Frito-Lay, and Allied Foods had marketed snacks nationally. Other large food manufacturers, including Kellogg, Quaker Oats, Reynolds Foods, and General Foods, had snacks in test market and were preparing to market those products nationally.

The three national snack marketers provided substantial advertising support for their products. In 1967 General Mills spent $4.4 million to advertise its puffed-shaped snacks; Frito-Lay spent $4.7 million, $3.9 million on Fritos Corn Chips and the remainder on Doritos Tortilla Chips. Allied Foods spent $139,000 on Popcorny. Of the approximately $9.2 million spent by these three manufacturers, $8.5 million (more than 92 percent) was devoted to television advertising.

Because General Mills was the most successful of the national marketers, and because their products resembled General Mills' snacks in many respects, Smith Foods decided to analyze General Mills' snack marketing activities. Smith Foods executives believed that if they could duplicate General Mills' early success, they would also enjoy the same rewards that General Mills enjoyed. Accordingly, Smith Foods officials purchased data on sales of General Mills snack items from 1965 through 1967 (see Exhibit 16).

By June 1968, Smith Foods executives believed they had ascertained a pattern in General Mills' marketing strategy. Essentially, the strategy called for bringing out a new line of snacks every nine to twelve months and accompanying that introduction with heavy advertising. Furthermore, each product was test marketed prior to introduction. General Mills' products were not simultaneously introduced into every major market in the United States, but rather were "rolled-out"; that is, they were introduced into one market, then another, and then another until national distribution was accomplished. Roll-out usually took six months. In late 1965, Bugles, Whistles, and Daisys were introduced and reached peak sales in 1966. New Daisys, Buttons, and Bows were introduced in late 1966 and achieved peak sales in 1967. Chipos, a flash-fried potato chip with a long shelf life, and Corn Chips were introduced in April 1967. Pizza Spins and Barbeque Vitales were introduced in May 1968. After the initial heavy advertising, General Mills cut back its advertising to a much lower sustaining level.

Robert Cecil, a market researcher who had worked for General Mills before coming to Smith Foods, noted that this snack food pattern was very similar to the strategy used by General Mills for breakfast cereals. Because breakfast cereals usually have short product lives, peak demand comes shortly after introduction. Test marketing is used to gauge the size of this initial peak, because the initial peak determines the total sales of the breakfast cereal during its entire product life. Heavy advertising accompanies introduction of new cereals, Cecil commented, in order to make the initial sales peak as high as possible.

Cecil noted that Smith Foods did not market breakfast cereals and that all Smith Foods' products had long product lives. The company's marketing personnel were accustomed to making five- and ten-year sales forecasts and marketing strategies for individual products. Robert Cecil wondered whether Smith Foods could adapt its marketing policies to fit a product with a short product life.

By early June 1968, Smith Foods officials had obtained data on consumer purchase patterns and snack uses from several different sources. These studies, results from which were all substantially in agreement, indicated that approximately 83 percent of all families used potato chips within the period of a year. About half of this number (41 percent of the total) used potato chips one to four times a month; 24 percent of the total ate potato chips more than once a week, and 18 percent of the total used potato chips less than once a month. Usage of potato chips and corn chips was greatest among persons under 35 in large households with median or higher income (see Exhibit 17). Data on total snack usage, as well as purchases of particular types and brands, was available from a panel of 576 households maintained by the *Chicago Tribune* (see Exhibit 18). The income distribution of the households in the panel resembled that of the United States as a whole.

ALTERNATIVES

If Smith Foods executives wished to introduce Snackers through a region by region "roll-out," they had to decide how large a snack manufacturing facility to equip and whether to purchase the snack press and specialized frying equipment so that Snackers could be made almost wholly from potato flour. To increase the present 900,000-case capacity to 2 million cases would require an investment of about $320,000 if Snackers were to be made from a mixture of corn and potato flour. If Snackers were to be made from potato flour alone, investment of $425,000 would be needed: $100,000 to convert present facilities and $325,000 for expansion. To increase present capacity to 3.2 million cases would require an investment of $440,000 if Snackers were made of corn and potato flour; $560,000 if potato flour only were used. Company officials believed that, for production in excess of 3.2 million cases per year, additional plant capacity as well as additional equipment would be needed.

Profits for operation at capacities of 3.2 million cases and 2.0 million cases were estimated, respectively, at $1,664,000 and $860,000. Proforma income statements for operation at each of these levels appear in Exhibit 19.

If the executives decided to delay Snackers' introduction pending further product development work, they realized that they would have to specify the criteria the product must meet for a "go" decision to be made, and the amount of time and dollars which could be expended on development work. Executives who favored this alternative argued that a few months of development and testing would be money well spent to ensure that Snackers were "right" for the market. Those who opposed this course of action feared the company would incur substantial opportunity costs. First, Smith Foods would lose the large revenues expected in the first year and delay receipt of revenues from subsequent years. Second, the company would lose competitive advantage. At present, several national manufacturers had snack products in test markets. Any delay in marketing Snackers would permit those firms to introduce their products into the national market first, making it much more difficult for Snackers to be marketed in the future.

Finally, Smith Foods executives could cancel the Snackers venture entirely. If they did so, the company would recover only a small portion of its investment to date in equipment, and none of its other expenditures on Snackers.

Exhibit 1
SMITH FOODS, INC. (B)
MICRO–MARKET BUDGET

Micro-market test		$26,500
Advertising	$14,000	
Diary panel (800 respondents)	10,000	
Awareness and penetration studies	2,500	
Evaluation of commercials		7,000
Evaluations of packages and price combinations		7,500
Contingency fund		9,000
		$50,000

Exhibit 2

SMITH FOODS, INC. (B)   DEFINITIONS OF IMPORTANT TERMS

Penetration—The number of people who *try* the product within a specified period of time. It is stated as the *percent* of total households in the panel, and is reported on a cumulative basis. It must always stay the same or increase—it can never decline.

Repeat rate—The percent of triers who made *at least one* purchase after their first purchase. It is reported on a cumulative basis. It can go up, down, or remain the same.

Depth of repeat—The number of total repeat *units* sold for every 100 people trying the product. Its purpose is to measure the repeat value of an average trier. It *reflects:*

1. the number of people repeating
2. the frequency with which repeaters are buying
3. the number of units purchased per transaction among repeaters. Depth of repeat is computed as follows:

$$\text{Depth of Repeat} = \frac{\text{Total repeat purchases (in units)}}{\text{Total triers}} \times 100$$

Average repeat consumption—measures the average number of repeat units purchased by each repeat buyer. Average repeat consumption (ARC) may be computed in either of two ways:

1. $$\text{ARC} = \frac{\text{Total units purchased by repeat buyers}}{\text{Number of buyers repeating}}$$

2. $$\text{ARC} = \left(\frac{\text{Depth of repeat}}{\text{Repeat rate}}\right) \div 100$$

Example

Sample size	Month 1 1000 households Households	Units	Month 2 1000 households Households	Units	Month 2 (cumulative) 1000 households Households	Units
Penetrators (Triers)	125	170	125	150	250	320
1st repeaters	30	50	15	40	45	90
2nd repeaters	15	40	5	15	20	55
3rd repeaters	—	—	5	20	5	20
Total repeat	45	90	25	75	70	165

From these raw data the following summary would be reported:

	Month 1	Month 2 (cumulative)
Penetration	$12.5\% \left(= \frac{125}{1000} \times 100\%\right)$	$25\% \left(= \frac{250}{1000} \times 100\%\right)$
Repeat rate	$36 \left(= \frac{45}{125} \times 100\%\right)$	$28 \left(= \frac{70}{250} \times 100\%\right)$
Depth of repeat	$72 \left(= \frac{90}{125} \times 100\right)$	$66 \left(= \frac{165}{250} \times 100\right)$
Average repeat consumption	$2.0 \left(= \frac{90}{45}; \text{ or } \frac{72}{.36} \div 100\right)$	$2.36 \left(= \frac{165}{70}; \text{ or } \frac{66}{.28} \div 100\right)$

Source: Company Records

Exhibit 3

SMITH FOODS, INC. (B)

SMITH SNACKERS MICRO-MARKET ADVERTISING FLOW CHART, 1967–1968

	September	October	November	December	January	February	March to May
Outdoor							
16 billboards	30 days						
Spot T.V.		452 GRPs/week 14 days			90–95 GRPs/week 28 days	40–45 GRPs/week 35 weeks	
Network T.V.							
Nighttime cut-ins			nine 60-second commercials 17 days				
Newspapers							
2 cities, 2 papers			1 page black and white apology ad				
Spot Radio							
Klamath Falls					35 GRPs/week		
60 seconds							
10 seconds							

(Notation in December column: SIX WEEK HIATUS)

Costs:	20 weeks	52 weeks	Cost of national campaign using same strategy
Billboards	$ 745	$ 745	$ 100,000
Spot T.V.	5,695	11,395	451,000
Network cut-ins	3,018	3,018	1,227,000 (includes daytime T.V.)
Newspapers	1,124	1,124	n.a.
Spot Radio	—	756	
	$10,572	$17,037	$1,778,000

GRP = Gross Rating Points
Source: Company Records

Exhibit 4

SMITH FOODS, INC. (B)
UNIT SALES OF SMITH'S SNACKERS FOR EIGHT WEEKS,
MAIL-ORDER PANEL

	Bag at 39 cents	Box at 39 cents	Bag at 49 cents	Box at 49 cents
Total units sold	362	378	323	346
Sales by purchase pattern				
Sales to repeat purchasers	154	159	103	133
Sales to triers who did not repeat	208	219	220	213
Sales by flavor				
Onion Snackers	196	186	164	180
Potato Snackers	166	192	159	166

Source: Company Records

Exhibit 5
SMITH FOODS, INC. (B)
BRAND SHARE, SPECIALTY SNACK MARKET
KLAMATH FALLS MICRO-MARKET

Period:	Oct. 23-Nov. 6	Nov. 7-20	Nov. 21-Dec. 4	Dec. 5-18	Dec. 19-Jan. 1	Jan. 1-15
Panel size (Families)[a]	393	383	378	374	374	374
Potato Snackers	23.2%	25.7%	7.7%	7.3%	6.7%	10.5%
Onion Snackers	37.3	27.2	21.4	28.1	21.5	21.1
Total Snackers	60.5	52.9	29.1	35.4	28.2	31.6
Bugles	14.2	24.0	35.0	22.9	25.2	35.7
Whistles	7.3	8.0	16.2	13.0	10.4	9.4
Daisies	3.4	2.0	5.1	2.1	3.6	2.1
Buttons	3.0	2.0	0.9	2.1	1.5	2.1
Bows	4.7	4.3	3.4	6.3	11.9	9.5
Total General Mills	32.6	40.3	60.7	44.4	52.6	58.8
Popcorny	2.1	2.0	3.4	9.4	9.6	7.4
Cornchippy	4.3	1.0	6.0	8.3	9.6	2.2
Total Allied Foods	6.4	3.0	9.4	17.7	19.2	9.6
Nibbits	0.5	3.8	0.8	2.5	—	—
Total specialty munching snacks	100.0%	100.0%	100.0%	100.0%	100.0%	100.0%

a Although 400 families agreed to join the panel, not all of them completed their purchase diaries for all six two-week periods. Such attrition is not uncommon in diary panels.

Exhibit 6

SMITH FOODS, INC. (B)
BRAND SHARE, SPECIALTY SNACK MARKET
MEDFORD MICRO-MARKET

Period:	Oct. 23-Nov. 6	Nov. 7-20	Nov. 21-Dec. 4	Dec. 5-18	Dec. 19-Jan. 1	Jan. 2-15	Jan. 16-29	Jan. 30-Feb. 12	Feb. 13-26	Feb. 27-Mar. 12
Panel size (families) [a]	381	380	365	366	371	368	298	294	283	295
Potato Snackers	35.0%	27.0%	22.7%	19.3%	22.7%	18.7%	22.2%	23.0%	17.5%	22.8%
Onion Snackers	42.2	35.8	22.7	21.9	37.0	34.6	27.3	19.5	20.0	15.8
Total Snackers	77.2	62.0	45.4	41.2	59.7	53.3	49.5	42.5	37.5	38.6
Bugles	7.0	14.5	18.4	20.2	19.4	19.5	22.2	24.1	21.3	22.8
Whistles	4.9	5.0	12.1	17.5	7.4	7.4	7.1	6.9	18.8	7.0
Daisies	0.6	2.5	0.0	0.9	1.9	1.9	2.0	1.2	1.3	1.8
Buttons	2.7	6.3	9.9	1.8	4.6	5.6	7.1	5.7	5.0	5.3
Bows	4.0	3.1	5.7	7.0	2.3	5.6	6.1	16.1	13.8	14.0
Total General Mills	19.2	31.4	46.1	47.4	35.6	40.0	44.5	54.0	60.2	50.9
Popcorny	0.9	1.9	2.8	3.6	1.4	5.6	—	1.2	2.3	3.5
Cornchippy	2.7	2.5	4.3	7.8	3.3	1.1	6.0	2.4	0.0	7.0
Total Allied Foods	3.6	4.4	7.1	11.4	4.7	6.7	6.0	3.5	2.3	10.5
Nibbits	—	1.2	1.4	—	—	—	—	—	—	—
Total specialty munching snacks	100.0%	100.0%	100.0%	100.0%	100.0%	100.0%	100.0%	100.0%	100.0%	100.0%

[a] Although 400 families agreed to join the panel, not all of them completed their purchase diaries for all six two-week periods. Such attrition is not uncommon in diary panels.

Source: Company Records

Exhibit 7

SMITH FOODS, INC. (B)
DIARY PANEL RESULTS
KLAMATH FALLS

		Oct. 23-Nov. 6	Nov. 7-20	Nov. 21-Dec. 4	Dec. 5-18	Dec. 19-Jan. 1	Jan. 2-15
Potato Snackers	Penetration (P)[a]	12%	20%	21%	22%	24%	27%[b]
	Repeat (R)[a]	11%	18%	20%	21%	21%	24%[c]
	Depth of Repeat (D)[a]	11 units	25	31	33	36	42[d]
Onion Snackers	P	19%	28%	31%	33%	35%	36%
	R	9%	16%	21%	26%	27%	28%
	D	9	21	31	46	59	165
Any Snacker	P	26%	38%	41%	43%	45%	46%
	R	24%	33%	35%	40%	42%	43%
	D	34	58	70	80	98	110
Any General Mills snack	P			DATA NOT AVAILABLE			
	R						
	D						
Any Allied Foods snack	P	3%	4%	6%	9%	11%	12%
	R	17%	36%	27%	24%	30%	38%
	D	25	50	40	42	69	82

Exhibit 7 (Cont.)

		Oct. 23–Nov. 6	Nov. 7–20	Nov. 21–Dec. 4	Dec. 5–18	Dec. 19–Jan. 1	Jan. 2–15
Fritos Corn Chips	P	28%	37%	42%	47%	49%	52%
	R	25%	45%	48%	52%	59%	62%
	D	30	76	103	135	168	197
Any potato chip	P	84%	94%	96%	99%	100%	100%
	R	56%	81%	87%	91%	96%	97%
	D	95	227	335	455	627	770
Any shaped snack	P	38%	56%	61%	64%	67%	68%
	R	32%	46%	56%	61%	66%	68%
	D	51	88	123	152	193	223

a For definitions, see Exhibit 2.

b 27% (= $\frac{101}{394}$) of panel families had purchased (tried) Potato Snackers one or more times.

c 24% (= $\frac{24}{101}$) of triers had made additional (repeat) purchases of Potato Snackers.

d The 101 families who tried Potato Snackers purchased a total of 42 repeat units, i.e., units (packages) in addition to their initial purchases. This calculation is performed in the following manner:

1. Depth of repeat = $\frac{\text{Total repeat units}}{\text{Total triers}}$ (100)

2. Substitution of known quantities yields the following:

$$42 = \frac{\text{Total repeat units}}{101} (100)$$

3. Solving for total repeat units, we find: $42 = \frac{42}{101}$ (100), rounding to nearest whole number.

Source: Company Records

Exhibit 8
SMITH FOODS, INC. (B)
DIARY PANEL RESULTS
MEDFORD MARKET

			Oct. 23–Nov. 6	Nov. 7–20	Nov. 21–Dec. 4	Dec. 5–18	Dec. 19–Jan. 1	Jan. 2–15	Jan. 16–29	Jan. 29–Feb. 11	Feb. 13–26
Potato Snackers	Penetration	(P)[a]	25%	31%	34%	36%	41%	43%	45%	47%	48%
	Repeat	(R)[a]	1%	15%	25%	32%	37%	37%	39%	38%	39%
	Depth of Repeat	(D)[a] 1 Unit	1	21	35	48	67	73	80	84	91
Onion Snackers		P	29%	38%	40%	42%	48%	49%	52%	54%	54%
		R	11%	19%	26%	29%	31%	36%	37%	38%	40%
		D	13	22	36	45	62	77	84	89	95
Any Snacker		P	39%	50%	53%	55%	61%	63%	65%	67%	68%
		R	41%	45%	50%	53%	55%	58%	60%	61%	61%
		D	57	72	95	111	139	156	168	177	186
Any General Mills snack		P	14%	21%	28%	31%	36%	39%	41%	43%	45%
		R	15%	35%	37%	46%	49%	48%	52%	53%	53%
		D	21	42	60	87	101	132	150	170	192
Any Allied Foods snack		P	3%	4%	7%	8%	9%	10%	11%	11%	11%
		R	—	6%	4%	32%	34%	37%	40%	41%	46%
		D	—	6	4	39	40	47	55	58	63
Fritos Corn Chips		P	19%	28%	32%	37%	42%	45%	48%	50%	53%
		R	26%	33%	45%	48%	50%	54%	57%	60%	60%
		D	41	61	91	109	122	142	168	190	209
Any potato chip		P	77%	90%	95%	98%	99%	100%	100%	100%	100%
		R	49%	76%	85%	89%	92%	96%	96%	96%	96%
		D	74	189	304	412	680	774	876	977	1065
Any shaped snack		P	48%	60%	66%	69%	73%	76%	79%	82%	n.a.
		R	n.a.	n.a.	n.a.	n.a.	n.a.	n.a.	n.a.	n.a.	n.a.
		D	n.a.	100	n.a.	175	n.a.	267	n.a.	350	n.a.

[a] For definitions, see Exhibit 2 and notes to Exhibit 7.
Source: Company Records

Exhibit 9

SMITH FOODS, INC. (B)—PERCENTAGE OF HOUSEHOLDS WHO
TRIED PARTICULAR SNACKS PRODUCTS IN MEDFORD, AND
NATIONAL PROJECTIONS BASED ON MEDFORD RESULTS

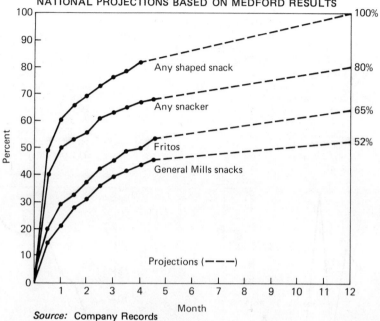

Source: Company Records

Exhibit 10

SMITH FOODS, INC. (B)—DEPTH OF REPEAT: NUMBER OF UNITS (PACKAGES) PUR-
CHASED PER 100 HOUSEHOLDS WHO TRIED PARTICULAR SNACK PRODUCTS IN
MEDFORD, AND NATIONAL PROJECTIONS BASED ON MEDFORD RESULTS

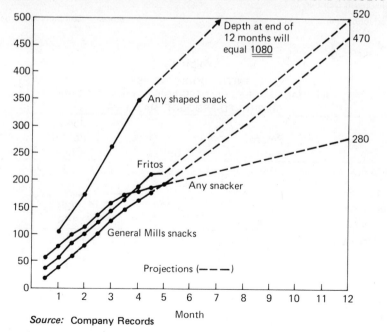

Source: Company Records

Exhibit 11

SMITH FOODS, INC. (B)
SHIPMENTS TO MICRO–MARKET OCTOBER 1967 THROUGH MAY 1968
CASES OF 12

6,176 — October[a]	6,176 — October
7,610 — November	13,786 -- November
1,110 — December[b]	14,896 — December
11,130 — January	26,026 -- January
514 — February	26,540 — February
1,306 — March	27,826 — March
1,066 — April	28,912 — April
2,902 — May	31,814 — May
31,814	

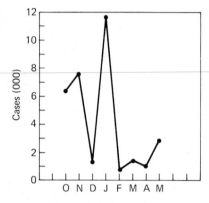

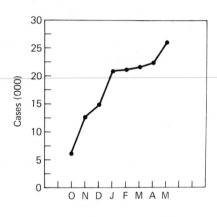

[a]Sales began October 23

[b]Production is interrupted

Source: Company Records

Exhibit 12

SMITH FOODS, INC. (B)
AVERAGE SCORES ON NINE–POINT "LIKING" SCALE
IMPROVED PRODUCT, MAY 1968

	Potato Snackers	Bugles	John's Potato Chips	Fritos
Average score	5.9	6.8	6.2	6.6
Sample size				
Purchasers	119	238	238	238
Repeat buyers	14	112	159	168

Source: Company Records

Exhibit 13

SMITH FOODS, INC. (B)
RESULTS OF IN-HOME TEST
MAY 10–24, 1968
REASONS FOR PREFERRING COMPETITIVE SNACKS

		Snacks liked more than Smith's Snackers	
	Fritos	Bugles	Potato chips
Better flavor/corn flavor	55%	49%	28%
Mild flavor	9	10	8
No artificial taste	2	2	—
No aftertaste	—	2	—
Right saltiness	6	5	1
Can use with dips	12	14	12
Right crispiness	17	11	17
Family/children prefer	18	19	12
Not as greasy	2	6	1
Old standby	—	—	16

WHAT WAS LIKED/DISLIKED ABOUT SMITH'S SNACKERS

	Liked	Disliked
Flavor	7%	39%
Saltiness	5	33
Greasiness	10	6
Aftertaste	1	7
Lack of flavor	—	8
Crispiness	33	6
Other, no response	44	1
	(n = 82)	(n = 82)

Source: Company Records

Exhibit 14

SMITH FOODS, INC. (B)
ESTIMATES OF RETAIL SNACK SALES, 1964 TO 1966
(MILLIONS OF DOLLARS)

Product	1964	1965	1966
Potato chips	$ 681.6	$ 748.4	$ 828.4
Cookies	653.6	700.0	736.4
Nuts	493.0	523.0	553.4
Corn chips	136.3	162.7	192.7
Pretzels	109.9	118.9	118.2
Unpopped popcorn	27.4	29.9	29.1
Daisys, Whistles and Bugles only	n.a.	n.a.	20.0
Total	$2,101.8	$2,282.9	$2,478.2

Source: Food Topics, September 1967

Exhibit 15

SMITH FOODS, INC. (B)

ESTIMATED SALES FOR POTATO AND CORN CHIPS, 1964 TO 1975

(MILLIONS OF DOLLARS)

Year	Manufacturer's price	Retail prices
1964	$486	$ 663
1965	524	716
1966	566	774
1967	606	828
1968	648	886
1969	694	948
1970	743	1005
1971	780	1065
1972	826	1129
1973	868	1185
1974	911	1245
1975	957	1307

Source: *Snack Foods,* January 1968

Exhibit 16

SMITH FOODS, INC. (B)

SALES TO RETAILERS OF GENERAL MILLS SNACKS

(THOUSANDS OF UNITS)

	1965	1966	1967
Bugles	2,184	60,096	32,856
Whistles	504	36,744	12,960
Daisys	452	27,948	6,648
Buttons	—	2,496	11,808
Bows	—	2,544	13,738
Total	3,140	129,828	78,010

Source: Company Records

Exhibit 17

SMITH FOODS, INC. (B)   CONSUMPTION OF SNACKS BY ALL USERS IN HOUSEHOLD
BY CHARACTERISTICS OF HOMEMAKER (1968)

Characteristics of homemaker	Percent of total U.S. homemakers %	Percent using past month	Index U.S. = 100	Percent using past year	Index U.S. = 100
Total	100 %	65.1%	100	54.4%	100
Homemaker age					
18–24	9.5	80.0	123	60.2	111
25–34	19.1	79.6	122	70.1	129
35–49	32.2	73.4	113	65.3	120
50–64	24.4	} 47.4	} 73	45.3	83
65 and older	14.8			21.8	40
Household income					
Under $5,000	33.8	48.8	75	39.2	72
$5,000–$7,999	26.6	70.3	108	57.0	105
$8,000–$9,999	14.0	78.4	120	64.1	118
$10,000–$14,999	17.6	78.7	121	66.6	122
$15,000 and over	8.0	71.3	110	66.6	122
Number of persons in household					
1–2	40.2	45.4	70	38.1	70
3–4	35.3	76.0	117	62.3	115
5 or more	24.5	80.9	124	70.0	129
Age of children					
Under 6	26.7	80.8	124	67.7	124
6–11	27.5	} 79.7	} 122	71.7	132
12–17	27.8			67.7	124
No children under 18	46.2	48.4	74		
Marital status					
Married	77.9	} n.a.	} n.a.	58.6	108
Not married	22.1			39.8	73

Source: Company Records

Exhibit 18

SMITH FOODS, INC, (B)

DATA ON SNACK SALES REPORTED BY CHICAGO TRIBUNE CONSUMER PANEL

	1966						1967						1968
	Jan.	Mar.	May	July	Sept.	Nov.	Jan.	Mar.	May	July	Sept.	Nov.	Jan.
Percent families buying snacks	69.6	73.1	75.9	74.8	75.5	73.5	66.7	68.2	71.9	69.1	70.5	69.7	68.4
Percent by family income													
Under $5000	11.0	11.6	11.8	12.5	11.0	19.3	10.2	9.5	11.1	11.0	10.7	10.2	9.5
$5000–$10,000	47.3	45.9	50.1	50.3	50.4	52.2	51.9	53.0	49.8	50.5	50.4	50.0	49.3
over $10,000	41.7	42.4	38.1	37.3	38.4	38.6	37.9	37.5	39.2	38.6	38.9	39.8	41.2
Total snack units purchased	1,659	1,921	1,931	1,567	1,860	1,816	1,618	1,672	1,761	1,536	1,731	1,645	1,619
Percent sales by volume[a]													
All potato chips	70.9	65.8	75.0	77.6	73.0	77.0	78.3	74.5	78.0	77.6	76.5	75.6	74.7
All corn chips[b]	29.1	34.2	25.0	22.4	27.0	22.9	21.7	16.8	21.2	13.0	13.8	14.6	15.2
All General Mills	11.4	16.9	9.4	8.1	8.5	6.8	5.8	7.0	5.9	7.7	6.9	7.8	7.6
Fritos Corn Chips	11.1	9.3	9.4	7.1	10.3	10.0	9.2	9.2	6.2	6.7	7.2	7.6	8.3
All Allied Foods	2.0	3.2	1.6	1.5	1.8	2.0	1.7	1.8	2.3	1.7	1.8	2.0	2.5
Bugles						n.a.	3.5	4.4	3.2	4.4	3.7	3.2	2.7
Whistles						n.a.	1.8	2.2	2.1	2.6	2.0	1.6	1.6
Daisys						n.a.	0.5	0.4	0.6	0.7	0.6	0.5	0.4
General Mills Corn Chips							n.a.	6.9	5.8	7.7	6.9	7.8	7.7

Exhibit 18 (Cont.)

Exhibit 19

SMITH FOODS, INC. (B)

COST AND REVENUE PROJECTIONS FOR SMITH'S SNACKERS FOR FIRST YEAR OF OPERATION AT CAPACITY

Sales				
Number of cases		3,200,000		2,000,000
Total revenues		$10,720,000		$6,700,000
Revenues per case		3.35		3.35
Less costs per case				
Ingredients	$0.50		$0.50	
Packaging	0.86		0.86	
Manufacturing and direct overhead	0.12		0.13	
Distribution and warehousing	0.24		0.24	
Cash discounts	0.07		0.07	
Administration and sales	0.11		0.12	
Research and development[a]	0.10		0.15	
Advertising[b]	0.45		0.45	
Promotion	0.35		0.35	
Market audits	0.03		0.05	
Total cost/case	$2.83		$2.92	
Total costs		$9,056,000		$5,840,000
Profits		$1,664,000		$860,000

[a]Research and development expenses charged against each product included charges for development of new products which would extend the present product line, and a share of the company's total R & D expense.

[b]Advertising expenses amount to $1.44 million and $0.9 million respectively at the 3.2 million and 2 million levels of capacity. These figures correspond to a national advertising budget of $4.2 million, which Smith Foods would spend when Snackers achieved national distribution. These figures are based on the premise that Snackers would be "rolled-out" region by region.

Source: Company Records

THE GREEN GIANT COMPANY

Frozen Fruits

In December 1967, marketing executives of The Green Giant Company met to decide whether or not to add to the company's line a new group of frozen fruit products in a "Quick Thaw" package. They knew that Birds Eye Frozen Fruits were beginning to appear on test market in the "Quick Thaw" pack, but were as yet unsure how well that new entry was faring.

THE COMPANY

Green Giant is a Minnesota-based company which processes and markets a wide variety of canned and frozen vegetables through the grocery trade to households throughout the United States and Canada. Green Giant also markets its products to hotels, restaurants, and hospitals.

The company had grown consistently for more than ten years in sales and earnings. In 1957, Green Giant had sales of $55.4 million with net earnings of $1.2 million. Its profits of 2.16 percent of sales was above average for the industry at that time. Ten years later, in 1967, sales had grown to $173 million, with net earnings of $5.7 million. The profit of 3.3 percent of sales remained above average for the industry. The company had historically earned 10 to 15 percent on invested capital. Abridged financial statements for 1966 and 1967 appear in Exhibits 1 and 2.

In 1967, the company's product line included such items as corn, peas, beans, brussels sprouts, broccoli, sweet potatoes, asparagus, mushrooms, carrots, onions, and spinach. These products were marketed under the brand names Green Giant, Niblet, and LeSueur, all of which were highly regarded by consumers and the trade. According to Green Giant executives, their products were intended to meet three objectives: (1) command attention in the marketplace, (2) provide excitement for the consumer, and (3) bring a reasonable return on investment for the company. Officials attributed the company's success in achieving these objectives to Green Giant's practice of continuously improving widely consumed vegetables.

Throughout the early 1960s Green Giant management had given considerable thought to expanding the company's product line. To date the greatest expansion and success had come through the use of a butter-sauce packing method, whereby frozen vegetables were packed in a butter sauce. Executives believed that this packing advantage had almost exhaused the company's possibilities for expanding its product line, and therefore in the mid-1960s sought to enter additional markets through development of new products.

MARKETING ORGANIZATION

The Green Giant marketing organization was responsible for developing and carrying out marketing and sales plans for both existing and new products. As part of its responsibility, the marketing group evaluated new products. Ideas for new products came from the company's research department, the sales force, executives, or anyone within the organization. Those ideas that survived a preliminary screening received extensive analysis by the marketing research department. This analysis typically included considerable consumer research.

With the exception of four cities (Atlanta, Cleveland, Detroit, and Indianapolis) in which Green Giant operated its own sales offices, the company sold its consumer products to supermarket chains and grocery wholesalers through food brokers, who in a particular geographic area sold five to ten noncompeting product lines and serviced these lines in the individual stores that stocked them. This service typically involved such activities as maintaining adequate stocks and arranging for special displays. For their services, brokers received a commission equal to 2.5 percent of their sales of Green Giant products. Company executives noted that Green Giant products typically were among the top three revenue producers for the brokers, and in many cases ranked first. Company officials also commented that the Green Giant brokerage network was considered one of the most highly motivated and effective in the industry. To support the activities of its brokers and salespeople, Green Giant conducted an extensive consumer advertising campaign. The company typically spent a higher proportion of its sales dollars on advertising than was common in the industry.

HISTORY OF FROZEN FRUIT INTEREST BY GREEN GIANT

Executives noted that the company's interest in frozen fruits began in 1962, when Green Giant acquired Sterling Industries in California. The original purpose of this acquisition had been to make use of Sterling's facilities for vegetables. Sterling was experienced with brussels sprouts and other vegetables, and also packed frozen fruits. Sterling's frozen peaches, melon balls, and mixed fruit servings were sold to private labelers who in turn sold the product through retail outlets.

Although Green Giant had no experience with frozen fruits, company executives believed that Green Giant's reputation and marketing expertise, when coupled with Sterling's technical expertise in frozen fruits, could result in profitable new products.

Green Giant had previously developed a new packaging technique for frozen vegetables, a boil-in-bag pouch. Research and development was able to transfer this principle to frozen fruits, and Green Giant was now able to offer a product that cut thawing time from several hours to less than 15 minutes. The consumer merely put the frozen pouch in warm water for 10 to 15 minutes, opened the pouch, and then served the fruits. No longer would consumers have to plan dessert several hours ahead to allow defrosting time.

FROZEN FRUITS

Frozen fruits were currently packed in 10-ounce and 16-ounce fibrous paper containers with metal ends called Sefton containers. The small package size allowed the container only limited space in frozen food cabinets.

A 10-ounce package of strawberries or raspberries was typically sold for around 30 cents at retail. A 16-ounce package sold for 40 cents to 45 cents.

Newspaper studies revealed the presence of many private label and few national brands in the frozen fruit market. Advertising expenditures on frozen fruits were limited.

Frozen food products required different transportation methods from nonfrozen products. After packing, frozen products were shipped by refrigerated vehicles to refrigerated warehouses and then by refrigerated trucks to the supermarket. Frozen foods typically were shipped in smaller lots than nonfrozen food products. Because of these special transportation requirements, transportation costs usually comprised a higher proportion of total product cost for frozen foods than for nonfrozen foods.

COSTS

Preliminary cost estimates indicated that direct manufacturing costs (including packaging) would amount to at least $5.75 for a case of 24 16-ounce containers of frozen fruit. Transportation to stores in major markets would add 50 to 75 cents a case. Industry sources estimated that manufacturers typically sold frozen fruit to retailers at a price equal to approximately 115 percent of delivered cost. Retail markups of 25 to 30 percent of the retailers' selling price were common in the industry.

Using available facilities in its Sterling Division, Green Giant could produce approximately 1¾ to 2 million cases of frozen fruit, depending on the particular mix of fruits to be packed. A "rule of thumb" in the industry was that incremental capacity for packing 750,000 to 1 million cases of frozen fruit could be added to an existing facility at a cost of $1.2 to $1.5 million for each such increase.

MARKETING RESEARCH INFORMATION

Green Giant marketing research personnel had prepared for executives a list of marketing data they considered pertinent, together with the costs—in time and dollars—of obtaining the information. The executives agreed that their upper limits on spending should be $90,000 and 15 months, but were eager to spend less and to bring the matter to a conclusion much more promptly. One executive noted that conducting several studies simultaneously could reduce the total time required for a decision, although the dollar costs of particular studies would not be reduced.

Research personnel also provided samples of the tables the several studies would yield. The table numbers, titles, and costs are listed in Exhibit 3; the blank tables are appended to the case.

Exhibit 1

THE GREEN GIANT COMPANY
INCOME STATEMENT FOR THE YEARS ENDING MARCH 31
(000)

	1966	1967
Net sales	$139,500	$173,033
Cost of goods sold	91,418	115,859
Marketing, distribution, and general expense	38,989	43,990
Earnings before taxes	9,093	13,184
Other income (loss)	21	(2,438)
Income taxes (net of investment credit)	4,423	5,012
Net profit	4,649	5,734

Source: Annual Report

Exhibit 2

THE GREEN GIANT COMPANY
BALANCE SHEET, MARCH 31
(000)

	1966	1967
Cash	$ 1,791	$ 3,796
Accounts receivable	11,600	13,596
Inventories	47,080	53,722
Prepaid expenses	1,397	1,593
Plant and equipment	27,519	34,671
Other fixed assets	6,646	5,976
Total assets	$96,033	$113,352
Accounts payable	$ 8,535	$ 5,736
Notes payable (including current maturities of long-term debt)	13,009	21,328
Accrued expenses and taxes	8,869	7,442
Long-term debt	23,458	23,595
Stockholders equity	41,750	55,251
Total liabilities and capital	$96,033	$113,352

Source: Annual Report

Exhibit 3

THE GREEN GIANT COMPANY
MARKETING INFORMATION AVAILABLE

Tables	Titles	Cost in: Dollars	Months
1–3[a]	Market Data	$ 300	1.0
4	Use of Frozen Fruits	50	0.5
5	Consumer Attitudes: Frozen Fruits	50	0.5
6	Advertising Expenditures: Frozen Fruits	50	0.5
7–8[a]	Consumer Taste Tests	1,250	1.5
9–16[a]	Two-City Taste Test	4,000	1.5
17	Consumer Reaction: Ollalieberries	1,500	1.0
18	Consumer Package Preferences	1,000	1.0
19	Three-City Taste Test	4,000	1.5
20	Package Test	2,500	1.5
21–24[a]	Store Audits: Three Cities	15,000	12.0
25	Pricing Study	1,000	1.0
26	Competitive Information	500	0.5
27–29[a]	Two-City Test Market	80,000	8.0
30	Nielsen Data and Projections	5,000	1.5

[a]Multiple tables constitute a single research study. Cost Figures are for *all* tables in a single study. For example, Tables 1, 2, and 3 may all be purchased for $300 and made available in a month. Purchase of only Table 1, for instance, would result in negligible savings in dollars and time.

Source: Research Data

APPENDIX

Green Giant—Frozen Fruits

TABLE 1 — AMOUNT SPENT IN GROCERY STORES FOR FRUIT IN 1966

	$ MILLION	PCT OF TOTAL
CANNED		
FROZEN		
FRESH		
TOTAL FRUITS		

SOURCE: AD AGENCY STUDY

TABLE 2—IMPORTANCE OF FROZEN FOODS BY TYPE IN 1966:

FROZEN FOODS	PCT OF RETAIL SALES		FROZEN FOODS	PCT OF RET SALE	
	UNITS	DOLLARS		UNITS	DOLLARS
VEGETABLES	PCT	PCT	FRUITS*	PCT	PCT
JUICES			PIZZA		
BAKED GOODS			PKGD MEATS +		
PREPARED ENTREES + SOUPS			POULTRY		
PREPARED COMPLETE DINNERS			OTHER		
PREPARED SEAFOOD					
ICE CREAM/ICE DESSERTS			TOTAL	PCT	PCT

* FROZEN STRAWBERRIES ACCOUNTED FOR 80PCT OF FROZEN FRUIT SALES: MIXED
  RASPBERRIES, PEACHES + MELLON BALLS TOGETHER ACCOUNTED FOR 10 TO 12 PCT

SOURCE: AD AGENCY STUDY

TABLE 3--AMOUNT SPENT IN RETAIL GROCERY STORES 1961-1966 IN $MILLION

	1961	1962	1963	1964	1965	*	1966
TOTAL FOODS							
INDEX							
TOTAL FRUITS							
INDEX							
FRESH							
FRESH							
INDEX							
CANNED							
INDEX							
FROZEN							
INDEX							
FROZEN FOODS							
INDEX							
FROZEN VEGETBLS							
INDEX							
FROZEN FRUIT							

*INDUSTRY SOURCES ATTRIBUTED DECLINE IN 1965-66 SALES LARGELY TO WEATHER
CONDITIONS AFFECTING FRUIT CROPS.

SOURCE: AD AGENCY STUDY

TABLE 4--PERCENTAGE OF HOUSEHOLDS SERVING FROZEN FRUITS
          PERCENTAGE:
          MAJOR USE:

SOURCE: CHICAGO TRIBUNE PANEL

TABLE 5A—FACTORS INFLUENCING POPULARITY OF FROZEN FRUITS:

TABLE 5B—DISADVANTAGES OF USING FROZEN FRUITS:

SOURCE: STUDY BY LIFE MAGAZINE

TABLE 6—COMPETITIVE ADVERTISING EXPENDITURES, 1966-67
   BRAND   ALL MEDIA   MAGAZINES   NEWSPAPERS
     BIRDS EYE
       1966
       1967 (FIRST 6 MONTHS)
     STOUFFERS
       1966
       1967 (FIRST 6 MONTHS)

SOURCE: AD AGENCY STUDY

TABLE 7A—BLIND TASTE TESTS: GREEN GIANT VS. BIRDS EYE
   EVALUATION ON: PREFERENCE:
       'LIKING' SCALES
       'READINESS TO BUY' SCALES
       INDIVIDUAL FRUIT BASIS

TABLE 7B—BLIND TASTE TESTS: GREEN GIANT AND BIRDS EYE FROZEN FRUITS VS.
DEL MONTE CANNED PRODUCTS
   EVALUATION OF: PREFERENCE:
       PEACHES
       MIXED FRUIT

SOURCE: COMPANY-CONDUCTED STUDY

TABLE 8—TASTE TESTS ON GREEN GIANT'S QUICK-THAW PACKAGE
   EVALUATION OF: COMMENTS:
       QUICK-THAW PACKAGE
       MIXED FRUITS

SOURCE: COMPANY-CONDUCTED STUDY

TABLE 9--OVERALL PREFERENCE FOR MIXED FRUITS

	HOMEMAKER	HUSBAND	CHILDREN	OTH FAMILY	TOT FAM
NUMBER OF RESPONDENTS	(138)	(121)	(154)	(15)	(428)
	PCT	PCT	PCT	PCT	PCT
PREFERRED GREEN GIANT	PCT	PCT	PCT	PCT	PCT
PREFERRED BIRDS EYE	PCT	PCT	PCT	PCT	PCT
LIKED BOTH	PCT	PCT	PCT	PCT	PCT
LIKED NEITHER	PCT	PCT	PCT	PCT	PCT

SOURCE: DENVER + SAN FRANCISCO TASTE TESTS

TABLE 10A—REASONS HOMEMAKERS GAVE FOR DISLIKING MIXED FRUIT PRODUCT

	GREEN GIANT	BIRDS EYE	
NUMBER OF HOMEMAKERS	(138)	(138)	
	PCT	PCT	(18)
HOMEMAKERS MENTIONING DISLIKES	PCT	PCT	
FLAVOR/TASTE	PCT	PCT	
GENERAL	PCT	PCT	
TOO SWEET	PCT	PCT	
TOO SOUR		PCT	
BLAND/TASTELESS	PCT	PCT	
ODD/ARTIFICIAL TASTE	PCT	PCT	
OTHER		PCT	
INDIVIDUAL FRUITS	PCT	PCT	
MELON BALLS	PCT		
CHERRIES		PCT	
GRAPES	PCT	PCT	
RASPBERRIES		PCT	
PEACHES	PCT	PCT	
PINEAPPLE	PCT		
MISCELLANEOUS	PCT	PCT	
METHOD OF PREPARATION	PCT	PCT	
COMBINATION OF FRUITS	PCT	PCT	
TEXTURE/TENDERNESS	PCT	PCT	
PACKAGE TOO SMALL	PCT	PCT	
SYRUP	PCT	PCT	
APPEARANCE	PCT	PCT	
OTHER	PCT	PCT	

TABLE 10B--REASONS HOMEMAKERS GAVE FOR LIKING MIXED FRUITS

	GREEN GIANT (138)	BIRDS EYE (138)	
NUMBER OF HOMEMAKERS			
HOMEMAKERS MENTIONING LIKES	PCT	PCT	
FLAVOR/TASTE	PCT	PCT	
GENERAL	PCT	PCT	(PCTS MAY
FRESH TASTING	PCT	PCT	NOT ADD TO
SWEET	PCT	PCT	100 DUE TO
TANGINESS/NOT TOO SWEET	PCT	PCT	MULTIPLE
INDIVIDUAL FLAVORS	PCT	PCT	RESPONSES)
RIGHT SWEETNESS	PCT	PCT	
TEXTURE/TENDERNESS	PCT	PCT	
GENERAL	PCT		
FIRM/CRISP	PCT	PCT	
TENDER	PCT		
OTHER			
COLOR/APPEARANCE	PCT	PCT	
GENERAL			
COLOR	PCT	PCT	
APPEARANCE	PCT	PCT	
OTHER			
INDIVIDUAL	PCT	PCT	
MELON BALLS	PCT		
CHERRIES		PCT	
RASPBERRIES		PCT	
PEACHES	PCT	PCT	
PINEAPPLE	PCT		
GRAPES	PCT	PCT	
MISCELLANEOUS	PCT	PCT	
COMBINATION OF FRUITS	PCT	PCT	
METHOD OF PREPARATION	PCT		
GOOD FOR SALADS	PCT	PCT	
SIZE	PCT	PCT	
SYRUP	PCT	PCT	
OTHER			

SOURCE: 2 CITY TASTE TEST--DENVER + SAN FRANCISCO

TABLE 11--PREFERENCES FOR PACKING METHOD

	HOMEMAKERS
PREFERRED QUICK-THAW PACKAGES	PCT
PREFERRED 'SEFTON' PACKAGE	
PREFERRED 'SEFTON' PACKAGE	PCT
WITHOUT PREFERENCE	PCT

SOURCE: TWO CITY TASTE TEST; DENVER + SAN FRANCISCO

TABLE 12--REASONS HOMEMAKERS GAVE FOR THEIR PREFERENCE ON TYPE OF PKG

PACKAGE:	QUICK-THAW NUMBER	'SEFTON' NUMBER	
COMMENTS ON PRODUCT QUALITY			NUMBER OF RESPONSES
KEPT FRESHER/BETTER			MAY EXCEED NUMBER
NO DISCOLORATION			OF RESPONDENTS DUE
OTHER			TO MULTIPLE RESPONSES
COMMENTS ON PACKAGE OR METHOD			
EASY			
EASY TO OPEN/HANDLE			
FAST			
NO SPILLING			
FAMILIAR PACKAGE			
EASY TO STORE			
CAN SEE CONTENTS			
OTHER			

SOURCE: 2 CITY TASTE TEST

TABLE 13--HOMEMAKERS PREFERENCES ON SPECIFIC ATTRIBUTES OF MIXED FRUITS

	OVERALL FLAVOR	APPEARANCE	COMBINATION OF FRUITS	SWEETNESS
NUMBER OF HOMEMAKERS	(138)	(138)	(138)	(138)
PREFERRED GREEN GIANT	PCT	PCT	PCT	PCT
PREFERRED BIRDS EYE	PCT	PCT	PCT	PCT
NO PREFERENCE	PCT	PCT	PCT	PCT

SOURCE: 2 CITY TASTE TEST

TABLE 14--HOW HOMEMAKERS RATED MIXED FRUIT PRODUCTS

	GREEN GIANT	BIRDS EYE
NUMBERS OF HOMEMAKERS	(138)	(138)
LIKE EXTREMELY	PCT	PCT
LIKE VERY MUCH	PCT	PCT
LIKE MODERATELY	PCT	PCT
LIKE SLIGHTLY	PCT	PCT
NEITHER LIKE NOR DISLIKE	PCT	PCT
DISLIKE SLIGHTLY	PCT	PCT
DISLIKE MODERATELY	PCT	PCT
DISLIKE VERY MUCH	PCT	PCT
DISLIKE EXTREMELY	PCT	PCT

SOURCE: 2 CITY TASTE TEST

TABLE 15--HOMEMAKERS INDICATIONS OF WILLINGNESS TO BUY MIXED FRUIT

NUMBER OF HOMEMAKERS	GREEN GIANT (138)	BIRDS EYE (138)
'I AM GOING TO BUY SOME RIGHT AWAY'	PCT	PCT
'I AM GOING TO BUY SOME SOON'	PCT	PCT
'I AM CERTAIN I WILL BUY SOME SOMETIME'	PCT	PCT
'I PROBABLY WILL BUY SOME SOMETIME'	PCT	PCT
'I MAY BUY SOME SOMETIME'	PCT	PCT
'I MIGHT BUY SOME BUT I DOUBT IT'	PCT	PCT
'I DON'T THINK I'M INTERESTED IN BUYING ANY'	PCT	PCT
'I PROBABLY WILL NEVER BUY ANY'	PCT	PCT
'I KNOW I'M NOT INTERESTED IN BUYING ANY'	PCT	PCT
'IF SOMEBODY GAVE ME SOME I WOULD GIVE IT' AWAY JUST TO GET RID OF IT'	PCT	PCT

SOURCE: 2-CITY TASTE TEST, DENVER + SAN FRANCISCO

TABLE 16--PRICE HOMEMAKERS WOULD EXPECT TO PAY FOR MIXED FRUIT PRODUCTS

NUMBER OF HOMEMAKERS	GREEN GIANT (138)	BIRDS EYE (138)
LESS THAN 16C	PCT	PCT
16-20C	PCT	PCT
21-25C	PCT	PCT
26-30C	PCT	PCT
31-35C	PCT	PCT
36-40C	PCT	PCT
LESS THAN 41C	PCT	PCT
OVER 41C	PCT	PCT
41-45C	PCT	PCT
46-50C	PCT	PCT

SOURCE: 2-CITY TASTE TEST

TABLE 17--CONSUMER REACTION TO OLALLIEBERRIES

	CURRENT TEST	AVERAGE PAST FROZEN PRODUCTS TEST
LIKE-DISLIKE		
LIKE EXTREMELY OR VERY MUCH	PCT	PCT
READINESS TO BUY		
WILL BUY SOON OR RIGHT AWAY	PCT	PCT

SOURCE: AGENCY CONDUCTED TASTE TEST AMONG HOUSEWIVES

TABLE 18—RESULTS OF CONSUMER REACTION ON TYPES OF PACKING SAUCE + QUICK
THAW POUCH   RESPONSES:
                        GENERALLY FAVORABLE   GENERALLY UNFAV

STRAWBERRIES, PEACHES, +
BLUEBERRIES PACKED WITH:
  CREAM SAUCE
  SYRUP SAUCE
  QUICK-THAW POUCH

SOURCE: 150 CONSUMER EVALUATIONS IN 1-CITY TASTE TEST

TABLE 19A—TASTE TEST SCALE RATINGS, GREEN GIANT VS. BIRDS EYE
                LIKE-DISLIKE: READINESS TO BUY:
                LIKE EXTREMELY OR VERY MUCH   WILL BUY SOON OR RIGHT AWAY

FRUIT:	GREEN GIANT	BIRDS EYE		GREEN GIANT	BIRDS EYE
MIXED FRUIT	PCT	PCT		PCT	PCT
RASPBERRIES		PCT			PCT
COMBINAGE		PCT			PCT
STRAWBERRIES	PCT	PCT		PCT	PCT
BLUEBERRIES	PCT			PCT	
PEACHES	PCT			PCT	

TABLE 19B—SCALE RATINGS FOR SWEETNESS OF GREEN GIANT PRODUCTS

	MIXED FRUIT	BLUEBERRIES	PEACHES	STRAWBERRIES
TOO SWEET	PCT	PCT	PCT	PCT
NOT SWEET ENOUGH	PCT	PCT	PCT	PCT
ABOUT RIGHT	PCT	PCT	PCT	PCT
TOTAL	(PCT)	(PCT)	(PCT)	(PCT)

SOURCE: 3-CITY CONSUMER PAIRED-TASTE TEST

TABLE 20—BLIND PLACEMENT TEST OF COMPETITORS' RASPBERRIES + MIXED FRUIT
WITH QUICK-THAW POUCH

TYPE OF PACKAGE, DO YOU THINK YOU:	RASP	MIXED
DEFINITELY WOULD BUY IT	PCT	PCT
PROBABLY WOULD BUY IT	PCT	PCT
MIGHT BUY IT — MIGHT NOT	PCT	PCT
PROBABLY WOULD NOT BUY IT	PCT	PCT
DEFINITELY WOULD NOT BUY IT	PCT	PCT

SOURCE: MARKET RESEARCH STUDY; N=60,30 EACH IN NEW JERSEY + CALIFORNIA

TABLE 21--FROZEN FRUIT SALES (PERCENT OF TOTAL DOLLARS)

	1ST AUDIT				FINAL AUD	
MONTH #	1	2	3	4	5	6
MIAMI						
BIRDS EYE QUICK THAW	PCT	PCT	PCT	PCT	PCT	PCT
OTHER BIRDS EYE	PCT	PCT	PCT	PCT	PCT	PCT
TOTAL BIRDS EYE	(PCT)	(PCT)	(PCT)	(PCT)	(PCT)	(PCT)
PRIVATE LABEL	PCT	PCT	PCT	PCT	PCT	PCT
ALL OTHERS	PCT	PCT	PCT	PCT	PCT	PCT
TOTAL FROZEN FRUIT	PCT	PCT	PCT	PCT	PCT	PCT
BUFFALO						
BIRDS EYE QUICK THAW	PCT	PCT	PCT	PCT	PCT	PCT
OTHER BIRDS EYE	PCT	PCT	PCT	PCT	PCT	PCT
TOTAL BIRDS EYE	(PCT)	(PCT)	(PCT)	(PCT)	(PCT)	(PCT)
PRIVATE LABEL	PCT	PCT	PCT	PCT	PCT	PCT
ALL OTHERS	PCT	PCT	PCT	PCT	PCT	PCT
TOTAL FROZEN FRUIT	PCT	PCT	PCT	PCT	PCT	PCT

SOURCE: STORE AUDITS

TABLE 22--PERCENT OF RESPONDENTS INTENDING TO REPURCHASE IN PHILADELPHIA
     TEST MARKET (48 WEEKS, 10 STORES) + MIAMI

GREEN GIANT (PHILADELPHIA, N=105)		BIRDS EYE (MIAMI, N=96)	
BLUEBERRIES	PCT	RASPBERRIES	PCT
MIXED FRUIT	PCT	MIXED FRUIT	PCT
PEACHES	PCT	STRAWBERRIES	PCT
		PEACHES COMBINAGE*	PCT
		*STRAWBERRIES + PEACHES	

TABLE 23--NATIONAL SALES OBJECTIVES FOR GREEN GIANT (NO. OF CASES)

    STRAWBERRIES
      SLICED
      WHOLE
    MIXED FRUIT
    BLUEBERRIES
    PEACHES
    RASPBERRIES
      TOTAL

SOURCE: COMPANY RECORDS

TABLE 24--CASES OF TEST ITEMS SOLD PER PERIOD PER STORE STOCKING* 66-67

MONTH #   1   2   3   4   5   6   7   8   9   10   11

GREEN GIANT:
FROZEN FRUIT
  MIXED FRUIT
  BLUEBERRIES
  PEACHES
  STRAWBERRIES
  RASPBERRIES

BIRDS EYE:
  MIXED FRUIT

*BASED ON SALES IN 10 PHILADELPHIA PENN FRUIT STORES

TABLE 25--PRICE SUMMARY FOR FROZEN FRUITS BY REGION

BIRDS EYE: RETAIL: EAST WEST WHOLESALE(PER DOZ) EAST WEST
  STRAWBERRIES   CTS   CTS
  OTHERS   CTS   CTS

SOURCE: SURVEY OF GREEN GIANT BROKERS

TABLE 26A--ADVERTISING USED BY BIRDS EYE (METHOD)

    SPACE INITIALLY ALLOTTED BIRDS EYE DURING INTRODUCTORY OFFERS

TABLE 26B--COMMENTS OF BROKERS REGARDING BIRDS EYE

SOURCE: COMPANY RECORDS

TABLE 27--6 MONTH RESULTS OF CLEVELAND + MIAMI TEST MARKETS FOR GG PRODS

        SALES   CS/YR

        SALES PROJECTIONS FOR TEST MARKETS   CS/YR

        TOTAL NATIONAL SALES PROJECTIONS: CS/YR

        TOTAL FROZEN FRUIT MKT PROJECTIONS: CS/YR

TABLE 28—FROZEN FRUIT SALES IN CLEVELAND TEST MARKET

MONTH #	1	2	3	4	5	6	7
GREEN GIANT TOTAL	PCT	PCT	PCT	PCT	PCT	PCT	PCT
BLUEBERRIES	PCT	PCT	PCT	PCT	PCT	PCT	PCT
MIXED FRUIT	PCT	PCT	PCT	PCT	PCT	PCT	PCT
PEACHES	PCT	PCT	PCT	PCT	PCT	PCT	PCT
RED RASPBERRIES	PCT	PCT	PCT	PCT	PCT	PCT	PCT
STRAWBERRIES	PCT	PCT	PCT	PCT	PCT	PCT	PCT
BIRDS EYE TOTAL	PCT	PCT	PCT	PCT	PCT	PCT	PCT
B.E. QUICK THAW	PCT	PCT	PCT	PCT	PCT	PCT	PCT
BLUEBERRIES	PCT	PCT	PCT	PCT	PCT	PCT	PCT
CHERRIES	PCT	PCT	PCT	PCT	PCT	PCT	PCT
MIXED FRUIT	PCT	PCT	PCT	PCT	PCT	PCT	PCT
PEACHES	PCT	PCT	PCT	PCT	PCT	PCT	PCT
RED RASPBERRIES	PCT	PCT	PCT	PCT	PCT	PCT	PCT
STRAWBERRIES	PCT	PCT	PCT	PCT	PCT	PCT	PCT
OTHER BIRDS EYE	PCT	PCT	PCT	PCT	PCT	PCT	PCT
ALL OTHER FRUIT	PCT	PCT	PCT	PCT	PCT	PCT	PCT
TOTAL UNITS							
TOTAL PERCENT	PCT	PCT	PCT	PCT	PCT	PCT	PCT

TABLE 29A—HOW HOMEMAKERS SERVED TEST PRODUCTS—MIAMI

	BLUE-BERRIES	STRAW-BERRIES	MIXED FRUIT	RASP-BERRIES	PEACHES
NO. OF HOMEMAKERS	44	140	118	70	47
SAUCE	PCT	PCT	PCT	PCT	PCT
PLAIN	PCT	PCT	PCT	PCT	PCT
WITH WHIPPED CREAM	PCT	PCT	PCT	PCT	PCT
WITH MILK/CREAM	PCT	PCT	PCT	PCT	PCT
WITH OTHER FRUITS	PCT	PCT	PCT	PCT	PCT
WITH SOUR CREAM	PCT	PCT	PCT	PCT	PCT
TOPPING	PCT	PCT	PCT	PCT	PCT
ON ICE CREAM/SHERBERT	PCT	PCT	PCT	PCT	PCT
ON CEREAL	PCT	PCT	PCT	PCT	PCT
ON PANCAKES	PCT	PCT	PCT	PCT	PCT
ON SHORTCAKES/CAKE	PCT	PCT	PCT	PCT	PCT
ON PUDDING	PCT	PCT	PCT	PCT	PCT
OTHER	PCT	PCT	PCT	PCT	PCT
SALAD	PCT	PCT	PCT	PCT	PCT
IN JELLO	PCT	PCT	PCT	PCT	PCT
IN SALAD/FRUIT SALAD	PCT	PCT	PCT	PCT	PCT
MISCELLANEOUS	PCT	PCT	PCT	PCT	PCT

(PCTS MAY ADD TO > 100 DUE TO MULTIPLE RESPONSES)

TABLE 29B--HOW HOMEMAKERS SERVED TEST PRODUCTS--CLEVELAND

	BLUE-BERRIES	STRAW-BERRIES	MIXED FRUIT	RASP-BERRIES	PEACHES
NO. OF HOMEMAKERS	401	130	105	85	71
SAUCE	PCT	PCT	PCT	PCT	PCT
PLAIN	PCT	PCT	PCT	PCT	PCT
WITH WHIPPED CREAM	PCT	PCT	PCT	PCT	PCT
WITH MILK/CREAM	PCT	PCT	PCT	PCT	PCT
WITH SUGAR	PCT	PCT	PCT	PCT	PCT
WITH OTHER FRUITS	PCT	PCT	PCT	PCT	PCT
WITH SOUR CREAM	PCT	PCT	PCT	PCT	PCT
WITH LIQUER	PCT	PCT	PCT	PCT	PCT
TOPPING	PCT	PCT	PCT	PCT	PCT
ON ICE CREAM-SHERBERT	PCT	PCT	PCT	PCT	PCT
ON CEREAL	PCT	PCT	PCT	PCT	PCT
ON PANCAKES	PCT	PCT	PCT	PCT	PCT
ON SHORTCAKES/CAKE	PCT	PCT	PCT	PCT	PCT
ON PUDDING	PCT	PCT	PCT	PCT	PCT
ON PIE	PCT	PCT	PCT	PCT	PCT
ON COTTAGE CHEESE	PCT	PCT	PCT	PCT	PCT
SALAD	PCT	PCT	PCT	PCT	PCT
IN JELLO	PCT	PCT	PCT	PCT	PCT
IN SALAD/FRUIT SALAD	PCT	PCT	PCT	PCT	PCT
MISCELLANEOUS	PCT	PCT	PCT	PCT	PCT
IN UPSIDE DOWN CAKE	PCT	PCT	PCT	PCT	PCT
IN TARTS	PCT	PCT	PCT	PCT	PCT
IN PANCAKES	PCT	PCT	PCT	PCT	PCT
IN PIE	PCT	PCT	PCT	PCT	PCT
OTHER	PCT	PCT	PCT	PCT	PCT

SOURCE: CLEVELAND AND MIAMI TEST MARKETS

TABLE 30A—SUMMARY AND PROJECTIONS--FROZEN FRUIT

	TOT $ RETAIL SALES--60 STORES		PCT CHG 66-67	IN NO. STORES 66 67	EST'D ANNUAL NAT'L VOLUME RET CASES (24'S) $MIL
	JUNE-JULY 1966	JUNE-JULY 1967			
TOTAL MARKET					
BIRDS EYE QUICK-THAW					
BLUEBERRIES SUPREME					
CHERRIES SUPREME					
MIXED FRUIT SUPREME					
PEACH COMBINAGE					
SELECT RASPBERRIES					
SELECT STRAWBERRIES					
BIRDS EYE OTHER FRUIT					
STRAWBERRIES					
OTHER FRUITS					
TOTAL BIRDS EYE					
ALL REMAINING BRANDS					
STRAWBERRIES					
OTHER FRUITS					

TABLE 30B—BI-MONTHLY DATA FOR TOTAL FROZEN FRUIT MARKET/UNITS + RETAIL $'S

	AUG—SEP65	OCT—NOV65	DEC—JAN66	FEB—MAR66	APR—MAY66	JUN—JUL66
UNITS						
DOLLARS	AUG—SEP66	OCT—NOV66	DEC—JAN67	FEB—MAR67	APR—MAY67	JUN—JUL67
UNITS						
DOLLARS						
CHANGE IN						
UNITS	PCT	PCT	PCT	PCT	PCT	PCT
DOLLARS	PCT	PCT	PCT	PCT	PCT	PCT

SOURCE: STORE AUDITS—NEW PROD SVC REPORTS

LAND-O-LAKES, INC.

In August 1971, Paul Johnson, executive vice-president of food processing and marketing for Land-O-Lakes, a large midwestern cooperative, wished to develop preliminary test market objectives for Land-O-Lakes margarine, the newest product to be considered for the Land-O-Lakes product line. The primary objective of the test market was to evaluate the market acceptance of the product and the profit potential for Land-O-Lakes. A key concern was the possible cut-in effect that a Land-O-Lakes brand margarine, produced mainly from soybean and corn oils, might have on Land-O-Lakes butter. There was also a need to identify alternative marketing programs for the new margarine.

Although sales of Land-O-Lakes brand butter had remained fairly stable, the total market for butter was decreasing. Land-O-Lakes executives doubted that the cooperative could increase significantly its penetration of the butter market, because of the well-entrenched positions of numerous regional and private brands. (Land-O-Lakes and other national brands together held less than 30 percent of the butter market; regional and private brands, in which Land-O-Lakes did not participate, held more than 70 percent.) The margarine market, on the other hand, was growing, and Land-O-Lakes had recently acquired one firm that, as a very small part of its business, marketed margarine. Land-O-Lakes had also merged with a large cooperative that, apart from its other activities, crushed soybeans, a principal ingredient of margarine, into oil. Many of the dairy farmer members of Land-O-Lakes grew soybeans.

THE COMPANY

Land-O-Lakes produces butter, cheeses, fluid milk, and ice-cream products, dry milks and dry-milk blends, whole and processed turkeys, and whole and processed eggs. The cooperative also operates wholesale and retail milk routes in the upper Midwest. The home office is located in Minneapolis. Regional and branch offices are located in Minnesota, Iowa, the Dakotas, and Wisconsin; the Land-O-Lakes selling organization covers the eastern half of the United States.

Land-O-Lakes' image among consumers is primarily that of a producer of quality products. The Indian Girl symbol, originally used as both the brand and the symbol for the cooperative's premium butter, is now used to identify all Land-O-Lakes products.

In 1970, Land-O-Lakes had sales of $654 million and net worth (members' and patrons' equities) of $91 million. Sales had increased more than $168 million over 1969, largely as a result of a major acquisition (see Exhibit 1). The cooperative had grown substantially since 1960, when sales were $183.5 million, and net worth $32.7 million.

Land-O-Lakes is a cooperative owned by members who use the organization both to market their farm products and to purchase farm supplies. Stock in the cooperative is owned by the members, and the organization's profits are returned to the members in proportion to the amount of their patronage. Thus, there is no accrued profit and the stock never changes in value.

Members of cooperatives are involved in the decision-making process of the organization. They can reject company policy either by voting a change in the board of directors or by passing resolutions at the annual conventions. Most members of Land-O-Lakes take an active interest in the organization, and a decision by "the country's largest butter-maker" to enter the margarine business would require the support of the membership, many of whom are dairy farmers.

BUTTER AND MARGARINE

Although per capita consumption of table spreads (principally butter and margarine) has remained relatively stable at 16 to 17 pounds during the past 20 years, butter consumption has declined from 11 pounds in 1950 to 5 pounds in 1970. Margarine use has increased from 6 to 11 pounds per capita in that same period. Exhibit 2 shows sales of butter and margarine from 1950 to 1970. Estimates of margarine sales for 1971 ranged from 1.6 to 2.0 billion pounds. Each estimate provided for some growth in the margarine market. Most analysts believed that such growth would occur at the expense of butter. Industry sources attributed the shift from butter to margarine to the lower price of margarine, to removal of restrictions on the sale of (yellow) colored margarine, and to the interest of some consumers in reducing their intake of butterfat to reduce cholesterol (presumably to lessen risks of heart attack). In 1970, margarine sold on average for about 30 cents a pound less than butter.

Sales of both butter and margarine peaked in November–December and were lowest in July and August. Exhibit 3 shows a seasonal index of sales for both products.

Sales of butter and margarine exhibited considerable regional variation. Margarine outsold butter almost seven to one in the trade area surrounding Atlanta, but sales were approximately equal in the Boston trading area (see Exhibit 4).

Margarine typically accounted for 10 percent of sales in the dairy department of a supermarket, and 8 percent of the department's gross profit. Butter, in contrast, produced about 6 percent of department sales, and less than 3 percent of dairy gross profit. Retailers' gross margins on margarine averaged 15 percent, versus 8 to 9 percent on butter. Margarine had three times the shelf space of butter, and the inventory turnover and gross margin per foot of shelf space of margarine were slightly below those of butter.

Butter was used chiefly on the table and in special recipes; margarine, mainly for cooking and baking, according to a study in which 100 users of table spreads were asked in an open-end question to list the uses of each and (subsequently) the reasons for preferring margarine. Exhibit 5 contains results from that study.

Additional research indicated that 87 percent of female heads of households used margarine in the past month, while 35 percent used butter. About half of the users of each type reported using at least one pound during the week preceding the survey. Approximately 73 percent of both margarine and butter users considered brand loyalty important. The research noted that 87 percent of Land-O-Lakes butter users were strongly loyal to their brand.

The research developed the profile of a typical butter user as a female over 50, un-employed, with few (if any) children at home. She had a minimum of a high school education, a household income of $10,000, and lived in a northeastern city. However, a Land-O-Lakes butter user was more likely to be 25 to 49, and probably had young children at home; her household income was the $10,000+ range. In contrast, the typical heavy user of margarine was a female aged 35–49, with children under 18 at home, five or more in the household, probably not a high school graduate, with a household income of $5,000–$10,000, and lived in the southern or central United States.

MARGARINE

In 1971, most brands of margarine were made primarily from a blend of vegetable oils. Soybean oil accounted for more than 72 percent of the ingredients in margarine (see Exhibit 6). Product ingredients began to shift from animal oils (e.g., oleo, or beef fat) to domestic vegetable oils in the 1930s. During World War II cheaper margarines were made from lard (pork fat), while the more expensive margarines used vegetable oils. Since that time, the use of vegetable oils has continued to increase.

Margarine was available in three basic combinations of ingredients and four package forms. The most common set of ingredients, used in "regular" margarine, included a blend of vegetable oils, of which soybean oil was typically the major component. Some brands of margarine contained only a single vegetable oil, e.g., corn or safflower. Other margarines contained animal fats, sometimes in combination with vegetable oils. Approximately 80 percent of margarine was purchased in the familiar one-pound package of four individually wrapped quarter-pound sticks. Most of the remainder was comprised of "soft" and "whipped" margarine which was purchased in one-pound plastic tubs or packages of two half-pound tubs. A small amount of margarine was sold in "soft stick" or liquid form. Exhibit 7 includes data on price, distribution, and sales of margarine by ingredient and package type.

Almost three-fourths of the dollar sales and well over half of the poundage of margarine came from national brands, manufactured by large multiproduct food companies, e.g., Kraft, Lever Brothers, and Standard Brands. The importance of these national brands has increased considerably since World War II. Most national brands were classified by trade sources as either "premium-price" or "medium-price" margarines. Although the two classifications overlapped, premium margarines ordinarily retailed from 45 cents to 59 cents a pound, while medium-price margarines retailed at prices from 29 cents to 50 cents a pound. Private label margarines generally overlapped the lower price range of the medium-price margarines, and occasionally retailed for as little as 21 cents a pound; some few private labels retailed for as much as 55 cents a pound. Sales of lower-priced brands (both national and private) were greater on a per capita basis in the South than in other parts of the United States. Company officials considered the southern market much more price-oriented than other regions. Margarine packaged in stick form generally sold for a price 4 to 12 cents a pound under the prices of products with comparable ingredients packaged in other forms. Diet margarine and corn oil margarine were priced within a cent or two of "regular" margarine for most brands.

Although premium-price margarines in some instances contained combinations of ingredients which were slightly more costly than those in medium-price and some private-label margarines, it was not clear whether consumers could taste any differences among brands of vegetable-oil margarine. Both premium-price and medium-price margarines, as well as many private labels, were available with "regular" ingredients (combinations of vegetable oils), corn oil, and stick and soft packages.

Retailers earned margins of about 15 percent on most national brands, and 10 to 13 percent on private brands. These margins reflected some sales at markups higher than 15 percent, as well as sales on "deals." These deals usually involved either a coupon, placed in the retailers' advertisements, which entitled the customer to a reduced price on presentation of the coupon or a discount off the regular price to the retailer. Such discounts might require retailers to promote the brand, or to offer a reduced price to the customer, for a specified period of time. Deals typically cost manufacturers 4 to 6 cents a pound, but could amount to 13 cents a pound.

Industry sources agreed that a considerable amount of "dealing" was occurring in the marketplace, but did not agree on whether the amount of dealing had increased or decreased during the past three years.

Virtually all sales of manufacturers' brands of margarine were accounted for by very large food manufacturers, whose products enjoyed wide distribution and favorable reputations in the grocery trade. Products of these manufacturers had support from large sales organizations and, in some cases, from advertising of different products under the same corporate name (e.g., Kraft) as the margarine.

In 1970, the eight leading advertisers of margarine that accounted for more than half of the industry's sales together spent more than $26.8 million in advertising their brands of margarine. Although this total figure had changed little during the past three years, the budgets of some individual brands had varied substantially. For example, Kraft's budget for Miracle margarine in 1970 was about half of its average budget for the three preceding years. Fleischmann's 1970 budget was more than $2 million greater than its 1969 spending. The 1970 Chiffon budget, although 35 percent greater than the brand's 1969 budget, was only two-thirds as large as the 1968 budget for the brand. Finally, Swift's budget for Allsweet, which had declined steadily since 1967, was almost four times as high in 1969 as it was in 1970.

Although television consumed some 80 percent of major advertisers' media dollars, Parkay spent more than 40 percent of its budget on radio, and Fleischmann's devoted almost 30 percent of its funds to magazines. Most major advertisers placed some advertisements in newspapers and magazines.

Exhibit 8 shows retail price ranges, typical retailer margins, market share estimates, and advertising expenditures for major brands of margarine.

Analysis of margarine advertisements revealed three principal themes used by major advertisers: (1) taste, (2) resemblance to butter, and (3) health value. Parkay and Imperial stressed the taste theme. Imperial used the slogan, "America's favorite-tasting premium margarine." Mazola, Blue Bonnet, and Chiffon emphasized butterlike taste, with slogans like, "You'll think you're tasting butter," and "If you think it's butter but it's not, it's new Chiffon." Fleischmann's was the largest advertiser to stress the health theme. Its ads emphasized "100% Golden Corn Oil" and "low cholesterol."[*]

Information which Land-O-Lakes had obtained on the consumer profiles of several leading brands of margarine indicated that across most brands diet margarine usage was highest in families whose head was 35 to 49 years old and in the middle-to-higher income bracket. For all types of margarine combined, the profiles for Imperial and Parkay differed in that the latter were younger and better-educated; had lower incomes ($5,000–$8,000 for Parkay vs. $8,000–$12,000 for Imperial) and smaller households (no children for Parkay; small families for Imperial). Profiles of consumers of Mazola and Blue Bonnet differed substantially. Mazola users were older (50 and above) and college educated; they had no children living at home, and income over $15,000. In contrast, the Blue Bonnet customer group cut across all ages. Blue Bonnet users typically had grade-school educations, large families (five or more) and incomes under $8,000. Chiffon's customer profile fell between those of Mazola and Blue Bonnet; Fleischmann's customer group paralleled the profile for Mazola.

LAND–O–LAKES MARGARINE

If Land-O-Lakes were to test market margarine, Mr. Johnson thought that the product should be tested in three forms: regular stick, regular soft, and corn oil stick. If test results warranted, Mr. Johnson planned to expand the line to include corn oil unsalted stick, corn oil soft, and regular whipped margarine. If he decided to recommend positioning Land-O-Lakes as a premium-price margarine, Mr. Johnson thought that regular retail shelf prices in the range of 47 to 53 cents a pound would be appropriate. Regular stick margarine would be priced at 47 to 49 cents a pound; corn oil soft, at 53 cents. Alternatively, Mr. Johnson knew that some Land-O-Lakes executives favored a "sell it cheap and sell a heap" approach.

Mr Johnson had two specific objectives for Land-O-Lakes' margarine advertising: (1) to maximize sales of margarine, and (2) to minimize the cut-in effect of margarine on butter. One study commissioned by Land-O-Lakes projected a decline of 23 percent in the Cooperative's butter sales as a result of introducing Land-O-Lakes margarine. The study was conducted in a major midwestern market in which Land-O-Lakes butter was a dominant national brand.

To ascertain the effect on consumers' reactions to margarine packaged in the familiar Land-O-Lakes package bearing the Indian Girl symbol, the Cooperative arranged to have 50 Minneapolis housewives each receive a pound of Imperial margarine wrapped and

---

[*]Consumption of animal fats or certain vegetable oils, e.g., coconut oil, was thought to increase levels of cholesterol in human blood. Elevated cholesterol levels were, in turn, linked to the accumulation of fatty deposits in blood vessels. These deposits narrowed the blood vessels, increasing blood pressure and the risk of circulatory system disorders such as heart attacks and strokes.

labeled in the traditional Land-O-Lakes package. The women used the product for a week, and were then asked to participate in panel discussions. The data showed that consumer predisposition toward Land-O-Lakes margarine was far stronger than for leading national brands of margarine.

Land-O-Lakes also tested four alternative advertising themes: (1) "for all-around use," (2) "without oily taste," (3) "from the number one butter maker," and (4) "perfect for baking." There was virtually no difference in responses to any among these four themes with respect to consumers' intentions for trial or repeat purchases.

Mr. Johnson realized, however, that an advertising program for Land-O-Lakes margarine might have to be varied by region. For example, in areas where Land-O-Lakes butter had lower penetration and where lower-priced margarines predominated, such appeals as "perfect for baking" and "no oily taste" might be more appropriate than such claims as, "A number one margarine from the number one butter maker."

Mr. Johnson thought that introductory advertising, which might last for several months in a particular market, would cost on a national basis about $500,000 for each percentage point of market share Land-O-Lakes obtained. He estimated that the cost would double if introductory "deals" to retailers were included. Mr. Johnson noted that introductory advertising and promotion efforts frequently cost one and a half to three times as much as did the continuing advertising and promotion necessary to maintain market share.

A survey of retailers conducted earlier in the year indicated that introduction of Land-O-Lakes margarine was unlikely to influence retailers' attitudes or merchandising behavior toward Land-O-Lakes butter. On the whole, retailers seemed indifferent to the prospect of another margarine entry.

In order to estimate costs of servicing retail stores that would carry Land-O-Lakes margarine, the Cooperative made a detailed analysis of the coverage required in a midwestern metropolitan area with a population of 1.1 million; this metro area was comparable to those ranking twenty-fifth to thirtieth in size within the United States. The analysis indicated that three salespeople in addition to the present force of three persons who serviced primarily the wholesale trade would be necessary to provide adequate coverage of retail outlets if Land-O-Lakes obtained distribution in stores which accounted for 75 percent of margarine sales. Salary and expenses were estimated at $18,000 per person per year. Land-O-Lakes officials believed that some additional personnel would be needed in almost all of their sales offices, because margarine required greater attention at the retail level than butter, in which both variety and interbrand competitive activities were lower than for margarine. In markets where Land-O-Lakes already had representatives calling on retailers in support of the Cooperative's cheese and frozen turkey products, only modest additional direct sales expense would be incurred.

Mr. Johnson knew that the minimum manufacturing facility considered economical would produce at least 30 million pounds of margarine a year. To build such a plant new would cost approximately $5 million; remodeling an obsolete or unused butter plant would cost one-third to one-half that amount.

An industry study had estimated that, for a facility producing 100 million pounds of margarine per year, costs of labor and materials for manufacturing and packaging would come to 15 cents a pound for premium margarine, and very little less for the lowest-cost vegetable margarine. This study also stated that three marketing expense categories—sales and distribution, advertising, sales promotion (including "deals")— would each cost five cents a pound. Fixed costs for such a facility were thought to exceed $5.5 million.

Although it was not possible to estimate precisely from published data the profitability of margarine, industry sources typically quoted a range of one to four cents a pound as pretax profitability for margarine, versus about two cents a pound for butter.

Exhibit 1

LAND–O–LAKES—ABRIDGED OPERATING STATEMENTS
INCOME STATEMENT FOR YEAR ENDING DECEMBER 31
(000)

	1970	1969
Products marketed and sales to patrons	$655,067	$487,186
Costs of products and expenses:		
Payments to patrons and cost of products sold	548,086	408,829
Warehousing, processing, and packaging	51,139	36,827
Selling and distribution	22,344	16,191
Office and administrative	10,855	8,625
Depreciation	4,811	3,609
Interest, net	2,814	1,652
Total costs	$640,050	$475,733
Net profit before income taxes	15,017	11,453
Federal and state income taxes	995	229
Net profit after income taxes	$ 14,022	$ 11,224

BALANCE SHEET DECEMBER 31 (000)

	1970	1969
Assets		
Cash	$ 6,335	$ 7,153
Accounts receivable, net	56,174	36,998
Inventories	51,858	36,521
Investment (principally in cooperatives)	15,607	13,344
Plant and equipment, net	45,916	32,743
Other assets	6,507	5,311
Total assets	$182,397	$132,070
Liabilities and equity		
Current liabilities	$ 70,871	$ 34,921
Long-term debt	20,345	15,171
Members' and patrons' equities	91,181	81,978
Total liabilities and equity	$182,397	$132,070

Source: Annual Report

Exhibit 2

LAND-O-LAKES
GROCERY INDUSTRY SALES
ANNUAL CONSUMER EXPENDITURES
MARGARINE VS. BUTTER

	Butter (millions)	Percent of change from previous year	Margarine (millions)	Percent of change from previous year
1947	$583	—	$246.5	—
1948	510	−12.2	328.6	+33.3
1949	496	− 2.6	238.7	−27.3
1950	482.5	− 2.8	225.6	− 5.5
1951	495.5	+ 2.7	263	+16.6
1952	452	− 8.8	276	+ 4.9
1953	434	− 4.0	288	+ 4.4
1954	432.7	− 0.3	310	+ 7.6
1955	453	+ 4.7	307.5	− 0.8
1956	464.5	+ 2.5	308	+ 0.3
1957	473.8	+ 2.0	339	+10.0
1958	478.6	+ 1.0	355	+ 4.7
1959	490.8	+ 2.5	354	− 0.3
1960	508	+ 3.6	376	+ 6.3
1961	496	− 2.4	392.9	+ 4.4
1962	501.7	+ 1.1	389.8	− 0.8
1963	478	− 4.7	390.6	+ 0.2
1964	476.7	− 0.3	387.5	− 1.8
1965	469	− 1.6	417	+ 7.5
1966	474	+ 1.1	467	+12.2
1967	479.5	+ 1.1	479.5	+ 2.6
1968	474	− 1.1	488	+ 1.8
1969	451	− 4.8	516	+ 5.8
1970	448	− 0.6	565	+ 9.5

Source: Supermarketing/Food Topics

Exhibit 3

LAND–O–LAKES
INDEX OF SALES OF BUTTER AND MARGARINE, BY MONTH

	July–August	September–October	November–December	January–February	March–April	May–June
Pounds						
Butter	81[a]	104	128	100	98	90
Margarine	86[a]	101	119	104	103	111
Buyers						
Butter	92	100	118	96	98	96
Margarine	98	101	104	97	102	98

[a]The index numbers for butter and margarine are independent of one another. Comparisons may, therefore, be made for each product from month to month, but *not* butter and margarine within a particular time period. For example, the index of "81" for butter for July–August means that 81 percent as many pounds of butter were purchased by panel members in July–August as in January–February.

"81" does *not* necessarily imply that purchases of butter were slightly lower than those of margarine during July–August.

Source: Chicago Tribune study

Exhibit 4

LAND–O–LAKES
USAGE OF MARGARINE AND BUTTER BY REGION

Area	Margarine	Butter
Atlanta	87%	13%
Boston	50	50
Chicago	68	32
Cincinnati/Indiana	77	27
Cleveland	62	38
Minneapolis	58	42
Philadelphia	55	45

Source: Company Records

Exhibit 5

LAND–O–LAKES

USES OF BUTTER AND MARGARINE

Butter	Number of responses from 100 users
On the table (unspecified)	23
In special recipes	21
Bread/toast/rolls/sandwiches	17
Vegetables	16
For guests/company	10
Frying	6
Potatoes	5
Baking (unspecified)	5
Popcorn	4
Cooking (unspecified)	2
	109

Margarine	Number of responses from 100 users
Baking	46
Cooking	35
Family member requests it (husband)	31
	(13)
Frying	5
Toast	2
On the table (unspecified)	1
	120

Reasons for preferring margarine	
Cheaper	50
Lower in cholesterol	30
Lower in calories	7
Spreads easier	4
	91

Source: Company Records

Exhibit 6

LAND–O–LAKES

INGREDIENTS USED TO MANUFACTURE MARGARINE

Type of oil	1965	1968
Soy	72.4%	72.1%
Corn	10.5	10.5
Cottonseed	7.4	4.1
Animal fat	6.4	9.8
Other	3.3	3.7

Source: U.S. Department of Agriculture

Exhibit 7

LAND-O-LAKES
SALES DATA ON MARGARINE, BY PRODUCT TYPE, 1970

Average retail price per pound		Percent of stores purchasing major brands	Number of brands	Lbs. (000)	%	$ (000)	%	Major brands
35–50 cents	Regular (stick)	75	49	1,002,696	64.6	272,688	53.8	Private label, Blue Bonnet, Imperial
48–52	Soft	64	9	206,788	13.3	93,774	18.5	Imperial, Parkay, private label
33–54	Corn (stick)	82	11	205,050	13.2	80,601	15.9	Fleischmann's, private label, Parkay
46–54	Diet (soft)	43	6	45,834	3.0	21,250	4.2	Imperial, Parkay, Fleischmann's
37–54	Whipped	26	7	46,520	3.0	17,666	3.5	Blue Bonnet, Miracle, Parkay
49–54	Soft corn	13	2	12,446	0.8	5,745	1.1	Mrs. Filbert's, Parkay
50–55	Unsalted (stick)	43	4	8,110	0.5	3,974	0.8	Fleischmann's
40–47	Safflower (stick)	7	6	9,497	0.6	3,705	0.7	Hollywood, Saffola
47	Soft whipped	18	1	5,917	0.4	2,583	0.5	Mrs. Filbert's
45–52	Soft stick	28	1	5,637	0.4	2,491	0.5	Chiffon
41	Flavored (stick)	12	1	2,855	0.2	2,193	0.4	Chiffon
45–49	Liquid	3	3	744	—	331	0.1	Parkay
	Total	100		1,552,094	100.0	507,131[a]	100.0	

[a]This total differs from that of $565 million in Exhibit 2 because of the inclusion in Exhibit 2 of some private labels not included here, and because of different methods of measuring market size.

Source: Company Records

Exhibit 8

LAND–O–LAKES

PRICE, RETAIL MARGIN, AND ESTIMATED MARKET SHARE,
BY BRAND OF MARGARINE

Brand	Manufacturer	Retail price per pound (cents)	Retail margin	Market share	Advertising expenditures (000)
Premium price					
Chiffon	Anderson-Clayton	48–54	15.3%	4.2%	$2,560
Fleischmann's	Standard Brands	45–49	14.9	11.4	5,212
Imperial	Lever Brothers	45–50	17	11.5	5,394
Kraft Deluxe	Kraft	45–49	n.a.	1.3	n.a.
Mazola	Corn Products Co. (CPC International)	49–57	n.a.	2.7	2,578
Medium price					
Allsweet	Swift	33–36	n.a.	1.6%	$ 136
Blue Bonnet	Standard Brands	35–49	15.1%	10.4	4,631
Good Luck	Lever Bros.	36	n.a.	n.a.	
Golden Glow	Greggs	31–35	n.a.	1.8	
Miracle	Kraft	38–43	n.a.	1.6	792
Mrs. Filberts'	J. H. Filbert	29–50	n.a.	6.6	
Nucoa	Shedd-Bartush (Beatrice	34–39	n.a.	2.7	
Nu-Maid	Miami Margarine Foods)	37–52	n.a.	1.9	
Parkay	Kraft	33–50	14.7%	10.3	5,505
Private labels		21–55	10.3–12.5%	26.0%	
			Total	94.0%[a]	

[a]The remaining 6 percent of the market was held by brands whose shares could not be measured reliably.

Source: Company Records

JOSTEN'S, INC.

**Commercialization of Computer-Aided
Design and Manufacturing System**

In March 1975, Mr. Robert Leslie, vice-president and general manager of Josten's Scholastic division, had to decide whether the division's computer-aided die-making system (CAD–CAM) should be made available to other firms or kept solely for use within Josten's. If Josten's were to make the CAD–CAM system available, executives would also have to determine whether the system itself should be sold or leased, or whether Josten's should sell products made by the CAD–CAM system.

Josten's had originally developed the system to enable its designers to develop a large number of designs which could be combined and modified as needed to produce a wide range of custom dies to manufacture rings and other products made by the company's Scholastic division. The system enabled the Scholastic division to produce a virtually infinite variety of custom designs quickly and at far lower costs than traditional handwork methods.

The developer of the CAD–CAM system, whom one Josten's official described as "our resident genius," saw almost unlimited potential for the system, and believed that it offered Josten's significant profit opportunities. As they developed CAD–CAM and became aware of its applications outside the Scholastic division's own activities, Josten's personnel had begun to work with local firms in an effort to ascertain how such a system might help them meet their needs. But by the spring of 1975, internal company use had grown to the point where outside work could no longer be accommodated without major expansion of facilities, equipment, and personnel.

THE COMPANY

Josten's manufactured and distributed a wide line of custom-designed motivation and recognition products to scholastic and commercial markets. Company executives stated that Josten's planned to increase its penetration in existing markets, and to diversify in areas that utilized the company's marketing and production strengths. For the year ending June 30, 1974, Josten's had sales in excess of $130 million, and net income of $7 million (see Exhibits 1 and 2). The company had experienced consistent gains in sales and income since 1958, when Josten's earned $829,000 on sales of $14.3 million.

Responsibility for Josten's product line was divided among five operating divisions: Scholastic, Yearbook, Recognition, Library Services, and Fashion Jewelry.

The Scholastic division was a dominant producer of college, high school and championship rings, which were sold primarily to students through colleges and schools. The division also marketed graduation announcements, diplomas, awards, trophies, and caps and gowns. In 1974, the Scholastic division accounted for 52 percent of Josten's sales and

53 percent of the company's earnings. Division sales had grown from $43 million in 1970 to $64 million in 1974.

The Yearbook division was a leading supplier of yearbooks to schools, colleges, and the military. That division accounted for 28 percent of Josten's sales and 30 percent of the company's earnings in 1974.

The Recognition division sold to business firms, associations, and other organizations custom-designed jewelry, awards, plaques, stationery, and travel plans. Organizations used these products and services to recognize service anniversaries, sales achievements, and performance in special incentive programs. Recognition products and services produced about 8 percent of Josten's sales and earnings in 1974. Division sales had increased almost two and a half times since 1970.

The Library Services division sold books, library supplies, and a computer-based card catalog service to libraries. The division currently produced about 6 percent of Josten's sales and 3 percent of the company's profit. Sales had more than doubled in the past three years.

The Fashion Jewelry division, formed with the acquisition of the Traub Company in 1973, sold diamond engagement rings, wedding bands, and fashion jewelry under the "Orange Blossom" brand name through 1,400 retail jewelry outlets. In 1974, the division accounted for 4 percent of Josten's sales and 3 percent of its profits.

THE CAD–CAM SYSTEM

The CAD–CAM system (Computer-Aided Design and Computer-Aided Manufacturing) was a method of machining dies used to manufacture products. There were two principal methods for using dies to make end-products: (1) die striking using conventional punch presses, and (2) lost-wax (investment casting). The lost-wax process was used more commonly for intricate and complex dies. The CAD–CAM system could be used to make dies for both methods.

The dies used in the lost-wax casting process were typically composed of four metal parts securely joined together to form a mold. The two primary pieces of the mold contained intricate detail which was the reverse image of the detail on the end product. This intricate detail was painstakingly placed in the mold by manual (hand-crafting) methods unless a computer-assisted die-making system was available. Molten wax was poured into the mold to form a pattern for investment casting.

Patterns for the end product were assembled together in tree form, and surrounded with a material similar to plaster of paris for investment casting. Next, the wax was burned out, leaving a hard cavity for molten metal. There was no loss of the intricate detail; any detail that was in the mold was retained. Molten metal was poured into the cavity, and allowed to cool.

After removal of the plasterlike material in which the end product was cast, the end product received further processing, and was then ready for assembly into a final product. Although the wax pattern was destroyed or "lost" in the process, the mold itself could be used to make several hundred identical patterns. Exhibit 3 shows molds illustrative of those used to make ring subassemblies and a completed class ring.

If the end product were plastic instead of metal, plastic could be injected directly into the pattern mold in place of the wax. No investment casting was necessary, since the plastic part yielded was immediately ready for further processing or assembly as an end product.

The CAD-CAM system of making dies coupled numerically controlled (N/C) machining with computer graphics. The Josten's system consisted basically of three subsystems: (1) a data translation subsystem, (2) a data manipulation subsystem, and (3) a numerically controlled (N/C) machining subsystem.[1] (See Exhibit 4.)

The data translation subsystem converted information about the die to be manufactured into measurements in two or three dimensions. This conversion was most commonly accomplished by a machine known as a digitizer.[2] Typically a sketch or modeled sculpture was placed on the bed of the digitizer. The tracing tool mounted on the top of the digitizer was guided by an operator through and around the sketch outline or surface of the sculpture. Through a small computer, movements of the tracing tool were converted into a mathematical representation on computer tape. Tapes made in this manner were stored in the computer for use in the data manipulation subsystem. By 1975, Josten's had accumulated a substantial library of such tapes. This system provided a means of preparing data which minimized utilization of the data manipulation. Use of the data translation subsystem was far more economical than use of the data manipulation subsystem.

The data manipulation subsystem consisted of a computer and computer console, which included a visual display device, an electronic pen, and a typewriterlike keyboard. The computer converted into a visual presentation the data supplied to it by the tape produced on the digitizer.

The designer seated at the computer console could call up for visual display any of the die designs stored in the computer, and modify those designs quickly and easily by means of the electronic (light) pen. The original design could then be sent back to storage within the computer, and the new design stored separately. Either could be used subsequently. One computer program permitted the designer to view the proposed product from virtually any angle; another, to enlarge or reduce in size the representation of the actual model. A designer could, for example, have the visual representation of a class ring enlarged several times and rotated in order to more easily examine, and—if he or she wished—change, some of the details on that ring. In addition, the designer could add such information as manufacturing tolerances and allowances for shrinkage, tool offset, and finishing. Josten's experience indicated that its own designers could, with the assistance of an experienced operator, learn to operate the computer graphics console within a very few hours. Operator assistance was ordinarily needed infrequently once a designer had spent two or three sessions at the console.

---

1. The description of the system is abridged from a paper, "Applying 3-D Computer graphics to the N/C Production of Sculptured Tools," by John Titus, Tool & Process Research Engineer, Josten's, Inc., presented to the Numerical Control Society in Washington, D.C., on May 20, 1975.

2. Other methods for translating into mathematical terms data about the object to be made included drawings and templates. Use of the digitizer itself, however, provided a fast and efficient method of converting into digital (i.e., mathematical) form complex three-dimensional surfaces.

The data manipulation subsystem produced a tape which was then fed into an N/C milling machine, which constituted the third subsystem. The tape controlled the movements of the cutting tool on the milling machine, and consequently determined the shape of the die that was cut. After machining operations were completed, necessary finishing operations were performed on the die, which was then ready for use in a manufacturing process.

According to Josten's personnel, what was unique about the CAD–CAM system was not the hardware, but its application and the proprietary computer programs themselves. The computer, digitizer, and N/C milling machine were readily available on the market for less than $500,000, but company officers estimated that it would take more than a year of intensive effort by skilled technicians to duplicate the company's operating system and programs.

Josten's personnel believed that the CAD–CAM system offered little economic advantage in the production of two-dimensional surfaces, which could be produced more economically by conventional methods, but provided a significant, and in many cases a dramatic savings in time, money, and effort in the preparation, design, and production of complex three-dimensional (sculptured) surfaces.[3] In addition, Josten's personnel believed that the CAD–CAM system afforded a much higher quality, precision, and ease of duplication of sculptured surfaces than the manual methods traditionally employed. Some die-makers had begun to program two and two-and-one-half axis N/C machines to make sculptured dies. But the CAD–CAM system could, according to its developers, guide an N/C machine to produce a sculptured surface with 50 percent less tape and, therefore, far less time than that required by two-dimensional programming methods.

According to Josten's personnel, the principal savings in using the CAD–CAM system came from reducing substantially the time required to design and, if necessary, redesign and modify a die. Additional savings accrued through the use of N/C milling operations, which took considerably less than half as long as traditional (hand-guided) metal cutting. The design and milling operations combined accounted for approximately half to three-quarters of the total cost of dies less than a cubic foot in size. The remaining cost, on which use of the CAD–CAM system had negligible effect, was comprised of activities such as heat treating and finishing, and the cost of materials. In several common types of dies, Josten's personnel had observed that the CAD–CAM system took only one-fifth to one-sixth the time for designing and milling as traditional methods. In other cases, the CAD–CAM system had performed in one and one-half to two hours what conventional procedures had required ten hours. In one instance, a die was designed and machined on the CAD–CAM system in 40 hours instead of the 400 hours traditional methods would have required.

Josten's officials considered market potential for the CAD–CAM system greatest in producing dies with sculptured surfaces in situations in which: (1) the die was intricate,

---

3. Dies with sculptured surfaces were needed to produce a virtually infinite variety of products, including (but by no means limited to) plastic dials, toys, pen barrels; metal parts for musical instruments, medical instruments, appliances and sculpture; and a variety of paper, leather, and jewelry products.

complex, sophisticated, and therefore normally difficult and costly to design or produce; (2) time to create designs or make dies was critical in terms of product development costs or in orderly assembly line production of a new product; (3) dies had to be developed quickly and at minimum cost to build prototypes for technical or market testing; (4) substantial competitive advantage might be maintained by dramatic reductions in cost or delivery time of existing products; (5) skilled die-makers were no longer available; (6) costs of die-making had to be reduced sharply without a sacrifice in the quantity or quality of the product, or the product line had to be expanded substantially without increased personnel; (7) exact duplicates of dies were needed quickly to replace worn or damaged dies; (8) dies had to be redesigned quickly.

In an effort to learn more about the need and market for the CAD-CAM system, Josten's personnel interviewed several knowledgeable individuals in the machine tool and die-making industries. Without exception, interviewees responded that CAD-CAM offered advantages over systems currently in use, and that in many applications in which current systems were employed businesses would benefit from using a system like CAD-CAM.

THE DIE-MAKING INDUSTRY

Although many firms which used large numbers of dies operated their own ("captive") shops, most users of dies purchased them from independent shops. When manufacturers (or any buyers) needed a product made from a die, and did not have their own die-making facilities, they ordinarily requested bids on the product from an outside part-making shop, which might or might not make its own dies. Shops that lacked die-making capability subcontracted the die-making function to independent tool-and-die shops. In 1974, some 9,500 independent (noncaptive) tool-and-die companies did an annual business estimated in excess of $5 billion, most of which was done by small shops. Josten's officials estimated that about $2 billion of independent shops' output represented sales of dies.

Independent tool-and-die shops typically priced dies by multiplying by a standard rate—usually $15 to $25—the number of hours required to make a die. The time required depended on the size, complexity, and hardness of metal used. A small, simple aluminum die might cost $1,000; a large, complex die with sculptured surface made from hardened steel, up to $40,000.

Josten's personnel had learned from an industry association that the average tool-and-die shop needed to have sales volume of approximately $22,500 per employee to make a pretax margin equal to 8 percent of sales. For most shops, this 8 percent margin on sales implied a 12 to 15 percent return on assets. Analysts pointed out that these figures might vary rather dramatically from shop to shop, particularly among small shops. Josten's personnel combined this information with what they had learned from trade association sources about the number of shops in each employee-size category to produce a chart showing total sales volume and profit for independent shops within each size range (see Exhibit 5).

Industry sources estimated that far more than half of the total market for dies was comprised of dies the size of one cubic foot or smaller. Independent tool-and-die shops with fewer than 50 employees were far more likely to be able to produce dies for these small parts than for larger ones. In fact, there were twice as many independent shops able to provide dies for these smaller parts as there were for larger parts. (Shops that could produce dies for large parts could also generally produce dies for parts smaller than one cubic foot.)

When a manufacturer determined that a die was needed he or she would ask a designer to make either a model or detailed drawings or, in some cases, both. This design process often had to be repeated several times, particularly for products new to the firm, i.e., those with which design and production personnel had limited experience. Once the completed design was sent to a captive or independent shop, the manufacturer would ordinarily have to wait from two to twelve months for the die to be completed. Waiting time depended primarily upon the number of unfilled orders a shop had in its "backlog." Almost all shops had large backlogs in times of peak economic activity and small backlogs during times of slow economic activity. In many instances, the die for a product new to a firm would be completely made up, mounted, and used before the need for redesign became evident. In such cases, manufacturers might have to wait as long for a replacement die as a new one. Dies were also needed to replace those which had become worn in production. In addition, duplicate dies might be required for a manufacturer wishing to expand production.

Most dies were made by hand with the use of hand tools and the assistance of basic metal-cutting machinery. N/C machining was used in some instances. In addition to cutting, dies could be made by electron-discharge machining (EDM) and electrochemical machining (ECM). EDM and ECM were specialized processes, used far less frequently than metal cutting to make dies. Along with the use of EDM or ECM, some manual or N/C machining was typically also required.

Operators of machine shops with 20 or more employees could ordinarily tell fairly quickly whether a particular job could be done more economically by hand, by N/C machinery, or by an EDM or ECM process. Most shops with 20 to 50 employees, and almost all shops with more than 50 employees had the facilities to use all these methods.

According to the National Machine Tool Builders Association, there were, in independent and captive shops combined, over 30,000 N/C machines in use in 1974, approximately 19 percent of which were milling machines. (The other 81 percent performed various operations, including turning, grinding, and boring.) CAD-CAM was used only with milling machines. Most of these machines were two-dimensional and could not provide sculptured surfaces. Government sources estimated that the number of N/C machines would likely double within five years. The average milling machine without N/C ranged in cost from $4,000 to $6,000. N/C capability might add as much as $95,000 to the cost of each machine.

Most N/C equipment was installed in large independent shops and in captive shops. An estimated 12 to 20 percent of all independent shops had N/C capability; an industry representative believed that only 5 to 10 percent of the independent shops with fewer than 50 employees could ". . . both afford and understand the N/C concept." Some independent tool-and-die shops which had numerical control capability were beginning to experiment with computer graphic systems that resembled CAD-CAM. To Josten's knowledge, none of these shops had developed a system anywhere near as sophisticated and reliable as CAD–CAM.

An industry association estimated that approximately 90 percent of the large companies that required substantial numbers of dies each year owned their own N/C equipment. Most of these large companies were in the automotive or aerospace industries. They included such well-known firms as Westinghouse, Rockwell International, Litton, General Electric, and Bendix Aircraft. Many captive shops had been using multiaxis N/C systems (two axes at a time) which did not, however, provide full three-dimensional simultaneous motion capability for sculptured surfaces.

Some of these large firms also bought dies from independent shops. Both large firms and many of the smaller firms which purchased dies from independent tool-and-die shops frequently sent out to those shops not blueprints, drawings, or models, but rather programmed tapes intended to run on milling machines. In such cases, the independent shop simply mounted the tape onto the N/C machine, produced the part required, and returned the finished part and tape to the customer.

If an independent shop with N/C capability received a print or a model instead of a tape, it could have a tape made from that print or model, or acquire a standard tape for a die which might be substituted for the design on the print or model. Some independent shops made their own tapes and maintained libraries of tapes. Others acquired tapes from computer manufacturers, machine tool manufacturers that made tapes, or computer service organizations. Manufacturers and distributors of N/C machine tools that could not themselves provide tapes took an active role in bringing together tape-producing companies with owners of N/C machines. One specialized service firm that sold tapes to firms that owned N/C machines had been producing two and a half axis tapes since the early 1970s. In 1974, the firm had 1,400 subscribers and was said to be adding subscribers at a rate of 180 per month.

There were currently seven languages in which numerical control machines could be programmed. Each language differed with respect to its capabilities and the time required to develop and run particular programs. None of the programs was fully developed for the production of sculptured surfaces.

Several industry observers expressed concern that the increasing technological sophistication within the milling machine industry would gradually force out of business small shops that lacked N/C capability. In fact, a report by a respected consulting firm indicated that, by 1980, 25 percent of all the parts made in the United States would be made by N/C machinery and that, by 1988, 50 percent of all parts would be made by machinery under numerical control. Another industry source commented that this forecast increase, coupled with the fact that most N/C machinery was going to larger firms, would result in a "parts monopoly" in the United States in the late 1980s.

ALTERNATIVES

Josten's executives had identified five alternative means by which they might market the CAD–CAM system: (1) they could sell the hardware and software as a complete system to a customer; (2) they could lease the hardware and software to a customer on the customer's premises; (3) Josten's could lease the use of its system at Josten's facilities or at other locations; (4) the company could sell tapes to guide N/C milling machines; (5) Josten's could sell the completed dies themselves.

1. Selling the system: Josten's officials estimated that, if they were to sell the entire system to a customer, they would have to charge approximately $500,000. Up to three quarters of this amount would be spent on the basic hardware which Josten's would have to purchase from manufacturers of digitizers, computer equipment, and milling machinery. The remainder would represent fees charged by Josten's for continuous consultation, installation, programming, and servicing. Josten's personnel estimated that the direct costs of providing those services would amount to $50,000–$75,000. The total purchase price of $500,000 included no markup on the basic hardware, because Josten's personnel believed that prospective customers would buy the hardware directly from the hardware manufacturers if Josten's attempted to take a markup on it.

In addition to the purchase cost of the system, a customer would incur internal training costs of up to $10,000. Continuing operating costs, such as those for space, maintenance, salaries of operating employees and costs of updating the technology, would range upwards from $20,000, depending upon the customer's requirements and internal costs.

For those initial and continuing costs, however, customers would gain complete mobility and flexibility of use of the system on their own premises. The performance of the system would be guaranteed for the first year of operation at no risk beyond the specified costs.

2. On-premise leasing: Because they recognized that many potential users of their technology might lack the capital to purchase an entire system, Josten's officials explored the possibility of leasing the system to customers on the customers' premises, instead of requiring them to purchase it. Because the useful life of technical equipment was considered to be two to three years, Josten's officials believed that lease payments had to cover, within a period of 24 to 36 months, the purchase price of hardware plus fees charged by Josten's and basic maintenance costs (estimated at $1,500 per month). On that basis, at prevailing costs of funds, Josten's accountants estimated they would have to charge at least $23,500 per month for a two-year lease, and $18,500 per month for a three-year lease.

Under this alternative, the customer would enjoy the benefits of purchasing the system, without having to make the initial investment and with no risk beyond the contract price.

3. Leasing time: Josten's personnel believed that an expansion of the temporary arrangements the company had with local firms might appeal to a broader market. Under this alternative, customers who did not need a system dedicated entirely to their own uses could take advantage of the benefits of the CAD–CAM system on a basis that could be shared by others. The customer's design staff and engineers would come to a Josten's facility to use the CAD–CAM system themselves. These personnel would learn how to use the system from digitizer through computer graphics console through N/C milling machine.

Josten's officials believed that this alternative would require them to spend considerable time with individual customers to interpret each customer's needs, as well as to instruct customers' personnel in the use of the CAD–CAM system. Furthermore, they recognized that scheduling conflicts among customers might occur. They thought, therefore, that companies that planned their needs well in advance or had relatively long lead-time requirements would find the service more attractive than those that had short lead times.

Josten's personnel identified as most likely prospects fabricators that required original and duplicate replacement dies on their equipment for production. Such manufacturers were typified by the plastic injection industry, in which hundreds of local shops made molds for various plastic parts. Another major source of business was thought to be companies that used their own equipment to produce customized parts designed and used by other manufacturers. For example, one firm that had used the CAD–CAM system on an experimental basis produced typewriter keys for a leading American manufacturer. Such parts-makers might use CAD–CAM to explore different ways of making a particular die, or to make slight modifications, which it might then recommend to its customers. These parts-makers would also benefit from the use of N/C machining to make the die, once the design was set. A third example cited by company officials were manufacturing firms that did their own designing but sent out die-making to independent shops on a bid basis. These firms would use CAD–CAM primarily to gain design flexibility. Finally, small and medium sized tool-and-die shops appeared to be good prospects for this alternative.

According to Josten's officials, small companies for which there could be no hope of purchasing or leasing on premise were the best and most logical prospects for leasing time. One executive declared that, "companies like these are listed by the hundreds in virtually any phone book in the land." These companies typically lacked large design and engineering staffs, and ordinarily had to purchase tooling made by traditional methods. Josten's officials believed that such manufacturers—and many small tool-and-die shops— by simply leasing time and working during that time with experienced operators at a set price, could enable themselves to compete successfully with larger firms by producing superior work at an adequate and known margin of profit.

Josten's officials estimated that the fixed costs for a facility that could be leased to outsiders would run about $95,000 per year. Of this amount, depreciation on the equipment would account for $60,500; maintenance, for $18,000; rent, for $10,000; and other fixed expenses, for $6,500.

Josten's personnel estimated that variable operating expenses would range from $76,500 to $212,500, depending upon the utilization of the 12,000 hours available on the system each year. (On three-shift operation, the system could provide 6,000 hours on the computer console and 6,000 on the N/C milling machine, both of which could be used simultaneously, each on a different job.) Company personnel estimated expenses for each of three utilization rates, 25 percent, 50 percent, and 90 percent as shown in Table 1.

Table 1

ESTIMATED VARIABLE EXPENSES

	Utilization rate		
	25% (3000 hours)	50% (6000 hours)	90% (10,800 hours)
Payroll—staff and administration	$ 6,000	$ 12,000	$ 36,000
Payroll—operators and supervision	30,000	65,000	90,000
Indirect payroll costs	4,500	9,750	13,500
Supplies	6,000	9,500	13,000
Selling and sales support	30,000	40,000	60,000
Total	$76,500	$136,250	$212,500

Josten's officials believed that it would take them six to eight months to put in place a facility that duplicated their present one and to train additional personnel.

Josten's charges to local companies with which it had worked on an experimental basis were approximately $25 per hour. Company officials did not, however, regard that as a final price and were exploring other alternatives. They knew that General Motors, which used internally a system like CAD–CAM, had publicly stated that its internal cost for time on that system was $50 per hour.

4. Selling tapes: Josten's could also enter the market by selling edited tapes, i.e., tapes that had been developed on the digitizer from an original model or drawing and played back on the graphics console for changes, corrections, or modifications to meet exactly the specifications desired by the customer. The edited tape would then be ready for mounting on a computer-guided (N/C) milling machine.

Customers who owned computer-controlled milling machines in a language compatible with that used on the CAD–CAM system could purchase the tape and use it with no additional investment. Customers whose N/C milling machines were programmed in a language not compatible with that used for CAD–CAM would require a program to make the languages compatible. Costs of developing such software were estimated at about $8,000 to $10,000 for each different language. Modifying an existing two and a half axis milling machine to handle the infinite-axis operation made possible by CAD–CAM would cost an additional $25,000 to $30,000. Prospective customers who needed to purchase numerically controlled milling machines might have to invest $40,000 to $100,000 in such equipment. In addition, they would incur continuing costs of approximately $15,000 per year for an operator. Firms that already had N/C equipment normally carried qualified operators on their regular payrolls.

Customers who wanted revisions, changes, or duplications of their tapes could have them done very quickly by sending the tape back to Josten's with a statement of necessary changes referenced in the original drawings or model. Josten's designers could play back on the graphic console the revisions, edit them if necessary, and return the tape to the customer. Josten's officials believed that the tape service might permit customers to reduce their design staffs because in many cases there would be no need to "go back to the drawing boards," because the same work could be accomplished on the graphics console. The one limitation from the customer's point of view, according to Josten's officials, was that customers who wanted tapes revised would have to wait their turns, depending upon how fully utilized the CAD-CAM system was.

Josten's officials believed that to market a "tapes" service they would have to prepare a basic guide for prospective customers. This guide would include suggestions for those customers who did not possess N/C equipment with respect to the kind of equipment they ought to purchase, depending upon their needs, costs, and programming requirements. Josten's would guarantee to supply the tapes as required to assure customers that their investments in such N/C equipment would not be jeopardized. One Josten's executive argued that the marketing of tapes might best be accomplished by a joint venture with an established supplier of milling machines.

Josten's executives were considering two pricing alternatives if they were to enter this "tapes" market. The first involved a flat rate of $75 per hour, with a minimum charge of $250 plus materials for generating tapes. The second approach involved charging 20 cents or more per foot for paper tape generated. Company officials knew that one large purchaser of N/C tape was paying $1 per foot. Josten's costs for generating paper tape ran approximately 10 cents per foot. Current output of the system exceeded a mile of tape per day on three-shift operation.

5. Selling dies: Finally, Josten's officials were considering the possibility of manufacturing and selling finished tools and dies. To produce dies up to one cubic foot in size, Josten's would have to add up to $250,000 worth of equipment, including additional N/C milling machine capacity, and the facilities needed to finish, heat treat, and process the dies before they could be mounted on the customer's fixture and used to produce parts. In addition, the company would have to duplicate its present CAD-CAM system.

With this additional equipment, and a duplicate of their present basic system, Josten's officials estimated that they could produce on average as many dies per year as a six- to twenty-employee shop currently produced by traditional methods.

These finished dies could be sold to manufacturers or to tool-and-die shops. Josten's officials believed that the price charged for such dies could range from market prices prevailing at the present time under current technology, down to a level that reflected the savings possible through the use of the CAD-CAM system.

No matter which alternatives were adopted, Josten's officials recognized that they would likely have to establish a separate division for CAD-CAM and have to add capable personnel. At present, executives believed that only the developer of the system really understood it thoroughly and could readily conceive ways of expanding and modifying CAD-CAM and of keeping the system abreast of technological changes. His time, however, was in demand for other projects in the company, and he personally expressed greater interest in advancing the technology of the system than in managing it as a commercial venture.

Josten's executives believed that, even though the basic technology of CAD–CAM was available to others (and being used internally by a few large firms), their experience gave them a one to two year lead over potential competitors. They recognized that competitors would likely enter the business if Josten's were successful in marketing CAD–CAM. They therefore wished to examine the consequences of each of these alternatives on a long-run basis in order to decide which, if any, of the alternatives to pursue.

Exhibit 1

JOSTEN'S, INC.
ABRIDGED INCOME STATEMENT,
FOR YEARS ENDING JUNE 30
(000)

	1974	1973
Net sales	$130,673	$110,907
Cost of products sold	73,282	59,461
Gross margin	57,391	51,446
Expenses, net of other income	43,015	38,916
Income before taxes	14,376	12,530
Income taxes	7,290	6,260
Net income	$ 7,086	$ 6,270

Source: Annual Report

Exhibit 2

JOSTENS, INC.
ABRIDGED BALANCE SHEET,
JUNE 30
(000)

Assets	1974	1973
Cash and securities	$12,129	$ 9,873
Receivables, net	22,767	18,242
Inventory	20,699	15,011
Property and equipment, net	24,086	24,944
Other assets and prepayments	1,159	1,189
Total assets	$80,840	$69,259
Liabilities and equity		
Current liabilities	$25,265	$19,332
Long-term debt and deferred taxes	14,042	14,261
Shareholders' investment	41,533	35,666
Total liabilities and equity	$80,840	$69,259

Source: Annual Report

Exhibit 3

JOSTEN'S, INC.

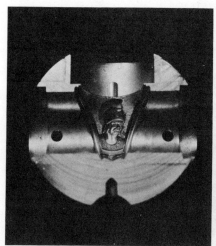 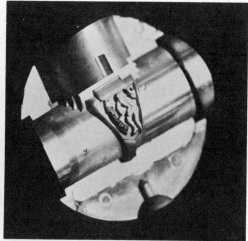

Molds used to make rings
(lost-wax process)

Subassemblies for class rings and completed class ring (center)

Source: Josten's, Inc.

Exhibit 4

JOSTEN'S, INC.
THE CAD–CAM SYSTEM

A: Data translation subsystem, showing digitizer and associated computer.

B: Data manipulation subsystem, showing designer using electronic pen to modify design displayed on graphics console.

Source: "Applying 3-D Computer Graphics to the N/C Production of Sculptured Tools," by John Titus.

Exhibit 4 (Cont.)

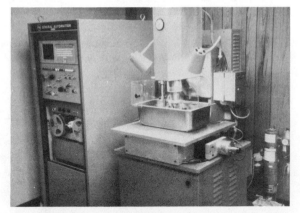

C: N/C machining subsystem, showing milling machine and associated computer.

Exhibit 5

JOSTEN'S, INC.

ESTIMATED AVERAGE AND TOTAL SALES AND PROFIT, BY SIZE OF SHOP, FOR INDEPENDENT TOOL–AND–DIE SHOPS, 1974

Number of employees	Number of shops	Average sales per shop (000)	Total sales (all shops combined) (000)	Average profit per shop @ 8% (000)
1–5	2,033	$ 67.5	$ 137,228	$ 5.4
6–10	2,026	180.0	364,680	14.4
11–20	2,232	360.0	803,520	28.8
21–30	1,235	585.0	722,475	46.8
31–45	826	855.0	706,230	68.4
46–60	427	1,170.0	499,590	93.6
61–80	294	1,575.0	663,050	126.0
81–100	161	2,025.0	326,025	162.0
101–130	95	2,587.5	245,812	207.0
131–160	57	3,285.0	187,245	262.8
161–200	38	4,072.5	154,755	325.8
Over 200	76	4,500.0	342,000	360.0
	9,500		$5,002,609	

Source: Company Records

ARCTIC ENTERPRISES, INC.

The "Wetbike"

In the late summer of 1977, officials of Arctic Enterprises, Inc., were faced with the need to develop a marketing program for the Wetbike, a new product planned for commercial introduction in 1978.

THE WETBIKE

The Wetbike is ridden like a motorcycle or snowmobile, but operates on top of the water riding on two in-line skis. After some instruction in mounting the vehicle, an individual can typically learn to operate the Wetbike in less than an hour. Two people can ride, or a driver can tow a waterskier. Maximum speed is 30 miles per hour. The Wetbike is pictured in Exhibit 1.

A 50 horsepower engine in the fiberglass body drives a jet pump which propels the Wetbike. This 50 horsepower jet pump delivers performance approximately equal to a 30 to 35 horsepower propeller-driven motor. Arctic officials consider the jet pump safer, because the operator would not be hurt by a propeller if he or she fell from the Wetbike. Power would shut off if the operator fell, and the Wetbike would promptly, but not abruptly, stop and settle down into the water. When stopped, the Wetbike draws about 30 inches of water; when operated from 12 to 30 mph, it planes atop the water, drawing only about four inches.

The noise level of the Wetbike is equal to a modern outboard motor to the bystander, although it may be a little louder to the operator. The Wetbike is as reliable as an outboard motor. Six gallons of fuel will generally last one-half day with normal use of the vehicle, although this time may be cut to less than three hours if the Wetbike is driven continuously at full throttle. The Wetbike has Coast Guard approval, and must be licensed as a boat in most states.

For $250,000, plus a royalty of 4 percent of the factory price on each unit sold, Arctic obtained from the product's inventors an exclusive, worldwide license to manufacture and market the Wetbike. The engine and pump will be supplied by Suzuki Motor Co., Ltd., of Japan, with which the company holds an exclusive worldwide license, and which supplies the engine for Arctic's snowmobiles and outboard motors. Arctic already has available production facilities, but an initial investment of approximately $200,000 will be needed to refine product engineering, prepare the vehicle for manufacturing, and purchase tooling sufficient to produce 10,000 units. Plant capacity to produce 50,000 to 80,000 units per year is presently available. Direct manufacturing costs for the Wetbike are expected to total $885 per unit for annual production of 3,000 or more units. In addition, Arctic has historically budgeted an amount equal to two-tenths of one percent of sales for the self-insured portion of its product liability insurance, and five- to six-tenths of one percent of sales for warranty fulfillment costs. Apart from expenses, investment in inventory and receivables for the Wetbike will come to $400 to $500 per unit, based on the company's experience with snowmobiles. Accounts payable are typically paid within 30 days. Company officials believed that, to duplicate the Wetbike, a competitor not in the business would need to invest more than a million dollars.

Three devices similar to the Wetbike have been introduced within the past three years, but to date have achieved only limited sales. Kawasaki introduced its "Jet Ski" in 1974. Arctic personnel estimated that Kawasaki sold 1,000 units to dealers in 1974, 2,000 in 1975, and 7,000 in 1976 through an intensive "dealer loading" program. Sales in 1977 are not known. Dynafoil and Power-Ski have each recently introduced propeller-driven machines. To date, however, only limited quantities have been manufactured. Exhibit 2 summarizes comparative data on the Kawasaki, Dynafoil, and Power-Ski units and the Wetbike. Exhibit 3 contains sketches of the three devices. Arctic management believes that the Wetbike is superior to these competing products because of the Wetbike's front steering, high performance, second-passenger capability, ability to pull a water skier, and passenger comfort.

Arctic officials became interested in the Wetbike because it appeared to meet the criteria established for the company's diversification program, whose objective was to have, within five years, half of Arctic's sales and earnings coming from products not related to snowmobiles. The criteria laid down for new product lines included the following: (1) substantial long-term earnings potential; and (2) earnings dependent upon seasons, geographic areas, and customer groups different from those of snowmobiles. Financial criteria for the diversification program were summarized in the Company's 1977 annual report:

> We intend to retain cash in the business in order to take advantage of opportunities for diversification that will provide a return on investment of at least 10 percent after tax. We are also prepared to borrow capital to finance new ventures and thereby increase our debt-to-equity ratio. We believe this ratio should not exceed 1:3 since we intend to sustain profits even during downturns in the cyclical industries in which we participate.

Company executives believed that certain recreational products could meet these criteria, and cited an article in the February 21, 1977 issue of *U.S. News & World Report* which stated in part:

> The recession of the past two years put no visible dent in total spending for leisure. Outlays for everything from tennis balls and snowmobiles to speedboats and foreign vacations soared to 146 billion dollars in 1976. . . . Few people realize the sturdy prop that such spending provides for U.S. business. . . . The total far exceeds annual outlays for national defense, or for home building. If past trends are a guide, leisure-time expenditures can be expected to double every eight or nine years. . . .

Among recreational products, marine-type products appeared attractive for three reasons, according to John C. Penn, President of Arctic Enterprises:

> (1) The marine market is very large with more than $5.3 billion spent each year in boating, including sales of new and used craft, accessories, safety devices, club memberships, launching fees, and insurance; (2) we already have experience in the marine

industry with Silverline (boats); and (3) our engineering, marketing, and distribution expertise is compatible with these products.

THE COMPANY

Arctic Enterprises, Inc., has been engaged in the manufacturing and marketing of outdoor recreational products since 1962. Its principal products are "Arctic Cat" snowmobiles, snowmobile parts, and accessories; "Arcticwear" clothing; snowmobile trailers and "Heavy Hauler" boat trailers. Arctic also manufactures and markets, under the "Silverline" name, a variety of outboard and inboard/outboard motor boats, ranging from 15 to 26 feet in length. The company markets "Spirit" outboard motors, ranging from 2 to 65 horsepower, which are manufactured for it by Suzuki Motor Co., Ltd., Japan. All these products are marketed throughout the United States and Canada, and in parts of Europe. In addition, the company recently began manufacturing and marketing in Canada a line of aluminum fishing boats, runabouts, and canoes. Although Arctic at one time manufactured lawnmowers and garden tractors, those lines have been discontinued. Because snowmobiles and related products constitute a major portion of Arctic sales, the company experienced losses in 1974 and 1975 when the snowmobile market declined sharply (see Exhibit 4). In 1977, however, Arctic earned more than $1.5 million on sales of almost $99 million. Capital expenditures were increased from $1.4 million in 1976 to $2.9 million in 1977. The company planned capital expenditures of $1.7 million in 1978 for existing lines of business. Income statements and balance sheets appear in Exhibits 4 and 5, respectively.

In 1977, Arctic sold just under 25 percent of the 192,000 snowmobiles sold by the industry as a whole. Company officials believed that Arctic Cat snowmobiles held the largest share of the United States snowmobile market. Arctic's sales have increased from 44,200 units in 1976 to 47,200 units in fiscal 1977 against a 20 percent industry decline (see Exhibit 6).

Arctic personnel expect their snowmobile sales to increase, along with those of the industry, about 5 percent annually for the next several years. Company officials expect profits to increase as a result of reductions in manufacturing costs; these reductions are not expected to require substantial additional capital investment. Arctic executives foresee no new competitors entering the industry. The number of manufacturers has declined steadily over the past five years; currently six manufacturers produce 13 brands. (Some companies manufacture snowmobiles for others who market those snowmobiles under their own brand names. Arctic manufactures both its own brand of snowmobiles and a separate brand marketed by another company.)

Distribution

About 70 percent of Arctic's snowmobiles and related products are presently sold through eight company-owned distributorships to more than 1,400 retail dealers. This percentage has increased from 50 percent in 1975. These company-owned distributorships are located throughout Canada, and from Michigan west throughout the northern snowbelt. The remaining 30 percent of sales are made through three independent authorized distributors who serve other regions of the United States. Limited sales are made through independent distributors in Norway and Sweden. Sales to all distributors are handled directly by a small staff at company headquarters. Approximately 40 percent of Arctic's snowmobile sales come from Michigan, Minnesota, Wisconsin, New York, and Pennsylvania. Arctic also uses its company-owned distributors plus one independent distributor, who does not handle snowmobiles, to distribute Silverline boats to almost 300 retailers. Approximately 15 percent of the retailers who carry Arctic snowmobiles also handle Silverline boats.

A sample survey of Arctic's snowmobile dealers revealed that most of them sold between $25,000 and $100,000 worth of snowmobiles per year at retail (see Exhibits 7 and 8). Most Arctic dealers do more volume in snowmobiles than in any other product line. Twenty-nine percent of Arctic's dealers carry at least one competitor's snowmobile, and many handle product lines in addition to snowmobiles.

Exhibit 9 lists the total number of marine, motorcycle, and snowmobile retailers by state, along with the number of Arctic snowmobile dealers in each state. There is no consistent relationship between Arctic's share of snowmobile dealers and the company's share of the market by state.

Approximately 44 percent of the dealers are located in towns of fewer than 10,000 persons; 12 percent, in towns of 10,000 or more. Almost 40 percent are located outside of towns, but within 50 miles of towns of at least 10,000 population. The remaining dealers are more than 50 miles away from a town of 10,000.

Advertising and Sales Support

Although they had not yet prepared an advertising plan for the Wetbike, Arctic officials knew that the company ordinarily budgeted 5 percent of the snowmobile sales for advertising and promotion of snowmobiles. Approximately two-thirds of that budget was spent on media advertising. (Illustrative media costs appear in Exhibit 10.) Somewhat more than half the media budget was devoted to television; radio and print advertisements split the remainder about equally. Dealers could claim up to 20 percent of the total budget for cooperative advertising (each dealer could claim an amount equal to 1 percent of his or her purchases). Arctic paid 50 percent of the cost of dealer cooperative ads. If the cooperative advertising allowance were not claimed by dealers, Arctic could use the funds for media advertising or other purposes.

Arctic provided its dealers with in-store display materials and a variety of sales aids in dealer kits, which required 5 to 10 percent of the total budget. The remainder covered production costs and administration. Arctic's own advertising and sales promotion efforts were augmented somewhat by those of its independent distributors.

Because dealers were reluctant to carry large inventories of snowmobiles, Arctic held inventory at its own and independent distributors' warehouses. In addition, the company provided inventory loans to dealers through a "floor planning" program. Arctic was, however, liable to repurchase inventories financed under the program up to a specific dollar limitation. Because the production cycle for large quantities of snowmobiles exceeded six months (from ordering raw materials and components to delivering the finished product) and the selling season lasted only the winter months, Arctic had to forecast demand as accurately as possible to avoid losing sales during the peak selling season or carrying large stocks of a previous year's models over to the next selling season. Arctic officials knew that the production cycle for Wetbikes would be similar to that for snowmobiles, but thought that the length of the selling season might vary by geographic region.

Prices and Margins

In 1977, Arctic Cat snowmobiles carried list prices ranging from $995 to $1995. The most popular model had a list price of $1425. Arctic's list prices positioned the company in the middle to upper range of industry retail prices. In addition to the price of the snowmobile, the customer paid freight costs from the factory to the retailer. This practice prevailed throughout the snowmobile industry. (Although Arctic officials had not determined price for the Wetbike, they planned to have customers pay freight from the factory to the Wetbike dealer.)

Retail dealers earned margins of approximately 25 percent on sales of Arctic Cat snowmobiles at list prices. Distributors earned margins of 20 percent on their sales to retail dealers. The company's discount structure was similar to that of other snowmobile manufacturers.

Snowmobile Owners

A survey of snowmobile owners conducted in 1976 by an industry source showed that the average number of snowmobiles owned was 2.5 per household, up from 1.8 in 1972. Far more than half of the machines were less than five years old. When buying additional snowmobiles, two-thirds of the buyers sold or traded in an older machine; one-third kept it for the family. Almost three-fourths of all snowmobiles purchased were bought new. More than 70 percent of all snowmobile purchases (new and used combined) were made for $1200 or less. In deciding whether to purchase a snowmobile in the future, personal financial situation was the single most important determinant. Two-thirds of all snowmobilers rode at home, i.e., without transporting their snowmobile(s) to another site.

A separate survey of Arctic's snowmobile consumers revealed the characteristics shown in Table 1. When Arctic owners were asked what types of recreational equipment

Table 1

	Percent of respondents
Age 25–49	67
Married	85
Have children	76.3
Live in or near city of less than 25,000	80
Earn more than $10,000	90
Earn more than $15,000	65.5

Table 2

	Percent who plan to buy within two years	Percent who currently own
Motorcycle	24.0	39.4
4-wheel drive vehicle	15.7	26.9
Pick-up truck	13.4	58.8
Chain saw	7.7	60.0
Inboard/outboard boat	7.0	15.5
Pick-up camper	6.6	16.1
Motorhome	6.1	4.7
Riding lawnmower	5.0	43.4
Cabin or second home	4.6	25.3
Garden tractor	4.6	37.5
Outboard motor	4.6	42.9
Live-in travel trailer	3.3	10.4
Hunting equipment or guns	2.0	86.1
Fishing equipment	1.8	84.6

they owned or were planning to buy within the next two years, they responded as shown in Table 2.

THE BOAT INDUSTRY

Because Arctic officials expected the Wetbike to appeal to users of water-ski equipment and motorcyclists, they reviewed information on both the boat and motorcycle industries.

Total United States marine equipment and service sales in 1976 were $5.3 billion, of which recreational boats (both motorized and nonmotorized) and motors represented more than $1.9 billion. Sales by category of boats and motors appear in Exhibits 11 and 12. The major segments of the industry have been growing steadily since 1972. One forecast for the continuing growth of the industry placed volume at $8 billion and 1,550,000 units by 1990. A major industry source stated that the primary reason for the continuing growth over the last thirty years has been that manufacturers have designed and built equipment to suit every taste and budget. Competition in the industry was extremely intense, particularly in pricing and advertising. A large number of companies manufactured and marketed boats.

Marine sales and dealerships have traditionally been concentrated in the East, North Central, South Atlantic, West South Central, and Pacific regions (see Exhibit 13). Florida and Texas held top ranking as outboard equipment consumer states. In 1976, significant gains in consumer sales were recorded in California, but both Wisconsin and Minnesota dropped sharply.

More than 94 percent of boat dealers are one-establishment firms. Eighty-five percent have fewer than 10 employees, and the average establishment has annual sales between $100,000 and $300,000. The typical marine dealer is thought to be quite conservative with respect to new products, particularly those that might either be inconsistent or competitive with his present lines. Marine dealers ordinarily earn margins of 20 to 30 percent, and buy through distributors who maintain margins of 10 to 20 percent.

The majority of boat consumers is between 25 and 45 years old, with an average age of 43.5. Most buyers are part of a two-person family, although a four-person family is the second largest group of purchasers. About two-thirds of the boat and motor purchases are made by skilled workers, managers, proprieters, and professionals. These consumers expect to use their purchases for a variety of activities. Approximately one-half expect to fish, cruise, and water ski (see Exhibit 14).

THE MOTORCYCLE INDUSTRY

Industry sources estimated that some 20 million Americans used more than 8 million motorcycles in 1976, and spent $4.7 billion on motorcycling. Of that amount, $1.3 billion went to sales of new motorcycles. Used motorcycles, parts, and accessories amounted to $1.8 billion. The remaining $1.6 billion went to services, state taxes, and license fees.

Motorcycle registrations have increased four-fold since 1965, and two-thirds of the motorcycles now in use were purchased new within the past five years. Although unit sales of motorcycles have declined from a 1973 peak, sales in units and dollars have increased since 1975 (see Exhibit 15).

Japanese manufacturers dominate the American motorcycle industry. Of the new motorcycles registered in 1976, 87 percent were manufactured by four Japanese firms. Honda accounted for 38 percent of the new registrations; Yamaha, 20 percent; Kawasaki, 17 percent; and Suzuki, 12 percent. (Harley-Davidson had 7 percent of the new registrations in 1976; five other manufacturers divided the remaining 6 percent.) This pattern of market share has prevailed for several years.

Within the United States, the motorcycle population is concentrated most heavily in the West, least heavily in the East (see Table 3).

Table 3

	Total motorcycle population	Motorcycle population per 1000 persons
West	1.9 million	5.1
East	1.1 million	2.3
Midwest	2.5 million	4.3
South	2.7 million	4.0

The number of franchised motorcycle dealerships in the United States has grown significantly over the last few years (see Exhibit 16). In addition to the 8,390 franchised dealers, in 1976 there were 1,912 other retail establishments that handled motorcycle replacement parts and accessories. A recent industry survey revealed that the typical motorcycle dealer has been in business seven years and employs six persons. Almost half of the dealers have total annual sales between $100,000 and $500,000 while about 19 percent have retail sales less than $50,000, and 5 percent have sales in excess of $1,000,000. Fifty-three percent of dealers' sales come from new and used motorcycles; 47 percent, from accessories. Financing for both dealer inventories and customer purchases comes primarily from banks.

Ninety percent of all motorcycle owners are male, and 60 percent are married. The median age of the motorcycle owner is 27.6 years. Fifty-two percent of owners have a high school education and 38 percent have some college education. The largest group of owners is students (23 percent), while 20 percent of motorcycle owners work in professional or technical positions. The median income of the motorcycle owner in the United States is $14,200; 49 percent of the owners have incomes between $10,000 and $19,999. The annual cost of owning and operating a motorcycle was estimated at $313 in 1976.

If Arctic were to use motorcycle dealers for the Wetbike, the company would sell to those dealers through its existing distributors, or through comparable distributors that served retail motorcycle dealers, if satisfactory arrangements could be made with the latter.

THE TASK

Mr. John C. Penn, President of Arctic, had asked the executives responsible for developing the market program for the Wetbike to prepare a five-year plan and budgets. (The year ending March 31, 1979, which Arctic termed "fiscal 1979," constituted the first year.) The plan was to include all major marketing activities envisioned for the Wetbike, supported by statements of objectives and brief descriptions of the market environment foreseen. Mr. Penn and the executives involved recognized that the objectives and environment might change from time to time throughout the planning period, and that plans for the first few years could be more detailed than those for later years.

The budgets were to include, for each year, estimated income statements and assets committed to the Wetbike line. Mr. Penn reminded the executives responsible for preparing the budgets that investments for the project had to be consistent with the financial capabilities of the company.

"This is a difficult forecasting and planning task," Mr. Penn stated, "for we must pioneer a new sport with the Wetbike."

Exhibit 1

ARCTIC ENTERPRISES, INC.
THE WETBIKE®

Source: Company Records

Exhibit 2

ARCTIC ENTERPRISES, INC.
COMPARATIVE DATA ON MOTORIZED WATERBIKES

	Arctic	Kawasaki	Dynafoil	Power-Ski	
Propulsion	jet	jet	propeller	propeller	
Passengers number position	1 or 2 seated	1 standing	1 or 2 seated	2 seated	or	1 standing or seated
List price to consumers	not yet determined	$1595	$2400	$2295	
Maximum speed	30 mph	30 mph	up to 30 mph	30 mph	
Engine	50 hp	27 hp	26 & 36 hp	35 hp	
Carriage	trailer or van	station wagon or van	trailer	trailer	
Distribution	not yet determined	motorcycle dealers	n.a.	n.a.	

Source: Company Records

Exhibit 3

ARCTIC ENTERPRISES, INC.
ILLUSTRATIONS AND COPY HEADLINES
FROM BROCHURES FOR OTHER WATER VEHICLES

Kawasaki Jet-Ski®
'discover the most exciting sport that ever hit the water.'

Dynafoil®

——'its different and it's dynamite'

PowerSki®   'water sports enters a new era'

Source: Drawings based on published brochures

Exhibit 4

ARCTIC ENTERPRISES, INC.

FIVE YEAR SUMMARY OF OPERATIONS

(YEARS ENDED MARCH 31)

(000 OMITTED EXCEPT ON PER SHARE AMOUNT)

	1977	1976	1975	1974	1973
Net sales	$98,911	$85,156	$79,625	$84,371	$107,185
Cost of sales	79,791	69,154	69,552	72,919	86,302
Gross profit	$19,120	$16,002	$10,073	$11,452	$ 20,883
Expenses					
Selling, administration, and others	$14,250	$11,988	$12,107	$14,515	$ 11,608
Interest	1,797	1,812	3,470	3,210	1,540
Total expenses	$16,047	$13,800	$15,577	$17,725	$ 13,148
Income (loss) before income taxes	3,073	2,202	(5,504)	(6,273)	7,735
(Provision for) benefit from income taxes	(1,550)	(1,186)	2,717	3,048	(3,982)
Income (loss) from continuing operations	1,523	1,016	(2,787)	(3,255)	3,753
Credit related to (loss on) discontinued operations	- 0 -	150	125	(5,024)	(1,615)
Net income (loss)	$ 1,523	$ 1,166	($ 2,662)	($ 8,249)	$ 2,138
Depreciation	$ 1,745	$ 1,558	$ 1,683	$ 3,484	$ 2,172
Sales by product line					
Snowmobiles	$66,003	$52,412	$47,872	$53,170	$ 75,595

Exhibit 4 (Cont.)

	1977	1976	1975	1974	1973
Snowmobile parts, accessories, and Arcticwear clothing	19,036	19,715	17,254	17,379	18,543
Silverline boats and related lines	12,121	9,002	9,287	9,645	9,669
Other	1,751	4,027	5,212	4,177	3,378
General leisure division (Discontinued 1973)	- 0 -	- 0 -	- 0 -	- 0 -	12,916
Earning (loss) by product line					
Arctic (snowmobiles, related lines, and other)	$ 1,166	$ 834	($ 2,928)	($ 3,012)	$ 3,466
Silverline	357	182	141	(213)	287
Discontinued operations	- 0 -	150	125	(5,024)	(1,615)
Snowmobiles manufactured	56	54	37	61	99
Position at year end:					
Working capital	$23,946	$23,007	$21,301	$22,226	$ 26,391
Current ratio	2.7	2.8	2.8	1.8	1.7
Property and equipment, net	$13,064	$12,237	$12,614	$14,722	$ 17,711
Goodwill, net	$ 602	$ 699	$ 780	$ 923	$ 2,692
Total assets	$52,664	$49,540	$47,347	$67,215	$ 85,185
Long-term debt	$ 7,781	$ 7,394	$ 7,625	$ 8,221	$ 9,138
Shareholders' investment	$30,003	$28,449	$27,277	$29,904	$ 38,151
Outstanding common shares	3,065	3,053	3,050	3,050	3,049
Shareholders' investment per share	$ 9.79	$ 9.32	$ 8.94	$ 9.80	$ 12.51
Share price, November 1	$ 6.25	$ 2.38	$ 3.75	$ 4.38	$ 5.38

Note: No cash dividends have been paid by Arctic during the five years ending March 31, 1977.
Source: Arctic Enterprises, Inc., 1977 Annual Report

Exhibit 5

ARCTIC ENTERPRISES, INC.

CONSOLIDATED BALANCE SHEET

MARCH 31

(000)

Assets	1977	1976
Current assets		
Cash	$ 945	$ 2,735
Receivables	4,061	2,957
Inventories	31,481	29,222
Prepaid expenses	1,639	1,008
Total current assets	38,126	35,922
Property and equipment (Net of depreciation of $7,958)	13,064	12,237
Other assets	1,474	1,381
Total	$52,664	$49,540

Liabilities and Equity	1977	1976
Current liabilities		
Current maturities of long-term debt	$ 1,131	$ 411
Accounts payable	9,112	9,107
Accrued expenses and income taxes	3,937	3,397
Total current liabilities	14,180	12,915
Long-term debt	7,781	7,394
Deferred income taxes	700	782
Shareholders' investment	30,003	28,449
	$52,664	$49,540

Note: The company must be free of all short-term debt for a period of 60 consecutive days during any calendar year; for the year ending March 31, 1977 the maximum short-term borrowing was $23 million, and the company has arranged total short-term bank lines of credit of $26 million for the year ending March 31, 1978.

Source: Arctic Enterprises, Inc., 1977 Annual Report

Exhibit 6

ARCTIC ENTERPRISES, INC.
TOTAL INDUSTRY
SNOWMOBILE RETAIL SALES
1963–1977

Year	Units
1963	10,000
1964	18,000
1965	30,000
1966	45,000
1967	65,000
1968	85,000
1969	255,000
1970	425,000
1971	495,000
1972	460,000
1973	450,000
1974	435,000
1975	305,000
1976	242,643
1977	192,000

Source: 1963–1967 Company Estimates, 1968–1977 Industry Association Tabulations

Exhibit 7

ARCTIC ENTERPRISES, INC.
PERCENTAGE DISTRIBUTION OF ARCTIC SNOWMOBILE
DEALERS BY VOLUME CATEGORY

Snowmobile retail sales volume	Percent of dealers
less than $25,000	18%
$ 25,000–$ 50,000	26
$ 50,000–$ 75,000	15
$ 75,000–$100,000	16
$100,000–$150,000	13
More than $150,000	12
	100%

Source: Sample Survey of Arctic Dealers

Exhibit 8

ARCTIC ENTERPRISES, INC.
PERCENT OF ARCTIC SNOWMOBILE DEALERS
HANDLING OTHER PRODUCT LINES

Product line	Percent of dealers
1. Marine	26.1% [*]
2. Lawn and garden equipment	25.6
3. Motorcycle sales and service	31.3
4. Farm equipment	9.3
5. Bicycle sales and service	9.3
6. Camper sales and service	10.9
7. Automobile sales and service	10.6

[*] Approximately 15 percent carry Silverline boats
Source: Company Records

Exhibit 9

ARCTIC ENTERPRISES, INC.

MARINE, MOTORCYCLE, AND SNOWMOBILE
DEALERS BY STATE

State	Total marine dealers	Total motorcycle dealers	Total snowmobile dealers	Arctic snowmobile dealers
Alabama	181	159	0	0
Alaska	107	40	45	33
Arizona	91	96	10	3
Arkansas	155	99	0	0
California	815	777	77	10
Colorado	92	145	390	15
Connecticut	248	78	148	12
Delaware	32	20	7	2
Florida	688	326	0	0
Georgia	252	201	0	0
Hawaii	41	13	0	0
Idaho	63	88	172	25
Illinois	643	375	287	27
Indiana	393	264	94	13
Iowa	236	180	241	44
Kansas	128	150	10	0
Kentucky	225	121	0	0
Louisiana	182	138	0	0
Maine	183	73	123	38
Maryland	227	90	31	2
Massachusetts	362	130	197	19
Michigan	780	459	1,183	118
Minnesota	375	224	895	112
Mississippi	98	82	0	0
Missouri	223	186	5	0

Exhibit 9 (Cont.)

State	Total marine dealers	Total motorcycle dealers	Total snowmobile dealers	Arctic snowmobile dealers
Montana	65	110	154	23
Nebraska	70	93	43	9
Nevada	41	30	11	3
New Hampshire	93	71	110	24
New Jersey	311	136	129	7
New Mexico	51	61	158	2
New York	882	416	658	144
North Carolina	245	187	1	1
North Dakota	46	61	79	29
Ohio	413	416	168	19
Oklahoma	173	117	0	0
Oregon	163	149	78	10
Pennsylvania	297	452	521	100
Rhode Island	55	25	12	1
South Carolina	119	89	0	0
South Dakota	49	57	92	19
Tennessee	176	168	1	1
Texas	537	456	1	1
Utah	84	70	94	17
Vermont	74	39	84	15
Virginia	210	156	5	2
Washington	333	169	81	25
West Virginia	57	89	9	0
Wisconsin	479	237	1,199	105
Wyoming	46	50	166	18
D.C.		2		
Canadian dealers			3,428	396
Total	11,889	8,390	11,197	1,444

Source: Recreation Industry Mailing List (Totals) and Company Records (Arctic and Suzuki)

Exhibit 10

ARCTIC ENTERPRISES, INC.
ILLUSTRATIVE MEDIA RATES*
TELEVISION
30–SECOND ANNOUNCEMENT

	Network	Top 10 markets (34% of T.V. homes)	Markets 11–20 (12%)	Markets 21–30 (9%)	Top 30 markets (55%)
7:30–11:00 P.M.	$50,000	$10,000	$4,300	$2,700	$17,000
6:00– 7:30 P.M. Mon.–Fri.	20,000	3,500	1,500	1,000	6,000
11:30– 1:00 A.M. Mon.–Fri.	15,000	1,800	750	450	3,000
Daytime	10,000	1,200	500	300	2,000

MAGAZINES
ONE–PAGE

	Black-and-white	Four-color
Newsweek, Time, Playboy	$25,000	$40,000
Sports Illustrated	20,000	30,000
Field & Stream, Outdoor Life, or Esquire	10,000	15,000

(*Note:* Rates for half-page approximately 60 percent of full-page costs; rates for regional editions 15–20 percent higher per household.)

SUNDAY SUPPLEMENTS
ONE–PAGE

	Black-and-white	Four-color
To reach 20 million families	$100,000	$135,000

Outdoor

To reach 89 percent of adult males 17 times, $430,000 per month for top 30 markets

*These costs are rounded average estimates based on quoted media rates, and are considered useful for illustrative purposes, though not precisely reflecting actual individual media rates.

Source: Estimates based on Standard Rate and Data Service, 1976

Exhibit 11

ARCTIC ENTERPRISES, INC.
ESTIMATED ANNUAL RETAIL DOLLAR VOLUME,
BOATS, MOTORS, AND TRAILERS 1972–1976

	1972	1973	1974	1975	1976
Motors					
Units (000)	535	585	545	435	468
$ volume (000)	432,300	501,300	463,300	411,100	514,800
Average cost ($)	808	857	850	945	1,100
Horsepower (% of total)					
0 – 7	21.5	21.6	24.0	24.6	21.0
7.1–19.9	18.0	16.7	17.0	17.8	18.0
20 and over	60.5	61.7	59.0	57.6	61.0
Outboard boats					
Units (000)	375	448	425	328	341
$ volume (000)	267,800	325,200	310,200	262,700	358,100
Average cost ($)	714	726	736	800	1,050
Inboard/outdrive boats					
Units (000)	63	78	70	70	80
$ volume (000)	307,800	410,400	386,700	420,000	576,000
Average cost ($)	4,885	5,261	5,524	6,000	7,200
Boat trailers					
Units (000)	265	330	325	255	285
$ volume (000)	72,100	94,400	98,100	87,700	121,100
Average cost ($)	272	286	302	343	425
Totals					
Units (000)	1,238	1,441	1,365	1,088	1,174
$ volume (000)	1,080,000	1,331,300	1,258,300	1,181,500	1,570,000

Source: Company Records

Exhibit 12

ARCTIC ENTERPRISES, INC.
ESTIMATED RETAIL SALES OF
NONMOTORIZED BOATS, 1976

Sailboats

Units (000)	86
$ volume (000)	$241,000
Average unit price	2,802

Houseboats

Units (000)	1.4
$ volume (000)	$ 34,300
Average unit price	$ 24,500

Pontoon and Deck Boats

Units (000)	12.5
$ volume (000)	$ 32,500
Average unit price	$ 2,600

Canoes

Units (000)	78
$ volume (000)	$ 22,600
Average unit price	$ 290

Rowboats, Fishing Boats, etc.

Units (000)	86
$ volume (000)	$ 32,680
Average unit price	$ 380

Source: Company Records

Exhibit 13

ARCTIC ENTERPRISES, INC.
BOAT INDUSTRY SALES BY REGION

	1972		1976	
	Retail sales ($000)	Number of dealers	Retail sales* ($000)	Number of dealers
Northeast	105,060	354	62,231	1,015
East N. Central	258,576	752	296,163	2,708
West N. Central	102,289	329	170,838	1,127
Middle Atlantic	175,785	542	163,803	1,490
South Atlantic	366,436	925	320,639	1,830
East S. Central	74,970	213	88,993	680
West S. Central	186,923	494	230,832	1,047
Mountain	46,420	109	96,356	533
Pacific	243,850	600	236,547	1,311
Total	$1,560,308	4,318	$1,665,402*	11,741[†]

*Sales figures include outboard motors, outboard boats, and inboard/outdrive boats, which together amount to 86.2 percent of total boat sales.

[†] Total differs from 11,889 in Exhibit 7 because of slight differences in definitions used and timing of counts.

Source: U.S. Census of Retailers, 1972, and Company Records

Exhibit 14

ARCTIC ENTERPRISES, INC.—INTENDED USES OF BOATS BY BUYERS, 1972-1976

Intended use	1972	1973	1974	1975	1976
Fishing (%)*	36.1	36.4	33.0	42.3	32.2
Cruising (%)	32.1	31.1	32.7	40.0	34.8
Skiing (%)	49.2	49.3	41.7	40.2	37.8
Hunting (%)	30.0	28.8	31.4	26.1	20.4
Other (%)	6.8	6.8	7.6	11.6	13.7

*Percentages do not total 100 percent because of multiple mentions.
Source: Company Records

Exhibit 15

ARCTIC ENTERPRISES, INC.—MOTORCYCLE SUPPLY AND DEMAND, 1969-1976

	U.S. motorcycle imports (units) (000)	Estimated U.S. production (units) (000)	Estimated retail sales (units) (000)	Estimated wholesale dollar volume (000)	Estimated retail dollar volume (000)
1969	640	40	670	n.a.	n.a.
1970	1,090	35	1,010	n.a.	n.a.
1971	1,540	25	1,240	n.a.	n.a.
1972	1,690	35	1,360	$ 782,910	$1,179,906
1973	1,210	45	1,520	984,684	1,305,994
1974	1,540*	40	1,200*	1,003,546*	1,320,200*
1975	950*	40	940*	912,654*	1,152,438*
1976	660*	80	1,050*	1,050,158*	1,300,000*

*Excludes estimated imports of mopeds: 1974—13,000 units; 1975—32,000 units; 1976—78,000 units.
Source: 1977 Motorcycle Statistical Annual

Exhibit 16

ARCTIC ENTERPRISES, INC.—MOTORCYCLE INDUSTRY SALES BY REGION, 1972 and 1976

	1972		1976	
	Retail sales new motor-cycles only (000)	Number of dealers	Retail sales new motor-cycles only (000)	Number of dealers
Northeast	$ 46,884	146	$ 59,500	416
East N. Central	260,965	667	283,500	1,751
West N. Central	110,277	326	137,400	951
Middle Atlantic	104,136	336	141,200	1,004
South Atlantic	184,282	481	167,000	1,160
East S. Central	55,622	194	78,600	530
West S. Central	105,985	345	122,300	780
Mountain	73,780	242	87,100	650
Pacific	237,975	679	223,400	1,148
Total	$1,179,906	3,416	$1,300,000	8,390

Source: 1972 U.S. Census of Retail Trade and 1977 Motorcycle Statistical Annual

MANAGING THE PRESENT PORTFOLIO

The basic question asked about businesses presently included in the portfolio is, "Should we continue to run the business as we do now (present strategies and investment level), change strategy and investment level (reallocate resources), or get out of the business altogether?" The decision to drop a line or to reallocate resources may arise from routine review of existing product lines and markets in the context of planning for future periods, from analyses of product lines or market whose performance appears to be significantly above or below managers' expectations, or from a general financial review of the portfolio. Conceptually, the decision to remove an investment from the portfolio is simpler than that to reallocate resources among multiple investments which must be analyzed simultaneously.

Removing Investments from the Portfolio

Removing from the portfolio a product line or business whose performance is disappointing or which appears not to fit appropriately with other businesses in which the firm is engaged represents a portfolio modification option that should be explored more frequently than it typically is. The analysis appropriate for a removal decision parallels that for a decision to reduce the breadth of an individual product line. Managers must identify candidates for removal from the portfolio, specify the benefits expected from removing the investment, set aside objections to removal, and plan a program for orderly removal of the product line from the portfolio.

Identifying Candidates for Removal from the Portfolio   To assure a continuing and systematic identification of candidates for removal from the portfolio, an organization may employ a product line audit of past and current performance, together with a forecast of probable future product line performance. Ideally, such an audit-and-forecast procedure should involve the entire portfolio of an organization.

Data for an audit ordinarily are available from internal records. The income statement for a product line will yield information on sales, direct costs, allocated costs, and profit. Most organizations have access to their own or outside studies of total industry sales from which a particular organization's market share can be estimated. Alert managers can ordinarily appraise competitors' positions fairly accurately. Low and/or declining industry and company sales, market share, and profits all constitute warning signals which a systematic audit should bring to managers' attention.

The same data incorporated into the audit, supplemented by appropriate marketing research studies, may be used to forecast sales, market share, and profits. The most useful forecasts will specify a range for each critical value, together with a statement of circumstances under which the low and high estimates, respectively, might occur.

One may identify four types of product lines or businesses that may be candidates for removal from an organization's portfolio: (1) businesses with disappointing returns; (2) businesses with marginal or adequate returns, but likely to offer limited future profit opportunities; (3) businesses that may be profitable in themselves, but should be "pruned" from the portfolio for the health of the organization as a whole; and (4) businesses for which a prospective buyer has approached the organization.

A business or product line may experience declining profits, or losses, for a variety of reasons, primarily because of low or declining sales and a small and declining market share. Product lines whose share of their respective markets is low frequently exhibit costs higher than those of competition, and may have distribution outlets, technical capabilities, or other resources that do not match those of competitors.

Rohm and Haas, a chemical company, sold its fiber business after several years of unsatisfactory performance. Many other firms from outside the fibers industry experienced similar problems, and subsequently removed fiber business from their portfolios because of declines in demand and intense competitive pressures.

Candidates for removal from the portfolio may also include product lines relatively new to the portfolio that may be marginally profitable, but require considerable investment before they are likely to yield adequate profits. Managers responsible for such product lines typically argue that additional resources are needed to bring the business up to a minimum size or "critical mass" necessary to capture adequate market share and generate suitable profits. Faced with the alternatives of substantial additional investment or continued inadequate profits, top management may well recommend withdrawing from the business.

A diversified manufacturer who had recently developed a novel filing system decided to discontinue investment after results from two years of regional sales indicated that a multimillion-dollar marketing effort would be necessary to build the business to a size and profit level satisfactory to the company.

Executives may also consider getting out of businesses that offer limited opportunity for future profit growth for their particular organizations. Such businesses frequently include product lines with which the organization's personnel lack familiarity, which require substantial amounts of executive time, which lack a basis for growth through horizontal or vertical integration, or which lack a basis for continuing development of new products to maintain the vitality of the business and to expand it.

A manufacturer of food products acquired and subsequently sold a chain of restaurants. The manufacturers' personnel experienced difficulty in learning how to manage the restaurant business, and finally concluded that growth prospects for this particular restaurant chain were limited. Even though the chain remained profitable, the manufacturer foresaw only modest growth opportunity, and therefore sold the restaurants.

Managers may choose to remove from an organization's portfolio businesses which are profitable and have growth potential, but which do not contribute directly to the organization's marketing strategy objectives, its corporate mission, or its optimum portfolio. In such instances, managers seek to use resources committed to these businesses in ventures which fit more centrally into the organization's mission and portfolio.

A midwestern manufacturer of sophisticated electronic equipment developed a simple, inexpensive device to measure and control air flow through air-operated paint spraying systems. Because the new device appeared promising, the company developed a different salesforce and marketing support effort, which the new product required, and organized a separate division for it. Although the new division had operated profitably for almost three years, corporate management sought a buyer for it, in order to release resources for the companys' rapidly-growing "core" business of sophisticated equipment.

Occasionally an organization may be forced to sell a profitable part of its operations, perhaps even one deemed central to the organization's overall mission, simply because the funds generated from such a sale are required to keep the organization viable. For example, White Motor Co. sold several of its divisions when the company was forced to retrench.

Even though they may have no plans to remove a particular product line from an organization's portfolio, managers may be pressed to consider such action by a prospective buyer of the product line or business. One executive of a large diversified company stated that the acquisitions that had fared best in his company had not been for sale at the time his company acquired them; rather, he and his staff had carefully analyzed the types of businesses they wished to buy from other large companies, and then pursued those that appeared most attractive as prospective purchases. His experience points up the fact that a product line that may not suit one organization's portfolio may fit well with that of another organization.

Benefits from Removing Investments   The principal benefit from removing an investment from the portfolio is to free resources, which can be employed—presumably more advantageously—in other product lines. Resources may be released because an unprofitable business is no longer consuming funds through operating losses, inventory, and receivables; because production and technical facilities and personnel are available for other product lines; because marketing dollars and personnel may be concentrated more heavily on remaining product lines; and because executives have more time to devote to building the remaining businesses. Heublein's withdrawal from the poultry raising and processing business, and Warner Communications's closing of its Jungle Habitat zoo in New Jersey represent typical attempts of parent organizations to stop losses and release resources.

In some instances, removal of a product line may enhance the image of the organization and facilitate sales of its remaining lines. Bell and Howell decided to close down its home-study division rather than attempt to rebuild its profitability, in large part because of adverse publicity generated by a Federal Trade Commission investigation of the whole home-study industry, even though Bell and Howell had not been charged with any wrongdoing.

Barriers to Removing Investments from the Portfolio   Notwithstanding the benefits of removing certain product lines from an organization's portfolio, few companies systematically "prune" their portfolios unless forced to do so. A study of 96 of the largest manufacturing firms in the United States showed that the typical company had eliminated fewer than 20 products—and presumably even fewer product lines—during a five-year period. This low "drop" rate may be attributed in large part to the barriers within organizations to product line removal which are varied and very strong. The objections to removing product lines progress from problem denial to retention justification.

A typical method of denying the existence of a problem (and therefore refusing to consider removing a product line from the portfolio) is the belief that current economic conditions and/or lack of familiarity with the product line have depressed performance. Once conditions improve, or now that our learning period is behind us, so the argument goes, the performance of this product line will reach satisfactory levels. Another common method of denial consists of arguing that available accounting data fail to show the existence of any problem, and that the data needed for analysis of a particular product line cannot readily be obtained.

In some instances, managers will admit the existence of a problem with a product line, but argue that corrective marketing action, rather than disinvestment, is the appropriate remedy. A change in the marketing program, perhaps including repositioning the line, and even product modification, may be recommended. Such methods are typically tried before serious consideration is given to removing the product line from the portfolio. To the argument that no matter what the strategy employed the line will still have only a small market share and suffer the low profit typically associated with a small share, managers often respond by claiming for the line a large share of a smaller and much more precisely defined market. This argument may be persuasive, provided that the smaller entity itself constitutes a viable market and that the product line in question possesses a distinct advantage in competitive position with the smaller market.

The next stage of argument against disinvestment consists of admitting that a particular product line or venture is unprofitable, but claiming that the line must be retained for the good of the company. Arguments such as, "We need it to sell our other lines," or, "We have to retain 'full-line' capability," are frequently made. These arguments are often rather difficult to support, as is their companion, "We built our company on this line," or, "We've always had the line; our customers expect it of us." Somewhat more persuasive is the argument that discontinuing one product line would lead customers to believe that the company might drop other lines, and therefore make them unwilling to depend upon it as a supplier. This argument may be important in industrial markets in which a small number of suppliers compete.

If the previous level of argument fails, adherents of a line that is being considered for removal may argue that dropping it will free no resources. They argue that physical resources committed to the line will still continue to generate overhead expense even if the line is dropped. This argument can result in the retention of any product line that is absorbing overhead. If the overhead-absorption argument fails, a fall-back position is to argue that dropping the product line would result in unemployment and would undermine organizational morale. In fact, most managers find it very difficult to fire personnel or to offer employees transfers they're unlikely to accept.

Finally, those involved with management of the product line considered for removal may acknowledge that its removal would indeed free resources, but that the organization could not employ those resources more appropriately within the forseeable future. Therefore, the argument runs, we might as well keep this line, because at least we know it better than another venture we might select, and we might find some way to make it more profitable. This argument often carries undue weight in organizations that have experienced difficulties with new ventures.

Because of their involvement with a product line, managers often consider a proposal to remove that line from the portfolio a personal indictment, even when management may not intend it so. Nevertheless, proposals for disinvestment typically encounter strong opposition from managers closely associated with lines that are candidates for removal from the portfolio. This intraorganizational resistance likely constitutes the single most important reason for the failure of organizations to "prune" their portfolios.

Methods of Removing Investments If managers can agree to remove a product line from the portfolio, there are several methods by which an organization may withdraw from a business. (1) The firm may plan to discontinue the product line over a fairly long period of time, and begin to do so by "milking" the line, i.e., withdrawing all promotional support to win new and retain present customers, and simply continuing to make the product line available through normal channels until demand dwindles entirely or the channels refuse to stock the product. (2) The product line, including manufacturing and service capabilities and personnel, may be sold intact as a "going concern" to another organization which will continue to offer the line. This option may not be a viable one for unprofitable product lines, unless a prospective buyer believes that he or she can take certain actions that the selling firm could not in order to make the line profitable. Even when selling a profitable product line, firms may discover that the value prospective buyers place upon that line is far less than they themselves believe the line to be worth. In many instances, assets the selling firm values highly on its books will have much lower worth to prospective buyers. A central question for a firm contemplating the sale of a portion of its business is, "From the point of view of an interested buyer, what is this business worth?" To answer this question, the seller may have to speculate on how the prospective buyer might operate the business, once purchased. (3) The organization may stop making the product, either retaining existing inventories or liquidating them. (4) The firm may simply abandon the business altogether. This alternative may have favorable tax consequences under certain circumstances, but it requires that the abandoning organization take action to secure any physical facilities, so that they constitute neither active danger nor "attractive nuisance."

The choice among these options depends in part on the nature of the product line and the market. Consumable products for which no replacement parts or postpurchase services are needed, and for which substitutes exist on the market, may be withdrawn by any of these options. Product lines for which spare parts and/or service are required ordinarily are not dropped abruptly. If such products are not sold intact with their associated organizations, the original manufacturer or reseller will ordinarily notify customers of intent to discontinue, and then retain inventories sufficient to provide spares through the normal life of the most recently sold products. The original manufacturer may retain responsibility for service, or train users or independent service organizations to handle maintenance and repair. Similarly, a manufacturer who constitutes a sole source of supply may make arrangements to supply current users for an extended period of time.

Because the objective of removing investments from the portfolio is to increase return and/or to decrease variability, the forecast performance of a product line may influence the withdrawal option chosen. Product lines and markets for which significant losses are forecast should be dropped promptly to increase return. To avoid abrupt drops in return, profitable businesses that are to be removed should be removed gradually, unless resources made available can be shifted immediately to other investments that will promptly yield an increased return. Gradual removal, either by "milking" a product line or market, or by selling a set of businesses off over an extended period of time, also avoids marked changes in returns, or variability, for the portfolio as a whole.

Reallocating Resources within the Portfolio

Reallocation involves shifting resources among existing product lines within the portfolio to withdraw resources from lines that are using them less productively and apply them to product lines that can employ them more efficiently. Reallocation is a more frequently used, but less radical, method of modifying the portfolio than adding or dropping product lines. Decisions to increase or decrease investment in a particular product line ordinarily involve reallocations of financial, technical, marketing, and managerial resources among product lines.

Resources to be Reallocated When we think of allocating resources, most of us think immediately of capital funds for purchase of plant and equipment. Because decisions to obtain land and erect a facility generally involve long lead times and significant long-term financial commitments for an organization, such decisions receive careful scrutiny. Decisions to buy new equipment, to replace existing machinery, or to remodel manufacturing and quality control facilities are often just as significant. Because plant and equipment are often specialized, conversion from intended use to use for a different product line may be difficult, or nearly as costly as investment in new facilities. Because of the size and visibility of these plant and equipment decisions, managers generally recognize that pursuit of one project—commitment to one product line—will delay or preclude commitments to other lines.

Less visible, but frequently larger in dollars than plant and equipment commitments, are investments in working capital for a particular product line. A product line may require additional working capital to support planned increases in marketing budgets and sales, to support extension of credit terms through increases in receivables, or to permit more prompt delivery through maintenance of higher inventory levels. Commitment of working capital funds, which are scarce in most organizations, to one product line will necessarily limit the working capital available to finance other product lines.

Similarly, a decision to work on modifications and/or extensions of one product line must mean that technical activity in behalf of other lines will be postponed or simply not done at all. Even if an organization supplements its internal technical staff with outside specialists, most firms can manage effectively only a limited number of such outsiders at one time. Therefore, engineering time to make modest changes in the product line, and research and development laboratory time for more sweeping changes, constitutes a scarce resource which forces an organization to choose among projects.

The most visible resource the marketing manager can allocate is typically the marketing communications budget. Both manufacturers and resellers can and do vary that budget among product lines. The marketing communications budget may include advertising; sales promotion in the form of catalogs and trade shows; reseller support through direct mail, displays, brochures, and the like; and the time of the sales force, purchased through commissions, intracompany transfer payments, or persuasion and negotiation between sales and product management groups. Marketing communications budgets generally are allocated more heavily to product lines that have some element of "newness," lines about which customers would be interested in having additional information.

One of the most important resources—and most difficult to measure—is managerial time. An organization that undertakes a program to, say, improve the competitive position of a particular product line in an important market in fact commits the time of executives and managers at many levels to that task. Because the total time of the executive and managerial staff is limited, concentration on that program necessarily means that other ongoing or prospective programs will receive less attention, or none at all. The costs of inattention may include erosion in market share and competitive strength, lost customers, missed opportunities, and lost profits. The question that too few managers weigh carefully is whether the gains from a proposed program will exceed probable losses because of time taken away from other programs.

Bases for Reallocation of Resources   Among the bases most frequently used to allocate resources among product lines are (1) the organization's marketing strategy, corporate mission, and portfolio objectives; (2) primary demand for each product line; (3) competitive opportunity for each line; (4) generation of/need for funds; (5) profit opportunities; and (6) resources available.

(1) Product lines that are considered most likely to advance the organization's movement toward its marketing and corporate objectives and toward its optimum portfolio of products and markets may receive more resources than those lines considered marginally related to the organization's primary mission. For a product line that appears not to fit with others in the portfolio, but is nonetheless sufficiently profitable to be retained, managers have three options: to treat the misfit as an orphan, providing only minimal resources; to invest resources in an effort to develop the organization's expertise in handling that type of business and integrating it more closely into the portfolio; or to provide resources needed to change the business to fit with the manner in which other product lines in the portfolio are operated. The third option is commonly employed by organizations that acquire going concerns to integrate them into the parent organization. If the new business does not fit well after these initial efforts, most organizations are reluctant to invest heavily to "learn the business," unless substantial profit growth appears imminent.

(2) Product lines in which primary demand, i.e., demand for the entire product class, is increasing ordinarily represent more attractive opportunities for allocation of available resources than do product lines that face stagnant or declining primary demand. In general, the greater the growth rate, the longer the time period for which growth is forecast to continue, and the larger the size of the market, the more attractive the opportunity.

(3) Product lines that face opportunities to increase market share or penetration, or to strengthen competitive position, may also attract resources. Such opportunities may accrue to a product line with a proprietary feature, cost advantage, or exceptionally strong customer acceptance compared to competition. Occasionally, opportunities arise to exploit a particular competitive weakness, to obtain a unique "niche" in the marketplace, or to forestall competition. Investment of additional resources against such opportunities may prove profitable.

(4) Some managers seek to reallocate resources to achieve a balance between product lines that generate cash and those that consume cash. This approach, sometimes termed a "portfolio strategy," calls for resource allocation and marketing strategy to vary among classes of product lines. A taxonomy used by the Boston Consulting Group divides product lines into four groups, based on market growth rates and market shares: (a) low growth/dominant share (cash cows), (b) high growth/dominant share (stars), (c) low growth/subordinate share (dogs), and (d) high growth/subordinate share (problem children). The strategy advocated for "cash cows" is to milk them of all resources in excess of those needed to maintain market dominance. "Stars" are to receive resources needed to support their growth. Some firms (e.g., General Electric) differentiate potential "stars" according to the type of resources needed to support growth. Some product lines may require primarily technical support; others, working capital. The type of resource needed may vary as the "star" grows, e.g., technical support may be needed in early stages; working capital later. "Dogs" are to be dropped promptly or gradually, or else repositioned to a more profitable and defensible niche in the market. "Problem children" are to be dropped, or repositioned as "stars" in more narrowly defined markets.

(5) Perhaps the most direct measure of attractiveness for investment of available resources is profit opportunity, which ordinarily results from favorable primary demand trends and competitive advantages. Profit opportunity may be defined as dollar profit, percentage return on sales, or return on investment; the last term is itself subject to a variety of definitions. Allocation of resources often depends in large part on the particular measure of profitability an organization uses, because any project may rank differently on different measures.

(6) The availability of resources may restrict the allocation procedure. No matter how attractive several opportunities may be, most organizations require a year or more to increase substantially their expertise and resource base in marketing and technical areas, or to augment substantially their fixed or working capital funds. Even though the existing resource base may be large, in most organizations much of that resource base will be committed to ongoing programs, and therefore unavailable for shifting among product lines. Even over long periods the amount of resources not required to maintain a continuing business, and thus available for reallocation, may be modest.

Implementing Reallocation Decisions   Once top management has decided to withdraw resources from one product line and invest them in another, executives may attempt to implement that decision by altering the objectives and compensation of product line managers accordingly. For example, the manager of the line from which resources are to be withdrawn may be given targets of return on capital or of cash flow to meet. In contrast, the manager of the line to which added resources are to be committed may be evaluated on his or her success in gaining market share, rather than on return-on-capital criteria.

One risk in evaluating managers on return-on-capital criteria is that they will emphasize short-run return so much that they'll skimp on asset-replacement programs. Some companies have found it helpful to forecast return both on the basis of replacing assets in the current period and on the basis of deferring such replacement. Although returns in the present period may be higher if replacement is deferred, forecast cost increases may make the deferred replacement (which may also be necessarily broader in scope) so much more costly that the stream of returns over the multiyear period will be greater if assets are replaced during the current period.

Another risk that top management must accept in withdrawing resources from a product line is that managers of that line will consider their line a "zero-growth" business and ignore opportunities for growth and revitalization of the business. In other words, identification of a business as a "cash generator" or "dog" may become a self-fulfilling prophecy. Many mature businesses are not lacking in opportunity, and can benefit from stable or even increased resources. For example, Gould committed resources to the automobile battery business (a mature and highly competitive field). They developed a new battery, aggressively solicited major accounts, and increased their market penetration significantly.

Perceptive executives recognize that development of annual plans provides an opportunity to reallocate resources within the portfolio and to alter individual managers' goals. But to exploit that opportunity, executives must have a clear idea of the portfolio they consider appropriate for the firm for the coming several years.

SELECTED REFERENCES

ALEXANDER, R.S. "The Death and Burial of Sick Products." *Journal of Marketing,* April 1964.

ANDERSON, LANE K. "Expanded Break-even Analysis for a Multi-Product Company." *Management Accounting,* July 1975, pp. 30–32.

BUZBY, STEPHEN L. and LESTER E. HEITGER. "Profit Contribution by Market Segment." *Management Accounting,* November 1976, pp. 42–46.

CORR, A.V. "A Cost-Effectiveness Approach to Marketing Outlays." *Management Accounting,* January 1976, pp. 33–36.

DAY, GEORGE S. "Diagnosing the Product Portfolio." *Journal of Marketing,* April 1977.

ELLIS, DARRYL J., and PETER P. PEKAR, JR. "Linking Resources to Strategic Marketing Plans." *Industrial Marketing Management,* vol. 6 no. 1, 1977, pp. 3–7.

KOTLER, PHILIP. "Phasing Out Weak Products." *Harvard Business Review*, March–April 1965.

McGINNES, MICHAEL A., and RICHARD T. HISE. "Product Elimination: Practices, Policies and Ethics." *Business Horizons*, June 1975.

WIND, YORAM, and HENRY J. CLAYCAMP. "Planning Product Line Strategy: A Matrix Approach." *Journal of Marketing*, January 1976.

(See also bibliography on Expansion and Reduction of the Product Line, page 57.)

CASES ON MANAGING THE PRESENT PORTFOLIO

INTERNATIONAL MULTIFOODS

Decorative Accessories Division

Early in 1975 Mr. Lloyd Workman, vice-chairman of the board of International Multifoods, was reviewing the long-range strategy for the company's Decorative Accessories division. Mr. Workman wished to decide how the company could best meet its original goals for the division of $50 million in sales and 5 percent profit (after taxes) on sales. The question was a significant one for Multifoods, because Decorative Accessories represented the company's first major diversification into nonfood businesses.

THE COMPANY

Multifoods manufactured a wide variety of industrial and consumer food products, which it marketed worldwide. For the fiscal year ending February 28, 1974, Multifoods earned more than $25 million (before taxes) on sales of $740 million. Earnings before taxes had increased more than three-fold, and sales almost two-fold, since 1968. Sales and earnings for each division appear in Exhibit 1; consolidated income statements and balance sheets, in Exhibits 2 and 3, respectively.

For more than half a century after its founding in 1892, Multifoods derived its revenues almost wholly from flour-milling activities. Although the company branched out during the 1950s and 1960s into production of animal feeds and agricultural processing, in 1968 some 75 percent of Multifoods' business still came from flour and flour products, e.g., bakery mixes. Because per capita consumption of flour had been declining steadily for many years, and because margins in the flour business were very limited, in 1968 Multifoods hired William G. Phillips, president of the Glidden-Durkee division of SCM Corp., as president and chief executive officer, with a mandate to diversify the company's product line.

Mr. Phillips reorganized Multifoods into divisions, which reported to Darrell Runke, executive vice-president of Multifoods, who had had extensive line management experience with the company. Responsibility for development of new activities was given to Mr. Workman, who had more than 25 years' marketing experience with Multifoods. Once new ventures or acquisitions became viable, they were integrated into existing divisions or established as new divisions reporting to Mr. Runke. Until then, Mr. Workman continued to be responsible for them. (Mr. Workman continued to oversee the activities of the Decorative Accessories division, as he had since Multifoods entered that business in 1972.)

In 1975, Multifoods was organized into six divisions in addition to Decorative Accessories. The company's six largest divisions included: Industrial Foods, Agricultural Products, Consumer Products, Away-From-Home-Eating, Canadian, and International.

Industrial Foods, the company's oldest division, marketed bakery flour and mixes for commercial and institutional bakers as well as durum products for pasta manufacturers. The division also marketed bakery equipment. The company held an estimated 20 percent share of the domestic market for institutional bakery mixes, and was the fifth largest flour miller in the United States (Multifoods' milling capacity was about 50 percent of that of the largest domestic miller). Multifoods was the world's largest miller of rye flour. The division had expanded its higher margin specialty flour business, because margins (before taxes) on bulk flour typically averaged less than 4 percent of sales.

Agricultural Products produced formula feeds and health products for livestock and veterinary supplies. The division also processed and merchandised table eggs. Multifoods had an estimated 8 percent of the feed market in its served area, concentrated primarily in the corn belt.

The *Consumer Products* division, formed in 1969, produced and marketed flour, cheese, cereal products, specialty meats, and bird food through food-distribution systems to consumers. Brand names included Robin Hood (flour) and Kaukauna Klub (cheese); Kretschmer Wheat Germ and Sun Country Granola (cereal products); Reuben (meat); and Sherwood Forest, Milford, and Tweetie Pie (bird food). The division also operated 18 Hickory Farm specialty cheese stores in seven states. Robin Hood flour had a considerably smaller market share than brands of the market leaders but Kretschmer had an estimated 90 percent of the sales of wheat germ through supermarkets. Commenting on the Consumer Products division, Mr. Phillips stated: "The Consumer Products group developed a specific marketing approach—which we've referred to as the 'niche' theory. Essentially, that is finding an immature product and accelerating its development to fit a special position in the grocery store, settling for a relatively solid basic sales base and maximizing profitability."

The *Away-From-Home Eating* division included King Foods, which produced portion-control frozen meat and meat products for sale to the food-service industry, as well as three "fast food" chains. Mr. Donut, the largest of these three chains, included 320 drive-in franchised and company-owned donut shops in the United States and 169 outside the country. The division also franchised thirty and operated four Sveden House Smorgasbord low-cost family restaurants and two premium-level T. Butcherblock restaurants in the United States.

The *Canadian division* ranked among the six largest consumer foods companies in Canada. Some 35 percent of its sales were consumer food products; 45 percent, industrial foods; and about 20 percent, agricultural products.

The International division, expanded from a single flour mill in 1958, operated primarily in Latin America. This division currently marketed bakery, durum, and family flour; precooked corn flour and rolled oats for consumers; and formula feeds for livestock and poultry. The division operated a trading department to export and import products among more than 70 countries.

ACQUISITIONS

Multifoods officials typically received dozens of proposals for mergers or acquisitions each month and pursued as far as interest warranted those proposals in businesses in which Multifoods was involved. Multifoods personnel also sought prospective acquirees and frequently approached executives of companies that appeared to offer potential for growth and profit and that complemented Multifoods' existing product lines.

Analysis of potential acquisitions among smaller companies was often complicated by their lack of detailed, reliable accounting data by which the performance history and prospects of the company might be evaluated. In such instances, Mr. Workman and his staff had to rely upon their appraisal of the basic soundness and potential of the business and of its management. Although Multifoods ordinarily attempted as part of the terms of acquisition to negotiate management contracts with owner-executives of such companies, those individuals frequently left after one to three years, in some cases because they could not accustom themselves to working within a larger organization, and in other cases because proceeds from the sale of their businesses enabled them to pursue alternative careers. The high probability of executive turnover required Mr. Workman and his staff to decide whether a prospective acquisition could be operated fairly promptly by executives from other Multifoods divisions.

From the beginning of the diversification program in 1969 through February 1973, Multifoods had made twenty-one major acquisitions, including one in the decorative accessories industry. From March 1973, through January 1974, the company made eight acquisitions, including three decorative accessories firms. No major acquisitions occurred during the remainder of 1974.

An analysis of seventeen Multifoods' acquisitions from 1969 through February 1973, indicated that the acquired businesses in general experienced increased sales, earnings, assets, and return-on-assets between the year before acquisition (different for each company) and February 1973. As a group, acquisitions in Agricultural Products showed increases in sales from $7.3 million (before acquisition) to $8.8 million; earnings, from $0.2 million to $0.7 million; and assets, from $1.7 million to $2.4 million. The two acquisitions made in the Consumer Products division increased their combined sales from less than $10 million before acquisition to more than $16 million by February 1973, although earnings decreased by almost one half as a result of one acquisition which was subsequently divested. Assets increased from under $4 million to almost $7 million. Companies acquired in Away-From-Home Eating nearly doubled in sales, from $26 million to almost $50 million. Earnings increased from a loss of $0.4 million to a profit of $1.3 million, on a near-doubling of the asset base. Companies acquired in Canada and Latin America had shown increases in sales, earnings, and assets.

DIVERSIFICATION INTO NONFOODS

In 1970, company executives, who believed that they had gained some experience in the consumer area, wished to reduce the company's dependence on food products by finding another area for growth. The objectives set for such an expansion included: (1) sales potential of $25–$50 million in three to five years; (2) net after-tax profit of 5 percent on sales; and (3) growth in excess of 10 percent per year.

The size objective was deemed necessary in order to provide a large enough sales base to support a qualified management team. The profit objectives were set in order to assure that any added businesses would contribute to Multifoods' stated objective of an after-tax profit margin of 3 percent of sales. The growth objective was necessary to assure expansion in nonmilling operations.

In addition, Multifoods executives sought an industry with sound but overlooked opportunities and a lack of concentration among manufacturers and buyers. Furthermore, they were particularly interested in industries that were marketing and innovation intensive, rather than capital or labor intensive, and in which the company could be a "dominant force."

These objectives led Multifoods executives to explore five possible areas of expansion, including nonprescription pharmaceuticals, decorative accessories, specialty mail order, art supplies and materials, and handicrafts. After analyzing these industries and comparing their characteristics with Multifoods' objectives, company executives decided to enter the decorative accessories business through acquiring companies in that industry. They planned to acquire first a company large enough to support its own sales and distribution organization, and subsequently to acquire and merge into that organization promising smaller companies.

DECORATIVE ACCESSORIES

Decorative accessories are accent pieces used in furnishing homes, offices, and other commercial establishments. Multifoods personnel estimated the wholesale value of sales by the entire industry at $1.15 billion in 1970, divided as shown in Table 1.

With one exception (1970), industry sales increased at least 12 percent per year from 1965 through 1972. From 1965 to 1969, the annual growth rate varied from 12 to 25 percent; in 1971 and 1972, between 12 and 15 percent. Multifoods personnel forecast that the industry would continue to grow substantially as large numbers of young people in the family-formation age group entered the market.

The industry was comprised of many small manufacturers. There were, for example, more than 1,200 lamp manufacturers in the United States. Some concentration was beginning to take place in the industry as firms outside the industry acquired manufacturers of decorative accessories. For example, Beatrice Foods and Time-Life had recently acquired manufacturers of pictures and lamps. Simmons, well-known for its Beautyrest ® mattresses, has entered the markets for wall decorations, statuary, imported ceramics, and lamps.

Historically, decorative accessories manufacturers earned net profits after taxes amounting to 3 to 15 percent of sales. Profits of 5 to 10 percent of sales were typical.

Table 1
WHOLESALE SALES OF DECORATIVE ACCESSORIES, 1970

	millions
Lighting (decorative only)	$ 350
Decorative mirrors	90
Picture frames	80
Framed picture reproductions (domestic)	50
Framed pictures (imported originals and reproductions)	80
Decorative clocks	40
Statuary, sculpture, and figurine reproductions	
Domestic	12
Imported	28
Pottery and ceramic novelties	50
Ornamental glass	30
Subtotal	810
Miscellaneous [1]	340
Total	$1,150

[1] *Miscellaneous* includes fireplace accessories, desk accessories, metal sculpture, and indoor-outdoor accessories, such as fountains.

Most production in the industry was craft-oriented, rather than mechanized. Casting and forging were still used for a variety of pewter, polished brass, and antique-finished items. Items made of wood involved considerable hand crafting. In many cases, 60 to 80 percent of the cost of production was labor expense, and gross margins (net sales less direct costs of manufacturing, packaging, and freight, if paid by the manufacturer) ranged between 15 and 30 percent of sales for firms working with wood, pottery, and some metal items. The industry was characterized by many old plants, poor material flows, little automation, and low capital investment.

Manufacturing costs were closely tied to design and varied with the ease of reproduction and the ability to exchange parts among various designs. Design talent was also the determining factor in whether a particular item would be accepted by a retailer and by the ultimate consumer. Designs tended to be quickly "knocked off" or copied by other firms in the industry if the designs were not copyrighted. Few firms in the industry copyrighted their designs because of the rapid turnover in product designs caused by a constant demand at the retail level for new products to show.

Very low finished-goods inventories were carried either at the retailer or manufacturer levels of the industry. Manufacturers typically produced to orders, and thus carried only raw material inventories. Retailers had a low turnover rate on accessories, and thus carried very limited back-up stocks on most items.

The size and breadth of product lines in the industry varied. Some manufacturers offered a wide line with many products in various styles over a wide price range, while others offered relatively few products in a narrow price range.

Manufacturers of decorative accessories typically sold directly to major chains such as Sears and Penney's, and through either their own sales force or manufacturers' representatives to small chains and independent accounts. Manufacturers that employed their own sales forces supported their selling efforts with exhibits at trade shows and in showrooms in major markets, and with trade advertising. The smaller manufacturers, which sold through representatives, typically provided limited sales support. Representatives in many instances operated their own exhibits at trade shows, representing in their displays merchandise from all the manufacturers they represented. Representatives typically had close relationships with customers, and some retained customers, even if the representatives themselves changed the manufacturers they represented. Commission schedules for sales representatives in the decorative accessories industry depended upon the territory, ease of selling the product, and expected dollar volume, and ranged from 5 to 20 percent of wholesale sales.

Decorative accessories were sold through thousands of gift shops, 32,000 furniture stores, 3,000 individual department stores and chains, and 10,000 interior decorators. In addition, decorative accessories were available through direct-mail promotion and house-to-house sales organizations. Approximately two-thirds of retail furniture stores' sales were concentrated among some 20 percent of the stores; half of the stores accounted for 90 percent of retail furniture stores' sales. A respected trade association reported that department stores sold approximately $300 million (at retail prices) of decorative accessories. Retailers generally earned markups of 50 percent of the price at which they sold decorative accessories; in some instances, markups amounted to 60 to 70 percent of the selling price.

Retail buyers purchased a variety of styles of particular decorative accessories in each of several different price ranges. Retailers typically placed limited orders at semiannual regional and national furniture exhibitions, and ordinarily ordered stock as needed between these shows, for delivery six to twelve weeks later. Many retailers expected manufacturers' representatives to inventory their stocks and suggest fill-in orders.

Many large retailers were willing to commit themselves to a limited number of suppliers in order to garner price breaks, reduce ordering costs, and attempt to gain exclusive distribution in a trade area for a particular design or line. Mail-order operations such as Sears and Penney's required that prices be maintained for periods ranging from six to eighteen months on merchandise sold through their catalogs. Most small retailers were interested in the availability of lines and minimal order requirements, in addition to service.

THE DECORATIVE ACCESSORIES DIVISION

The Decorative Accessories division consisted of four companies (Turner, Freeman-McFarlin, Nadler, Niepold/Borghese) acquired between December 1972 and January 1974. For the year ending February 28, 1974, the division earned $51,000 on sales of

$15.1 million. Approximately 87 percent of division sales was contributed by Turner; another 11 percent, by Freeman-McFarlin. Gross margin percentages of the division's constituent companies ranged, as they had before acquisition, between 15 and 20 percent of sales. Profits generated by Turner more than offset losses incurred in the other three companies. Multifoods' executives forecast that the division might experience significant losses in fiscal 1975, but that it would be operating at a profitable level by the end of fiscal 1976.

Turner, largest of the four companies in the division, was acquired in December 1972 for cash and stock of $3.7 million. Turner had sales of $12 million during the year prior to its acquisition and was the largest domestic manufacturer of framed pictures and mirrors. Approximately half of Turner's volume came from framed pictures, prints, and lithographs. The art works themselves were acquired from artists-suppliers. Turner then designed and produced frames for particular groups of pictures. Some 25 percent of Turner's sales came from a wide variety of framed mirrors and wall shelves in a broad range of prices. Remaining sales came from tables and other items produced by other manufacturers and sold by Turner. There were more than 5,000 different items in each of Turner's spring and fall lines.

Two salespeople working out of Turner's headquarters in Chicago handled sales to major accounts such as Sears, Penney's, and Woolworth. Sales to chain accounts amounted to about 25 percent of Turner's sales. Thirty company salespeople handled sales throughout the country to more than 3,500 other accounts, which included furniture and department stores.

Freeman-McFarlin, a manufacturer of ceramic sculpture and decorative ashtrays, was acquired in January 1973 for Multifoods stock with a market value of $837,000. Freeman-McFarlin employed about 120 artisans to make molds and to produce and finish pottery from those molds. The company sold its products through twelve manufacturers' representatives to more than 12,000 retailers. Principal accounts included gift departments of such stores as Sears, Penney's, Macy's, and the like. Independent gift shops constituted the next most important group of accounts. Freeman-McFarlin had sales of approximately $1.5 million in the year before its acquisition.

Nadler Lighting designed and manufactured modern lamps which were sold through manufacturers' representatives to a variety of retail accounts. Nadler was purchased for $500,000 at the end of 1973, during which it had sales of $1 million and earnings of about $111,000 before taxes.

Niepold/Borghese, a pottery manufacturer, was acquired for $153,000 in January 1974, after the firm had experienced financial difficulty. Despite its problems, Niepold/Borghese possessed an inventory of well-designed molds and enjoyed a good reputation in the industry. Marketing of Niepold/Borghese products was absorbed into Freeman-McFarlin's sales organization.

In commenting on the history and prospects of the Decorative Accessories division, Mr. Workman noted that Multifoods had three goals in establishing the division: (1) sales of $50 million in five years; (2) profits (after taxes) of 5 percent of sales; (3) growth in excess of 10 percent per year.

"Our strategy," continued Mr. Workman, "was to acquire a solid base company for the division and add to it smaller units with unrealized growth potential. Our plan included the creation of a single sales and marketing organization for all product lines of the division.

"To date, the performance of this division has been disappointing. The calendar year 1973 was one of rapid inflation. Raw materials and labor costs increased in accelerating fashion. In a normal situation, product prices could be pushed up to keep pace with costs. But the home-furnishings industry didn't work that way, partly because major buyers such as the catalog companies have to have firm prices for their catalogs well in advance of order shipments. So we were locked in to fixed prices while costs were climbing. While we did allow for an inflation factor in our pricing, it was not sufficient to let us keep pace with rising costs.

"To make the situation even more critical, wage and price controls were initiated in 1971. The companies we acquired were not—as long as they operated as small independent firms—covered by price controls. As part of International Multifoods, they were—and attempts to get price relief based on increased costs always lagged behind the impact of the cost price disparities—if price increases were approved.

"As we moved into 1974 with its recession and high unemployment, new changes impinged on our division's operations. The American people sharply reduced their buying of home furnishings along with many other types of durable products. Home-furnishings dealers, faced with slow sales movement and high interest rates, slashed their buying to reduce their inventories. The compounded impact of reduced consumer buying and curtailed dealer buying cut our sales volume. Our projections for market growth simply did not and could not materialize.

"But those externally caused difficulties were not the full extent of our problems. Frankly, we discovered that the existing management often did not react firmly and with timeliness to the changes taking place. Some were not profit-oriented. Additionally, we had inadequate cost and inventory control systems.

"To solve these problems (in 1974) we established a centralized sales and marketing organization covering all four product lines; appointed a solidly qualified general sales manager; revitalized our sales force, changing some assignments in the direct sales force and weeding out and replacing weak personnel with stronger ones; installed a system of sales quotas and tighter supervision to obtain a strengthened sales effort; and extended our marketing into the institutional field. We also expanded our product line and adjusted prices where necessary.

"We have also reduced inventories by nearly $1 million; consolidated our computer services to improve order processing, production planning, and inventory control; and established tight operating budgets for all operations based on reduced sales. This program will generate savings of nearly $750,000 at the Turner plant alone.

"In addition, we have replaced managers at Turner and Freeman-McFarlin, and have retired several senior executives for a savings of more than $150,000 per year.

"My personal belief is that our strategy in acquiring the components and assembling our Decorative Accessories division was sound when the decision was made, and remains sound today, and that our long-range goals are attainable."

ALTERNATIVES

Mr. Workman and a task force of Multifoods executives were reviewing alternative courses of action with respect to the Decorative Accessories division. These alternatives included (1) continuing the division largely in its present form, but expanding the range of items within present product categories; (2) broadening the Decorative Accessories line through acquisition of product lines not presently included in the division's offering; and (3) selling the division.

The first alternative, expansion within present product categories, was based on the assumptions that Multifoods' original premises in establishing the Decorative Accessories division had been sound and that the division would become profitable as the operating changes initiated by Mr. Workman became effective. The similarity of product lines among companies within the division was expected to facilitate management of division operations. The units which made up the division could broaden their product lines to attain the size and growth initially planned.

The second alternative, broadening the division's offering through acquisition, also assumed that Multifoods' original objectives in establishing the Decorative Accessories division had been sound, but that the limited product line and the small size of most of the constituent companies had prevented the company from meeting those objectives. The reasoning in favor of this second alternative was that the funds needed to broaden the lines and increase the volume of the present Decorative Accessories companies would earn a greater return if invested in acquisition of medium- and large-size companies in such product lines as tables, lamps, and giftware.

While the task force was engaged in its review, Multifoods officials learned that two companies, Glasscraft[*] and Windsor Ceramics,[*] might be available for purchase. Glasscraft purchased and merchandised table glassware and crystal decorator pieces through wholesale floral-supply houses, hotel and restaurant-supply houses, retail gift shops, and department and chain stores. Ten company salespeople and twenty manufacturers' representatives sold the line to more than 8,000 customers. Glasscraft had sales in 1974 of approximately $13 million and pretax earnings in excess of $2 million. Multifoods officials believed that Glasscraft officials would accept a purchase price of $5-$7 million.

Windsor Ceramics, a manufacturer of pottery artware and table lamps, has an excellent name in the industry. Windsor products were sold through manufacturers' representatives to furniture, gift, and department stores. Last year the firm earned approximately 5 percent before taxes on sales of $8.5 million. The family owners of the company would, in the opinion of Multifoods officers, accept $1.5-$2 million for Windsor Ceramics.

---

[*] Names disguised. Any resemblance to actual names or trademarks is unintended and entirely coincidental.

The task force also concerned itself with the alternative of selling the Decorative Accessories division. The logic of following this course of action was that the original premises on which the division had been established were unsound and should be reversed and that division performance was unlikely to reach, in the foreseeable future, the goals initially set for diversification into nonfoods.

If Multifoods were to sell the division, the company could either concentrate on improving performance and expanding offerings in its food product lines or investigate alternative opportunities in nonfood businesses. The task force knew that diversification outside of food products had initially been unprofitable for many large food manufacturers, but had subsequently proved to be more profitable than the food business. For example, sales of nonfood lines constituted 29 percent of sales and 33 percent of earnings for General Mills, 24 percent of sales and 40 percent of earnings for Beatrice Foods, and 40 percent of sales and 51 percent of earnings for Consolidated Foods.

Exhibit 1
INTERNATIONAL MULTIFOODS
SALES AND EARNINGS BY DIVISION, 1968–1974
FISCAL YEAR ENDED LAST DAY OF FEBRUARY
(DOLLAR AMOUNTS IN MILLIONS)

Sales	1974 Amount	%	1973 Amount	%	1972 Amount	%	1971 Amount	%	1970 Amount	%	1969 Amount	%	1968 Amount	%
Industrial Foods	$263.0	36	$191.9	36	$175.8	38	$170.9	39	$157.2	41	$146.9	41	$170.0	44
Agricultural Products	120.8	16	81.5	15	62.8	14	70.0	16	60.5	16	58.1	16	59.0	15
Consumer Products	66.3	9	47.1	9	44.0	10	32.3	7	30.5	8	26.8	7	22.4	6
Away-From-Home Eating	58.3	8	48.6	9	37.6	8	32.4	7	21.8	5	18.3	5	17.5	5
Decorative Accessories	15.1	2	3.8	1	1.2	—	1.1	—	1.1	—	1.1	—	—	—
Total United States	523.5	71	372.9	70	321.4	70	306.7	69	271.1	70	251.2	69	268.9	70
Canada	158.4	21	111.5	21	100.1	22	98.8	23	89.3	23	85.2	24	91.0	24
International	58.5	8	46.0	9	37.9	8	33.3	8	26.7	7	25.1	7	22.8	6
Total net sales	$740.4	100	$530.4	100	$459.4	100	$438.8	100	$387.1	100	$361.5	100	$382.7	100

Exhibit 1 (Cont.)

Sales	1974 Amount	%	1973 Amount	%	1972 Amount	%	1971 Amount	%	1970 Amount	%	1969 Amount	%	1968 Amount	%
Earnings														
Industrial Foods	$ 15.4	41	$ 7.5	30	$ 7.2	32	$ 6.1	28	$ 5.8	29	$ 2.7	18	$ 4.2	32
Agricultural Products	4.6	13	4.4	17	2.9	13	4.4	20	3.7	18	3.2	21	1.1	8
Consumer Products	3.9	11	1.5	6	2.5	11	1.0	4	1.4	7	1.2	8	.5	4
Away-From-Home Eating	1.1	3	.7	3	1.0	4	.8	3	1.2	6	.7	5	.5	4
Decorative Accessories	.1	—	.2	1	—	—	—	—	—	—	—	—	—	—
Total United States	25.1	68	14.3	57	13.6	60	12.3	55	12.1	60	7.8	52	6.3	48
Canada	10.6	28	6.6	26	6.0	27	6.7	30	5.3	26	4.8	31	4.8	36
International	1.6	4	4.5	17	2.9	13	3.2	15	2.8	14	2.7	17	2.2	16
Operating earnings	37.3	100	25.4	100	22.5	100	22.2	100	20.2	100	15.3	100	13.3	100
Unallocated expenses	(3.3)		(2.4)		(1.9)		(2.4)		(2.9)		(2.3)		(2.1)	
Interest expense	(8.9)		(5.2)		(5.0)		(6.1)		(4.3)		(3.9)		(3.8)	
Earnings before income taxes	$ 25.1		$ 17.8		$ 15.6		$ 13.7		$ 13.0		$ 9.1		$ 7.4	
Earnings after taxes per $1.00 of sales	1.6¢		1.9¢		1.9¢		1.7¢		1.7¢		1.4¢		1.1¢	

Source: Annual Report

Exhibit 2

INTERNATIONAL MULTIFOODS
INCOME STATEMENT
YEAR ENDED FEBRUARY 28, 1974
(DOLLARS IN THOUSANDS, EXCEPT AMOUNTS PER SHARE)

Net sales	$740,380
Costs and expenses, net:	
Cost of sales	642,827
Selling, general, and administrative expenses	65,258
Interest expense	8,949
Interest and other income, net	(1,780)
Total	715,254
Earnings before income taxes	25,126
Income taxes	13,166
Net earnings	$ 11,960
Net earnings per share of common stock	$ 3.27

Source: Annual Report

Exhibit 3

INTERNATIONAL MULTIFOODS
BALANCE SHEET
FEBRUARY 28, 1974
(DOLLARS IN THOUSANDS)

Assets		
Cash	$ 6,614	
Accounts and notes receivable	84,984	
Inventories	105,788	
Prepayments	7,703	
Total current assets		$205,089
Investments in foreign companies	5,036	
Other investments and sundry assets, at cost	3,925	
Total investments and sundry assets		8,961
Net property, plant, and equipment		59,359
Intangibles		15,517
Total assets		$288,926

Liabilities and stockholders' equity		
Notes payable	$ 47,976	
Accounts payable	38,337	
Accrued expenses and taxes	18,716	
		105,029
Total long-term liabilities		70,378
Total preferred stock	7,520	
Common stock	26,183	
Retained earnings	79,816	
Total stockholders' equity		113,519
Total liabilities and equity		$288,926

Source: Annual Report

ROBERTSON ELECTRONICS (A)

In the spring of 1968, Mr. John Hodges, group vice-president for the Electronics Group of Lustrex Corporation, met with Mr. Everett Coughlin, president, and Mr. Robert Franklin, marketing manager, of the Robertson Electronics division of Lustrex to discuss marketing plans for the division's line of home television receivers. Mr. Hodges expected to discuss two types of plans. The first plan involved direct sales to large retailers that had not previously carried Robertson TV; the other plan called for a substantial increase in consumer advertising of the Robertson line, coupled with a price reduction and strengthening of the division's distributor network. Mr. Hodges considered this discussion particularly important because home television receivers had accounted for two-thirds of Robertson's sales in 1967.

Division officials considered Robertson Electronics' position unique in the home television industry. (The industry is described in an Appendix to the case.) The officials stated that Robertson's monochrome (black-and-white) and color television receivers employed advanced and costly features which improved the performance and serviceability of Robertson sets and resulted in prices somewhat higher than those of competitors. The division distributed its line of home television receivers through channels different from those used by major television manufacturers and, unlike competing manufacturers, did not spend large sums to promote its products. Although Robertson home television receivers were sold throughout the United States, the company had historically been most successful in Cincinnati and the trading areas within a 200-mile radius of Cincinnati. Although Robertson's share of the national home receiver market was no more than 2 percent, some 12 of every 100 home receivers in use in the Cincinnati metropolitan area (1968 estimated population 1.5 million) were Robertson sets. This percentage had risen steadily since 1963.

THE COMPANY

Robertson Electronics had recently been acquired by the Lustrex Corporation, a financial and manufacturing conglomerate whose sales in 1967 exceeded $300 million. Robertson was one of four divisions that formed the Electronics Group headed by Mr. Hodges. Sales of the Electronics Group were just under $60 million in 1967 and were expected to increase substantially through growth of each of the constituent divisions. Mr. Hodges knew that funds to finance that growth would have to be generated within his group. Lustrex corporate management had emphatically ruled out the possibility of providing corporate funds for the next three to five years. Because the other three divisions, all of which had histories of steady sales and profit growth, had already requested more funds than were available, Mr. Hodges had informed Mr. Coughlin that the Robertson division would have to finance its activities itself.

Robertson Electronics was founded in 1926 by William E. Robertson, an engineer, to produce automobile radios. Sales grew slowly to about $3 million in 1949, the year in which Robertson Electronics began production of monochrome television sets for home use. By 1960, sales had increased to $10 million. In 1962, the company began to manufacture educators, television receivers built especially for classroom use. Educators were the first products in the company's commercial line, which Mr. Robertson considered a by-product of home receiver production. In 1963, the company added home color television receivers, sales of which helped to increase volume to about $16 million in 1964. In that year Robertson began to manufacture stereo radio-phonographs under the private brand of a large local appliance retailer. In 1966, however, the retailer withdrew from the appliance business and discontinued its contract with Robertson Electronics.

Early in 1966, Mr. Robertson withdrew from active participation in the firm and brought in a new president, Mr. Everett Coughlin, who subsequently hired Mr. Franklin. Reporting directly to Mr. Coughlin, in addition to Mr. Franklin, were the treasurer and the managers of purchasing, engineering, and manufacturing.

During the summer of 1967, Mr. Robertson had discussed informally with a Lustrex executive, whom he knew socially, the possibility of selling Robertson Electronics. Lustrex officials immediately contacted Mr. Robertson, who agreed to sell his company to Lustrex for cash and Lustrex stock which together amounted to approximately $4.5 million. Lustrex formally acquired Robertson on January 1, 1968.

Robertson had earned a $2.2 million profit during 1966, but had lost almost $2.3 million in 1967 (see Exhibit 1). At the end of the first quarter of 1968, however, losses had been reduced substantially, largely by reductions in overhead expenses.

Division officials attributed the 1967 losses to a dramatic decline in sales, coupled with an increase in fixed costs from an expansion program begun in 1966. Sales in 1966 of home color receivers (the company's largest selling product) exceeded $18 million, which represented almost a three-fold increase over home color sales in 1965. In 1967, however, sales of home color receivers declined to $6.6 million. According to management, the 1966 peak in color television sales was caused by an unexpected sharp increase in total demand for color television during that year. Because the large manufacturers could not satisfy this demand, many customers were willing to buy less well-known brands. Consequently, many smaller manufacturers, including Robertson, sold as much as they could produce.

By the end of 1966, however, total demand for television receivers had declined somewhat. Large manufacturers had expanded and were beginning to operate below full capacity. Mr. Franklin thought that as the better known (and typically less expensive) brands of home color receivers became readily available, consumers were choosing them in preference to the brands of smaller manufacturers. In addition, Mr. Franklin believed that 1967 sales had been depressed because many distributors who had ordered heavily from Robertson and other smaller manufacturers during 1966 found themselves with high inventories of these sets. During 1967, distributors attempted to reduce their inventories before ordering new models from the manufacturers.

THE PRODUCT LINE

In 1967, Robertson sold monochrome and color home television receivers in various screen sizes and styles, commercial receivers used in schools and industry, and stereo phonographs and radio phonographs. Table 1 shows sales by product for 1966 and 1967.

Table 1
SALES BY PRODUCT LINE

Product	1967		1966	
	Dollar sales (000)	Unit sales	Dollar sales (000)	Unit sales
Home television receivers				
Color	$ 6,616	15,088	$18,016	41,636
Monochrome	1,422	13,200	2,620	24,030
Commercial receivers	3,340	19,262	1,878	12,470
Stereo phonographs[a]	198	896	2,646	13,360
Service	512	–	488	–
Total	$12,088	48,446	$25,648	91,496

[a]Note: The company discontinued the manufacturing of stereo equipment in 1967. These sales represent liquidation of accumulated inventory, almost all of which had been sold by the end of the year.

COLOR HOME RECEIVERS

Robertson offered color television receivers for home use in three screen sizes, 18V, 22V, and 23V.* The 18V and 22V models were available in three different styles. Suggested retail prices ranged from $500 for the 18V screen set to $660–$690 for the 22V screen receiver. The 23V unit was available in a variety of styles. The retail prices for these 23V sets ranged from $700 to $870, with an average price of about $760 for a console and $820 for a console lowboy. (The principal difference between these styles was in the cabinet work.) In addition, the company made a 23V color television, AM-FM stereo radio and phonograph combination which carried a suggested retail price of $1,200.

Suggested retail prices of Robertson color home receivers were somewhat higher than those of other manufacturers (see Exhibit 2). Robertson's factory selling price was also higher than the average for the industry. In 1967, Robertson received an average price of $438 for each color home receiver sold; the average manufacturers' price in the industry was $362. The industry average had declined slightly over the past three years.

In 1967, Robertson departed from its custom of changing styles on one model at a time and hired a furniture design specialist to redesign its complete line of home television receivers for 1968. Such annual restyling was common in the television industry. According to management, the Robertson restyling had proved very expensive and caused

---

*18V, 22V, and 23V were standard industry measures of picture-tube size. An 18V tube had 180 square inches of viewing area, a 22V tube had 272 square inches, and a 23V tube had 295 square inches. The 23V tube was the largest color television tube currently available.

a delay in the presentation of the new models. Management was contemplating a more modest restyling for the 1969 product line.

MONOCHROME HOME RECEIVERS

The company produced monochrome television receivers from 15V to 22V in screen size. The line included portable table and console models. The suggested retail price for Robertson monochrome sets ranged from $150 to $250. For sets of comparable screen size, Robertson-suggested retail prices typically ran about $50 higher than those of the largest selling American manufacturers. Robertson's average factory selling price per set was $108, $13 higher than the industry average of $95. The industry average had declined steadily since 1963.

MODULAR CONSTRUCTION

For the past several years, Robertson television sets had employed the modular construction originally developed by the company's founder. The electronic components of each set were divided into several circuit units and a "mother board" chassis. According to Robertson personnel, modular construction had the advantage that a set need not be removed to a repair shop for service. Repairs did not require that the defective component itself be located while in the set. Instead, a service representative needed only to identify the faulty circuit unit and replace it. The defective unit could be repaired or returned to the factory where Robertson would then provide a new unit or a factory-rebuilt unit which carried a new-unit guarantee.

Management believed that the faster, and usually less expensive, service made possible by modular construction represented a substantial benefit to the consumer. Officials stated that servicing a color receiver was a much more complex task than servicing a monochrome set. Increased sales of color sets, together with a shortage of people capable of providing service, had resulted in consumers having to wait two weeks or more for service calls in many metropolitan areas. If a set had to be removed to a shop for repair, an additional 7–10 days might be required.

MANUFACTURING COSTS

Executives estimated that Robertson's standard profit contribution[*] on the home receiver line was about 20 percent. The percentage was believed to be slightly higher for color than for monochrome. As an example, division accountants stated that direct manufacturing costs for a home television receiver with a list price of $677 and a factory price of $438 were approximately $310. Related variable marketing and administrative costs

---

[*] Standard profit contribution was defined by the company as net sales revenue minus variable administrative, selling, and manufacturing expenses. Variable manufacturing expenses included materials, direct labor, and variable overhead costs.

were estimated at $25 to $30 per receiver. Officials believed that the company's costs were about $70 higher than those incurred by the major manufacturers in producing home receivers in the $350–$450 range (factory prices).

Management cited several reasons why Robertson's costs were higher than those of larger television manufacturers. Executives believed the division designed its receivers to meet more rigorous performance standards than those of competitors. Modular construction required more direct labor and in some cases more costly materials than did typical television manufacturing methods. These increased costs were not completely offset by the use of circuit units common to many different receivers. (Use of common circuit units permitted greater flexibility in production scheduling and facilitated quality control procedures.) In addition, Robertson manufactured its own cabinets, whose quality was acknowledged to be higher than that of most other television manufacturers. These cabinets required considerable hand crafting and finishing. Although the company had considered buying high-quality cabinets instead of making them, investigation of alternative sources indicated that cost savings would be slight.

One executive stated that the division could increase its contribution to fixed expenses by $50 to $70 on many units if volume were increased and longer, less flexible production runs employed. In addition, he argued that increased volume would make practical the installation of highly automated production equipment, which would reduce unit labor costs.

Robertson produced all of its products in facilities located just outside Cincinnati. The company's total capacity for production of both home receivers and commercial equipment was approximately 40,000 color receivers, or 100,000 monochrome receivers, per year on a one-shift operation.

SALES AND DISTRIBUTION

Robertson sold its products through independent sales representatives and the headquarters sales staff. Representatives handled sales to distributors outside of the company's home market and to smaller OEM (original equipment manufacturer) customers. Robertson's headquarters staff handled sales to distributors in Ohio, Indiana, and Kentucky; direct sales to retailers in metropolitan Cincinnati; sales to large OEM accounts; and sales to government, export and miscellaneous accounts. Sales of home receivers to government and foreign purchasers usually involved some product modifications, and negotiated prices and delivery dates. The headquarters staff handled such sales of home receivers as it did sales of the commercial line.

Distributors sold home receivers to retailers or consumers, and sold the commercial line to end users. Robertson's distribution system is diagrammed in Exhibit 3; sales by market and product line are shown in Exhibit 4.

SALES REPRESENTATIVES

According to division executives, the typical Robertson representative employed up to five salespeople. In addition to Robertson home and commercial receivers, they sold radio equipment for home and amateur broadcast use, stereo high-fidelity components, and electronic parts (tubes, transistors, etc.). Some representatives also sold other component parts for closed-circuit television systems. Representatives who carried the Robertson line did not carry competing merchandise. These independent sales representatives received a commission of 4 percent on sales of Robertson products. Management estimated that in 1967 the typical representative earned about $25,000 in gross commissions on sales of Robertson products. Out of their gross commissions on all lines the representatives had to cover operating expenses and their own compensation.

Each of the division's twenty representatives covered a specific geographic territory and was the exclusive Robertson representative within that territory. Of these twenty representatives, five sold $700,000 or more of Robertson merchandise in 1967. Sales of the remaining fifteen were approximately evenly distributed between $200,000 and $700,000.

The division's home receiver line typically accounted for more than two-thirds of a representative's sales of Robertson products. The remainder came from sales of Robertson's commercial line.

Although some of the smaller television manufacturers used sales representatives, other small manufacturers employed salaried salespeople. All the major television manufacturers employed their own sales forces.

DISTRIBUTORS

In 1966, sales representatives sold Robertson products to 550 parts and service distributors. Of these distributors, 450 carried the division's home television receiver line; 100 carried the commercial line of educators and monitors. Distributors could, but seldom did, order Robertson products other than those they customarily handled. Historically one-eighth of these distributors had accounted for almost half of Robertson's sales.

The parts and service distributors that handled the company's home receiver line ranged from one-person repair shops, often located in the owner's home, to moderate-sized wholesaling operations. At the retail level, Robertson had no distribution through department stores or other high-volume outlets, except in Cincinnati.

The larger distributors resold Robertson television sets, along with other manufacturers' radios, stereo sets, parts, and service equipment, to a variety of smaller radio and T.V. retailers and repair shops. The smaller distributors derived most of their income from repair of small appliances, radio, television, and stereo equipment. These small distributors typically sold Robertson home television receivers directly to consumers.

Distributors who sold Robertson home receivers to retailers at the company's suggested dealer price received a margin of 17 percent of the dealer price. Retailers who purchased receivers at these suggested dealer prices and then resold to consumers at the company's suggested list price earned a margin of 22 percent. Based on the company's suggested prices, distributor and retailer margins together amounted to approximately 35 percent of the list price to consumers. Management believed that this discount structure was comparable to that prevailing in the television industry.

Robertson officials believed that distributors and dealers did not, however, always follow the company's suggested prices. They thought that the smaller distributors who sold directly to consumers generally charged consumers the dealer price, or even less. In addition, many distributors who resold Robertson receivers to retailers were thought to earn only a 10 percent margin on sales to their larger retail accounts. Officials believed that these larger retailers, as distinct from the aforementioned small distributors who sold direct, maintained their margins at about 20 percent.

DISTRIBUTION IN THE CINCINNATI METROPOLITAN AREA

Since July 1967, the company had sold its home receiver line direct to retailers in the Cincinnati metropolitan area and to distributors in Indiana, Kentucky, and Ohio (outside of the Cincinnati metropolitan area). Sales of home receivers during all of 1967 in Ohio, Indiana, and Kentucky amounted to $1.12 million, of which 25 to 30 percent came from Cincinnati. Direct sales were undertaken in Cincinnati when the distributor who served that market decided to expand his line of television receivers to include products competitive with Robertson.

Upon terminating its agreement with this distributor, the company sought to sell its home receiver line directly to retail stores with high potential volume. Stores of this type typically carried six brands of television sets, although some carried as few as two or three and others as many as nine. Industry sources believed that in stores that offered six or more brands, the three largest selling brands usually accounted for nearly 70 percent of total sales of television sets. These sources estimated that in stores that carried only two or three brands, sales would be split about evenly among them, unless one of the brands were Zenith or RCA, the market leader. In such instances, which occurred frequently in the stores with higher volume, Zenith or RCA alone might account for 65 percent or more of the store's television sales.

In Cincinnati, a large multiunit, high-quality department store and a few smaller specialty stores agreed to carry the Robertson line. Sales, including initial stock and display orders, to these accounts during the last four months of 1967 approached $250,000. Management estimated that 1968 sales to these accounts would approach $600,000.

Management believed these stores had accepted the Robertson line for three reasons: (1) the company's stated policy to sell only to a few selected retail stores in the Cincinnati area; (2) a direct factory service program, in which a Robertson factory technician installed every Robertson color receiver sold by the store, and provided at no cost to the store or customer any service needed during the first 90 days after purchase; and (3) the need for only a few floor samples to show all 16 combinations of screen size and style available in Robertson home color receivers (RCA offered more than 150 combinations). For other brands of color receivers, retailers had to provide installation and warranty service through their own service departments or arrange for part or all of the service to be provided by factory-authorized service stations. Robertson officials believed that their direct factory service was faster and superior in quality to that provided by such service stations.

On direct sales to retailers the company sold its products at distributor prices plus 10 percent. Thus retailers who purchased directly from the division and sold Robertson products to consumers at the list prices suggested by the company could earn margins up to 28 percent. Management believed that its policies of limited distribution and close cooperation with these retailers would enable them to maintain margins at this level. These retailers were also eligible to receive promotional support from the division.

DEALER SUPPORT PROGRAMS

Robertson offered its distributors and their dealers financial assistance in carrying inventory and in promoting the division's products. To encourage retailers to display and stock Robertson products, the division financed a "floor-planning" program. In effect, this program allowed Robertson and a distributor to share equally the cost of lending retailers money to finance their purchases of Robertson products. Since June 1967, when a revised floor-planning program began, nearly 20 percent of the retailers that carried Robertson products had participated in it. Floor planning was particularly popular among the smaller distributors and retailers. Few, if any, large retailers requested floor-planning assistance.

To provide promotional support through its distributors and dealers, the division set aside a fund equal to 2 percent of gross sales of home receivers in each sales territory. Costs of point-of-purchase and catalog material accounted for about 25 percent of the fund; the remaining 75 percent was available to distributors for cooperative advertising. Distributors that claimed funds for media advertising had to match Robertson's fund dollar-for-dollar with their own promotional expenditures and furnish proof of advertising in newspapers or other media.

In addition, the division offered to retailers who purchased direct, promotional support funds equal to 4 percent of their purchases. Management expected these "key accounts" to sell a substantial volume of Robertson products and to lend prestige through their advertising to the division's products, thereby increasing sales in smaller outlets in the same market.

In 1967, the division spent $260,000 on cooperative advertising of the home receiver line and $72,000 on national advertising of home television receivers. According to management, the primary objective of the national advertising campaign had been to support Robertson dealers, rather than to build extensive consumer preference for Robertson products.

SERVICE

Like most television manufacturers, Robertson offered consumers a one-year warranty on parts. In the Cincinnati market, during the first 90 days following purchase, factory service personnel replaced parts free of labor or materials charges. After that period in the Cincinnati market, and from the date of purchase in all other markets, a nominal charge was made for the service involved in parts replacement.

Warranty and postwarranty service outside Cincinnati on Robertson products was the responsibility of distributors and dealers. Management believed, however, that some of the smaller distributors and dealers did not stock adequate inventories of parts, and that in many cases they did not employ a sufficient number of service personnel.

Officials also thought that the division had to have an adequate service network in order to attract new dealers. Accordingly, management was planning to establish Robertson maintenance stations. These stations would be independent of the division's distributors and dealers, who would still be allowed to perform services. Although owned and operated by local technicians, these stations would be franchised by the division. To obtain a franchise, a station would have to meet minimum inventory and staffing standards.

Robertson maintenance stations would bear primary responsibility for warranty service, for which they would be compensated by the division. Franchised maintenance stations would purchase parts from the company at the distributor's price less 15 percent.

PLANS

Based on discussions within the Robertson executive group, Mr. Coughlin and Mr. Franklin had drafted two plans to discuss with Mr. Hodges. The first proposal was to extend the direct selling approach Robertson employed in Cincinnati to selected accounts in major American cities through a direct sales staff. In each major city, a company salesperson and service assistant would be located in a branch office, which would also serve as the franchised service station for that city. Company officials believed that a qualified salesperson could develop new accounts among department stores and a limited number of quality specialty stores. The salary required to attract people with the desired background was expected to be in the $25,000 range, plus up to $15,000 in expenses. An additional $8,000 would be required for a service assistant and $1,000 a month for office space and operations. It was anticipated that profits from the parts and service operations would cover all other overhead costs. In addition to the field costs, Robertson would incur expenses associated with supervision of the direct sales efforts.

Company officials estimated that sales in the twenty largest metropolitan United States markets could exceed $30 million, if Robertson achieved the same penetration in each of those markets that was forecast for Cincinnati in 1968. At that level of sales, promotional support funds would amount to $1.2 million. Under this proposal direct media advertising would not exceed $250,000.

If he proceeded with the direct distribution plan, Mr. Franklin expected to move into three to six markets in the first year, and up to twelve per year thereafter. Historically, Robertson's market penetration had been greatest in the northcentral region, particularly in the division's home market, and in the Northeast. Robertson did very little business in the Southeast and Pacific Northwest.

The other proposal under consideration called for upgrading the present distributor network, advertising directly to the consumer, and reducing the suggested retail price of Robertson home receivers. If accepted, this plan would be implemented region by region, and cover the entire United States within two years.

Although Robertson executives considered the direct sales program in Cincinnati promising, many believed that the continued use of distributors would be preferable for selling to retailers outside the Cincinnati area. They proposed that the present distribution system be strengthened throughout the United States by replacing independent sales representatives with salaried company salespeople, who would call on distributors. These officials hoped that the salaried salespeople would enable Robertson to upgrade the present distributors and be more selective in choosing new ones. As a result, the selling operations at the retail level and the quality of retail outlets would be improved. It was also expected that the company salespeople could gain cooperation from distributors through performing missionary work at the retail level.

Robertson officials who favored selling through company salespeople and distributors considered direct selling to retailers inefficient. One executive commented as follows:

If we could find the right distributors—particularly in the major markets—we would prefer to sell our products through them. We do not like the close contact with numerous small retail dealers who order only 10 to 15 sets per year. This creates additional work and makes the operation costly. We would like to work together with distributors who have experience in T.V. or similar equipment retailing, who are well-known in the community for carrying high quality, reliable products, and who are able to provide the necessary support to the dealers.

The objective of the proposed advertising campaign was to "... increase consumer awareness of the Robertson name and develop preference for Robertson quality television receivers." Advertisements were to be run in regional editions of national magazines and on local spot T.V. Company officials expected the advertising budget to stabilize around 4 percent of sales (as in the alternative previously described), or even less, but recognized that more funds might have to be invested in the early stages of the program. Accordingly, they contemplated spending at a rate equivalent to almost $2 million on a national basis during each of the first two years of the program.

Coupled with the proposed distribution and advertising plans was a suggestion that Robertson lower the suggested retail price of its home receivers by approximately 10 percent, to make them more competitive with RCA and Zenith. No immediate changes in factory prices were contemplated under this plan.

Exhibit 1

ROBERTSON ELECTRONICS (A)
INCOME STATEMENT
FOR YEAR ENDING DECEMBER 31
(000)

	1967	1966
Sales	$12,088	$25,648
Variable expenses:		
Direct manufacturing costs	8,640	17,710
Factory administration and overhead	446	884
Commissions to sales representatives	514	860
Other expenses:		
Advertising	342	662
Indirect labor	1,806	1,686
General administration and overhead	2,634	1,626
Total expenses	$14,382	$23,428
Net profit (loss) before taxes	($ 2,294)	$ 2,220

BALANCE SHEET, DECEMBER 31, 1967
(000)

Assets

Cash and negotiable securities	$ 954	
Accounts receivable	3,000	
Inventories	4,082	
Total current assets		$ 8,036
Plant and equipment		886
(Net of accumulated depreciation)		
Total assets		$ 8,922

Liabilities and net worth

Current liabilities	$ 1,892	
Term loan (due 1972)	2,000	
Stockholders' equity	5,030	
Total liabilities and net worth		$ 8,922

Source: Company Records

Exhibit 2

ROBERTSON ELECTRONICS (A)
SUGGESTED RETAIL PRICES OF SELECTED
COLOR TELEVISION RECEIVERS

| Manufacturer | 18V = 180 sq. in. | Table or console models | | | Console-lowboy models 23V |
		20V = 227 sq. in.	22V = 272 sq. in.	23V = 295 sq. in.	
Robertson[a]	$500	$ –	$660–690	$690–790	$770– 870
Zenith	370–500	400–550	–	470–875	875–1120
RCA	370+	400–500	–	500–850	800–1600
Admiral	–	–	–	450–795	895–1250
Magnavox	340–450	450	400–480	470–795	650–1200
Motorola	–	400–500	–	470–875	700–1200
Multiplex	350–460	–	–	500–850	800–1350
General Electric	450–470	450–500	580–670	675–780	–
Sylvania	–	420	–	450–750	–
Panasonic (Japan)	400–440	–	–	–	–
Sears	290	–	–	390–560	600– 680

[a]Company Records
Source: *Merchandising Week*, August 28, 1967, pp. 30–40

Exhibit 3

ROBERTSON ELECTRONICS (A)
DISTRIBUTION SYSTEM FOR ROBERTSON PRODUCTS

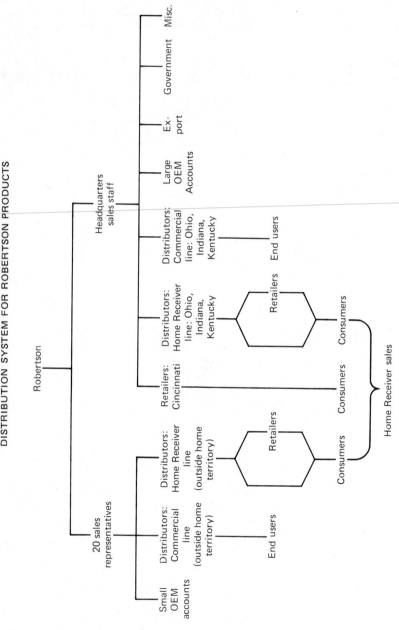

Source: Company Records

Exhibit 4

ROBERTSON ELECTRONICS (A)

1967 SALES BY MARKET AND PRODUCT LINE

(000)

| | Through reps | | Direct | | | | | |
	To distributors	To OEM	To distributors in Ohio, Indiana, and Kentucky (including Cincinnati)	To OEM	Export	Government	Miscellaneous	Total
Home receiver line	$6,398	–	$1,120	–	$ 86	$338	$96	$ 8,038
Commercial line	1,656	122	196	322	444	600	–	3,340
Total	$8,054	$122	$1,316	$322	$530	$938	$96	$11,378*

*Income of $710,000 from service and stereo sales made up the difference between $11,378,000 and total division sales of $12,088,000.

Source: Company Records

APPENDIX

ROBERTSON ELECTRONICS (A)

The Television Industry

The home television receiver industry was composed of two distinct segments: color and monochrome. The color television segment differed considerably from the monochrome segment, although the major manufacturers competed in both. One industry source stated: "The money and technology required to stay ahead in color T.V. is incomparably greater than in monochrome. In monochrome you had companies in a loft turning out sets and selling them almost by intuition while they benefited because someone else reduced the cost of components. With color you just can't survive that way."

Total industry sales of color television receivers during 1967 exceeded 5.5 million sets, or almost $3 billion at current retail prices. Industry sources forecast sales of 6 to 6.5 million color sets during 1968. Exhibit A.1 shows unit sales for the industry for both color and monochrome television sets from 1947 to 1967.

While reliable forecasts of sales of monochrome television sets were not readily available, it was known that virtually every home in the United States that was wired for electricity contained a monochrome television receiver. In contrast, the markets for multiple sets and color receivers were much less heavily saturated. Exhibit A.2 shows percentage saturation of monochrome, color, and multiple set markets from 1947 to 1967.

Nearly 300 companies had manufactured television sets in the United States since 1947. By 1967, however, only about twenty remained. *Forbes* Magazine (March 15, 1968) estimated that in 1967 four of these companies accounted for 75 to 80 percent of the national market. *Forbes* put RCA's share at close to 40 percent; Zenith at 20-25 percent; Magnavox at just under 10 percent; and General Electric at about 5 percent. The remainder was divided among several firms, none of which had more than 3 to 4 percent of the national market. Many of these firms, including Robertson Electronics, were important only in particular local or regional markets.

Among the three market leaders, Magnavox placed the most emphasis on developing and controlling the operations of its distribution system. Zenith and RCA were more widely known in the television field, and devoted considerable effort to the promotion of their product images with the general public.

PROMOTION

Most major television manufacturers spent substantial sums to advertise their products. For example, in 1967 RCA spent $5.9 million to advertise color television sets. This figure did not include advertising of monochrome television sets, nor did it include dealer cooperative advertising or other dealer promotional aids for color or monochrome receivers. Industry sources estimated that in 1967 Zenith spent $9.2 million on national advertising, almost all of which was devoted to its line of television receivers. Zenith sales of these items were estimated between $450 and $500 million in 1967. It was estimated that for the same year Magnavox had spent in excess of $3 million to advertise its television sets, radios, and phonographs through national media. This amount represented about 1 percent of Magnavox's sales of these products. About half of Magnavox's advertising budget was devoted to color television.

In addition to national advertising, Zenith spent an estimated $8.8 million on other promotional programs, including dealer cooperative advertising and dealer merchandising aids. Magnavox's spending on dealer cooperative advertising of color television receivers was estimated at more than $10 million. Although the cost to Magnavox of dealer merchandising aids was not known, one industry source estimated it to be at least as great as the company's expenditures in cooperative advertising.

Both RCA and Zenith offered retailers a promotional allowance equal to 2 or 3 percent of the retailers' purchases. General Electric allocated its advertising and promotional funds in a pattern similar to that used by RCA and Zenith. It was believed that Magnavox dealers could claim between 2.5 and 7.5 percent of their purchases as promotional funds. To obtain promotional allowances, retailers were expected to match the funds provided by the manufacturer with equivalent expenditures of their own.

DISTRIBUTION

Most large manufacturers of television sets had one or more distributors and a large network of retailers in each major metropolitan market. Some of these distributors were wholly owned subsidiaries of the manufacturer; others were independent organizations. Some manufacturers that owned distributors in particular markets also used independent distributors in those same markets. In all cases, both types of distributors received equal prices and services from the manufacturer. RCA, Zenith, and other major television manufacturers maintained a sales staff to call on independent and wholly owned distributors. Both types of distributors in turn used their own salespeople to call on retailers, which included department and specialty stores and large "discount" appliance dealers.

Magnavox employed a somewhat different distribution system and sold directly through its own salespeople to franchised dealers. Franchisees were expected to adhere to Magnavox's suggested retail prices and to carry specified inventories. Magnavox had been known to withdraw franchises from retailers who sold below suggested list prices. Magnavox franchisees included both highly regarded department and specialty stores and some smaller, more aggressive dealers for whom Magnavox was typically the major line of television and stereo equipment carried.

In most markets, the number of retailers offering Magnavox products was only one-third to one-fourth the number carrying RCA or Zenith. In Cincinnati, for example, RCA supplied one independent distributor, who in turn supplied more than 50 retailers. Zenith used an independent distributor to reach 65 retailers. General Electric sold to both a GE wholesale subsidiary and to an independent distributor. Together these GE distributors supplied an estimated 45 to 55 retailers. Magnavox sold directly to 17 franchised retailers in Cincinnati.

Officials of Robertson characterized the marketing activities of Magnavox as being more dealer-oriented than those of the other major manufacturers. The Magnavox sales force provided extensive merchandising and planning assistance in addition to advice on the effective use of advertising and in-store aids. Robertson officials also believed that Magnavox's dealer conventions at the start of each model year were effective for developing loyalties and interests in the line.

Margins earned by retailers on home television receivers varied by type of set and by brand. In late 1967, industry sources estimated that the average gross margin earned by retailers on all brands was about 23 percent for color television receivers, and 27 percent for monochrome sets. Other industry sources indicated that margins earned on RCA and Zenith sets were typically somewhat lower than the average, perhaps around 21 percent for color sets of these manufacturers. The margins earned on Magnavox sets by franchised Magnavox retailers were believed to be somewhat greater than the industry averages.

Exhibit A.1

ROBERTSON ELECTRONICS CORP. (A)
BLACK AND WHITE, AND COLOR TELEVISION UNIT SALES (1947–1967)

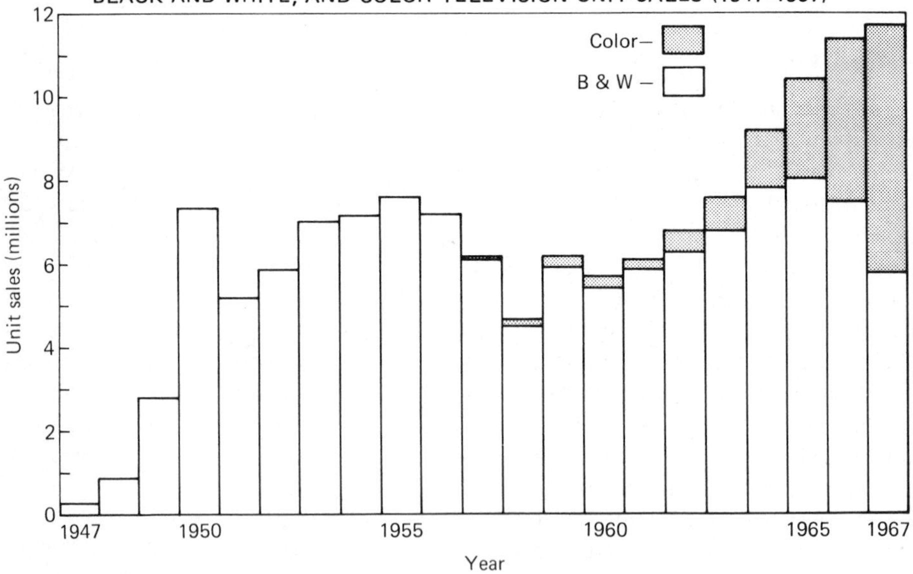

Source: Company Records

Exhibit A.2

ROBERTSON ELECTRONICS CORP. (A)
PERCENT SATURATION OF BLACK AND WHITE, MULTIPLE,
AND COLOR TELEVISION SET MARKETS

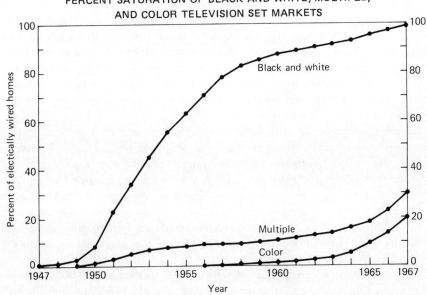

Source: Company Records

ROBERTSON ELECTRONICS (B)

At the same time they were developing plans for Robertson home receivers (see Robertson Electronics (A)), Mr. Hodges asked Mr. Coughlin and Mr. Franklin to review the competitive position of Robertson's commercial line and to recommend alternative courses of action for the commercial line. Mr. Hodges believed that the market for commercial (as opposed to home) television equipment was growing rapidly, and might therefore offer greater opportunity than the home receiver market. Mr. Hodges also believed that the commercial market was not, like the home receiver market, dominated by a few large firms and that Robertson had considerable freedom to choose a particular competitive position or "niche" in this market.

Robertson's commercial television line included both educators and monitors. Educators were monochrome television receivers, which, like home receivers, accepted programs transmitted by commercial television stations. Educators could also receive broadcasts from educational television stations, and from closed-circuit television (CCTV) systems into which they were incorporated. Educators were used in schools, hospitals, and institutions. Monitors were visual display devices which did not receive audio signals. Unlike educators, monitors could not receive broadcasts from commercial television stations. Monitors received only the visual transmissions that originated within the CCTV systems in which they were installed.

Sales of Robertson commercial receivers in 1967 totalled $3,340,000, representing almost a two-fold increase over commercial sales in 1966 (see Robertson Electronics (A)). Division officials forecast commercial sales of $4.5 million in 1968. Exhibit 1 shows historical sales in units and dollars by product type.

Although commercial receivers were manufactured in the same facilities as home receivers, the standard profit contribution[*] on the company's commercial line was calculated at 30 percent, ten points higher than the 20 percent obtained on the home receiver line. Within the commercial line, standard profit contribution varied between monochrome and color sets. Monochrome educators and monitors yielded a contribution of 27 percent, while color monitors produced a contribution in excess of 54 percent.

SALES AND DISTRIBUTION

Robertson sold its commercial products through the division's headquarters staff and through the independent sales representatives who carried the division's home receiver line (see Robertson Electronics (A)). The headquarters staff handled commercial sales to distributors in the division's home market of Ohio, Indiana, and Kentucky, as well as government and export sales. In addition, headquarters personnel worked with sales

[*]Standard profit contribution was defined by the company as net sales revenue minus variable administrative, selling, and manufacturing expenses. Variable manufacturing expenses included materials, direct labor, and variable overhead costs.

representatives to solicit business from OEM accounts that were likely to offer the division substantial sales volume. (For sales by channel and product line, see Robertson Electronics (A), Exhibit 4.)

Within the division's home territory, the headquarters staff sold the commercial line to fourteen distributors, of which six were based in Cincinnati and eight in other large cities in Ohio, Indiana, and Kentucky. These distributors, in turn, sold Robertson and related but noncompeting equipment to ultimate users in their respective trading areas.

The headquarters staff negotiated and fulfilled government contracts that called for installation and service of Robertson home or commercial receivers in several cities widely scattered throughout the United States. In such cases, none of the division's sales representatives had the capability to handle the entire transaction. In addition, the headquarters staff took complete charge of government contracts that required special testing and inspection procedures. Such orders occasionally included guarantees permitting the government to purchase up to several hundred units, but not obligating the government to do so. Under those circumstances, no one distributor was willing to assume the risk of carrying excess inventory of specialized products.

According to management, the division's export business involved relatively small, special orders in which few American manufacturers were interested. Virtually all the television receivers made by Robertson and other American manufacturers had to be modified for use overseas, and required special testing, inspection, and packaging. The company had to estimate its costs and quote a special price for each prospective order.

Apart from these direct sales activities, headquarters personnel worked with the representatives in sales to large OEM accounts. In such cases, the representative functioned primarily as a contact, while the headquarters staff negotiated the supply agreement itself. Representatives received a negotiated commission (less than 4 percent) on any OEM sales that resulted from those cooperative ventures. Sales representatives handled by themselves, and received full commission on, sales to distributors and small OEM accounts. OEM sales consisted primarily of monitors, which manufacturers incorporated into the original equipment they manufactured.

Sales representatives themselves sold the commercial line to distributors outside the division's home market and to small OEM accounts. Most of the revenue sales representatives received from sales of Robertson products came from the division's home receiver line, rather than the commercial line. Late in 1967, division officials were exploring the possibility of dividing sales representatives' responsibilities within each territory by product line. Under such a plan, educators and monitors would be sold by one representative, home television receivers by another. The two representatives in a territory could either be independent of one another or members of the same sales representative organization, each heading a different department (i.e., home receiver sales and commercial sales). While proponents of this plan believed that it would increase the effectiveness of each representative by permitting him or her to specialize only in one market (home or commercial), these executives recognized that finding additional qualified, aggressive representatives would be difficult.

Separation of the division's two lines already existed among the 550 distributors that purchased Robertson products: 450 of these distributors handled the division's home receiver line; 100 carried the commercial line.

Distributors that sold Robertson educators and monitors usually employed at least two salespeople, and typically carried a broad line of audiovisual equipment, broadcasting equipment, and components for CCTV systems. These distributors sold to schools, institutions, and a variety of commercial and industrial establishments. In some cases, these distributors sold individual components to original equipment manufacturers.

Robertson supported distributors' selling efforts with catalog material, product-description handouts, and advertisements in broadcasting journals and school magazines, e.g., *School Product News*. In 1967, the division spent $10,000 on such advertisements.

POSITION IN THE EDUCATOR MARKET

The market for educators had grown rapidly in recent years as secondary schools and colleges began to use television in a variety of instructional applications. Nevertheless, in 1967, a survey of 15,600 educational institutions, which accounted for more than 85 percent of total enrollment in precollegiate and collegiate institutions, revealed that only about 4 percent of those institutions had installed educational television systems (see Exhibit 2). Most installations were in large urban areas.

Almost 90 percent of educational television systems transmitted either on special broadcast frequencies reserved for educational transmission or through cables which connected the transmission point with each school in the CCTV system. Use of special broadcast frequencies was greatest in large, densely populated urban areas, where the costs of cable installation were considered prohibitive, and in small rural school systems, which picked up educational television programs, often by relayed transmission, from distant cities. Cable transmission was used most frequently in locations where transmission and receiving locations were close together, such as large universities or colleges.

In contrast to larger firms in the industry (e.g., General Electric, RCA), which sold a modified version of a home reciever as an educator, Robertson manufactured television receivers designed in consultation with school officials and built specially for institutional use. Robertson offered a variety of features that could be incorporated into the basic educator chassis to meet specific customer needs. These features included an additional audio amplifier, command microphone feature, "student-proof" locks, and a stand-by power circuit. According to management, these features enabled the division to offer an entire line of educators, whereas other manufacturers typically sold one or two models that did not include many of the features available on Robertson educators.

Prices of Robertson educators to school systems and other ultimate users ranged from $220 to $290, depending on the product type and application. The division's prices ran about $100 higher than those of manufacturers such as General Electric and RCA. Distributors earned margins of 30 to 35 percent on sales of Robertson educators. Such margins were similar to those earned by distributors on related CCTV equipment, but somewhat higher than margins offered by competing educator manufacturers.

Division officials estimated that nearly seven out of every ten Robertson educators sold by distributors were sold to an individual school or relatively small school system. These schools or systems almost always purchased the educators with funds provided by federal government grants. In addition to public schools, most private and parochial schools were eligible to receive such grants.

Mr. Franklin thought that the primary decision maker in individual schools or smaller school systems was a teacher or administrator who, in addition to his or her other duties, was responsible for audiovisual equipment, including acquisitions. In recent years, these schools had to an increasing extent sought advice on the purchase of audiovisual equipment from consultants who specialized in this area. Mr. Franklin believed that consultants were, in general, quite favorably impressed with Robertson educators, and would frequently recommend their purchase.

Although the lack of comprehensive and reliable data made it very difficult to estimate the total market for educators, management believed that in the first half of 1967 Robertson sold 10 to 20 percent of all the educators sold during that period. Division officials also believed that Robertson's share of the market for educators among smaller school systems might be much higher, inasmuch as Robertson made few sales to larger school systems. Management attributed its position to several factors, including the superior quality of the Robertson educator, the distributors' knowledge of total audiovisual systems, and the status of the distributor as a member of the local community. In this latter role, distributors often assisted local school boards and administrators in applying for government grants with which audiovisual equipment could be purchased.

Division officials stated that, while larger school systems also received government aid for purchasing audiovisual equipment, Robertson could not compete as effectively for their business. As one executive put it:

Larger school systems have both specialized audiovisual personnel with budget responsibility and centralized purchasing departments. These large systems usually ask for proposals from various manufacturers or write specifications which may fit only the large producers, who can offer the product much cheaper than we do. The audiovisual director and the purchasing agent do not listen to engineers, who may recommend our product. They simply compare the prices and choose the cheaper product. In addition, we find it very difficult to communicate with audiovisual and purchasing personnel in large school systems, because they insist on talking directly to manufacturers. Our distributors may not even have a chance to see the responsible person. In dealing with small customers, however, our distributors have proved to be very successful.

The executive also stated that the division had on occasion been led to believe that gifts to individuals influential in the purchase decisions in larger systems would result in orders being given to Robertson. He declared, however, that under no circumstances would the division engage in unethical practices to obtain business.

POSITION IN THE MONITOR MARKET

Original equipment manufacturers and ultimate users purchased monitors as components of complete CCTV systems which also included cameras, videotape recorders, and installation equipment. The minimum cost of a complete system ranged from two to three thousand dollars. Customers who wanted to install a complete CCTV system could either assemble it themselves from the products of different manufacturers and distributors or buy a standard system. Robertson officials believed that most customers assembled their own systems. Management believed that fewer than ten distributors in the United States—all of which carried Robertson's commercial line—presently had the capability to assemble complete CCTV systems. Among manufacturers of CCTV equipment, only RCA offered all the components necessary to assemble a complete system. Sylvania sold both cameras and monitors, and other manufacturers specialized in either cameras, monitors, or videotape recorders. Robertson made no CCTV equipment other than educators and monitors. Most makers of cameras and videotape recorders had the necessary technical ability and capital to build monitors, but many monitor manufacturers lacked the resources to enter the camera or videotape fields.

Closed circuit television systems typically found their greatest use in broadcasting and specific industrial applications. The industrial market was expected to grow more rapidly than the broadcast market (see Exhibit 3).

Commercial television broadcasters used CCTV extensively within their own systems in the preparation and transmission of broadcasts. Individual broadcast applications each typically contained several monitors.

Among industrial users, applications of CCTV were most frequent in manufacturing (see Table 1). To date, manufacturers in the chemical, metallurgical, food, and paper industries had been the major users of CCTV. Applications in those industries included security, training, quality control, and research and development. Retailers also made use of CCTV, primarily for purposes of security, training, and monitoring traffic flows. Medical and municipal service users made similar use of CCTV.

Table 1

APPLICATIONS OF CCTV
SYSTEMS

Manufacturing	67%
Retailing	17
Medical services	8
Municipal services	5
Others	3
	100%

According to industry sources, increased use of CCTV depended upon two factors: new applications and the growth of industries that currently utilized CCTV. A major trade association official stated, "CCTV fits in perfectly with advanced technologies that require immediate feedback of activities. We see no plateau in the growth of these industries or limitations to possible applications. Moreover, the current trend toward increased security of premises as well as safety of employees creates endless opportunities for CCTV systems. Applications of CCTV are only limited by an individual's creativity. One merely has to conjure the different ways a person may use a tape recorder to appreciate the limitless opportunities or applications possible."

Robertson first offered monitors in 1967, when executives recognized a need in the market for an economical visual display device for use in CCTV systems. According to management, this need was growing because of increased interest in industrial applications of CCTV and because of price reductions on CCTV equipment other than monitors. Until 1967, most monitors on the market had been designed for use in laboratories and television studios. In these applications a visual display device had to be able to reproduce details up to three times as precise as the reproduction possible on a home television receiver. List prices for these high quality monitors ranged from $300 to $1,400 for a monochrome monitor, and ran about $2,500 for a color monitor.

In 1967, Robertson management responded to distributors' requests for a less expensive monitor. The company offered monochrome monitors in 15V and 18V[*] screen sizes, and color monitors with 18V screens. List prices for Robertson monitors were considerably lower than those of competitors, and ranged from $220 for the simplest 15V monochrome units to $950 for the deluxe 18V color unit. The division sold these monitors for $120 to $700, respectively. In 1967, Robertson sold to OEM purchasers all of the color monitors it manufactured.

Management estimated the division's share of the total market for monitors at less than 10 percent, but believed Robertson to be the largest manufacturer of monitors for applications outside of laboratories and television studios. According to management, competition in the market for less expensive monitors came primarily from other manufacturers of home television receivers. Executives did not consider this competition to be a significant threat at the present time, since monitors accounted for only a very small portion of the total sales of those manufacturers.

Manufacturers who purchased Robertson monitors included the largest suppliers of CCTV equipment in the industry. These OEM customers in some cases competed for sales to broadcasters and industrial purchasers with distributors who carried Robertson monitors. The distributors were nevertheless able to compete quite successfully, management believed, because they assembled components from several manufacturers and could offer a wider variety of customer-tailored systems.

Management planned to increase sales of monitors to OEM accounts in 1968. The division had approached several large manufacturers to get Robertson equipment established as part of the CCTV systems and other equipment made by these firms. Some officials believed the increased OEM sales would provide an excellent opportunity to obtain wider exposure for the division's products. As one executive expressed it, "They can see that it is Robertson from the back, no matter what kind of nameplates you put on the front." Other executives were, however, concerned that Robertson would gradually

---

[*]15V and 18V were standard industry measures of picture-tube size. A 15V tube had 125 square inches of viewing area; an 18V tube, 180 square inches.

be forced into the position of a contract manufacturer of a component for a CCTV system, and would have to compete on a price basis. These executives thought that the division should seriously consider manufacturing or assembling complete CCTV systems.

SERVICE

Service on educators and monitors was typically negotiated as part of the original sales contract for such equipment. At that time, service on Robertson commercial products was provided by distributors. Division officials planned to turn responsibilities for service on commercial lines over to its franchised maintenance stations as they came into operation (see Robertson Electronics (A)).

Management believed that service on Robertson educators and monitors could be performed at a cost to the manufacturer of about three cents per unit per day, whereas competitors' costs typically ran considerably higher, in some cases up to nine cents per unit per day. This difference, according to division officials, came about because of Robertson's modular construction.

PLANS

Mr. Coughlin and Mr. Franklin knew that Mr. Hodges wanted them to have proposals for the commercial line drafted for discussion within six to eight weeks. They knew also that Mr. Hodges would insist on seeing a complete marketing plan, including pro forma budgets, and would require that all figures in those budgets be supported. Such extensive, formal planning was a new experience for Mr. Coughlin and Robertson personnel. Although they considered these planning and review procedures demanding, Mr. Coughlin and Mr. Franklin knew that Mr. Hodges had a reputation for fairness and that he encouraged the refinement and revision of plans and budgets.

In a preliminary meeting with Mr. Coughlin and Mr. Franklin, Mr. Hodges noted that development of marketing plans and budgets for Robertson's home receiver and commercial lines represented only the first steps in the planning and budgeting process Lustrex required of each division. The corporate review board, composed of senior staff personnel, group vice-presidents, and Lustrex's president and executive vice-president, would examine not only estimates of operating profit, but also the investments required to generate those profits. Forecasts of investments in equipment and working capital, and of depreciation, would be combined with profit estimates to produce projections of net cash flow for each product line within the corporation. This planning procedure had led Lustrex to attempt to assign responsibility for profits and investments down to the product line level, if possible; or to the operating division level, for product lines that shared assets.

Mr. Hodges observed that this practice had resulted in organization by product line, rather than by function (e.g., marketing, production), within most Lustrex divisions. He suggested that Mr. Coughlin explore the possibility of reorganizing Robertson into "home receiver" and "commercial" operating groups. Because five individuals constituted the division's executive staff, the relative strength of the "home receiver" and "commercial" groups could be affected substantially by such a reorganization and by the particular assignments made.

Mr. Coughlin believed that planning for the commercial line had far-reaching implications for the division. "We have to decide whether we're going to be a component manufacturer or a systems builder," he stated. "We're a small, flexible operation, which can respond quickly to changes in technology and market opportunities. We're capable of producing a wide variety of equipment, specially customized for individual customers' needs. I'm not sure how big we should try to be in this commercial market. In the past, we've concentrated on home receivers and sold commercial equipment essentially as a by-product. We'd better decide whether we should continue to reverse that position." Mr. Hodges added, "The basic budgetary issue is whether to expand our base in home receiver sales—especially to Cincinnati—or to 'milk' the home receiver line to generate funds for growth in the commercial line."

Exhibit 1

ROBERTSON ELECTRONICS (B)
SALES OF COMMERCIAL TELEVISION EQUIPMENT BY PRODUCT TYPE

Product Type	1967 Dollars (000)	Units	1966 Dollars (000)	Units
Educators (monochrome only)	$2,706	17,088	$1,878	12,470
Monitors	634	2,174	nil	nil
Color	350	700	nil	nil
Monochrome	284	1,474	nil	nil

Source: Company Records

Exhibit 2

ROBERTSON ELECTRONICS (B)
NUMBER OF EDUCATIONAL INSTITUTIONS
WITH INSTITUTIONAL TELEVISION SYSTEMS
1956–1967

Year	Total number of using institutions Elementary/ secondary	College/ university	Total
1956	2	17	19
1957	4	32	36
1958	7	44	51
1959	12	57	69
1960	21	71	92
1961	41	97	138
1962	59	116	175
1963	83	145	228
1964	106	168	274
1965	141	203	344
1966	196	249	445
1967	308	310	618

Source: National Education Association, "A Survey of Instructional Closed Circuit Television," 1967

Exhibit 3

ROBERTSON ELECTRONICS (B)
MANUFACTURERS' SHIPMENTS
OF TELEVISION MONITORS
1963–1967

Year	Estimated dollar shipments by application (millions) Broadcast/ studio	Industrial	Total
1963	2.7	3.0	5.7
1964	3.2	3.4	6.6
1965	4.2	3.9	8.1
1966	7.0	7.0	14.0
1967	5.5	7.7	13.2

Source: Trade estimates based on U.S. Department of Commerce, "Current Industrial Reports"

DESIGNING THE OPTIMUM PORTFOLIO

Discussion in the preceding sections has assumed the existence of a desired or optimum portfolio and argued that decisions to add, drop, or reallocate resources among product lines should move an organization toward that optimum portfolio. The present section relaxes that assumption and poses, in turn, two questions: (1) What is an optimum port-folio? and (2) How may an optimum portfolio be designed?

What Is an Optimum Portfolio?

An "optimum" portfolio reflects the most appropriate balance of return and risk (vari-ability of return) for a particular organization. Theoretically, an optimum portfolio should provide maximum return for any level of risk, or a minimum of risk (uncertainty) for any level of return. Most organizations that attempt to apply a portfolio approach do so by attempting either to minimize variations in net cash flow or to maximize net cash flow.

Most established organizations try to improve their historic rates of return, but rec-ognize that dramatic increases are unlikely in the short term. Established organizations are accustomed to managing particular types of risk at certain levels. Managing lower levels of uncertainty represents an inefficient use of managerial resources if the lower level of uncertainty is associated with a lower expected return. Attempting to manage a higher level of uncertainty or a different type of risk ordinarily increases the uncertainty around the level of return.

The combination of return and risk considered most appropriate varies among organi-zations because management groups differ with respect to their return goals and the amount and type of risk they are willing to accept in pursuit of those return objectives. Some organizations deliberately seek portfolios of product lines and markets that are diversified so that the portfolio includes a mixture of high-risk/high-return combinations and low-risk/low-return combinations. Other organizations seek to diversify portfolios among different product/market combinations either at the high-risk/high-return end of the continuum or at the low-risk/low-return end. Their reasons for seeking diversification ordinarily are to reduce as far as possible variation in expected returns. Such organiza-tions do not always select their portfolios so that earnings from individual investments will correlate inversely with one another to minimize variation. Some deliberately accept higher levels of variation in the hope of increasing total returns.

In contrast to organizations that seek diversified portfolios are those that deliberately concentrate their portfolios in closely related product line/market combinations. Such organizations ordinarily believe they will obtain higher returns through specialization, synergy, and dominance than by spreading their resources more broadly. In addition, man-agers in such firms may consider themselves quite capable of estimating accurately returns from investments concentrated in their areas of expertise, and thereby reduce the risk associated with any level of return in ventures closely linked to existing activities. These managers may also believe that they have little skill in managing or forecasting returns from businesses unlike their present ones, and therefore forecast a high level of variability of returns (i.e., high risk) in businesses with which they lack familiarity. The breadth of portfolios in such organizations depends in part on how broadly the managers involved define their businesses.

Some organizations manage risk by limiting commitments to a particular product line to sums below a certain level. For example, in one firm with $50 million in sales, an investment of half a million dollars to redesign a product line appeared virtually certain to result in increased sales, profits, and market share, yet was turned down because executives were afraid to commit so large a sum to a single product line.

In other organizations, modest investments may be rejected because of lack of certainty over the outcome. Some management groups prefer ventures that have a low probability of earning less than a particular level of return, and will accept such ventures in preference to those whose forecast distribution of returns offers greater opportunities for returns much higher and much lower than the expected level.

The optimum portfolio for a particular organization, then, includes investments consistent with the return objectives and risk preferences of the management group. These goals and preferences may be stated explicitly, or reflected in risk management styles and through the historic pattern of decisions on prospective additions to and deletions from the portfolio.

Even though one may identify the dimensions of an optimum portfolio for a particular organization, there does not exist a single set of product lines and markets that may be considered the unique, optimum, or ideal portfolio for that organization. As with portfolios of investment securities, several different combinations of product lines and markets might appropriately constitute the portfolio for a particular organization. An important corollary to this point is that no one business is ideally suited to all portfolios. A business whose level and variability of return is inappropriate for one organization's portfolio may be well suited to that of another organization.

Despite the lack of a unique solution to portfolio design problems, managers can attempt to define portfolios that approximate optimum portfolios, and can design certain portfolios that appear superior to others for their particular organizations.

How to Design the Portfolio

Portfolio design involves specifying return objectives and risk preferences, identifying sets of investments, forecasting future environmental conditions, estimating returns and variability of returns for each set of investments, and choosing as the optimum portfolio that whose distribution of returns most closely matches managers' desired combinations of return and variability. This approach to portfolio design, which incorporates techniques from decision theory, facilitates choice among sets of investments available to the organization within the planning period of interest, typically several years.

Return Objectives and Risk Preferences   Managers may usefully begin the procedure by articulating their objectives or goals for levels of return and the amount and type of variability they are willing to tolerate in pursuing those levels of return. For this procedure to be useful, the return objectives must be reasonably attainable within the level of resources the organization can be expected to commit. Past successes and failures in managing particular types and levels of risk provide a starting point for determining the amount of variability or uncertainty the management group can expect the organization to tolerate. Individual managers' risk preferences should be made clear. Historic strategies employed to manage uncertainty (e.g., limitation of investment, extensive evaluation of new ventures), as well as operationally meaningful objectives, should be identified in order to limit somewhat the range of portfolios that might be examined. Interests of the management group in exploring new businesses or learning new technologies, markets, and the like should also be articulated.

Investments A useful first step is to define the "investments" under consideration. These definitions should include the type and level of resources required. For example, an investment in a novel food-preservation technology would initially require technical personnel, laboratory and test facilities, marketing planning and research personnel, some managerial time, and commitments of funds for personnel, materials, and equipment. At later stages, that project might require substantially larger amounts of all those resources, plus funds for pilot production facilities and extensive market testing. Once technical feasibility and commercial viability were demonstrated, personnel and funds for full-scale manufacturing and market development would be required. At each stage, the requirements of the investment in terms of the organization's scarce resources of technical, sales, marketing, and managerial personnel, facilities, and funds should be specified. Once requirements for individual investments are specified, the analyst should identify those sets of individual investments that, taken together, would fit within the organization's resources.

As an illustration,[*] consider the set of alternative investments available to a large food-processing company in a recent year:

1. expansion of a manufacturing facility

2. acquisition of a distributor

3. development of a proprietary technology for processed foods

4. acquisition of three "Campus Deli" premium sandwich and fast-food restaurants located near colleges.

This set of investments included one for building the company's base business (plant expansion), one for market development (distributor), one for product development (food technology), and one that represented a departure from the company's traditional product lines and markets into new areas ("Campus Deli"). The manufacturing-facility expansion would increase the company's capacity to make its existing lines of processed foods. Acquiring the distributor, who served primarily low- and medium-priced restaurants and fast-food outlets as well as other institutional food service operations, would

---

[*] Certain data in this illustration have been disguised.

enable the company to develop a market for its institutional lines in a region of the country that was growing, but in which the company had been unable to penetrate the institutional market. The new technology, intended to improve nutritional content and taste, and to reduce preservatives, in processed foods, appeared likely to be appropriate for premium-priced food lines for both consumer and institutional uses. The company could use the technology in its own operations and could sell raw materials based on the technology to other processors, as well as finished products to distributors and restaurants. Although the Campus Deli shops did not by themselves represent a significant investment, company managers believed that these restaurants offered an opportunity to enter the restaurant business (in which they were not presently engaged) through expansion into a chain of owned and franchised Campus Deli shops.

Funds for expanding the plant would come to $1.5 million; for acquiring the distributorship and augmenting its facilities, approximately $0.5 million. Company research personnel estimated that at least $0.5 million would have to be committed to the food technology project before they could be sure whether they had something worth backing with additional funds (in a subsequent planning period) or whether the project should be curtailed. Acquisition of the three Campus Deli's and development of a central organization to expand the chain through a combination of company-owned and franchised units was estimated to require approximately $1.0 million during the present planning period; thereafter additional funds would be needed to expand the chain if it appeared to be successful.

Because company officials expected to be able to commit no more than $2.0 million to whatever set of projects were chosen, the prospective investments had to be grouped into sets, each of which totaled $2.0 million. Negotiations within the company resulted in the combination of plant expansion and "Campus Deli" purchase being included as a possible set, in case the $2.5 million necessary for that combination should become available.

Forecasting the Environment   At the same time they estimated the resource requirements for these four investments, company personnel identified three factors that they considered among the most powerful influences on the company's fortunes during the coming three years (the planning period under consideration). These factors included general economic conditions, changes in the structure of the food service industry, and changes in consumers' preferences for food served through fast-food outlets. Specifically, analysts identified the following ranges of outcomes on each of these environmental influences as follows:

1. Economic Conditions: (a) Severe recession, perhaps accompanied by inflation
    (b) "Stagflation"—little or no real growth, 5–10 percent annual inflation
    (c) Significant real growth, accompanied by a modest inflation rate

2. Structural changes: (a) Food service operations concentrate their resources at the retail level, demanding more supporting services from suppliers

                                              (b) Food service operations integrate backwards to become their own distributors and, in some cases, their own processors

3. Consumers' preferences: (a) The number and percentage of fast-food customers who seek premium-quality (at a higher price) increases measurably

                                              (b) No increase—and perhaps a decrease—in the size of the consumer group interested in premium-quality fast-foods.

These outcomes may be combined into twelve mutually exclusive and collectively exhaustive individual outcomes, and arrayed as follows:

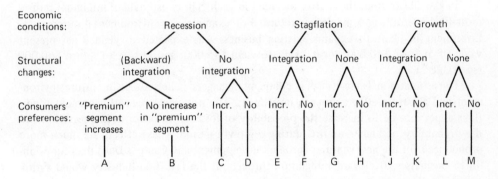

For convenience, each individual outcome may be designated with its own letter, as above.

Estimating Returns and Variability The next—and perhaps most crucial—step is to estimate a range of returns likely to occur for each investment for each individual environmental outcome. It is useful to begin this task by organizing outcomes, or possible future environmental states, and investments into a payoff matrix like that shown in Table 1.

Completion of the matrix involves placing into each cell the range of returns expected from each investment under the specified set of environmental conditions. In practice, most managers will find it difficult to generate a complete probability distribution of returns. One of the techniques frequently used to elicit managers' estimates and to stand as a proxy for a complete distribution is to request a range of estimates: a minimum return, defined as one that will be met or exceeded nine times out of ten; a most likely return, one that is about as likely to be exceeded as missed; and a maximum return, one that will be exceeded only one time in ten. The returns themselves should be expressed in terms of net present value of a stream of cash outflows and inflows associated

Table 1

PAYOFF MATRIX

| Investments | Environmental outcomes ("states of nature") | | | | | | | | | | | |
	A	B	C	D	E	F	G	H	J	K	L	M
Plant expansion												
Market development (distributor acquisition)												
Product development												
Campus Deli shops												

with that investment throughout its expected life, and discounted at the rate customarily used by the company for prospective investments. (A procedure for computing net cash flows is described in the Appendix to this chapter.)

In this illustration, the matrix included in each cell an estimate of minimum return, most likely return, and maximum return. For example, for environmental outcome A, investment in plant to expand existing business was expected to yield a net present value of at least $40,000; most likely to yield $45,000; and at best to return $60,000 (see Table 2).

The estimates in Table 1 display company managers' beliefs about the future environment and about its effects on each investment. The principal effect of economic conditions appears to be to increase the probability of losses or low returns in a recession and the probability of higher returns during a growth period. These effects are much more pronounced for the new ventures (product development and Campus Deli) than for established businesses. Backward integration throughout the fast-food industry would shrink somewhat the market available for output from the expanded plant and from the distributorship; it would have no effect on the returns from the new food technology, presumably because raw materials could be sold to processors and finished products to distributors and retailers. Integration might enhance somewhat the opportunity for Campus Deli shops, insofar as integration forced existing fast-food retailers to concentrate resources and attention on operations and supply assurance, rather than on retail positioning. Increase in the size of the "premium" segment of fast-food customers would apparently operate to increase returns from the new food technology and the Campus Deli's, both of which are premium-price offerings. Change in size of that segment would presumably have limited impact on the company's or the distributor's existing businesses.

The variation in return, or risk, foreseen for the plant expansion and distributorship acquisition is relatively small. Evidently managers believe that these established businesses will experience a level of return affected only to a modest extent by the environmental conditions specified. In contrast, the variation for the product development project and for the Campus Deli chain are both substantial. Maximum estimates of return, however, for those new investments are dramatically higher than those for the plant expansion and

Table 2

ESTIMATED RETURNS (MINIMUM–MOST LIKELY–MAXIMUM)
NET PRESENT VALUES OF CASH INFLOWS AND OUTFLOWS FOR
INVESTMENTS UNDER SPECIFIED ENVIRONMENTAL OUTCOMES
(000 OF DOLLARS)

Investments (000)		Environmental outcomes											
		A	B	C	D	E	F	G	H	J	K	L	M
Plant expansion ($1500)	Minimum	40	40	50	50	50	50	55	55	55	55	60	60
	Most likely	45	45	60	60	55	55	65	65	60	60	70	70
	Maximum	60	60	70	70	65	65	75	75	70	70	80	80
Market development (distributor acquisition) ($500)	Minimum	(15)	(15)	15	15	5	5	30	30	5	5	35	35
	Most likely	0	0	20	20	10	10	35	35	10	10	40	40
	Maximum	5	5	25	25	15	15	40	40	20	20	50	50
Product development ($500)	Minimum	(200)	(200)	(200)	(200)	(200)	(200)	(200)	(200)	(200)	(200)	(200)	(200)
	Most likely	20	(100)	20	(100)	150	(50)	150	(50)	250	(20)	250	(20)
	Maximum	50	0	50	0	600	100	600	100	1000	150	1000	150
Campus Deli shops ($1000)	Minimum	(200)	(200)	(200)	(200)	(50)	(50)	(70)	(70)	(50)	(50)	(70)	(70)
	Most likely	25	15	20	0	250	50	200	250	500	150	300	50
	Maximum	100	50	50	25	1000	200	800	100	2500	600	1500	300

distributorship acquisition. Not surprisingly, return and risk levels are closely related: product development and the Campus Deli investments represent high-risk, high-return projects; plant and distributorship, low-risk, low-return investments. The variation in the return estimates for the product development project occurs in part because of the $0.2 million loss which appears across all environmental conditions. This loss evidently represents total failure of the project to develop a new technology, and illustrates the impact of a partially controllable factor—R & D success—on the level of return.

Selecting a Portfolio   Because the return on each investment was expected not to be affected directly by any of the other investments, total expected return for each set of investments could be obtained by summing respectively the minimum, most likely, and maximum return estimates for each set of investments for each combination of environmental outcomes. Table 3, which contains those sums, provides a basis for selecting among the alternative sets of investments, or portfolios, previously identified.

Individual executives' willingness to accept forecasts of environmental conditions, as well as their preference for using a range of forecasts instead of a single estimate, affect the portfolio-selection choices they make. If company managers were completely uncertain about which set of environmental conditions would prevail, and believed that the returns for particular sets of investments could fall anywhere between the minimum and maximum estimates, those whose risk preference was to minimize the likelihood of loss would invest in plant expansion and market development (through the distributorship acquisition). Indeed, even if they were quite certain that a particular outcome would occur, those who wished to minimize probabilities of loss would always choose that portfolio, because for every combination of environmental circumstances that portfolio has the highest values at the "low" end of the range of forecast returns (see Table 3). On the other hand, managers who were similarly uncertain about the environment and return estimates, but who wished to maximize returns, would choose the portfolio of market development (distributorship acquisition), product development, and Campus Deli, because for each environmental outcome, that portfolio offers the highest values at the "high" end of the return range (see Table 2). If those latter managers expected a particular environmental outcome, but were uncertain about where within the range estimated the returns would fall, they might choose the portfolio with the highest maximum estimate. Interestingly, that portfolio would be unlikely to be the plant expansion and market development distribution acquisition alternative, which the loss-minimizers would choose, because for any outcome except D, other portfolios have higher "high" values.

If managers worked only with the "most likely" estimates, those completely uncertain about the environment, but who wished to minimize probability of loss, would choose the plant expansion and Campus Deli alternative. Those who wished to maximize return would have to clarify their expectations about the future environment. In some instances, the plant expansion and Campus Deli have the highest "most likely" returns (e.g., F, K); in others, the market development (distributorship acquisition), product development, and Campus Deli portfolio are highest (e.g., E, G); in only two instances

Table 3

TOTAL RETURN FOR SETS OF INVESTMENTS
FOR SPECIFED ENVIRONMENTAL OUTCOMES
($000)

Investments

Environmental Outcome	Plant expansion, distributor acquisition ($2 million investment)			Plant expansion, product development ($2 million investment)			Distributorship acquisition, product development, Campus Deli shops ($2 million investment)			Plant expansion, Campus Deli shops ($2.5 million investment)		
	Low	Most Likely	High	Low	Most Likely	High	Low	Most Likely	High	Low	Most Likely	High
A	25*	45	65	(160)	65	110	(415)	45	155	(160)	70	160
B	25	45	65	(160)	(55)	60	(415)	(85)	55	(160)	60	110
C	65	80	95	(150)	80	120	(385)	60	125	(150)	80	120
D	65	80	95	(150)	40	70	(385)	(80)	50	(150)	60	95
E	55	65	80	(150)	205	665	(245)	410	1615	0	305	1065
F	55	65	80	(150)	5	165	(245)	10	315	0	105	265
G	85	100	115	(145)	215	675	(240)	385	1440	(15)	265	875
H	85	100	115	(145)	15	175	(240)	10	240	(15)	90	175
J	60	70	90	(145)	310	1070	(245)	760	3520	5	560	2570
K	60	70	90	(145)	40	220	(245)	140	790	5	210	670
L	95	110	130	(140)	320	1080	(235)	590	2550	(10)	370	1580
M	95	110	130	(140)	50	230	(235)	70	500	(10)	120	380

*Comprised of a gain of $40,000 from the plant expansion, and a loss of $15,000 on the distributorship (see Table 1).

(outcomes D and H) does the plant expansion and market development alternative have the highest "most likely" returns. Managers who were willing to base their decision on the "most likely" estimates and predicted that a particular environmental outcome would occur would choose the portfolio with the highest "most likely" net present value return for that particular outcome; under that decision rule, they would not choose the plant expansion, product development alternative.

But in fact that's what the company did, because executives made their decision not on the basis of the portfolio design approach just described, but by analyzing investments one by one and compromising on the risk preferences and perceptions of corporate goals of the members of the decision-making group. This portfolio analysis was applied after the fact, in part because managers were not satisfied with the compromise they had reached on the basis of one investment for the existing business and one for a new venture, and in part because the Campus Deli chain showed substantial growth after its acquisition by another company.

When to Use Portfolio Analysis   This approach to portfolio design yields far more useful results when applied before investment decisions are made than it does when used to assuage disappointment. The procedure should increase return and decrease variability when conscientiously employed to choose among alternative sets of investments. The example above dealt with a case in which managers were considering several new ventures. The approach may be used identically for decisions to reallocate resources among or to drop product lines, such as the decisions involved in Simon's, Inc. (page 19).

A management group may use this procedure to define an optimum portfolio and to generate criteria to evaluate new proposals which come along one at a time. To develop an optimum portfolio, managers may apply this procedure first to their existing products and markets to ascertain the outcome in the future if no new investments are added or present ones taken away. If the outcome appears unsatisfactory with respect to uncertainty or return, then characteristics of "ideal" and "acceptable" new investments may be specified, as well as candidates for divestiture identified.

Portfolio design procedures like those described here have their greatest payoff in situations in which managers have different risk/return preferences and in which managers have considerable uncertainty about the future, even though they may agree on the major forces that will shape that future; and in which flexibility is needed. This approach to portfolio design encourages managers to express their individual objectives for return and preferences for amount and type of risk, and to resolve with their colleagues differences in those objectives and preferences. Because the portfolio design procedure outlined here calls for managers to identify and predict the impact of specific environmental factors, the procedure narrows ranges of uncertainty. Note, for example, that without explicit consideration of environmental factors, the variation in return estimates for the plant expansion in the illustration above would be from $40,000 to $80,000; but specifying the impact of each of several environmental influences cut that variation in half, to a $20,000 spread (see Table 1).

Flexibility may be important to evaluate many sets of investments or to resolve differences of opinion among managers. This procedure may be repeated with different environmental influences added or deleted, and with any variety of investment/disinvestment alternatives. If the portfolio that results from this choice process appears unsatisfactory to the managers involved, they may reiterate the procedure, through modifying their preference criteria and/or seeking out additional or different investments. Caution: Managers who seek to alter the attractiveness of the chosen portfolio by revising their estimates of environmental outcomes should ask themselves searchingly whether they are determined on a particular portfolio despite the outcome or depending on whether additional information or new insights may sharpen their forecasts and analysis.

Because management groups seldom have the opportunity to design an entire portfolio from scratch, this procedure will typically be used to change an organization's existing portfolio, through adding or dropping product lines and markets, and through reallocating resources; these activities will gradually reshape the existing portfolio and move it toward the optimum portfolio. On occasion, managers may have the opportunity to design a portfolio of product lines for one particular market, or to choose a set of markets for a limited number of product lines. In such instances, when the resource commitment may be substantial, managers may find these portfolio design procedures helpful, even though this approach by no means guarantees selection of a portfolio that will in hindsight turn out to be the best of any of those evaluated.

SELECTED REFERENCES

COX, WILLIAM E. "Product Portfolio Strategy: A Review of the Boston Consulting Group Approach to Marketing Strategy." 1974 Combined Proceedings of the American Marketing Association, pp. 465–470.

KOTLER, PHILIP. *Marketing Management: Analysis, Planning & Control,* 3d ed. Englewood Cliffs, N.J.: Prentice-Hall, 1976, Chap. 9.

LOCANDER, WILLIAM B., and RICHARD W. SCAMELL. "A Planning Model for Multiple Product Introductions." *Journal of Business Administration,* Spring 1976, vol. 7, no. 2.

STAUDT, THOMAS A. "Program for Product Diversification." *Harvard Business Review,* November–December 1954.

WASSON, CHESTER R. *Dynamic Competitive Strategy and Product Life Cycles.* St. Charles, Ill.: Challenge Books, 1974, pp. 140–160.

WIND, YORAM. "Product Portfolio Analysis: A New Approach to the Product Mix Decision." 1974 Combined Proceedings of the American Marketing Association, pp. 460–464.

APPENDIX*

CALCULATING NET PRESENT VALUE

Investments in business capital assets are distinguishable from most consumer assets because business assets generally have earnings streams associated with them. Analysts define the value of such assets as the present value of future earnings generated by the asset.

The net present value of a proposed investment equals the time-adjusted cash inflows less the time-adjusted cash outflows associated with the investment. If the net present value at an appropriate interest rate of an investment is greater than or equal to zero, the project should be accepted. If the net present value is less than zero, the investment proposal should be rejected.

Cash inflows include revenues from sales and any other income such as service fees, as well as reductions in net working capital and terminal values of plant and equipment. Cash outflows include all fixed and variable cash outlays for costs of production and distribution, plus increases in net working capital and plant and equipment. Noncash charges, such as depreciation and amortization, are not counted as cash outflows. In most instances, it is convenient to consider as inflows the following:

net profit after taxes

+ depreciation (plus other noncash charges)

+ reductions in working capital

+ terminal value of current and fixed assets

Cash outflows, then, may be summarized as follows:

operating losses, less tax savings associated with the loss

+ increases in fixed assets

+ increases in working capital

Because inflows and outflows occur at different times throughout the life of a project and the timing of their occurrence affects the value of an investment, it is useful to specify inflows and outflows by time period, and to calculate a net cash flow per period.

---

*This Appendix was prepared with the assistance of Mary Bochnak, a Graduate Assistant in Finance at the University of Minnesota.

Table A.1

$000
Year

Inflows	Plant built 0	Plant in operation 1	2	3	4	5	Project terminated 6
Profit after tax	–	150	165	182	200	220	–
Depreciation (straight line, $\frac{\$1500}{5 \text{ years}}$)	–	300	300	300	300	300	–
Reduction in working capital		(none until project terminated)					153
Terminal value of fixed assets	–	–	–	–	–	–	–
Total inflows	–	450	465	482	500	550	153
Outflows							
Operating losses	–	–	–	–	–	–	–
Increases in fixed assets	1500	–	–	–	–	–	–
Increases in working capital	–	125	6	7	7	8	–
Total outflows	(1500)	(125)	(6)	(7)	(7)	(8)	–
Net cash flow	(1500)	325	459	475	493	512	153

(Terminal value above equals sum of increases)

Consider, for example, investment in plant capacity to reduce costs and expand sales of an existing product line. Assume that the plant will cost $1.5 million and have a useful life of five years, with negligible scrap or resale value at the end of that period; that this plant will enable profits on the product line to increase by 10 percent per year, beginning with an increase of $150,000 the first year; that working capital will increase initially by $125,000, and by 5 percent of that amount per year thereafter to support increased sales volume. Assume further that the plant construction activity will take place in one year, that the increased sales and profits will occur for the five subsequent years, and that the current assets contributed to the project will be withdrawn in the year following the five years of profit. Then the cash flows will occur as shown in Table A.1.

To obtain the present value of this stream of cash flows, one must choose an interest rate at which they are to be valued, or discounted. (The argument here is that a dollar received today is worth more than one received some years hence; that a dollar spent today costs more than the same expenditure postponed because of the return that the dollar could have earned had it not been spent.) Under capital budgeting theory, the discount rate applied should be equal to the investor's (firm's) marginal cost of capital. Some companies arbitrarily set "hurdle rates" to approximate their opportunity costs (cost of earnings opportunities foregone) as discount rates.

"Present value" tables (a variation of tables of compound interest) or a desk calculator can readily provide the present value, or equivalent value in year 0, of a dollar spent or received in each of several future years. In the example above, if one used a discount rate of 15 percent, the net flows shown above would be multiplied by the discount factor below, and the resulting time-adjusted stream of cash flows would be as follows:

	Year						
	0	1	2	3	4	5	6
Discount factor	1.000	.870	.756	.658	.572	.497	.432
Net cash flow discounted at 15% (000)	($1500)	$282	$346	$312	$281	$253	$ 66

The net present value of a series of payments is merely the sum of the present values of the individual payments. Therefore, to obtain the net present value (value in year 0) of this stream of discounted cash flows, one simply adds up the seven dollar figures above (000 omitted):

($1500) + $282 + $346 + $312 + $281 + $253 + $66 = $40.

This example shows how the net present value of $40,000 was calculated as the "pessimistic" (minimum) estimate for environmental outcome A in Table 1, page 365.

CASES ON PORTFOLIO DESIGN

ADAMS, INC. (A)

Hydraulics System Proposal

In May 1970, the management of Adams, Inc., a manufacturer of fluid-handling equipment, had to decide whether to add a line of pumps, powered by hydraulic pressure, to the company's existing line of pneumatic and electric-powered pumps and related equipment and, if so, what pricing strategy to follow for the new equipment. If the proposal were accepted, Adams would add to its line both the hydraulic pumps and accessory equipment designed specifically for use with those hydraulic pumps. Company officials regarded adding hydraulics as a major extension of the product line. (Adams, Inc., its product line, markets, and marketing activities are described in the Appendix to this case.) Adams officials were investigating hydraulics because prospects for growth in sales of air-powered systems were limited.

Although pumping systems that employed hydraulic equipment might enable Adams to enter some new markets, company marketing executives believed that in most applications the proposed line of hydraulic pump systems would compete directly with the company's existing products and those of Adams' competitors. Although the basic technology used in the design and manufacture of the proposed hydraulic pumps was by no means new, none of the company's competitors in the United States offered hydraulic pumps. A German manufacturer of pumps had, however, incorporated hydraulic pumps into fluid-handling systems for several years, and had gained a significant share of the German market for automobile painting with its hydraulic system. This firm had recently been acquired by one of Adams' principal domestic competitors, Leatroht Pump Company. Adams officials believed that Leatroht might soon attempt to introduce hydraulics systems into the United States. Two other competitors possessed hydraulic system capability, but were believed to require one and a half to two years to bring hydraulics to market. Adams officials doubted that hydraulic systems and components could be patented.

The hydraulic reciprocating pump system that Adams would manufacture resembled in function the company's current air-powered models, except that the power transfer medium was hydraulic fluid instead of compressed air. In a hydraulic system an electric motor operated a hydraulic pump, which forced hydraulic fluid from a reservoir through steel tubing to a hydraulically powered reciprocating pump ("hydraulic motor"), from which the hydraulic fluid returned through the hydraulic pump to the reservoir. The "hydraulic motor" in turn operated in a material pump (see Exhibit 1).

Both hydraulic and air-powered systems consisted of three principal sets of components; (1) the materials pump, (2) the power pack, and (3) the application equipment (sometimes called "accessories"). Material pumps used in hydraulic systems were similar or identical to those used in air systems, and could perform the same functions. Both air and hydraulic power packs could support from one to twelve materials pumps. Company officials estimated that a hydraulic power pack needed to support a twelve-pump system would cost approximately one and a half times as much as a hydraulic power pack necessary for a single materials pump. Power packs for air systems were priced between $2,000 (one pump system) and $10,000 (twelve-pump system). For comparable systems, hydraulic power packs were lighter in weight than air power packs. Hydraulic systems offered quieter operation than air systems. Application equipment was essentially the same for both hydraulic and air systems.

If Adams were to offer hydraulic pumps, the company would make complete hydraulic power packs, materials pumps, and necessary connecting and application equipment. Although hydraulic power packs and their components could be purchased separately, Adams management believed that the company should manufacture its own power packs to ensure a reliable supply of equipment that would complement the pumps. Company officials stated that the equipment distributors through which Adams sold more than 80 percent of its fluid-handling equipment and the end users themselves knew very little about hydraulic power packs, and would likely buy hydraulic systems only if a supplier provided a complete system including materials pumps and power packs. Adams officials estimated their costs to manufacture hydraulic power packs at $450-$900, depending on the size of the total system. Investigation of alternative sources of supply indicated that comparable power packs would cost as much or more to purchase.

Neither Adams nor its principal competitors manufactured or sold air power packs. Distributors and users of fluid-handling equipment bought air power packs separately. Adams officials characterized the air compressor and motor business as "very highly competitive."

Company officials noted that market estimates for pumping equipment included pumps and connecting equipment, but not air compressors. They reasoned that sales of hydraulic power packs would take business from air-compressor manufacturers, rather than from Adams' principal competitors in pumping equipment. Further, they argued that Adams would gain competitive advantage by offering a complete system for fluid handling, one that did not require separate purchase of an air compressor.

Hydraulic systems might require lower initial investment, depending upon the pricing strategy Adams chose, and appeared to offer operating cost savings compared to air systems. Costs of installation and application equipment were expected in general to be similar for both types of systems, but could well differ in particular situations. Installation of hydraulic systems required careful supervision to assure that fluid leaks would not develop. In instances where hydraulic systems were installed to replace or parallel existing air systems, installation costs could equal costs to the customer of the hydraulic equipment itself. In new or expanded facilities, costs of installation were slightly higher for hydraulics.

In two comparisons made by the company of medium-size painting systems in which either air or hydraulic powered pumps could be used, the hydraulic systems cost much less to operate. In one system, company engineers estimated that the electricity needed to operate an air system for one day would come to $13.92. The comparable hydraulic system would require only $2.64 in electricity per day. In the other case, the electricity needed to operate the hydraulic system amounted to $657 per year, against $3,154 for the comparable air system. The principal reason for this difference was that air systems required motors with approximately five times as much horsepower as those needed to operate the more efficient hydraulic systems. Because these tests had been conducted for a limited time under controlled conditions and under close supervision of Adams' technical specialists, many executives were skeptical about the results.

The potential savings in operating costs led some company personnel to recommend pricing hydraulics systems higher than comparable air systems. These men argued that premiums of $2,000 to $3,000 above air systems could be justified on the basis of savings in electricity costs alone.

Other executives believed that coming out with a hydraulic line would provide the company an opportunity to compete more vigorously against manufacturers of air systems, almost all of which priced their products 5 to 10 percent below the Adams air line. These executives argued that the hydraulic line should be offered at prices equal to competitors' comparable air systems. The advantages of hydraulics, they reasoned, would cause customers to switch to Adams' equipment from competitors' air systems. Adams would not be "cutting prices," because prices on the present air systems would remain unchanged.

According to Adams officials, hydraulic and air systems could compete with one another in the "middle 80 to 85 percent" of the air product line. For the 15 to 20 percent of applications comprised of very small and extremely large systems, however, hydraulic systems were not appropriate.

In 1970 the prices to users of air systems for typical finishing and coating applications were as shown in Table 1.

Distributors typically earned margins of 30 percent on pumps and accessories. Margins on air power packs, however, ranged from 5 to 10 percent of the price at which distributors sold to users. Distributors' margins on hydraulic power packs were ordinarily 20 percent.

Company officials believed that prices for 70 percent of all applications would be within 20 to 25 percent on either side of those for typical finishing/coating systems. A range of 35–40 percent above or below the prices for a typical finishing/coating system would include 85 percent of all applications. These ranges were thought to apply not only to prices of air systems but also to manufacturing costs of hydraulic systems.

Adams officials estimated manufacturing costs for hydraulics systems components, all of which the company could manufacture or assemble itself, as shown in Table 2.

Table 1

PRICES TO USERS OF ADAMS'
AND COMPETITORS' AIR SYSTEMS
(TYPICAL FINISHING/COATING APPLICATION)

	Small system (4 pumps)		Large system (10 pumps)	
	Adams	Competitors	Adams	Competitors
Pump assembly	$2,800	$2,400	$ 7,000	$ 6,000
Accessories	800	700	2,000	1,750
Air power pack*	2,200	2,200	7,500	7,500
	$5,800	$5,300	$16,500	$15,250

*Adams and its competitors did not manufacture air power packs. Distributors bought these power packs from compressor manufacturers, coupled them with pump assemblies, and resold them to users at the prices shown.

Table 2

ESTIMATED MANUFACTURING COSTS OF ADAMS
HYDRAULIC SYSTEM
(TYPICAL FINISHING APPLICATIONS)

	Small system (4 pumps)	Large system (10 pumps)
Pump assembly	$ 840	$2,100
Accessories	260	650
Hydraulic power pack	475	900
	$1,575	$3,650

Initially, Adams would manufacture hydraulic pumps for applications in the industrial and appliance markets. Within the industrial market, hydraulic pumps were thought to be especially well suited to applications in finishing or coating, food processing, metering, and original equipment manufacturing (OEM). Hydraulic systems reliably provided constant pressure, without the extensive system of regulators and frequent adjustment needed in many air systems. Hydraulic systems offered superior performance and decreased operating costs in comparison with the air-powered systems currently used in finishing applications. Manufacturers of furniture, of coated building materials (e.g., paneling), and of appliances and other metal products that required finishing were thought to be likely prospects for hydraulic systems. Company officials believed that food-processing firms would prefer hydraulic to air systems because the former had no exhaust, which could pose problems of sanitation in food manufacture. One OEM application considered appropriate for hydraulics was the installation of hydraulic ink transfer systems within printing presses that were themselves hydraulically powered. In the appliance market, which Adams served with its own direct sales force, principal applications were believed to be (1) finishing and coating, and (2) movement of viscous raw materials.

As demand increased, Adams would expand its hydraulic line to include pumps of different sizes and for other applications. Company personnel believed that few new service skills and new spare parts would be needed for either initial or later applications of the hydraulic line.

Adams executives thought that some 750 of the company's distributors which served the industrial market could handle the Adams hydraulic system effectively. Typically, these distributors had sales volumes of $250,000 to $1,000,000, and could provide sales, parts, and service support that Adams considered adequate for the new system. Many of these distributors would incorporate the hydraulic equipment into complete customer installations. Company officials believed that these distributors could, with little difficulty, learn to advise customers on the installation and operation of hydraulic systems, whose operating characteristics differed only slightly from air systems.

Adams would introduce the new line with sales training to its own sales force and distributors' salespeople, and with advertising to prospective customers. A budget of $30,000 was proposed for the first year. In addition, "missionary" sales help would be available from headquarters personnel at an estimated cost of $10,000. These expenditures were considered "start-up" costs and were not expected to recur. Company marketing specialists indicated that sales expense for new products typically ranged from 15 to 20 percent of sales for three to five years.

Apart from the initial marketing expenditures to launch the product, management expected to incur additional costs for manufacturing and carrying inventory. Design, engineering, and tooling costs were estimated at $125,000. Analyses of manufacturing costs indicated that hydraulic pumps might cost 1 to 5 percent less to manufacture than air-powered pumps. Some company engineers believed, however, that manufacturing costs of hydraulic systems might exceed those of air pumps by 1 to 2 percent. In 1969, manufacturing costs amounted to approximately 45 percent of sales of pumps and related equipment sold to the industrial market. Company analysts noted that historically every dollar of sales had required 20-40 cents of inventory support, and about 25 cents in receivables.

Adams officials attempted to derive sales projections for the hydraulics line from the company's forecasts of market growth and penetration of the current product line. These latter forecasts indicated that the total market for air-powered pumps would increase at an annual rate of between 5 and 10 percent, and that Adams' share might increase to 10-15 percent of that market within five years. Company personnel estimated that the market for hydraulics would initially increase more rapidly, at an annual rate of 20 percent, but that the annual rate of increase would be less than 15 percent by 1975. By that year, some Adams officials estimated that the company might be selling as many as 13,000 hydraulic pumps per year, which could account for 16 percent of the total market for hydraulic pumps.

The task of forecasting demand for both air and hydraulic pumps was complicated by the difficulty of estimating the extent to which hydraulic pumps might compete with air-powered pumps. One Adams executive estimated that as much as 50 percent of Adams' pump sales might be composed of hydraulic pumps within five years, depending upon the price relationships between hydraulic and air systems. Company officials believed that the impacts of hydraulics on sales of the company's current product line would be greatest in the industrial and appliance markets, somewhat less in the cleaning market, and least in the automotive and painting contractor markets. (These markets are described in the Appendix to this case.)

Proponents of the hydraulics project countered that the new product would increase sales of all Adams products. They argued that the hydraulics line would give Adams technical leadership in the market, and provide a new and exciting concept for their salespeople and distributors to present to customers. These executives pointed out that, until the early 1960s, Adams was highly regarded within the industrial and appliance markets as an innovative company, one that could help customers solve their problems. This reputation, in the opinions of those officers, gave Adams a noticeable competitive advantage in these markets. These men believed that during the past five to ten years competitors had closed this gap, and that Adams needed to introduce the hydraulics line to regain its prestige and competitive advantage. They also argued that offering a full line of fluid-handling systems—both air and hydraulics—would lead users to prefer Adams air systems over those of competitors.

Although they acknowledged the advantages of hydraulics, other Adams executives questioned the advisability of adding the hydraulics line. These executives argued that air systems were widely accepted, and that users had not found major dissatisfactions with air systems. Furthermore, once an air system was installed in a plant, additional pumps could be added up to the capacity limits of existing compressors, without installing additional connecting air lines. Company analysts believed, however, that up to 90 percent of the industrial plants currently in operation had little or no excess capacity in their present air systems. The executives pointed out that hydraulic systems were less flexible than air, because two sets of steel tubing for hydraulic fluid transfer had to be installed. If the tubing broke, the resulting spillage of hydraulic fluid could be messy and, in food-processing operations, unsanitary. The hydraulic fluid used in Adams systems was flammable, and could constitute a fire hazard. Finally, these executives were concerned about the effect of sales of hydraulics on the sales of air systems, and questioned whether the company needed two similar product lines.

If the decision to proceed with the project were made immediately, the hydraulics line could be ready for shipment by mid-1971. Some executives feared that, if the decision were delayed, enthusiasm within the company for the project might decline. Other officials argued that any competitive advantage Adams might have by being first in the market would be diminished if the hydraulic project were delayed. Company officials who favored hydraulics argued that the sooner Adams entered the market, the greater the competitive advantage the company would have. If the company proceeded with hydraulics, marketing personnel would have to develop five-year forecasts of sales and profits, based on a detailed marketing plan for each appropriate market. As part of their planning, marketing personnel would have to determine price levels for hydraulics systems of different sizes and for the components of hydraulic systems.

Exhibit 1

ADAMS, INC. (A)
OUTLINE OF HYDRAULIC AND AIR SYSTEMS

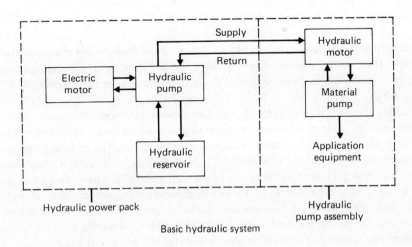

Basic hydraulic system

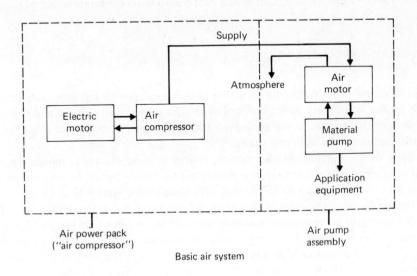

Basic air system

APPENDIX

ADAMS, INC. (A)

In 1969, Adams had sales in excess of $43 million, more than double the company's sales in 1964. 1969 earnings before taxes of $6.4 million were more than two and one-half times the company's earnings in 1964. Current financial statements appear in Exhibits A.1 and A.2.

During the past several years, Adams had developed products to meet the needs of specific markets, then taken those products to new markets whose requirements, in turn, prompted additional product modification and development. The company had in recent years undertaken only those new ventures that were expected to yield a return on investment of at least 25 percent after taxes. In the spring of 1970, Adams executives believed they would have more ventures that met this criterion than they could fund. According to one executive, ideas for new ventures surfaced easily at Adams; the problem, as he saw it, was to choose the best ideas, to avoid spending executive time and energy on programs that would not contribute significantly to the growth of the company, and to concentrate on those ventures that would continue to build corporate sales and profits.

THE CURRENT PRODUCT LINE

In 1970 Adams manufactured a wide line of pumping systems and other related equipment for use in a variety of applications in each of several different markets. According to management, no one of the company's 600 products or systems accounted for more than 10 percent of the company's sales.

Each Adams system included pumps, reservoirs (if appropriate), application equipment (e.g., spray guns or nozzles), and connecting equipment (hoses, fittings, and clamps). Some systems also included devices that would enable the system to store, mix, meter, and dispense a specified amount of a particular fluid compound at a predetermined rate.

According to company management, the most important single piece of equipment in a system was the pump. Both distributors and users of pumps and systems traditionally regarded Adams pumps as high quality, and frequently incorporated Adams pumps into systems sold by Adams' competitors. Most Adams pumps were of reciprocating double-action design, consisting of a power source and a fluid pump joined to the power source by a connecting rod, which caused the pumping action. Adams also manufactured electrically driven centrifugal pumps. Pumps were manufactured in a variety of designs and sizes to accommodate differences in the material to be handled, the required rate of delivery, and the type of container from which the material was to be pumped.

In addition to original equipment, the company offered replacement packings, seals, hoses, and metal parts for its pumps and related equipment. Periodic replacement of packings and seals was necessary to maintain efficiency and prevent loss of the material being handled. Because Adams equipment was often installed in production line operations where immediate availability of replacement parts was essential, many Adams customers maintained their own inventories of replacement parts. Sales of parts constituted 30 percent of Adams' total sales.

Adams systems and components were normally priced 5 to 10 percent higher than similar products of competitors. Company executives believed that the superior quality and features of Adams equipment justified this premium price. The officials believed that users paid full list price for parts, but were occasionally able to obtain discounts off the list price for equipment and systems.

Company officials estimated that approximately half of the company's sales of individual items carried list prices below $1950. Included in this group were small systems, many individual products, and all parts. The other half of the company's sales, comprised of products with list prices in excess of $1950, included larger individual pieces of equipment and. most systems. Unit prices ranged from a few dollars, for some parts, to more than $100,000 for complete large systems. A typical small spray painting or cleaning outfit carried a list price between $940 and $2275, depending upon the power of the pump employed. The pump itself represented approximately five-eighths of the cost of such an outfit.

MARKETS

In 1969, more than $9.8 million (approximately 23 percent) of the company's sales came from markets outside the United States. More than half of this amount represented equipment manufactured in the United States and marketed through the company's overseas facilities. The importance of overseas markets to the company had increased steadily during the past five years. Adams products were manufactured in Canada, France, and Japan. In addition, the company owned sales subsidiaries in Europe, South America, Hong Kong, and Canada.

Of the company's $33.2 million of domestic sales in 1969, all but $3.8 million were made to five major markets: (1) automotive maintenance, (2) industrial manufacturing and processing, (3) painting contractors, (4) cleaning, and (5) manufacturers of major household appliances. The remaining $3.8 million represented government sales and special contract work for one customer.

Of Adams' five major markets, the largest in 1969 was the industrial market, followed by the painting-contractor and automotive-maintenance markets. An index of sales to each of the company's five markets from 1965 through 1969 appears in Exhibits A.3 and A.4. [*]

---

[*] The company has authorized the use of figures which are judged to be useful for purposes of discussion, but do not necessarily reflect the company's experience.

Users of Adams equipment in the automotive-maintenance market, which consisted primarily of fleet operators, car dealers, and service stations, purchased Adams chassis lubricators, gear lube dispensers, and a variety of other special-purpose lubrication devices, including systems that contained remote pumps connected by supply hoses and overhead service reels to appropriate nozzles at the point of service. Many of these systems had the capability to store, meter, and pump a predetermined amount of lubricant.

Adams management estimated that the total automotive-maintenance market might be as large as $50 million in 1969, and placed the company's current share at just over 10 percent. Officials believed that Adams' penetration varied within the market from 5 percent in agricultural-equipment applications to 20 percent in hand-lubrication equipment. Adams was one of three companies that together accounted for about 25 percent of the automotive-maintenance market. Company officials expected the automotive-maintenance market to increase at the rate of 4 percent per year. Management forecast that Adams could increase its sales to the automotive-maintenance market more than 10 percent per year within the next three years, barring changes in the company's or competitors' offerings and activities.

Within the industrial market, Adams products were used by manufacturers of furniture, appliances, boats, and building materials; manufacturers and users of aircraft and railroad equipment; processors of food and a variety of chemicals; and graphic art shops. Manufacturers of durable goods used Adams systems to store, meter, mix, transfer, and dispense materials at different stages in the production process. The manufacturers also used Adams paint transfer and applications systems for coating and painting their products. In addition, makers and users of aircraft and railroad equipment used Adams equipment for exterior spray-cleaning of the products. Firms engaged in the processing of food and chemicals used Adams fluid transfer systems to move and control liquids and viscous fluids such as catsup and peanut butter within the production process.

Company officials estimated the industrial market for pumping equipment at about $150 million, approximately 60 percent of which involved finishing applications. Adams was believed to hold somewhat less than a 10 percent share of the total industrial market in 1969. That share varied, according to company estimates, from less than 4 percent among sales to manufacturers of metal products (primarily finishing applications) to more than 15 percent among sales of fluid-handling equipment to railroads (primarily cleaning applications). Approximately half of Adams' sales to the industrial market were for finishing applications.

In finishing applications within the industrial market, the Wellman and Ackler Company and Leatroht Pump together held more than half of the market. In applications involving cleaning and transfer of viscous fluids, company officials believed Adams to be the dominant firm. No competitor held a larger share of the market for those applications than Adams. Company officials expected that the industrial market would grow at approximately 10 percent per year for the next few years, and hoped to double their present penetration of that market.

The painting contractor market, estimated at $130 million, included the few large specialized painting contractors as well as numerous smaller painting contractors. This market also included a major paint manufacturer which offered Adams portable paint spray equipment, primarily for sale to small contractors and users, through its chain of more than 500 retail paint stores. Company officials believed Adams to be one of the largest firms in this market, which was divided among several firms.

Adams management expected the painting contractor market to grow to more than $350 million within the next five years, and hoped to increase the company's penetration of that market to 25 percent from the present level of slightly more than 5 percent.

The market for cleaning systems was composed of cleaning contractors who had contractual agreements with a variety of industrial customers to perform cleaning functions, and of large industrial users themselves. These customers in some cases bought complete cleaning systems, which incorporated Adams equipment, from manufacturers of chemical cleaning compounds. Adams' principal products in this market included air-powered and electric-powered pressure-washing equipment for use in cleaning food-processing plants, locomotives, airplanes, automobiles, buildings, printing presses and a variety of other items. Estimates of the size and growth potential of this market were unavailable.

The manufacturers of major household appliances and certain of their subsidiaries comprised the appliance market. Total sales of fluid-handling equipment to appliance manufacturers amounted to approximately $40 million, of which about $25 million involved finishing equipment. Adams sold fluid materials handling equipment, cleaning systems and complete paint spraying and finishing systems direct to appliance manufacturers. Slightly more than half of Adams' sales to appliance manufacturers involved finishing systems and their components. Management estimated that the company held almost 10 percent of the $40 million appliance market. Adams officials expected the total size of this market to increase between 5 and 6 percent per year, and believed that the company could increase its penetration to almost 15 percent by 1973. Management believed that Wellman and Ackler and Leatroht together dominated the appliance market for finishing applications, but that Adams was among the largest firms in supplying pumping equipment for other appliance applications.

In all markets combined, Adams faced competition from two larger companies, Wellman and Ackler ($65 million sales) and Leatroht ($40 million sales), and from twenty others, most of which, like Adams, held dominant positions in particular submarkets but had little penetration in other submarkets. According to management, this pattern of uneven market penetration came about because one manufacturer would develop a specialized product for a particular application and thereby obtain a dominant position in the submarket for that special product. Once customers had purchased such a specialized product, they would typically be reluctant to switch to a slightly modified version of that product offered by another manufacturer. Customers would, however, switch manufacturers and/or equipment if their own requirements changed or if products that were significantly superior technically or economically became available. Management believed that Adams and most of its largest competitors possessed the technical skill and products necessary to adapt to most special applications.

Throughout all markets company officials believed that competitive advantage could be gained primarily by product superiority, dependability, and service, combined with prompt identification of and response to new application opportunities. These officials thought that Adams' reputation had been built primarily on the durability and long life of its products.

MARKETING

Domestic sales of Adams products were handled through a national account sales force, the Appliance division, and a regional sales organization that covered the entire United States. In 1969, the company estimated that direct costs of selling activities related to the sale of products within the United States amounted to 12 to 13 percent of domestic sales. Advertising, sales promotion, and sales support activities added one to one and one-half percent of domestic sales.

The national accounts sales force of four men handled direct sales in the automotive, industrial, painting, contractor, and cleaning markets to all large customers and others whose purchasing was coordinated centrally, but whose operations were dispersed throughout several of Adams' sales territories.

The Appliance division sold directly to some 400 plants. Approximately 70 percent of the time of the 13 salespeople who served the Appliance market was devoted to seeking business from prospective customers. The remainder of the Appliance salespeople's time was spent in learning about new Adams products and their applications.

The regional sales organization, which handled sales of Adams products to government agencies and to the independent distributors who subsequently sold to users, included 5 Regional Managers, 10 Regional Sales Managers, and 100 salespeople.

Within a specified geographic territory, each salesperson typically concentrated his or her efforts on distributors that served particular markets. A salesperson who concentrated on the industrial market typically spent 60 percent of his or her time calling on the independent distributors that sold Adams products, 30 percent making calls with distributors' salespeople on present or prospective users of Adams products, and 10 percent at meetings and trade shows. Salespeople who concentrated on the automotive-maintenance, painting-contractor or cleaning markets spent most of their time with distributors' salespeople, making demonstrations to customers. Adams operated five regional headquarters offices and seven branch offices, all twelve of which included parts warehouses and service personnel, in addition to the administrative staffs.

The Adams regional sales force sold the company's products to more than 4,600 independent, nonexclusive distributors. Almost every one of these distributors specialized in a particular market (automotive, industrial, painting-contractor, cleaning) and, therefore, handled primarily the products designed by Adams and its principal competitors for the particular market the distributor served. Distributors that served the industrial market combined equipment from several different manufacturers, sometimes modified certain components, and then sold complete systems to users. Distributors that served the automotive, painting, and cleaning markets made available to customers a full line of products and systems from each of several manufacturers. Both types of distributors maintained salespeople, whose principal responsibilities were, in order, servicing present customers and seeking new customers. Adams officials estimated that each of the largest 75 distributors had three to six salespeople, but that smaller distributors seldom employed more than two or three and operated on very limited capital. Only the larger distributors were considered capable of selling complex fluid-handling systems.

In the industrial market, Adams' principal competitors sold both direct and through distributors to most of the customers Adams served through distributors. Management believed that competitors' salespeople might be more aware than Adams' salespeople of problems and opportunities in a particular industrial submarket, because competitors' salespeople spent more total time in contact with users. In other markets, however, both Adams and its principal competitors used similar channels and selling methods.

Sales to the largest 100 accounts in each of the company's five markets represented more than two-thirds of the company's sales. Company officials noted that the percentage of Adams' total business contributed by these top 100 accounts in each market had been decreasing during the past five years, although the total dollar volume of those sales had increased. Sales to distributors were made at list price less 30 percent. For an item whose list price was $1500, a distributor would pay $1050.

Exhibit A.1

ADAMS, INC., AND SUBSIDIARIES
CONSOLIDATED INCOME STATEMENT FOR THE YEAR
ENDING DECEMBER 31, 1969
(000)

		Dollars	Percent
Net sales		43,068	100.0
Cost of products sold		20,950	48.6
Gross margin		22,118	51.4
Expenses			
Product development	1,125		2.6
Selling and sales support	9,091		21.1
General and administrative	5,281		12.3
Interest and other expenses, less other income; net	269		0.6
Total expenses		15,766	36.6
Earnings before taxes		6,352	14.8
Taxes on income		3,415	7.9
Earnings after taxes		2,937	6.9

Exhibit A.2

ADAMS, INC. (A) AND SUBSIDIARIES
CONSOLIDATED BALANCE SHEET DECEMBER 31, 1969 (000)

Assets	
Cash	$ 1,221
Accounts receivable	10,261
Inventory	14,279
Property, plant, and equipment	10,303
Other assets	961
Total	$37,025

Liabilities and equity	
Accounts payable	$ 8,515
Notes payable	2,054
Taxes payable	3,987
Long-term debt	6,941
Deferred taxes	880
Minority interest in subsidiary	742
Shareholders' equity	13,906
Total	$37,025

Source: Annual Report

Exhibit A.3

ADAMS, INC. (A)—INDEX OF DOLLAR SALES BY MARKET[a], 1965-1969
(1969 TOTAL SALES = 100)

Market	1965	1966	1967	1968	1969
Automotive maintenance	18	16	16	17	18
Industrial	20	24	28	35	41
Painting contractors	10	12	13	19	25
Cleaning	4	4	4	3	3
Appliance	10	11	8	14	13
Total	62	67	69	88	100

[a] International sales, government sales, and miscellaneous domestic sales not included
Source: Company Records

Exhibit A.4

ADAMS, INC. (A)—INDEX OF UNIT SALES OF PUMPS[a], 1965-1969 (1969 TOTAL SALES = 100)

Market	1965	1966	1967	1968	1969
Automotive maintenance	30	26	24	21	20
Industrial	20	24	26	29	34
Painting contractors	18	19	18	24	31
Cleaning	14	14	13	11	12
Appliance	3	3	3	3	3
Total	85	86	84	88	100

[a] Includes pumps incorporated into systems as well as pumps sold individually.
Source: Company Records

ADAMS, INC. (B)

Proposal to Acquire the Lowell-Pearson Company

In the spring of 1970, senior corporate officers of Adams, Inc., a manufacturer of fluid-handling equipment, were deciding whether or not to attempt to acquire the Lowell-Pearson Company as a vehicle for entering the market for electrostatic finishing equipment. If they decided to acquire Lowell-Pearson, Adams officials would then have to determine whether they should pay almost $2 million for the company.

From time to time during the preceding five years, Adams management had considered adding electrostatic capability to the company's lines of conventional finishing and coating equipment. Adams currently marketed paint-transfer systems, pumps, spray guns, paint heaters, and other related products for the application of paints and coatings. (Adams, Inc., its product line, markets, and marketing activities are described in the appendix to Adams, Inc. (A).)

Company officials had explored two possibilities in addition to acquisition, namely: (1) developing Adams' in-house electrostatic capability, and (2) licensing the needed technology from another firm. To date, neither of these alternatives appealed to corporate executives. If Adams were to develop its own electrostatic capability, management believed that it would take the company at least four to five years to become current with the "state of the art." Adams presently lacked the technical capability in electrostatics, electrical engineering, and other expertise that would be necessary to develop an in-house capability and to train salespeople in electrostatic concepts and products.

Based on past experience, it was estimated that a staff of six full-time engineers plus appropriate supporting personnel and facilities would be necessary. Furthermore, if Adams decided to develop its own capability, it would also be necessary to work around existing patents in order to avoid patent infringement and resulting lawsuits. Although licensing would avoid legal proceedings, Adams would be in the position of requesting a license from a competitor already established in the market. Company officials believed that license fees would be prohibitively high and would put Adams at a severe competitive disadvantage.

FINISHING PROCESSES

By 1970 there were five different processes used in finishing and coating systems. Two processes, referred to in the industry as "conventional air spray" and "conventional airless," had been employed for many years in a wide variety of applications. The other three processes were incorporated into the newer, electrostatic systems which to date had been employed primarily in certain applications. These three processes were referred to, respectively, as "air-atomizing electrostatic," "airless (or hydraulic) electrostatic," and "centrifugal electrostatic."

Conventional Systems

Conventional air spray: In these systems, paint was atomized and deposited on a surface by a high-velocity stream of air. The air stream struck a free stream of liquid paint or other coating at high speed, breaking up the stream of liquid into tiny drops. The force of the air pressure then propelled these drops onto the surface to be coated. Conventional air-spray systems were used in literally hundreds of different finishing and coating applications, and were by far the most common in use in 1970. Their cost ranged from several hundred dollars for the simplest system to more than $100,000 for large, complex finishing systems. Company officials believed that typical systems ranged from $5,000 to $17,000.

Conventional airless: In the airless atomization process, hydraulic pressure was used to force the paint through a very small orifice under high pressure. Viscous and surface tension forces of a paint particle reacted with the velocity and air-drag forces to form a finely atomized fluid, which the hydraulic pressure then propelled to the surface to be finished. Airless systems were newer and far less prevalent than air-spray systems, and could not substitute for air-spray systems in certain applications. In general, airless systems might have somewhat higher initial costs, but lower operating costs, than comparable air spray systems.

Electrostatic Systems

All three electrostatic finishing processes operated under a fundamental law of physics that unlike charges attract and like charges repel one another. Paint particles were atomized (reduced from a liquid into separate drops) and then ionized (given a negative charge) as they left the dispenser. The negative charge of all the paint particles caused them to repel each other and therefore provided a wide dispersion of the spray. The object to be coated was grounded and therefore had a positive charge in relation to the paint spray. This difference in charges literally pulled the paint particles onto the object (see Exhibit 1.)

According to Adams technical specialists, all three electrostatic processes possessed certain advantages over conventional finishing processes, but shared characteristics that might make them less suitable than conventional processes in certain applications. Company officials estimated that electrostatic systems could in time account for one out of every four systems employed in finishing operations.

In electrostatic systems "overspray" was greatly reduced because paint that at first missed or rebounded from the object was still attracted to the grounded object and therefore returned to be deposited on rear or side surfaces. This phenomenon, "electrostatic wrap-around," made possible the finishing of many small items by spraying from one side only. In such cases, items that previously had to be finished by hand could be finished on automatic systems.[*] Reduced "overspray" had several benefits; namely: (1)

---

[*] In both conventional and electrostatic systems, coatings could be applied either by an automatic method or by a hand gun. In automatic systems the dispenser was preset to discharge coating automatically as the objects to be coated passed by the dispenser on a conveyer. Hand guns required an operator to apply the coating manually.

costs of finishing material might be reduced by 15 to 50 percent; (2) maintenance costs might be cut because of less booth cleanup and less strain on the plant ventilation system; (3) fewer paint particles in the air inside a plant would cut air pollution and enhance workers' health and safety.

Adams technical specialists also pointed out that electrostatic systems could use either liquid or powder coatings, whereas conventional systems could use only liquid coatings. Use of powder coatings could reduce material costs still further, because powder that did not adhere to the object to be finished could be recycled for further use. Furthermore, the absence of solvent reduced dangers to workers' health and made it unnecessary to install additional equipment to reduce solvent vapors to within acceptable legal limits. But because commercial application of powder coating was still in its infancy, precise identification of all applications in which powder coating might displace liquid could not be made, nor could the market potential for powder be estimated.

Despite the advantages of electrostatic systems, the electrostatic process had some inherent limitations. Because the paint particles were charged, they might migrate more readily to nearby surfaces than to more distant surfaces of the object being finished. This phenomenon could produce poor penetration of finish into corners and recessed surfaces. In some electrostatic systems, special provisions were required if electroconductive finishes were to be used, and in many electrostatic systems water-base paints could not be used at all. In manual electrostatic systems, dirt or lint particles surrounding the painter could be attracted to the surface being finished and might render the quality of the finished job unsatisfactory. In automatic systems, color change required a delay of several minutes more than that ordinarily needed in a conventional system. In any electrostatic system, the item being finished had to accept and hold a positive charge well in order for the finishing job to be effective. Finally, although electrostatic systems were designed to be inherently safe (they had low amperage characteristics, alarm circuits, and overload circuits), carelessness had caused serious accidents. A typical electrostatic operation required very high voltage (60,000-100,000 volts). With manual systems, there was always the danger that an electrical arc could strike the operator. Since the amperage was low, such an arc would not be fatal. However, if the operator jumped, injury was possible.

In 1970, electrostatic systems were used in a variety of applications. Stationary automatic systems were used for coating tubular furniture, automobile air cleaners, oil filters, motor starters, and numerous other products handled on overhead or spindle conveyers. Wax coatings were applied to automobiles with this type of system, and Teflon coatings on cookware were almost universally applied electrostatically.

Reciprocating (movable) automatic electrostatic systems were particularly useful in painting surfaces that could not easily be reached by hand sprayers, such as automobile hood and roof surfaces, refrigerator tops, or continuous steel sheets.

Manual electrostatic systems were employed in situations where human flexibility was necessary. Typical uses of manual systems included the painting of industrial machinery (e.g., bulldozers, trucks, and other vehicles), ornamental iron, wood furniture (e.g., baby cribs), and other situations where manual control was vital.

In "air-atomizing" or "airless" (hydraulic) electrostatic systems, a typical method of applying an electrostatic charge to the atomized particles was to use a needle-sharp electrode, which induced a negative charge on the paint particles.

Air-atomizing electrostatic: In this system, paint or other coatings were atomized by a stream of air as in the conventional system, and the atomized particles then received an electric charge. The attraction between the negatively charged particles of coating and the grounded object to be coated, rather than the force of the air stream alone, was the principal force responsible for depositing the coating on the object.

Airless (hydraulic) electrostatic: In this type of finishing system particles were atomized by hydraulic pressure (as in conventional airless systems). These fine particles received a negative charge, which led them to be deposited on the object to be coated, which was itself grounded (positively charged).

Adams technical specialists believed that use of either air-atomized or airless electrostatic processes in a finishing system could reduce direct labor costs, because the increased coverage efficiency of these electrostatic systems made possible production-line speeds that were higher than those of conventional finishing systems. Nevertheless, air-atomizing and airless electrostatic systems were generally substantially more expensive to install than conventional systems. Air-atomizing and airless electrostatic systems ranged from $6,000 to $260,000. Typical automatic systems of either type (air-atomizing electrostatic or airless electrostatic) cost from $40,000 to $50,000; comparable systems using hand guns cost approximately half that amount.

Centrifugal electrostatic systems: In this type of process, the coating material was atomized by the centrifugal force generated by a rotating disc or bell throwing globules of fluid off its periphery in a radial direction. These negatively charged globules of fluid were attracted, as in other electrostatic systems, to the positively charged object that was to receive the coating. Centrifugal electrostatic systems operated somewhat more slowly than air-atomizing and airless electrostatic systems, and were not well suited for building thick or heavy coatings on an object. Because particles moved at relatively low velocity, they could not penetrate remote surfaces and recesses as effectively as particles in an air-atomizing or airless electrostatic system. In some instances, the doughnut shape of the rotating bell could cause an uneven thickness of coating to be deposited.

Patents on centrifugal electrostatic systems were held only by Margrave, which leased its system directly to users. Manufacturers and users of centrifugal electrostatic systems had to lease the equipment from Margrave and pay Margrave a royalty on every gallon of material dispensed through the system.

Engineering personnel at Adams summarized their own comparative analyses of the three types of electrostatic systems in Table 1.

Company technical specialists believed the decisions to choose an electrostatic system over a conventional system and which electrostatic system to use depended

Table 1
COMPARISON AMONG ELECTROSTATIC SYSTEMS

Characteristic	Air-atomizing electrostatic	Airless electrostatic (hydraulic)	Centrifugal electrostatic
Wrap-around	Good	Good	Excellent
Penetration to recessed areas	Excellent	Fair	Poor
Fluid-flow rate	Medium	High	Medium
Quality of finish	Excellent	Fair	Good
Uniformity of film build	Excellent	Good	Good
Ability to handle variety of paint	Excellent	Fair	Fair
Paint reformulation necessary	Unlikely	Maybe	Likely
Relative cost	Least expensive	Medium priced	Leased from Margrave

primarily upon the amount of paint or coating used, the configuration of objects to be finished, and the standardization of types of paint and of colors. Exhibit 2, taken from a Lowell-Pearson brochure, shows the type of air-atomizing or airless electrostatic system that company recommended to replace conventional systems for particular types of applications.

THE MARKET FOR FINISHING EQUIPMENT

Adams marketing personnel estimated that in 1970 the total market for in-plant finishing systems, including royalty and lease payments, was approximately $115 million. Of this amount, some $80 million was believed to represent sales of conventional equipment. The remainder, approximately $35 million, was related to electrostatic finishing systems.

Of the $35 million market for electrostatic finishing, Adams officials estimated that some $10 million represented transfer payments from some of the industry's members for the right to use one or more of some other member's patents, and receipts from equipment leasing. The balance of $25 million represented sales of electrostatic finishing equipment.

An association of manufacturers of electrostatic finishing equipment predicted that by 1974 material used in electrostatic coating processes would increase to almost two times the amount used in 1970. This growth rate was expected to be greater than the growth for other types of coating.

Furthermore, sales of the electrostatic equipment necessary to attain these levels of material usage were expected to experience similar growth. In fact, Margrave officials stated that the industry association figures were too conservative, and predicted that the industry's sales of electrostatic equipment would increase more than four-fold from 1970 to 1975.

Margrave was clearly the industry's leader, as illustrated by the following estimates of market share compiled by industry observers:

Margrave	More than 50%
Wellman & Ackler	10–15%
Leatroht	10–15%
Tracht	5–10%
Lowell-Pearson	4– 5%
Six others	15%
Total	100%

Margrave and Lowell-Pearson sold both air-atomizing and airless electrostatic equipment. In addition, Margrave leased centrifugal electrostatic equipment. All the others except Tracht sold air-atomizing electrostatic equipment; Tracht had only airless equipment.

Margrave dominated the market for both automatic and hand-gun applications. Adams officials noted that Margrave's equipment possessed several advantages over that of its competitors, namely: greater compactness, greater ease of use (particularly the handgun), higher quality, and greater reliability and ease of service. In automatic applications, Lowell-Pearson was Margrave's dominant competitor; Leatroht and Wellman & Ackler were also major competitors in automatic electrostatic equipment. In the market for hand-gun applications, Leatroht, Tracht, and Lowell-Pearson—all of which utilized Margrave patents—constituted Margrave's principal competition.

Margrave pioneered the development of electrostatic technology and consequently held extensive patents. Margrave introduced an automatic system in 1944, more than 10 years after Curtis Margrave had begun work to develop an electrostatic finishing process. For the next 14 years, Margrave was alone in the market, except for minor competition from firms that had licensed Margrave technology at a fee for each gallon of coating applied. In 1952, Margrave introduced an additional system, which had less overspray than any other electrostatic system, but refused to issue licenses for the patents that covered this system. In 1958, Margrave introduced the first electrostatic hand-gun system, and within the next five years introduced additional hand guns as competitors began to become active in the market for hand-gun applications. Margrave's sales of $12 million (exclusive of royalty and lease receipts) came entirely from electrostatics.

Wellman & Ackler, one of Adam's major competitors in many product lines, was expected to become one of the larger competitors in electrostatics in the future. However, because their hand gun was inefficient and was therefore a low volume item, Wellman & Ackler was trying to circumvent Margrave's patents. As a result, Margrave was suing Wellman & Ackler for patent infringement.

Leatroht had historically produced conventional air-spraying systems, but in recent years the company had diversified into most other finishing methods. In fact, Leatroht was a major competitor of Adams in many different product lines. The company had entered the electrostatic finishing market in 1962 and had successfully developed air and airless electrostatic guns, incorporating Margrave's licensed technology. Leatroht had recently won a contract from a leading automobile manufacturer to supply approximately $1 million of electrostatic equipment.

Tracht produced under the Margrave license an exact copy of Margrave airless electrostatic equipment. Tracht had attempted to circumvent Margrave's patents, but Margrave had sued for infringement and won.

THE LOWELL-PEARSON COMPANY

The Lowell-Pearson Company manufactured electrostatic finishing equipment, color-dispensing equipment, and medical electronic equipment. In 1969, the company earned $36,000 (before taxes) on sales of $3.7 million. Earnings had declined from 1960 to 1968, despite increases in sales during the period. In January 1969, Robert Schuster was named executive vice-president to assist Mr. Al Pearson, the acting president. Adams management believed that the downturn in the profits of the company was attributable primarily to the costs generated by electrostatic products. Operating statements for Lowell-Pearson for 1969 appear in Exhibits 3 and 4; a historical summary of financial data appears in Table 2:

Table 2

LOWELL-PEARSON FINANCIAL SUMMARY—1964-1969
(000)

	1964	1965	1966	1967	1968	1969
Net sales	$2,956.7	$3,019.2	$3,370.9	$3,379.7	$3,488.9	$3,683.5
Earnings (loss) before taxes	92.7	49.1	(4.6)	(39.1)	(182.6)	36.1

Electrostatic Systems

In 1969, Lowell-Pearson sales of electrostatic systems amounted to slightly more than $1.2 million. An income statement for electrostatic products appears in Table 3.

Automatic electrostatic systems, which accounted for some 80 percent of Lowell-Pearson's electrostatic sales, were sold directly to users through eight field representatives. These eight individuals were manufacturers' representatives, each of whom received commissions of 10 to 25 percent of sales. Four of them were located in the field, and four operated out of the Chicago office. Serving the field representatives in the Chicago laboratory were two laboratory technicians and one service manager.

Table 3

INCOME STATEMENT FOR
LOWELL–PEARSON
ELECTROSTATIC PRODUCTS, 1969
(000)

Sales	$1,200.8
Cost of goods sold	567.7
Gross margin	633.1
Expenses	881.5
Operating income	(248.4)

Officials at Lowell-Pearson foresaw little change in the automatic electrostatic equipment field, but a dramatic turnabout was forecast for hand-gun sales. Mr. Schuster had instituted a crash program to develop a hand-gun that would be priced about 30 percent less than the present $1,000 gun, and expected to market the new hand gun sometime in 1970. Manual (hand-gun) electrostatic equipment was sold through distributors and represented roughly 20 percent of Lowell-Pearson's electrostatic business. Lowell-Pearson officials believed that its direct sales force lacked the numbers needed to promote hand-gun sales.

Adams officials also believed that Lowell-Pearson electrostatic systems had gained considerable acceptance in the marketplace because of the latter's reputation for quality, first-line merchandise. To evaluate the competitive strength of Lowell-Pearson equipment, Adams engineers compared Lowell-Pearson equipment with Margrave systems in a series of tests. The engineers concluded that the Lowell-Pearson equipment, which was competitive in price to that of Margrave, was "... a shade better (than Margrave) ...." However, the report pointed out that in evaluating this type of equipment it was very difficult to compare objectively the wrap-around and penetration characteristics of one piece of equipment to that of another. Also, one could not conclude that all Lowell-Pearson electrostatic equipment was as good or better than that of Margrave, because only one type of manual system was compared in the study.

Adams officials believed that Lowell-Pearson's electrostatic patents were strong enough to permit Adams to offer electrostatic systems without infringing upon competitors' patents. Furthermore, because Lowell-Pearson had obtained a license from Margrave, Lowell-Pearson was protected from suit by Margrave under all of Margrave's existing patents (except those covering electrostatic atomization). The patent agreement was assignable to any company acquiring Lowell-Pearson or its electrostatic technology.

Color-Dispensing Equipment

Lowell-Pearson also manufactured a high-quality line of color-dispensing equipment, which manufacturers and retailers used to provide their customers with a wide range of precisely selected colors—all from a minimum inventory of white paint. When a customer selected a particular color of paint in a retail store, for example, the clerk simply added to a can of white paint a small amount of one or more colorants, according to a precise and simple formula stated on the color chip from which the customer had made the selection. This small amount of colorant, measured and dispensed from the color-dispensing equipment, was then thoroughly mixed into the white paint to provide an exact match to the color chip selected by the customer.

In 1969, color-dispensing equipment generated sales in excess of $1.3 million, and profits of almost $500,000. Nevertheless, both sales and earnings of the color-dispensing equipment line had been declining in recent years. An income statement for the line for 1969 appears in Table 4.

Color-dispensing equipment was sold directly to large paint manufacturers by headquarters personnel. In the spring of 1969, Mr. Schuster had sent a single traveling salesman to visit large paint manufacturers to determine the reasons for decreasing sales, to disseminate product information to field personnel, and to visit new accounts. Mr. Schuster intended in 1970 to develop a marketing program directed toward manufacturers who used a variety of different colors in the finishing portions of their manufacturing operations.

Table 4	
INCOME STATEMENT FOR LOWELL–PEARSON COLOR–DISPENSING EQUIPMENT, 1969 (000)	
Sales	$1,318.7
Cost of goods sold	578.2
Gross margin	740.5
Expenses	250.8
Operating income	$ 489.7

Table 5	
INCOME STATEMENT FOR LOWELL–PEARSON MEDICAL EQUIPMENT, 1969 (000)	
Sales	$1,164.0
Cost of goods sold	1,040.1
Gross margin	123.9
Expenses	319.0
Operating income	(195.1)

Medical Equipment

The primary product in Lowell-Pearson's medical equipment line was X-ray machinery, supplemented by diathermy and miscellaneous medical equipment. Because X-ray machines had been the company's first product when the company began operations in 1912, Lowell-Pearson personnel had long considered the company "... in the X-ray business, with some additional products." Increased competition and lack of growth in the market had reduced profit margins over the years, and the line lost money in 1969. An income statement for that year appears in Table 5.

Medical equipment was sold to hospitals, clinics, and other users by one salesperson. Lowell-Pearson officials had contemplated concentrating their efforts on the veterinary and chiropractic segments of the medical market, because those appeared to be growing fairly rapidly, but had reached no final decision.

ADMINISTRATION

Since becoming executive vice-president, Mr. Schuster had personally directed every phase of company operations, making all of the decisions, right down to the hiring and firing of the lowest category of employee. In fact, within the last year he had reduced the employment from 165 to 106. Several of the released personnel were highly paid family members who were not, in Mr. Schuster's opinion, contributing to the growth of the company in any significant manner. At the same time he was releasing employees, Mr. Schuster was hiring individuals for positions deemed necessary for the proper growth of the company. Despite his vigorous approach to Lowell-Pearson's problems, Mr. Schuster was not interested in remaining in a top management position. He wished to return to the field as a salesperson.

Adams management believed that the major problems existing at Lowell-Pearson were the lack of a marketing plan and marketing organization, and the lack of an efficient production operation. From visits to the plant and conversations with Lowell-Pearson employees, Adams officers believed that Lowell-Pearson had no marketing personnel who could be retained if the company were acquired, and no more than three technical people who were capable of serving as a core of a technical service group.

FACILITIES

Lowell-Pearson had only one facility, the Chicago plant, which had usable floor space of 88,000 square feet. The building, constructed by Lowell-Pearson, was sold to the Prudential Life Insurance Company and then leased back for $15,000 per year until September 1973. From thereafter to the year 2003, it was leased for $9,000 per year. The lease was believed to be assignable upon the purchase of the Lowell-Pearson Company or its assets.

ACQUISITION ARRANGEMENTS

From preliminary conversations with Lowell-Pearson executives, Adams executives believed that they would have to pay $2 million to acquire Lowell-Pearson. Adams officials believed that certain of their competitors might pay that price if they themselves did not.

If they acquired Lowell-Pearson, Adams personnel estimated that an additional $600,000 or more would have to be spent to improve test facilities for electrostatic equipment, properly staff Lowell-Pearson, train Adams personnel, equip Adams branches, hire additional sales personnel, and reactivate advertising (which Lowell-Pearson had dropped). An undetermined amount would also have to be spent for incentives to attempt to persuade existing Adams distributors who were selling other brands of electrostatic equipment to switch to distributing Lowell-Pearson electrostatic products. Adams officials believed that most of the company's distributors that had experienced demand for electrostatic finishing equipment currently handled one or more brands of electrostatic equipment. Executives thought that at least 25 percent of their top distributors would not add Adams-made or Adams-acquired electrostatic products to their lines unless it were equal to or better than the equipment they were already representing.

Exhibit 1

ADAMS, INC. (B)

AN ELECTROSTATIC SPRAY GUN IN ACTION

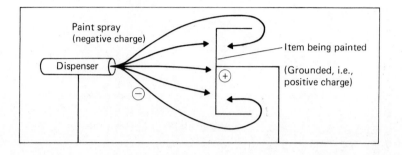

Exhibit 2

ADAMS, INC. (B)

LOWELL–PEARSON

SELECTION GUIDE FOR LOWELL–PEARSON AUTOMATIC ELECTROSTATIC SYSTEMS

(FOR PRODUCTS HAVING A WIDE VARIETY OF SHAPES AND SIZES)

Present finishing process	Required film thickness (mils)	Present minimum annual coating material consumption	Present number of hand sprayers	Recommended Lowell-Pearson electrostatic system	Estimated savings	
					Finishing material	Labor [a]
Conventional air or airless hand guns	0.1–2.5	$15,000	Two or more	Air-atomizing automatic	40–90%	50–90%
Conventional airless hand guns	2.5–12	$15,000	Two or more	Airless automatic	40–90%	50–90%
Conventional air or airless automatic system	0.1–2.5	$15,000	As needed for touchup	Air-atomizing automatic	40–90%	Up to 50%
Conventional airless automatic system	2.5–12	$15,000	As needed for touchup	Airless automatic	40–90%	Up to 50%

Note: For comparison with other electrostatic processes, dipping, flow-coating, electrophoretic coating, or other coating processes, contact Lowell-Pearson. For most automatic applications, *air-atomizing* electrostatic systems are recommended to provide the needed flexibility. Airless electrostatic systems are used for applying extra heavy film thicknesses, such as required for plastisol coatings. The product being coated must be conveyorized through the automatic electrostatic finishing process.

Exhibit 2 (Cont.)

SELECTION GUIDE FOR LOWELL–PEARSON ELECTROSTATIC HAND GUNS

Present finishing process	Product type	Required film thickness (mils)	Present minimum annual coating material consumption*	Present number of hand sprayers	Recommended Lowell-Pearson electrostatic system	Estimated savings	
						Finishing material	Labor[a]
Conventional air or airless hand guns	Small intricate shapes	0.1–2.5	$2,000	One or more	Air electrostatic hand gun	$800–1800	Up to 25%
Conventional air hand gun	Wide variety of shapes and sizes	0.1–0.7	$2,000	One or more	Air electrostatic hand gun	40–90%	Up to 25%
Conventional air or airless hand guns	Wide variety of shapes and sizes	0.7–2.5	$2,000	One or more	Air or airless electrostatic hand guns	40–90%	Up to 25%
Conventional airless hand gun	Wide variety of shapes and sizes	2.5–12.0	$2,000	One or more	Airless electrostatic hand guns	40–90%	Up to 25%

Note: In many instances, either air or airless electrostatic hand guns can be recommended for a specific application. Air guns will save coating material by holding closer tolerances on film thickness, and will apply somewhat higher quality of finish and handle more intricate shapes. Airless guns will provide higher speed of operation, produce greater labor savings, and apply a heavier film thickness.

*Based on an assumed average price of $5 per gallon

[a] Labor costs (direct and indirect combined) in a finishing operation typically averaged $3.25 per hour in 1970.

Source: Lowell-Pearson Brochure

Exhibit 3

ADAMS, INC. (B)

LOWELL–PEARSON INCOME STATEMENT FOR YEAR ENDING DECEMBER 31, 1969

		Percent
Net sales	$3,683,544	100.00
Cost of goods	2,186,005	59.35
Gross margin	1,497,539	40.65
Operating expenses		
Selling and advertising	966,645	26.24
Shipping and crating	100,078	2.72
General and administrative	384,603	10.44
Total operating expenses	1,451,326	39.40
Income from operations	46,213	1.26
Other (expense) or income	(10,096)	
Income before tax	36,117	0.98
Taxes on income	5,000	
Net income	31,117	0.84
Retained earnings beginning of year	837,820	
Credit sale of treasury stock above cost	3,163	
Preferred stock dividend	(4,587)	
Retained earnings at end of year	867,513	
Average earnings per common share	0.84	

Source: Company Records

Exhibit 4

ADAMS, INC. (B)
LOWELL–PEARSON
BALANCE SHEET   DECEMBER 31, 1969

Assets		
Cash		$ 86,974
Accounts and notes receivable, net of allowance for bad debts		1,005,685
Inventory[a]		925,764
Refundable tax from loss carry back		16,531
Prepared expense and other current assets		78,546
Total current assets		2,113,500
Property and equipment, net of depreciation		173,039
Deferred charges		58,500
Total assets		$2,345,039

Liabilities and equity		
Current liabilities		
Notes payable to bank		$ 418,357
Trade accounts payable		145,804
Commissions payable		171,032
Other current liabilities		177,107
Federal and state taxes; deferred income taxes on installment notes		73,218
Total current liabilities		985,518
Long-term debt		83,318
Shareholders' equity		
Preferred 7½%	$ 88,810	
Common	355,230	
Retained earnings	867,513	
	$1,311,553	
Less treasury stock at cost	35,350	1,276,203
Total liabilities and equity		$2,345,039

[a]Inventories (valued on a first-in, first-out basis, at lower of cost or market) consist 20 percent of finished goods; 10 percent of work in process; and 70 percent of raw materials.
Source: Company Records

THE HALL COMPANY

Superior Supermarkets

In August 1972, executives of the Hall Company, which operated three Superior Super-markets in Centralia, Missouri, met to decide whether to build a supermarket in a new shopping center in Centralia, and whether to adopt for that store a merchandising and pricing strategy different from that presently employed by existing Superior stores. If they built the new store, Hall officials would have to decide whether to close one or more of their present Superior stores. Discussion of these questions in turn precipitated a discussion of whether the present Superior merchandising and pricing strategy was appropriate. Executives had been concerned about Superior's present strategy because results from a series of store image studies indicated that Superior supermarkets did not have as favorable an image as their competitors.

THE COMPANY

The Hall Company, which operated wholesale and retail food outlets in several south central states, purchased the Superior Chain in 1950. Hall established its first general merchandise store in 1960, and added discount food outlets in 1967.

By 1972, the company distributed food and related products to approximately 150 corporate owned and operated supermarkets, discount food outlets, and general merchandise department stores. In addition, 25 distribution centers (wholesalers) supplied approximately 480 independently owned franchise supermarkets and more than 2,400 independent retailers and institutions.

The Hall Company had shown consistent growth over the past five years. In 1967, Hall had sales of $288.6 million with net earnings of $3.6 million, compared with sales of $384.9 million and net earnings of $5.4 million in 1971. Financial statements for 1971 appear in Exhibit 1.

Sales of Superior owned and franchised supermarkets in 1971 exceeded $44.6 million, about one-third of which was accounted for by corporate owned stores. The three Superior stores in Centralia were owned and operated by the Superior Division of the Hall Company. Any new Hall Company store in Centralia would be owned by the firm, rather than operated by a franchisee.

CENTRALIA, MISSOURI

Centralia was the primary trade center in central Missouri. The city's total retail trade area, which contained Scott county and portions of other counties northwest of Centralia, included approximately 5,500 square miles with a population of more than 122,500 persons in some 40,000 households (1970 Census).

Studies of traffic flow into Centralia indicated that the southern and western approaches to the city were the most heavily traveled. For every 100 cars traveling the major northern artery into Centralia, 140 traveled one of the two northwestern approaches (including the road from the suburb of Truman Heights); 160 used the major southwestern artery; and 190 traveled the major southern route, which carried traffic between Centralia and its airport. The major southeastern highway to Centralia had about the same traffic count as the northern artery; and the northeastern approach carried approximately 30 percent more traffic than the southeastern highway.

The immediate or primary trade area of Centralia included the city itself, the outlaying suburb of Truman Heights, and some small contiguous suburbs. Population data for 1970 and estimates of population in 1975 and 1980 appear in Exhibit 2. A demographic profile of Centralia residents, based on 1970 Census data and Hall research studies, appears in Exhibit 3.

During the 1960s, the population of Centralia itself increased approximately 20 percent. Most of this growth occurred in the northwest and southwest sections of the city. Most of the future growth projected was expected to occur in the northwestern portion of the city, but some increases in population were forecast for all sections of Centralia. Although the population of Centralia was expected to increase by almost 5,000 during the 1970s (see Exhibit 2), a slower growth rate was projected thereafter, resulting in a predicted population of approximately 40,000 for the city alone in the 1985-1990 period.

The most dramatic gains in population were projected for Truman Heights, a suburb to the northwest of Centralia. Truman Heights consisted principally of single-family homes in the $30,000-$70,000 range. The suburb had no business district and no food store, and Hall officials knew of no plans for retail development there. Truman Heights itself was expected to quadruple its size in the 1970s. In addition, the area between Truman Heights and Centralia was considered a prime area for residential development.

Income in the total Centralia trade area came principally from agriculture, but industrial employment was growing. In the 1960s, such industries as meat packing, farm machinery, and mobile homes located plants near the perimeter of the city; and in 1969, a government armaments factory was opened near Centralia.

In 1970, Centralia retail sales, excluding automobiles, were estimated at $110 million, an increase of 83 percent since 1960. Retail sales rose 30 percent from 1968 to 1971, compared with the state average of 23 percent for the same period. Retail food sales in Centralia for the period 1962-1972 were as follows:

Year	1962	1963	1964	1965	1966	1967	1968	1969	1970	1971	1972 (est.)
Millions	$7.2	$8.6	$9.7	$10.5	$11.5	$13.3	$14.2	$15.9	$17.3	$19.0	$20.3

By 1972, some 97 percent of Scott County food sales were made in Centralia; the city had accounted for less than 80 percent of total county food sales in 1960.

COMPETITIVE SITUATION IN CENTRALIA

In 1971 four major competitive food chains together accounted for approximately 83 percent of all food sales in Centralia (see Exhibit 4). The remainder of the retail food business was shared by three independent stores.

Each of three chains—Henny Penny, Grand American, and Payless—operated one store; Hall operated three Superior supermarkets in Centralia. Each of the three Superior stores was smaller than the other chains' stores. Grand American, Henny Penny, and Payless drew their customers from larger geographic areas than did each Superior store. Payless, in particular, enjoyed a strong trade from outside Centralia. Store locations are shown in Exhibit 5; selected statistical data on Superior stores and competitors appear in Exhibit 6.

HENNY PENNY

The Henny Penny supermarket, on West Main Street, was built about 1962 and completely remodeled in 1971 at a cost of approximately $100,000. Some 15 percent of the store's selling space was devoted to an extensive general merchandise assortment. According to Hall executives, most of the store's customers came from a residential area of one- and two-family homes with annual family incomes in excess of $6,000. Hall officials believed that Henny Penny had captured most of the business of the middle- and upper-income "in" group in Centralia, and that the store probably had the highest average sales of all the major stores.

Hall officials considered the Henny Penny store well managed, clean, orderly, and attractive. The decor was warm, the clerks friendly, and the physical layout easy to shop. Henny Penny's merchandising strength came from balanced variety in groceries, quality meat, and produce. The store was conveniently located with excellent parking facilities. Henny Penny's principal promotion theme was everyday low prices, as evidenced by its advertising slogan, "Save on the total." The store did not offer trading stamps. According to Hall officials, the Henny Penny store had an extremely favorable customer image.

The Henny Penny supermarket in Centralia was one of 65 Henny Penny supermarkets throughout Missouri and Illinois. Estimated sales in 1970 for the entire chain were $185 million.

GRAND AMERICAN

The Grand American store, at the corner of Fairview and West Main, opened early in 1972. This store replaced an older facility located several blocks northeast of the new site. The Centralia store was one of 148 supermarkets opened or remodeled in the last year by Grand American, one of the nation's largest food distributors and retailers. Hall officials believed that the Grand American store was the most modern store in Centralia, and had the finest fixtures and decor. It had wide aisles and was relatively easy to shop.

According to Hall executives, Grand American was a major competitor. The store was highly regimented and lacked innovative merchandising appeal. It had good variety in meat, produce, and groceries and its dairy department was highly acceptable to the consumer. The store carried a "skeleton" variety of general merchandise and offered no stamps. Grand American's weekly advertising approach emphasized variety of items and also attempted to create a low-price image by advertising competitive prices for the wide variety of items listed in each ad. The store's customers came from residential areas similar to those from which Henny Penny customers came; however, the income distribution of Grand American customers ranged from $3,000 to $15,000.

PAYLESS

According to Hall officials, Payless was number one in sales volume in Centralia and the principal competitor to the Superior supermarkets. Approximately 22 percent of Superior customers shopped Payless regularly. Most of Payless' customers were middle-age and older families whose annual incomes exceeded $6,000. Two-thirds of the store's selling space was allotted to general merchandise; one-third of its space contained food items. Managers of the three Superior stores maintained that Payless' primary merchandising strength was in groceries and special purchase displays. One manager stated that orderliness and cleanliness were sacrificed for production, and that the store lacked the quality and freshness present in the other supermarkets in Centralia. Payless' ads featured very low prices on particular items, which were displayed in large quantities at the ends of aisles in the grocery section of the store. Payless offered Green Gold trading stamps. Unlike Henny Penny and Grand American, the Payless store was part of a complex of other types of stores including several service shops, a bakery, a drug store, and a furniture store.

Payless Stores Company, the regional chain that built the Centralia store and operated it for many years, had recently sold that store to an independent businessman who continued to operate the store under the Payless name.

SUPERIOR

The three Superior supermarkets in Centralia were smaller and generally older stores than those of the major competitors. According to company officials, the stores' combined sales of almost $4.4 million in 1971 represented nearly the maximum that the present physical plants could produce.

Sales for the three stores combined had increased consistently during the past five years, as indicated in Table 1. Hall executives pointed out, however, that much of the increase in Superior sales, as in the sales of all food retailers, was attributable to price inflation. After adjusting for inflationary changes, executives estimated that Superior's sales had increased approximately 6 percent over the five-year period.

In 1972, sales of the three Superior stores were divided approximately as follows: grocery (including dairy), 68 percent; meat, 25 percent; and produce, 7 percent. These figures were similar for all three stores, and were typical of those for supermarkets throughout the United States. Because the Hall Company accounting system allocated gross profits approximately in proportion to sales, about two-thirds of Superior stores' gross profit was attributed to the grocery department (including bakery); approximately one-fourth, to meats (including delicatessen); and the remainder, to produce.

Company officials believed that Superior stores offered more limited variety than the major competitors, but that Superior carried high quality merchandise, particularly

Table 1

SALES OF SUPERIOR STORES IN CENTRALIA

1967–1971

Store	1967	1968	1969	1970	1971
North Fairview	$1,109,064	$1,164,958	$1,237,865	$1,310,423	$1,356,250
West Main	1,525,447	1,605,003	1,587,712	1,581,318	1,642,585
South Prospect	964,785	1,124,112	1,253,030	1,291,968	1,379,758
Total	$3,599,296	$3,894,073	$4,078,607	$4,183,709	$4,378,593

in canned goods and fresh produce. Officials recognized that the fresh meat departments of the three stores varied in consumer acceptance.

Superior stores offered S & H Green Stamps, and emphasized "Stamps and Price" in their weekly advertising. The stores often advertised high-volume items at very low prices, and occasionally featured "loss leaders."

North Fairview: Built in 1958, the North Fairview store was the oldest of the three Superior stores in Centralia. Since 1967, its sales had increased 6.6 percent beyond increases attributable to price inflation. The store was located less than two blocks from the center in which Payless was situated. Approximately 35 percent of the North Fairview store's customers came from outside Centralia. In 1972, the average transaction[1] amounted to $5.61. Financial and operating data for the North Fairview store appear in Exhibit 7.

Hall's lease at the North Fairview site was due to expire in 1974. Hall management believed that an extension of that lease could be negotiated for a period as short as five years or as long as twenty years.

West Main Street: The Superior supermarket on West Main Street was opened in 1959. In the next seven years the frozen food and dairy departments were expanded, and a "mini-deli" added. The deli prepared baked beans, potato salad, and similar items for sale on the premises, and for delivery to and sale at the Fairview and South Prospect stores.

Two competitors, Henny Penny and Grand American, were situated across the street. Although both were strong competitors, Hall executives believed the West Main Street store drew most of its customers from the area south of the store, and that Henny Penny and Grand American drew fewer customers than Superior from that area. Approximately 26 percent of the West Main store's sales came from people living beyond the city's limits.

---

1. Average transaction is an approximate measure of the dollar amount spent by each shopper on each shopping trip. The average is computed by dividing the number of "totals" rung on the cash register (i.e., the number of transactions per week) into the total dollar sales volume for that week.

When price inflation was factored out, sales had declined by 8.6 percent since 1967. Early in 1972, the average transaction was $5.80. Financial and operating data for the West Main Street store appear in Exhibit 8.

Earlier in 1972, Hall personnel had begun negotiations to acquire land adjacent to the West Main Steet store. If satisfactory terms could be arranged, Hall officials planned to expand both the parking lot and the store building. The expansion would nearly double in size both the parking lot and the selling space of the West Main Street store.

South Prospect: The South Prospect Superior supermarket was built in 1962 and substantially remodeled in 1966. Though no major competitors existed in the immediate vicinity, a K-Mart store, offering both general merchandise and food, was scheduled for construction across the street within the next two years. K-Mart stores typically included 15,000 to 20,000 square feet of selling space for food. The food section was ordinarily operated by a lessee. Hall officials expected the lessee in Centralia to be one of three major national chains not now operating in Centralia, each of which would offer vigorous and continuous price competition to existing food stores.

The South Prospect store had the only on-premise "scratch" bakery among the three Superior stores. Deliveries were made to the other stores daily. Company executives believed that the bakery did not offer as high quality or as much variety as the typical retail bakery shop in Centralia. Adjusting for inflationary price increases, sales had increased 26.2 percent in the last five years—the highest of the three stores. About 23 percent of the store's sales came from people who live outside Centralia. In 1972, the average transaction was $5.14. Financial and operating data for the South Prospect store appear in Exhibit 9.

MARKET RESEARCH STUDIES

In June 1971, Hall commissioned an independent marketing-research firm to conduct a series of studies for the Superior stores in Centralia. Hall executives sought to develop a profile of Superior shoppers and to determine the shopping behavior of these customers.

This information was to be used in making store relocation and modification decisions. Executives also hoped that, by questioning shoppers about what they liked and disliked about the Superior stores, they could establish what kind of retail "image" the stores projected. The question of store image had plagued corporate officials since 1964, when a retailing consultant to the company concluded that the stores had failed to reach their full profit potential because of the lack of a strong consumer image.

The first of three studies consisted of a telephone survey of 150 Centralia residents, who were asked to comment on the principal strengths of Superior Stores, Payless, Grand American, and Henny Penny. More than 30 percent of the interviewees considered Superior's prices "above average." In contrast, some 20 percent of the respondents thought the prices at Payless and at Henny Penny were "below average."

The respondents were also asked to associate the advertising slogans of the stores with the appropriate outlet. Forty percent of the respondents correctly associated the slogan "Stamps and Price" with Superior, and 60 percent of the respondents correctly named Henny Penny as the store using the slogan, "Save on the Total." But "Discount Prices" was correctly associated with Grand American by only 5 percent of the respondents, while 13 percent related the slogan to Superior and 26 percent associated the slogan with Payless. Additional data from this study appear in Exhibit 10.

A second study, conducted in September 1971, consisted of asking ten housewives, who were representative of the various geographic and income segments of Centralia, to discuss various aspects of food shopping in Centralia. A summary of their impressions appears below:

- *Meat*—Eight of the ten housewives stated that the quality of meat was the most important determinant of store choice. They liked to see cleanliness in the meat department and "bargains" which aren't necessarily poor cuts of meat. Meat display was also viewed as a salient consideration.

- *Produce*—Housewives wanted "home-grown" produce.

- *Superior bakery*—Housewives generally liked the bakery and particularly the freshness of the cakes, rolls, and bread at all three stores. However, several housewives believed that bread advertised as being fresh was in fact "day old" at the South Prospect store.

- *Consumerism*—Housewives were surprisingly aware of recent packaging proposals such as unit pricing and open coding and favored both. The housewives did not note any displeasure in seeing both national and private brands on shelves. They typically purchased private brands if these were less costly and regularly if they thought the quality was acceptable.

- *Advertising*—Eight of the ten housewives read all of the newspaper ads each week. They read the ads and compared prices regularly. Advertising emphasizing discount prices had little effect on customer intentions—they simply didn't believe it. Also, discount price slogans had little impact as all the stores claimed to offer such reduced prices. Stamps, however, received a favorable vote by the housewives.

- *Stores in general*—Distance did not seem to be a factor in determining customer patronage, rather meat was the most important factor. Housewives usually shopped more than one store regularly. They enjoyed having store services, i.e., sewing notions, deli, and greeting card sections. Also, "cents off" coupons appealed to many of the housewives.

  In general, the housewives believed that it was the "little things" that counted in generating loyal patronage, such as carry-out service, friendliness of store personnel, well-stocked shelves, and cleanliness.

- *Payless*—The typical housewife's comment, in reference to Payless, was that "you can't stick to your budget if you shop at Payless because there are so many things to buy." However, housewives didn't like the service at Payless, nor did they care for the quality of meat.

- *Grand American*—Most remarks about Grand American were in a negative view. Housewives stated that the store was often out of stock and the store usually "over-advertises." Housewives maintained that Grand American advertised specials were not, in fact, specials at all.

- *Henny Penny*—The housewives maintained that Henny Penny was winning the price war with Payless in Centralia. Henny Penny was recognized as being the best in price, courtesy, quality of merchandise, and service. In general, housewives believed Henny Penny's slogan of "Save on the Total."

- *Superior* (combined)—Almost all of the housewives liked the advertising of Superior, particularly its presentation. A strong criticism was that the stores were often out of stock. Housewives thought the Superior logo was imaginative and they liked the S & H Green Stamps.

A third study, conducted in January 1972, involved personal interviews with 587 Superior customers at the three store sites. Customers were asked to respond to specific questions asked by the interviewer and to comment on the store. Responses to questions are tabulated in Exhibit 11 for each store, and for all three stores combined.

In commenting on Superior stores, shoppers stated that lower prices and greater variety were needed in the departments that required the most improvement, namely, the health and beauty aids department and the deli. Shoppers suggested that the dairy section be cleaner, the price of meat be lower, the variety of goods in the bakery be greater, the out of stock situation in private labels be improved, and the quality and freshness of produce be enhanced.

Questions concerning the features of the Superior stores liked by shoppers generated a variety of responses. Appearance and cleanliness, friendliness, service, and trading stamps were liked most by the shoppers. Prices, parking, and checkout procedures were major features disliked by shoppers.

Previous customer studies had repeatedly shown that 65 to 75 percent of Superior customers lived within two miles of the particular Superior store at which they shopped. The personal interviews conducted in January 1972 with Superior shoppers indicated that some differences existed between Centralia residents and those who lived outside the city. Selected comparisons appear in Exhibit 12.

PROPOSED SHOPPING CENTER

The new regional shopping center was to be built on a rectangular site bounded on the east by Tank Road, the west by U.S. Highway 261, and by Independence Avenue and West Thirteenth Street on the north and south, respectively. (See map, Exhibit 5; Site plan, Exhibit 13.) The shopping center would face Tank Road with access points on Tank Road and Independence Avenue. According to Missouri Highway officials, U.S. Highway 261 was to be reconstructed to conform to Interstate Highway specifications within three years and would be designated Interstate Freeway 60. Entrance and exit points for Interstate Freeway 60 were planned for Independence Avenue and new Highway 20. Tank Road was to be widened and resurfaced as a frontage road.

The shopping center would cover approximately 30 acres and house three major tenants—F.W. Woolworth, J.C. Penney, and one other—in an enclosed mall. Also included within this mall would be barber and beauty shops, a drug store, a liquor store, and men's and women's clothing shops. The supermarket of approximately 22,000 square feet would stand by itself in a parking area southeast of the enclosed mall.

The cost of building the supermarket, including interior finishing, was estimated at $13.50 a square foot. Developers of the center would erect the building and lease it to the tenant for 20 years, with two- to five-year renewal options. Occupancy costs, which would be borne by the tenant, were forecast at $2.02 a square foot, or $44,440 per year. Of this amount, $39,600 would be rent; $2,640, common area maintenance; and $2,200, joint activities with other tenants in the center.

Tentative completion dates for the freeway and shopping center were set for Spring 1974.

Grand American, Payless, Henny Penny, and Superior had been mentioned as possible occupants for the supermarket. Hall executives believed that Henny Penny had no interest in the venture, and that the recent opening of a Grand American store at the West Main Street site precluded its management from making any formal commitment.

Hall executives were not sure whether a 22,000 square-foot store in the new center would be a community supermarket or a regional supermarket. A community supermarket typically drew 60 percent of its sales from families who lived within a two-mile radius of the store. A regional supermarket, in contrast, ordinarily drew more than 60 percent of its sales from families who lived more than two miles from the store. The present Superior stores were community supermarkets. Company officials believed that the 25,000 to 30,000 families who lived outside Centralia but shopped in the city might be an important source of revenue for a supermarket in the new center.

To assist company executives in developing a pro-forma income statement for a new 22,000 square-foot supermarket to be operated as a "conventional" supermarket in a manner similar to the existing Superior stores, Hall's accounting department had developed cost data from the company's own experience and from industry sources. The accountants arrayed that information in a worksheet format, as shown in Table 2.

Alternatives

At the end of a lengthy discussion of the Centralia market situation, one Hall executive summarized the problem as follows:

> If we decide to go into the new shopping center, we have to address the basic question, "What position do we want in this market?" We've got stamps, and people shop us even though they think our prices are high, so we could really go the premium route. We could go in there (the proposed shopping center) with a real palace— carpeted floors, a flower shop, an extensive gourmet section, premium meats—and signal our intention to be the "top of the line." We could, on a smaller scale, trade up our present stores too.

Table 2

PRO-FORMA INCOME STATEMENT WORKSHEET

	Percentage	Dollars
Sales	100.0 %	————
Cost of goods sold	81.6	————
(including freight in and warehousing)		
Gross profit	18.4	————
Controllable expenses		
Total salaries and wages	7.90	————
Advertising (including promotions)	1.25	————
Trading stamps	2.25	————
Administration (accounting, interest, bank charges, etc.)	1.50	————
Miscellaneous	2.00	————
Subtotal	14.90	————
Noncontrollable expenses		
Rent	————	$44,440.00
Insurance (and upkeep)	————	2,200.00
Utilities	————	14,000.00
Taxes	————	6,600.00
Depreciation (based on fixture cost of $220,000)	————	22,000.00
	————	$89,240.00
Total operating expenses	————	————
Net income (loss) before taxes[a]	————	————

[a] An industry study indicated that conventional supermarkets earned 1.5 to 2 percent of sales (before taxes) in 1972.

On the other hand, we could go just the other way: expand the (shopping center) store to 25,000 to 30,000 square feet and run it as a food warehouse—bare floors, bare walls, fixtures packed in and stacked to the top—and the lowest prices for 40 miles in every direction. Because our present stores aren't physically suited to this type of high-turnover, low-price operation, we'd probably have to run the "warehouse" under a different name, even though we could supply it through the same distribution center that serves the present Superior stores.

If the company chose the "premium" strategy for a new store in the shopping center, Hall operating personnel estimated that costs higher than those projected for a conventional operation would be incurred. Costs of trimming meat and selecting produce to maintain premium quality and freshness for a wider line (which would necessarily include some slower-moving items) were likely to amount to a sum equal to 2 percent of sales of perishables in a conventional supermarket. Added labor expense could equal a sum equivalent to ½ to 1 percent of sales in a conventional supermarket. Carpeting and other amenities could increase the cost of fixturing by $25,000 to $30,000. The impact of these added costs on net profit depended largely on the extent to which prices could be increased as part of the "premium" strategy.

If Hall were to upgrade its present stores, the cost of improved trimming and selection of meat and produce would amount to about 2 percent of present sales of perishables. The cost of additional labor was estimated at $10,000 per store per year. In addition, $25,000 of new meat fixtures would be needed for each store. If the bakery and deli sections of the present stores were to be upgraded at the same time, Hall officials estimated that about 250 square feet of additional space would be needed in each store for the two departments combined, and about $2,000 per store would be necessary for new fixtures. A continuing cost of approximately $7,500 per store per year would be incurred to enhance the freshness and variety in those departments. Company officials estimated that Superior stores would have to spend an additional $10,000 per year on advertising for two or three years to communicate effectively the stores' new offering and image.

Some executives favored a low-price strategy for a new store which might be built in the center, but doubted that the volume needed for a low margin "warehouse" operation could be attained. They favored a "discount" operation, which typically maintained a gross margin about four percentage points lower than that of a conventional supermarket, either by taking shorter markups than conventional stores or by taking similar markups and offering very substantial discounts on a wide variety of items in every department. Discount supermarkets offered no stamps, and earned net profits about one percentage point less than conventional supermarkets. Discount supermarkets ordinarily carried the same quality and variety of meat and produce as that found in a conventional store.

In contrast, a warehouse food market differed sharply in merchandise and operation from either a conventional or a discount supermarket. Warehouse markets carried no meat, a very limited selection of produce, and only high-turnover grocery items, which were displayed in manufacturers' boxes. Customers used warehouse-type dollies rather than typical supermarket shopping carts, and were required to mark prices on items they purchased. Warehouse markets had fewer checkout stands and offered little or no carry-out help. Although warehouse markets offered either individual items or case lots, many consumers believed that they had to buy whole cases and could not purchase individual items.

Warehouse markets had lower shelf prices and lower operating costs than conventional supermarkets. Hall officials believed that gross margins of warehouse food markets ranged from 10 to 13 percent. Operating savings came about primarily from lower labor costs. Operation of a warehouse market required 10–20 employees, rather than the 40–50 needed in a typical conventional supermarket. Laborers eliminated included highly paid butchers and price-marking employees. In addition, warehouse food markets offered no stamps. Costs of interior furnishings and fixtures were estimated to be 10-15 percent less than those for a conventional supermarket.

Because warehouse operations were a comparatively recent phenomenon, information on profitability was difficult to obtain. Company officials had, however, recently learned of one warehouse food market of about 25,000 square feet which had sales between $3 and $3.5 million and earned profits similar to those of conventional supermarkets of comparable size.

Many Hall executives expressed serious reservations about building the new store, no matter what merchandising strategy was used. They foresaw the possibility that Centralia would become "overstored," i.e., that the volume of retail food business available would not support the present stores plus the expected K-Mart food store and a new store in the shopping center. Although some Hall officials had proposed closing the North Fairview store if a new store were opened in the center, others were reluctant to close the North Fairview store or, for that matter, any of the existing Superior stores, which they believed served the needs of consumers who desired "convenience" stores for frequent, small purchases. Hall management had discussed the possibility of attempting to buy out a competing store, but had been advised by company attorneys that the federal government would likely prohibit such action under antimonopoly laws.

Company executives wished to resolve as promptly as possible the related issues of what network of stores to have in Centralia, and what marketing strategy to adopt for those stores. The developers of the shopping center had indicated to Hall executives that they would seek out another supermarket chain within three months if Hall were not interested in the site.

Exhibit 1

HALL COMPANY
INCOME STATEMENT
FOR THE YEAR ENDING DECEMBER 31, 1971
(000 OMITTED)

Net sales	$384,900
Cost of goods sold	327,200
Marketing, general, and administrative expenses	47,060
Earnings before taxes	10,740
Taxes on income	5,340
Net earnings	5,400
Earnings per share of common stock	9.76

BALANCE SHEET
DECEMBER 31, 1971
(000 OMITTED)

Assets	
Cash and securities	$ 7,538
Receivables	6,054
Inventories	34,564
Plant and equipment	13,653
Prepaid expenses and other assets	8,038
Total assets	$ 69,847
Liabilities	
Current liabilities	$ 20,764
Long-term liabilities	4,743
Stockholders' equity	44,340
Total liabilities and stockholders' equity	$ 69,847

Exhibit 2

HALL COMPANY
PRESENT AND PROJECTED[a] POPULATION FOR CENTRALIA
AND IMMEDIATE (PRIMARY) TRADE AREA

Year	Centralia	Truman Heights	Contiguous suburbs[b]	Total
1970	32,400	1,200	1,100	34,700
1975	34,800	2,200	1,400	38,400
1980	37,200	4,600	2,000	43,800

[a]Projections based on Census and State Planning Agency estimates.

[b]Approximately two-thirds of this population lived on the eastern edge of Centralia in 1970; that proportion was not expected to change through 1980.

Exhibit 3

HALL COMPANY
CENTRALIA CITY PROFILE

	Centralia	State of Missouri
Population	32,400	4,676,000
Housing units	11,476	1,484,286
Median housing value	13,400	12,400
Age breakdown (%)		
Less than 18	33.7	34.2
18–64	53.0	53.4
65 or older	13.3	12.4
Income breakdown		
$0–$2,999	15.6	17.3
$3,000–$4,999	10.2	12.4
$5,000–$7,999	17.0	21.3
$8,000–$9,999	15.5	14.7
$10,000–$14,999	28.9	19.4
$15,000 and over	12.9	14.9
Family income less than poverty level	7.4	10.1
Median family income	$8,933	$8,534
Employment (%)		
Blue collar	19.5	13.7
White collar	48.0	44.4
Federal government employment	14.6	15.5
Median age	29.2	28.6

Source: Company Records

Exhibit 4

HALL COMPANY
ESTIMATED SHARE OF MARKET

	1965	1966	1967	1968	1969	1970	1971	1972 (est.)
Superior	24%	26%	27%	27%	26%	24%	23%	23%
Grand American	22	13	7	7	7	7	7	9
Payless	25	25	26	28	30	33	33	33
Henny Penny	9	15	19	18	18	19	20	20
Others	20	21	21	20	19	17	17	15

Note: Share-of-market estimates were made by Hall Company executives on the basis of information they considered reliable. The total market (100%) represents all food sales made in Centralia.

Source: Company Records

Exhibit 5

LOCATION OF STORES, MAJOR TRAFFIC ARTERIES, AND PRINCIPAL
IN-CITY TRADE AREAS OF SUPERIOR AND COMPETING STORES

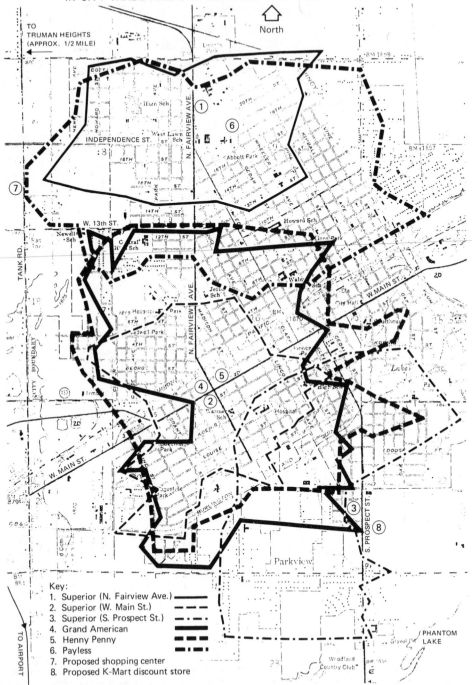

Key:
1. Superior (N. Fairview Ave.)
2. Superior (W. Main St.)
3. Superior (S. Prospect St.)
4. Grand American
5. Henny Penny
6. Payless
7. Proposed shopping center
8. Proposed K-Mart discount store

Note: Trade area boundaries were drawn on the basis of personal interviews with customers in each Superior store. The address of each interviewee was then plotted on the map, and boundaries drawn.

The trade area surrounding the North Fairview store includes 5330 persons (1970 census); that around the West Main store, 5650; and that surrounding the South Prospect store, 6400.

Source: Company Records

Exhibit 6

HALL COMPANY
CENTRALIA STORE COMPARISON
(1972 ESTIMATES)

	Weekly food sales/store	Avg. bldg. size (sq. ft.)	Avg. food selling area (sq. ft.)	Avg. food sales/sq. ft.	Avg. parking spots	Avg. number checkstands	Avg. advertising lines/month (1971)
Grand American	$ 35,135	22,000	15,400	$2.28	106	6.0+Exp.	1636
Henny Penny	78,077	22,500	15,750	4.96	151	8.0	898
Payless	128,846	110,000a	24,000	5.37	300+	17.0	2351
Superior (Avg. of 3 stores)	29,917	11,713	8,223	3.64	80	4.3	2006 (all 3 stores)
W. Main	32,939	10,842	8,090	4.07	76	5.0	
N. Fairview	27,989	11,756	8,625	3.25	84	4.0	
S. Prospect	28,821	12,540	7,954	3.62	81	4.0	

	Avg. number shopping carts	Courtesy counter	Avg. age of store(s)	Avg. bakery variety b	Avg. produce variety b	Avg. meat variety b
Grand American	110	None	1+	—	74	84
Henny Penny	90	1	10+	—	60	76
Payless	300+	1	10+	—	64	81
Superior (Avg.)	63	1	12+	40	67	75
W. Main	70	1	13	21	66	75
N. Fairview	66	1	14	29	68	66
S. Prospect	52	1	10	70	66	84

aNonfood items occupy approximately 48,000 square feet of the total of 72,000 square feet of selling space in the entire store.
bVariety refers to the number of separate items and the nature of the packaging. For example, rye bread is considered separate from whole wheat bread. Within the item class "rye bread" there may be two types of packaging—1 lb. and 1½ lb. loaves.

Source: Company Records

Exhibit 7

HALL COMPANY
SELECTED OPERATING AND FINANCIAL DATA
NORTH FAIRVIEW STORE

Year	Sales (000)	Gross profit (000)	Gross profit/ sales	Net profit (after tax) (000)	Return on investment
1967	$1,109	$219.8	19.8%	$22.1	33.8%
1968	1,165	224.3	19.3	21.1	28.4
1969	1,238	221.5	18.0	5.6	7.4
1970	1,310	235.2	17.9	7.6	7.3
1971	1,356	266.5	19.7	21.8	n.a.

Source: Company Records

Exhibit 8

HALL COMPANY
SELECTED OPERATING AND FINANCIAL DATA
WEST MAIN STREET STORE

Year	Sales (000)	Gross profit (000)	Gross profit/ sales	Net profit (after tax) (000)	Return on investment
1967	$1,525	$295.8	19.4%	$34.6	36.6%
1968	1,605	315.0	19.6	49.4	52.9
1969	1,588	291.1	18.3	22.3	22.9
1970	1,581	290.6	18.4	22.0	20.2
1971	1,643	321.4	19.6	37.2	n.a.

Source: Company Records

Exhibit 9

HALL COMPANY
SELECTED OPERATING AND FINANCIAL DATA
SOUTH PROSPECT STORE

Year	Sales (000)	Gross profit (000)	Gross profit/ sales	Net profit (after tax) (000)	Return on investment
1967	$ 965	$190.0	19.7%	$ 2.4	1.9%
1968	1,124	221.0	19.7	15.0	12.3
1969	1,253	232.3	18.5	9.2	7.8
1970	1,292	243.3	18.8	10.3	8.4
1971	1,380	268.2	19.4	15.6	n.a.

Source: Company Records

Exhibit 10

HALL COMPANY
ASSOCIATION OF PARTICULAR CHARACTERISTICS WITH
MAJOR FOOD STORES IN CENTRALIA
(TELEPHONE SURVEY, n = 150)

Characteristic	Grand American	Henny Penny	Superior	Payless	Apathetic, "don't know"
Most reasonable prices	11%	36%	7%	34%	12%
Most convenience	18	21	35	25	1
Best quality meat	20	27	18	11	24
Widest variety meat	22	25	20	18	14
Best quality produce	24	35	24	11	6
Widest variety produce	24	30	14	18	14
Best store service	12	30	28	13	17
Quality canned goods	12	24	14	14	36
Best specialty games, continuity programs, and trading stamps	5	2	26	52	15
Best overall variety	6	8	2	74	10
Best store layout	27	24	14	9	26
Best bakery	—	—	42	—	58
Best deli	—	—	9	—	91

Source: Company Records

Exhibit 11

HALL COMPANY
RESULTS FROM INTERVIEWS WITH 587 SUPERIOR CUSTOMERS
JANUARY 1972

	S. Prospect	W. Main	N. Fairview	Superior combined
Age of customer				
Over 65 years	7.5%	16.8%	9.7%	10.7%
64–50 years	13.7	25.5	28.0	21.6
49–35 years	33.0	35.8	33.1	33.8
34–25 years	18.9	15.3	24.0	19.7
24–18 years	21.2	6.6	4.0	11.6
Under 18 years and no response	5.7	nil	1.2	2.6
Average persons per household	3.5	3.1	3.4	3.3
Frequency of store visits				
4 times a week	18.1%	11.7%	9.7%	13.4%
3 times a week	10.6	11.2	9.2	10.3
2 times a week	19.9	21.2	22.7	21.2
Once a week	28.2	38.0	40.0	35.0
3 times a month	0.9	1.7	5.4	2.6
2 times a month	6.0	4.5	7.0	5.9
Once a month	9.7	8.9	5.4	8.1
Other	6.5	2.8	0.5	3.5
Length of patronage				
Less than 1 year	11.4%	10.0%	7.1%	7.6%
1–3 years	19.3	8.8	8.0	12.5
3 or more years	69.3	81.2	84.9	77.9
Proportion of total food needs purchased				
Almost all	50.0%	58.2%	47.2%	51.7%
About ¾	18.8	14.1	13.3	15.0
About ½	13.0	12.4	24.4	17.0
About ¼ to ½	6.7	7.9	7.2	7.1
Less than ¼	11.5	7.3	7.8	9.2
Amount of purchase				
$ 0 - 2.49	24.7%	21.6%	20.0%	21.3%
$ 2.50- 4.99	20.4	15.0	21.1	19.1
$ 5.00- 9.99	19.9	26.8	27.4	24.3
$10.00-14.99	13.7	11.1	8.6	11.3
$15.00-19.99	5.7	5.9	11.4	7.6
$20.00-24.99	5.7	4.6	4.6	5.0
$25.00-29.99	1.9	7.8	2.3	3.7
$30.00 and over	9.0	6.5	4.6	6.9

	S. Prospect	W. Main	N. Fairview	Superior combined
Departments shopped				
All three	35.8%	27.4%	41.8%	35.3%
Grocery, meat	10.7	10.4	13.6	11.5
Grocery, produce	11.2	7.3	5.4	8.2
Meat, produce	6.5	3.7	2.2	4.3
Grocery only	33.5	45.1	29.9	35.7
Meat only	1.4	2.4	4.3	2.7
Produce only	0.9	3.7	2.7	2.3
H & BA	15.2%	9.2%	7.5%	10.9%
Frozen foods	22.4	20.8	28.5	23.9
Dairy	39.6	37.6	49.7	42.3
Bakery	33.3	22.4	39.6	32.1
Other stores shopped most regularly				
Grand American	7.6%	7.8%	4.9%	6.8%
Henny Penny	15.8	10.8	6.8	11.2
Payless	14.0	9.0	43.8	22.0
Superior	0.6	0.6	—	0.4
Independent 1	5.8	—	0.6	2.2
Independent 2	4.7	0.6	—	1.8
Other	3.5	3.0	3.7	3.4
None	48.0	68.1	40.1	52.1
Liked best about other regular store				
Prices	33.8%	29.5%	19.5%	27.0%
Meat	8.8	22.7	7.8	11.6
Variety	10.3	9.1	6.5	8.5
Location	10.3	9.1	5.2	7.9
All Other (no one category accounted for more than 7% of the total)	36.8	29.6	61.0	45.0

Source: Company Records

Exhibit 12

HALL COMPANY

RESULTS FROM INTERVIEWS WITH 587 SUPERIOR CUSTOMERS

JANUARY 1972

	Centralia residents	Nonresidents		Centralia residents	Nonresidents
Age of customers			**Length of patronage**		
Over 65 years	10.1%	11.6%	Less than 1 year	8.6%	11.4%
64–50 years	21.5	21.9	1–3 years	15.4	5.6
49–35 years	29.6	43.2	3 or more years	76.0	83.0
34–25 years	20.7	17.8			
24–18 years	14.7	4.8	**Proportion of total**		
Under 18 years	3.5	0.7	**food needs purchased**		
Family shopping			Almost all	52.4%	48.8%
pattern			About ¾	16.9	11.4
			About ½	15.4	21.5
Man alone	14.3%	11.3%	About ¼ to ½	5.8	10.1
Woman alone	77.5	71.7	Less than ¼	9.6	8.2
Couple	8.1	15.1			
With children	18.7%	25.5%	**Amount of purchase**		
With car	93.1	98.7	$ 0 - 2.49	23.9%	17.1%
Size of family			$ 2.50– 4.99	21.5	13.8
1	13.4%	5.2%	$ 5.00– 9.99	25.7	22.4
2	29.7	33.5	$10.00–14.99	10.3	12.5
3	17.6	16.1	$15.00–19.99	6.4	10.5
4	16.6	17.4	$20.00–24.99	3.2	8.6
5	11.9	11.0	$25.00–29.99	3.2	5.3
6	6.7	7.1	$30.00 and over	5.8	9.9
7	2.0	3.2			
8 or more	2.1	6.4	**Departments shopped**		
Frequency of			All three	31.9%	43.2%
store visits			Grocery, meat	13.3	7.7
			Grocery, produce	7.8	9.0
4 times a week	15.8%	6.3%	Meat, produce	4.3	4.5
3 times a week	12.4	5.7	Grocery	38.2	29.7
2 times a week	22.1	18.9	Meat	3.0	1.9
Once a week	32.8	41.5	Produce	1.5	3.9
3 times a month	2.2	2.5			
2 times a month	4.1	10.7	H & BA	11.1%	11.0%
Once a month	7.1	10.7	Frozen foods	21.1	28.8
First time	2.4	1.3	Dairy	39.9	49.7
Other	1.0	2.5	Bakery	30.0	37.6
Other stores shopped			**Liked best about**		
most regularly			**other regular store**		
None	53.2%	47.8%	Prices	27.5%	25.0%
Payless	21.7	23.1	Variety	9.9	4.5
Henny Penny	11.8	9.7	Location	7.7	9.1
Grand American	8.2	3.7	Special promotions	2.1	9.1
Independent 1	1.7	3.7	All other (no one	52.8	52.3
Independent 2	1.7	2.2	category accounted		
Other	1.1	9.7	for more than 7%		
Other Superior	0.6	—	of the total)		

Source: Company Records

Exhibit 13

THE HALL COMPANY

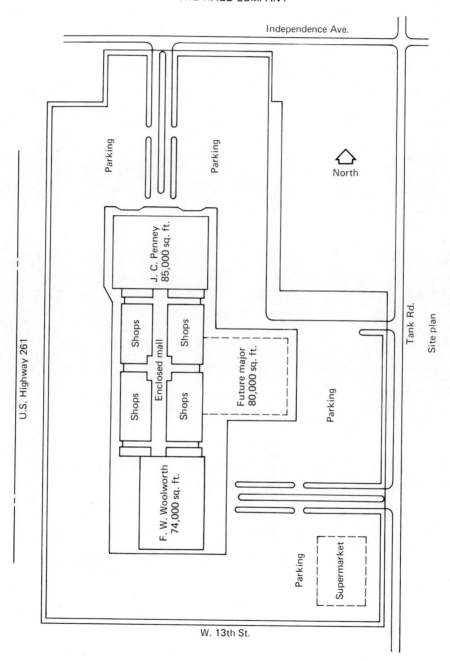